Just the book I've been waiting for!

As a retired librarian/archivist I've been dealing with the guilt of seeing family papers and photographs sitting in multiple storage boxes just waiting to see the light of day and a firm organizing hand. As the only family member who seems interested in genealogy and family artifacts, I have become the "keeper of the flame." And the years are ticking by rapidly. This book will give me the impetus to get my act together and plunge into those boxes. Yes, it is daunting. Start labeling those photographs ("Who are these people?"). Should I digitize a portion of them and distribute copies to all the relatives? Should I digitize them myself or pay someone to do it? What to do with the originals? All questions that I have been mulling over for years unsure about what to do. Now I know!

—**Clare Sheridan,** former Librarian/Archivist American Textile History Museum

A Must-Have Book for Preserving Family History!

Who isn't curious about the stories of family members who came before them? While it may be overwhelming to even think about how to capture these stories, both from the past and present, this book is your guide on how to do it. An easily understandable step-by-step guide, the book helps to take what can be a huge undertaking and break it into doable tasks. The author brings her extensive knowledge and years of experience as an archivist and history lover to help the average person organize and preserve their family histories, photographs, artifacts, and other treasures so that future generations may enjoy their ancestors' stories. But even more than that, these stories provide researchers with a window into the past, giving clues as to what everyday life was like and connecting the dots into many unanswered questions. Chadwick intersperses her personal observations to underscore the importance of passing along family history to keep these stories alive and makes the book not only instructional, but also a most enjoyable read! This invaluable book makes a perfect gift for historians and novices alike and for anyone who is interested in carrying on their family's history.

—**Kathy Hartley,** President Hearthside House Museum, Lincoln, RI

Do you worry about who is going to treasure your grandmother's wedding picture?

Are your family photos and papers saved for future generations or are they at risk of being destroyed forever by a natural or manmade disaster? Don't be afraid. Rhonda Chadwick's book will give you all the tools you need to make sure your grandchildren will be able to show their grandchildren the family history.

I've known Rhonda for many years and we worked together in our archival consulting business. I was always so impressed that she had all of this knowledge at the tip of her tongue when clients had questions about how best to preserve their material culture. She's the perfect person to write this book and provide people with clear steps to take to avoid a catastrophe of ancestral proportions.

—**Elaine Robinson,** Librarian/Archivist

The tried-and-true methods (the secrets) of professional archivists

Archivists have a unique place in the historical and genealogical worlds. They preserve and make materials available for future researchers. In *Secrets from the Stacks* Rhonda teaches family historians and genealogists the tried-and-true methods (the secrets) professional archivists use so they can preserve their own family and personal records for future descendants. It's not enough to save documents and research family trees. Knowing how to store, organize, categorize, and present both physical and digital information, is an integral part of maintaining a collection. Rhonda's attention to detail and passion for history comes through on every page. Family historians and genealogists who want to preserve their collection like a professional archivist should buy this book.

—**Karen Eberhart,** Manuscripts Processing Archivist, Brown University.

The Right Message for Our Times

Weather extremes have become part of life, and family photos, memorabilia, etc., are most at risk. Fires, tornadoes, hurricanes, extreme freezes, flooding are all happening every day. The message that gets missed in all the reporting is what to do before these events. That is why this book is the perfect resource for anyone motivated to preserve their family legacy.

—**Cathi Nelson,** CEO/Founder The Photo Managers

Library Lecture Attendees Testimonials

I attended this lecture because I wanted to learn more about keeping and organizing family photos and other family "treasures" from an expert archivist. I learned to think about the future people who would be seeing or using this information as I organized and documented things. Learning the best ways to care for and store material was useful and helpful. I refer to Rhonda's handouts whenever I am working on family archives projects. The lectures I attended were very interesting and helpful.

—**Helen**, attended lecture at Seekonk Public Library, MA

I attended this lecture because I am interested in genealogy. The favorite thing I learned was that pencil last longer than ink! I found the information interesting. I use pencil notes when working on my family archives now.

—**K.** attended library lecture in Milford Mass

I have been designated our family's historian, and other family members give me any related materials, rather than try to preserve them themselves. I attended the library lectures at the Wellesley Public library to learn the best way to preserve genealogical materials, documents, and information. The favorite thing I learned was that digitized information needs to be updated periodically to current technology. I liked the specific step-by-step procedures for preserving physical documents. After attending the lectures, I changed the procedures I use to preserve information.

—**Marilyn,** attended library lecture at Wellesley Free Library, MA

Copyright (C) 2023 Rhonda J Chadwick. All rights reserved.

No part of this publication shall be reproduced, transmitted, or sold in whole or in part in any form without prior written consent of the author, except as provided by the United States of America copyright law. Any unauthorized usage of the text without express written permission of the publisher is a violation of the author's copyright and is illegal and punishable by law. All trademarks and registered trademarks appearing in this guide are the property of their respective owners.

For permission requests, write to the below address:

PYP Academy Press
141 Weston Street, #155
Hartford, CT 06141

The opinions expressed by the Author are not necessarily those held by PYP Academy Press.

Ordering Information: Quantity sales and special discounts are available on quantity purchases by corporations, associations, and others. For details, contact the author at rhonda@lenasalina.com.

Edited by: Nancy Graham-Tillman
Cover design and formatting by: Nelly Murariu (PixBeeDesign.com)

Printed in the United States of America.

ISBN: 978-1-955985-25-3 (hardcover)
ISBN: 978-1-955985-24-6 (paperback)
ISBN: 979-8-88797-087-5 (B&W Softcover)
ISBN: 978-1-955985-26-0 (ebook)

Library of Congress Control Number: 2022905426

First edition, September 2023

The information contained within this book is strictly for informational purposes. The material may include information, products, or services by third parties. As such, the Author and Publisher do not assume responsibility or liability for any third-party material or opinions. The publisher is not responsible for websites (or their content) that are not owned by the publisher. Readers are advised to do their own due diligence when it comes to making decisions.

Publish Your Purpose is a hybrid publisher of non-fiction books. Our authors are thought leaders, experts in their fields, and visionaries paving the way to social change—from food security to anti-racism. We give underrepresented voices power and a stage to share their stories, speak their truth, and impact their communities. Do you have a book idea you would like us to consider publishing? Please visit PublishYourPurpose.com for more information.

Secrets from the Stacks

An archivist reveals
how to store, digitize,
and preserve documents to
create a family archive
and leave a personal legacy

Rhonda J. Chadwick

This book is dedicated to Al Tyas,
my little brother by choice,
and forever friend.

TABLE OF CONTENTS

Preface	xiii
Introduction	xv
Leaving a Legacy	xvi
Clearing the Clutter	xviii
In Defense of Archives	xxi

SECTION ONE: THE MATERIAL WORLD — 1

1: ARCHIVAL BASICS — 3
- The Goal — 3
- What is a Family Archive? — 5
- Prevention — 8
- The Environment — 8
- Location, Location, Location — 11
- Enclosures — 12
- Creating a Workspace — 15

2: ORGANIZATION — 19
- Respect du Fonds — 19
- Original Order — 21
- Intellectual vs. Physical Order — 22
- Other Parts of the Finding Aid — 33
- Appraisal — 36
- The Survey — 40

3: PHOTOGRAPHS — 45
- The Technical Stuff — 46
- Processing Photographs — 49
- Damage to Photographs — 57

4: 19TH-CENTURY PHOTOGRAPHS — 63
- Daguerreotypes — 64
- Calotypes — 66
- Ambrotypes — 68
- Tintypes — 69
- Cartes-de-Visite — 71

Stereoscopic Slides	72
Determining the Year of a Photograph	73

5: 20TH-CENTURY PHOTOGRAPHS — 75
- Color Prints and Film — 76
- Non-Chromogenic Film — 80
- 20TH-Century Paper — 80
- Processing Modern Photographs — 81

6: FILM — 83
- Nitrate Film — 83
- Acetate Film — 86
- Polyester Film — 88
- Storage of Slides and Negative Film — 89

7: PAPER — 91
- A Brief History of Paper Making — 91
- Paper — 93
- Maps, Blueprints, Drawings, Oversize Items — 100
- Processing Paper Documents — 101
- Books — 105

8: TEXTILES — 115
- Fiber Types — 118
- Synthetic — 119
- Caring for Textiles — 121
- Handling — 127
- Cleaning and Maintenance — 128
- Storage – General Considerations — 134
- Storage – Specific Items — 136
- Display — 140

SECTION TWO: THE DIGITAL WORLD — 147

9: DIGITAL BASICS — 149
- The Digital World — 150
- Born Digital vs. Digitized — 151
- Terms — 153
- Data Storage — 162

10: ORGANIZING, BACKING UP, AND STORAGE — 181
- Backing Up – The 3-2-1 Rule — 183
- The Problems of Long-Term Digital Storage and Access — 186
- The Problem with Commercial Services — 189
- Printing Digital Documents — 190

11: DIGITIZATION — 193
- Choosing a Scanner — 194
- Preparing Documents for Scanning — 197
- Dust and Canned Air — 197
- Scanning Documents — 198
- Scanning Photographs — 199
- Scanning Slides and Negatives — 200
- Scanning Objects — 202
- Photographing Objects — 203
- Videotaping Objects — 203
- Audio/Video — 204
- Converting Audio Tape to Digital — 207
- Converting Videotape to Digital — 208

12: BORN DIGITAL — 209
- Obsolescent Media — 210
- Born Digital Documents — 211
- Born Digital Photographs — 215
- Transferring Photos to Your Computer — 216
- Organizing Photographs — 217
- Digital Audio — 223
- Digital Video — 224
- Email — 225
- Websites and Social Media — 228
- Text Messages — 234

SECTION THREE: CREATING A LEGACY — 237

13: ESTATE PLANNING — 239
- The Non-Digital Afterlife — 240
- The Digital Afterlife — 241
- Email — 248

Facebook	249
Twitter	250
Deadman's Switch	251

14: DISASTER PREPAREDNESS, DISASTER RECOVERY & EMERGENCY MANAGEMENT — 253

Prevention	256
Personal Disasters	261
Recovery	270
Floods/Water Damage	272
Photographs	274
Paper	275
Textiles	276
Metals	277
Books	277
Furniture	278
Audio and Video Tapes	278
Framed Artwork	279
Glass, Ceramics, Pottery, Earthenware, Crystal	279

Conclusion	281
Notes	285
Family Historian Legacy Promise	289
Suggested Resources	291
Books	291
Websites	292
Genealogy Shows	295
Supplies	296
List of Terms	297
Bibliography	308
Photograph Credits	319
Acknowledgements	323
Index	325

PREFACE

The information presented in this book is designed to assist the layperson with enough knowledge to create a family or personal archive so that future generations will know where they come from and appreciate the choices their ancestors made. The curious may want to simply know what life in an earlier age was like. Many conservators refuse to offer any advice to non-professionals and several that I consulted in writing this book voiced that opinion. On the other hand, after giving library lectures for several years and speaking to the patrons who attended them, I am well aware of the great need in the community for knowledge of how to organize, store, and preserve materials for future generations. People have stuff. That's an undisputed fact. What they will do with it is negotiable. It's not uncommon for relatives to go into a home after someone has passed away and throw half of their things in a dumpster, while the other half is dropped off at second hand stores. I know many people fear this fate for their documents, photographs, books, and furniture.

I offer the information in this book as a guideline. I've tried to make a distinction between what you can do yourself and when you should seek the advice of an expert. As is true of any field, the information is always evolving, and this is particularly true of digital documents. While this book contains step-by-step instructions for digital preservation that will most likely change, the *principles* discussed will remain constant. I hope the advice given in the following pages will not only instruct you, but will inspire you to leave a legacy. Proceed with caution and when in doubt, do nothing and call an expert.

Rhonda J. Chadwick

October 30, 2021

INTRODUCTION

Hurricane Sandy hit the New York coast on October 29th, 2012, as a post-tropical cyclone with hurricane force, 70-mile-per-hour winds and a 14-foot storm surge. The devastation to the city and its boroughs was immense. Sandy was the second costliest storm in US history, created the largest power outage on record, and left 147 people dead in eight countries.[1] Americans have become all too familiar with these "super storms" and catastrophic events. The weather, which used to be broadcast locally in evening newscasts, is now a regular part of the national news. It seems almost every day the destruction and devastation from these weather-related events captures our national attention—hurricanes along the coasts, tornados in the Midwest, wildfires in the drought-stricken west, and floods everywhere.

Staten Island after Hurricane Sandy

A few days after Hurricane Sandy, Anne Curry from *The Today Show* interviewed Phyllis Puglia, a hurricane survivor from Staten Island. News crews followed Phyllis when she returned to her small home on the island, which was completely devastated. The next day, cameras captured Phyllis as she walked on a pile of rubble that stretched as far as the eye could see. Wearing black knee-high rubber boots, she balanced precariously on a wooden board perched on a gnarled mess of ocean reeds and household items that had washed ashore a mile from her home.

> America's heart broke watching that scene. I thought, "If only I could have told her how to save her memories, she would not have lost everything."

Spotting a photograph, Phyllis stooped down and picked up a 12" x 16" sepia toned photograph of a 1940s bride with a sweeping train pooling at her feet. The photograph was curled from the effects of being wet, it was dirty and warped, but miraculously not ripped. Phyllis looked at the photograph and cried, "My mother! My mother!" She immediately thought of her father and said, "There have to be more pictures of my father." In a heartbreaking plea she said, "I want to go home. I want to go home. But there is no home. There's nothing left."

America's heart broke watching that scene. I thought, "If only I could have told her how to save her memories, she would not have lost everything." As a trained archivist who has worked in university libraries and museums, I could have shown her how to preserve her memories so that when the hurricane hit, parts of her family legacy would be recoverable. While a relatively small portion of the American public is losing everything to these catastrophic weather events, the rest of us sit by watching horror-struck and wonder if we will be next. There are many reasons for getting your memories in order, losing everything in a super storm is one of the most compelling.

LEAVING A LEGACY

When you die, your stories and your memories die with you. This includes the stories you know about your grandparents and great-grandparents, the stories your mother told you about relatives you never met but were part of your family and meaningful to those you loved, and the stories your grandfather told about his time serving in the war. Unless you preserve these stories in a way that is meaningful and in a way that your family can access them, your legacy and your family's legacy will die—if not with you, then with your children.

When my Aunt Hope died, I took a box of photographs she had stored in her closet that my cousin was going to throw out. Aunt Hope had no children to leave her memories to, so any of her nieces or nephews were welcome to take them. I could not wait to get home to see what was in them, thinking there would be pictures of my father and aunts and uncles when they were children. I envisioned seeing my grandparents as young adults, or perhaps even as children themselves. I opened the box as if unlocking a treasure chest filled with secrets from my father's hidden past.

What I found was disappointing. I did not know who was in the pictures or where they were taken. I knew many of the pictures were of my paternal grandmother's relatives, none of whom I have ever met. Without any information accompanying the pictures, their meaning was lost to me. I knew who some of the people were, but for many of them, especially those from my aunt's teens and twenties, I had no idea. I did not even know the age of my aunt at the time the photographs were taken.

I brought the box of photographs to my Aunt Thelma, Hope's sister, in the expectation that she could identify them. She was helpful to a point, but dementia had already set in and I became aware that she was making up names just to please me. I had to decipher when she really knew someone and when she was pretending to know. Unless you take the time to write this information in, your descendants will be lost in identifying who is in the picture and knowing why that day or person may have been significant.

In another photo album belonging to my Auntie Edna, there is a young man with the name "Chocolate" written under his image. Why was he called Chocolate? He looks like a silly, happy-go-lucky kind of guy by his expression and the clothes he wears. I am curious to know why he was called Chocolate, but sadly will never know. I think I have identified him on the genealogical family tree, but I cannot be certain of that either since his nickname and his real name are not connected anywhere.

Chocolate

Have you ever gone to a flea market, yard sale, or church bazaar and found a box of photographs on the table ready to be sold to the next buyer? I have always wondered how those photographs end up in a place like that. After seeing my aunt's pictures, I understand why family members have no reason to keep them. Why not get rid of a box of photographs that are meaningless to you? Without an explanation of who is in the picture and what is going on, the pictures are just clutter. Unless you take the time to organize and preserve your photographs, they might end up in a flea market or antique shop someday too. On the other hand, if you take the time to describe your photographs and the other materials in your possession, you will create a family legacy that people in your family can appreciate for generations.

Many people own letters that have been handed down from one generation to another. A friend of mine was given a box of letters, photographs, journals, and artifacts that went back as far as 1835. Everything was in a couple of shoeboxes, and the letters were folded into little packets. The photographs had been put into plastic sheets—the kind that melt on a hot day. Everything was disorganized and erratic. My friend cared deeply about these items and wanted to take care of them in the best way possible, but she did not know what to do. We had a training session, and I showed her how she could store everything so that it could all be shared with the family and preserved for as long as possible. I am writing this book to share that same information with you.

CLEARING THE CLUTTER

Your main motivation for organizing your memorabilia might be that you cannot stand the clutter any longer. As we downsize and clear the clutter from our homes, cleaning out our memory drawers is part of the process. In looking over the boxes of materials we have saved, we must ask ourselves whether we really need to keep everything. The answer may be yes, the answer may be no. We will discuss more about what to keep and what to get rid of in Chapter 1, but disposing of certain items may be as simple as passing them on to a child or grandchild, or it may mean taking a photograph of something, digitizing it, and getting rid of the original.

There are many good reasons to get your family collection in order. Now onto the business of getting it done.

Chapter 1 discusses archival basics. You will learn about the importance of climate controls for archival collections and the best storage enclosures for specific items. In addition, you will consider the best place within your home to store materials and what types of materials belong in a family archive. This chapter also discusses how to gather the best archival supplies and how to create a workspace.

> "In Africa, when an old man dies, it is a whole library burnt down."
> (Keakopa 1998, 87).[2]

Chapter 2 explores how to organize materials both physically and intellectually and how to process a collection. It also teaches the importance of doing a survey and appraising what you have.

Chapters 3, 4, 5, and 6 teach how to store photographs, which are often the largest part of any family archive and are usually the most sensitive objects in our collections. You will learn how to store 19th-century daguerreotypes and tintypes, what the best storage enclosures for 20th-century photographs are, and what to do with film.

Chapters 7 and 8 show how to archive specific materials most common in family collections, including paper documents and books (Chapter 7); and textiles such as wedding gowns, christening gowns, or military uniforms and flags (Chapter 8).

Chapters 9, 10, 11, and 12 are all about the digital world. You will learn how to digitize photographs and documents in your collection and find out what to do with born digital documents including email, photographs, and audio/video files. We discuss how to preserve your Facebook pages, blog posts, and websites if you have any. You will learn how to backup materials, consider the best digital storage mechanisms, and determine which file formats are most likely to last into the future. Have you ever looked at your sister's or father's family photographs and wished you could have a copy for yourself? Chapter 11 specifically focuses on using digitization to expand your project and leave a legacy and family history that is inclusive of the photographs and memorabilia of others.

Chapter 13 helps you consider the steps you need to take so that the executor of your estate will have access to your digital footprint after your passing. What types of documentation and authorization will people need to settle your estate digitally? We talk about passwords, access, rights and ownership, online digital estate planning services, and what happens to email, Facebook, and Twitter after you pass. We also discuss what dead man switches are and how they work.

Chapter 14 considers how living in the age of global warming necessitates protecting our collections against the superstorms that are becoming commonplace. You will learn what you can do to safeguard your documents and memorabilia, what kinds of security systems you need to keep precious materials out of the hands of thieves, and what to do after disaster strikes—whether it is a natural disaster or a burst pipe within your home.

Extensive research went into this book. I have searched the most relevant websites, institutions, and experts in the field. I have consulted with archivists and conservators who have worked in archives and museums for many years and have integrated their advice and direction. Many of the websites and books I consulted were written by conservators or museum curators. New technologies are constantly being introduced into the marketplace. While it is impossible for a book to capture all these new advances, the archival principles in this book remain consistent. After reading this book, you will be able to assess whether new technology is something you should embrace or avoid.

I have tried to bring my unique perspective as an archivist to the information that is already available. Archivists strive to protect items before damage occurs. Conservators fix items after the damage has been done. Genealogists are great at showing how to collect and find information on your family tree, but they are not so great at teaching how to organize that material so that it makes sense and can be easily retrieved. I teach the tried-and-true methods that archivists around the world use to organize collections both large and small. Archivists are always thinking of future researchers who will come to the archive seeking organized and rehoused information. I try to instill this same perspective by helping you place your future descendants in the position of the archivist's researcher. They have both come to an archive seeking information. In your descendants' case, they are coming to the family archive seeking knowledge about your shared past.

Writing this book has forced me to step outside the bounds of the daily work I do as an archivist. I tried not to step out too much. With that in mind, the chapters I have chosen to write about are areas of archives and conservation with which I have had direct experience. Books, paper documents, and photographs have been part of every collection I have worked on. In other archives, I have become familiar with both metal objects and textiles. (Please note that in order to save space, the chapter on Metals has been moved to my website at https://lenasalina.com/secretsfrom-the-stacks-guides/).

I decided that it was not in the best interest of my readers for me to write about other types of conservation which I have not had exposure to or experience with. However, the suggested resources pages at the end points you in the right direction for gaining advice on how to care for specific items such as fine art, furniture, ceramics, musical instruments, ethnographic materials, toys, and many other types of materials.

I hope you are excited about taking on this project. By the end of this book, you will officially be "The Family Historian" of your clan. Not everyone in your family will want to take on this task, but everyone may be grateful that you have.

I watch many genealogy shows, and you will see quotes from those shows sprinkled throughout this book. One particular episode I watched told the story of an actress' great-great-grandmother who lived in Victorian England. The woman was poverty-stricken and her first husband abused her until she left him. She created a successful business that failed after several years due to circumstances beyond her control. For several years, she and her children lived through the horrors of England's poor house. The family became separated, one of her children died, and she nearly died herself. Having been knocked down repeatedly, she rose up one more time, pulled herself and her baby out of the poor house, and brought her family back together. She went to work and became successful again. While she was never wealthy, she restored herself and her family back to health and wellness. Her story was very inspirational. The actress felt sadness for her ancestor's downfalls and losses, and happiness for her successes. Ultimately, she felt a deep sense of gratitude and pride in the strength that her great-great-grandmother had demonstrated in the face of impossible odds.

I, too, was inspired by her story. But I wondered what would have happened if this woman's great-great granddaughter did not happen to be a famous person who was featured on a genealogy show for entertainment purposes? Her story, her suffering and pain, her conquest over a difficult life and impossible circumstances would have been lost in the annals of history forever. Not even a whisper of her dramatic life would have been heard. No one would know what she accomplished, or even that she existed.

Do not let this happen to your family. I know there are important stories and life lessons buried behind those serenely smiling faces in the photographs that fill your family's photo albums. It may take a while to put it all together, but it will be a worthy cause. I hope this book will help steer your family legacy in the right direction.

IN DEFENSE OF ARCHIVES

Watching genealogy shows makes it clear that we have a common history and a common past. Shows from different countries illuminate themes common to all who descend from a particular country or area. American genealogy shows tend to find relatives who were alive during the Civil War, and it is always interesting to see how they participated. If the genealogy goes back further, it bangs into the American Revolution. Other families arrived during the Industrial Revolution when America's population swelled exponentially or when their ancestors came unwillingly on slave ships. English genealogy shows find ancestors living in poor houses or working in the factories of Victorian England. The Irish cannot avoid the Great Famine, and Australian shows reveal crimes major and minor that brought relatives to the continent's penal colony.

Your family's history may be unique and important to your family, but the objects in your collection and your family's history may also be important to local history, state history, or national history. With that in mind, you might want to consider donating all or part of your collection to an archive. If you have a Civil War bayonet in your possession, or the plaque from your great-great-grandfather's textile mill, you might consider donating that piece to an archive. A professional archive may take care of the item better than you can, and if you document for the family that it has been donated, they will be able to visit it anytime. It may also go on display at times so others can enjoy a piece of history that came down the line in your family. Scholars and researchers will also have the benefit of examining and analyzing your piece and including it in the larger history of the community.

Having worked at a museum when it closed, I can tell you with certainty that historical objects cannot be destroyed. The worst that can happen is that they could be sold at auction, but that would be a last resort after all attempts to have them sent to another archive have failed and that would only be if the archive was closing, which is rare. Items donated to archives have great chances of survival and longevity.

By donating to an archive, you will have the ability to keep documents closed for a period of years if you so choose. If you write an autobiography that you think will cause embarrassment or heartache for someone, you can keep the records closed until well after they have passed.

Another thing to consider is that you do not have to do everything by yourself. In the following pages I teach you what needs to be done, but that does not mean you have to do it all—or do it alone. There are services available and professionals who can assist you in getting your documents in order, your photographs organized, and your stories told.

When people come to my library lectures, I find one of the biggest deterrents to them getting help with an archival or legacy project is the cost. Many people do not have the time or ability to put their archives together until they are retired, and by then they are living on a fixed income. Other people think spending money on this kind of project is like paying someone to wash your dishes or do your laundry. Many people pay for these services, but many others have the mindset that paying for such services is frivolous.

With that in mind, I would like you to consider how much money the last married couple in your family spent on their wedding. If they spent $10,000, that was a low-cost wedding. Couples typically spend $50,000 or more for a one-day event. Wouldn't it be worth it to spend 10% of that amount paying a few professionals and purchasing good materials to build a personal or family archive that will be a legacy for generations to come? You are worth the expense. Your family history is worth the expense.

Stop waiting for the perfect time to do this. Do it now. Clear a time in your schedule. You have the time; you just need to give it to this project. I was once invited to set up a table at a historic event given by a local town museum. I brought all my archival supplies and memory books and had a big banner with my company name on it. A silver-haired woman rolling an oxygen tank behind her walked past my table several times over the course of the day. Finally, at the end of the day, she came over to take a look at my supplies and offerings.

"I have to do this," she said. She went on to tell me that she had tons of photo albums and documents from her family's history. "I really need to put it in order," she said again. She explained that she had a son and a daughter who were not interested in family history and did not know the stories she knew about their grandparents and great-grandparents. I offered to go to her house and do a consultation to help her get started and point her in the right direction. She refused, saying she was too busy right now to focus her attention on it. As I looked at the rubber tube that extended from the oxygen tank up to her nose, I could not help but think, "Better hurry up."

Some African cultures believe that when a person dies a whole library is lost. For many people, the moment they become interested in family history is the moment the family member who has always been "The Keeper of the Lore" passes. That woman's uninterested son and daughter might become very interested on the day of her funeral when they know they can no longer call her up and say, "Remember you said your parents came over from Italy? Where did you say they lived when they were there? What was that story about your father's brother? How old was he when he came? How did he meet your mother? Were they part of a larger migration? Was there a war or a famine that drove them? I read something on the internet that made me think of him."

Imagine the gratitude they would feel if, when clearing out her home, they stumbled upon a family archive that she had quietly put together for them that told those stories, answered those questions, and connected them to their own history and the history of their people.

SECTION ONE

THE MATERIAL WORLD

CHAPTER 1

ARCHIVAL BASICS

Well, I've been afraid of changin'
'Cause I built my life around you
But time makes you bolder
Children get older
I'm getting older too.

—**Stevie Nicks,** *Landslide*

THE GOAL

Before we begin, let's consider who we are creating this archive for. If you are not one of those lucky people who have photographs and letters from a long-lost relative who lived during the Civil War or the American Revolution, it is probably not on your radar to think very far ahead when considering who you are creating the family archive for. You may think of creating it for yourself in the event of a disaster. You may think of creating it for your siblings and cousins with whom you can share it at the next family gathering. Most people think of their children and grandchildren when they contemplate preserving their documents. Typically, this is as far ahead as most people consider.

I want you to think of the person in your family who will be born after the last person who has known you directly has died. Assuming we do not blow ourselves up, we can imagine the human race will continue for another thousand years. I want you to think of your descendants who would think it cool to have memorabilia from the 20th and 21st centuries. You lived through a great time in history! People belonging to the Greatest Generation lived through the Great Depression and World War II. Baby boomers lived through the '60s; the assassinations of JFK, MLK and RFK; the Civil Rights Movement; the Feminist Movement; and Viet Nam. Gen Xers lived through the Gulf War, Reaganomics, the Berlin Wall coming down, and the end of the Cold War. Millennials grew up with school shootings and, as most of us remember, September 11th and its aftermath, the Crash of 2008, and more recently the worldwide pandemic. These are just a few of the major historical events that have touched our lives. We are all part of a generation and an era. A hundred years from now, people will be interested in knowing that their relative's lives were touched by these events in different ways. Even if you do not have evidence of how your life was touched by these events, your descendants will still be interested in who you were and what your life was like during this era.

Genealogy shows such as *Finding Your Roots, Who Do You Think You Are,* and *Genealogy Roadshow* bring to life how connected we are to our ancestors. Episodes show people crying because a great-great-great-grandparent that they never knew lived through a historical event or personal tragedy. In the same episode we see people puff up their chests after learning they are related to a great historical figure. Whether our history tells of a celebrated past or a painful circumstance, we are connected to it. We care deeply about our forebears' lives. We can often detect how what happened to them shaped who we are today. Stories and legends get passed down for generations—some true, some partially true. Today, we have the opportunity to tell the story of our ancestors and to add our story to the mix.

Why do I want you to expand your thinking about who you are leaving your archives to? Because if you change your mind from thinking only of your children or your grandchildren, you will tell your story in a very different way; you will describe a letter, a deed, a photograph, or a quilt much differently. Instead of indicating that a picture is of, "Aunt Mary and her friend, Lou," you would write, "Mary Louise Smith and Lou Johnson. They were a couple for many years, but never married." If you write for your children, you will assume they know who Aunt Mary is and that they know that Lou was the boyfriend she never married. The person who is born after the last person who knows you directly dies will not know that.

Here is a formula to help you conceptualize this:

- ✓ If you were born in 1945 and live to be 100, you will die in 2045.
- ✓ If your great-grandchild is ten years old when you die, they will have been born in 2035.
- ✓ If that great-grandchild lives to be 100, they will die in 2135.
- ✓ The person who is born in or after 2135 is the person I want you to think about when you preserve your family history. I call that person, Baby 2135.

I know that sounds crazy and is an extremely long time into the future. When I think of Baby 2135, the concept seems very remote and abstract. Even I, the archivist, thinks, "Who cares?" When I am working in the archives and I wonder whether I should save something, I always look back and think, "What don't we have that I wish we did?" or "What do we have that I'm glad we do?" Asking these questions changes our perspective. With that in mind, let's apply the formula to our ancestors.

Baby 2135

- ✓ Say you had great-great-grandparents who were born in 1800.
- ✓ If they lived to be 100, they would have died in 1900.
- ✓ Their 10-year-old great-grandchild would have been born in 1890.
- ✓ If the great-grandchild lived for 100 years, they would die in 1990.
- ✓ The person who was born in 1990 would now be in their thirties.

It does not seem that long ago when you put it that way, does it?

When you are creating your family archive, I want you to consider that you and your relatives are someone else's ancestors. You will be the great-great-great-great-grandparent to someone else. Leave your legacy to that person. Think about them when you are organizing your materials. Explain to them what is going on. Do not assume they know what you mean when you talk about the U2 concert you went to or how you had a "brush with fame" with David Letterman. Obviously, we can assume your great-great-great-great-grandchild will know something about history, and Google or its equivalent will most likely be around. Nevertheless, you want to be mindful that the person of the future is not necessarily going to know what Spanx or clogs are or who the mayor of your town is. Do you know who ran for president against Woodrow Wilson?

WHAT IS A FAMILY ARCHIVE?

Everything we own or use does not belong in a family archive. In the archival profession, we try to identify items that have enduring value. A family archive should retain records that show documentary evidence of a person's life. Collectively this forms the family history. I cannot say fully what would have enduring value in your family. To some extent the matter is very personal. But there are certain things that are typically more important than others and are worth saving.

ARCHIVES TIP

A family archive should retain records that show documentary evidence of a person's life.

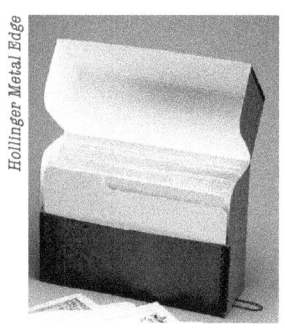

Hollinger Metal Edge

Fliptop boxes with archival folders can be used to store many paper documents including legal documents, financial papers, and even photographs.

Legal Documents

Legal documents include certificates of birth, death, and marriage; passports; immigration papers; military records; lawsuits; divorce decrees; wills; etc. Legal documents reveal a great deal about people, sometimes in ways we do not always think of. Typically, all legal documents should be retained.

Items with Financial Value

Stocks and bonds; deeds; purchase and sales agreements; loans; appraisals for jewelry, antiques, or equipment; and family heirlooms such as jewelry, silver, watches, and artwork may all have financial value. Keep documents that show evidence of value for items that are still active. Many people are very private about how much money they earn, but saving some of this information might be revealing to future generations. Tax returns need to be saved for a certain period of time but can then be discarded. Business owners may want to retain documentary evidence of their business' life cycle. For a family business, this would be particularly relevant to a family archive.

Functional Documents

Documents used to accomplish a specific task are considered functional documents. Some examples are blueprints, architectural drawings, maps, navigational records, scientific and observational documents, business plans, cookbooks, dress patterns, and knitting patterns. If something was created by a family member or shows evidence that it was important in their lives, you may want to save it.

Evidence of Events

Though legal documents provide evidence of some events, other events not legal in nature will be recorded through different means. Graduation diplomas, certificates of religious rites of passage such as first communion or bar mitzvah, greeting cards for birthdays, sympathy cards, thank you notes, awards or certifications for hobbies or sports, and course completions or professional training certificates are some examples. Even concert tickets, theater tickets, museum receipts, ski lift tags, and movie ticket stubs show proof that an event occurred. Photographs are the most explicit way we document an event. Photographs of family reunions, travels abroad, annual holidays, or baby's first tooth are all events we may find important to save and archive.

Some discrimination will be needed in this category of showing proof that an event occurred. Ask yourself, does this item have enduring value? Does it show evidence of a person's life? Is the event significant enough to keep evidence of it? In other words, do we need to keep every photograph from every holiday? It is probably not necessary to save every Christmas card you have ever received, but you might want to save all the sympathy cards you received when your father died. Think of what would be of interest to Baby 2135.

Sentimental Items

This is a tough category because, depending on how sentimental you are, everything could potentially be saved. Some things have more sentimental value than others. You may not want to save the McDonald's uniform you wore in high school, but you may want to save the baseball cap you wore if that was a big part of your high school experience. If you played baseball one season and were not very good at it or did not like it, keeping the cap does not really provide evidence of who you were and what was important to you. Many people save wedding dresses and christening gowns that are passed down to future generations. My family saved the fiddle my mother's Uncle Freddy played to entertain the family. He died many years before I was born, but I will keep the fiddle and include the stories my mother shared about his wild life.

Records of the Inner Life

Many people spend hours carefully creating records of their own thoughts, telling their own stories, or recording the lives of other family members. These documents include journals, scrapbooks, photograph albums, blog posts, videos, emails, letters, memoirs, oral histories, and books, especially those that are signed by the author or contain margin notes by the owner. You will want to save these documents since the owner took such care in creating them.

Accounts of Social Interactions

Most people have belonged to at least one social organization in their lifetime, whether it is the Boy Scouts as a child or a quilt group as an adult. Some of these social institutions form a big part of our identities and personal histories. In many cases, families participate in a social organization as a group. This is particularly true of many religious institutions. We may have in our possession minutes of meetings, programs of events, or membership rosters. Sports organizations also fall into this category, as do recreational activities such as boating, hiking, skiing, golfing, or bicycling. Evidence of political activity such as pins, banners, financial contributions, speeches, and campaign activities may have enduring value.

It is not necessary to save everything from every organization we have attended. We may not want to save any of it. But, if we have received special recognition for them, or if they formed a big part of our personalities, we may want to save a few treasured items. My sister belonged to a quilt group for over twenty years. She received recognition for some of her quilts, gave presentations, and participated in the group's annual events. Retaining some evidence of her participation in this group will show future generations what was important to her, provide evidence of her values, and document how others perceived her and her handicraft.

PREVENTION

When putting together your family archive, keep in mind that prevention is a better strategy for retaining family archives than restoration. A professional conservator can remedy much damage, but their methods are often expensive and not always complete. Damage can be permanent and irreparable. Some damage is done through improper handling, but the greatest amount of damage is often done through neglect. We store things away thinking that when we pull them out in five or ten years they will be in the same condition. Finding damage that has unknowingly occurred is a sad discovery.

Preventative measures include environment, location, enclosures, and handling. Taking the right preventative steps can give your materials the longest life. When considering the best way to store archival documents, think of bats, spiders, or vampires. They prefer the environment to be cool, dry, and dark, and they abhor sunlight. They like solitude—to be far from the maddening crowd—and are happiest when sleeping in the proper enclosure. They must be handled with care.

The Environment

The single most important thing you can do to preserve your documents over the long term is to find or create an environment that provides the best surroundings for your treasures. Look around your house and determine where the best storage facility is. Different materials in your collection will have different needs, but the rule of thumb is cool, dry, dark. As stated earlier, your historical artifacts, like vampires, hate sunlight and sunlight hates them. It destroys them. When you expose an archival item to direct sunlight, imagine it giving out a long high-pitched scream like Boris Karloff. Shield it and no one gets hurt. Understand? Archival items like it cold and dry. Damp cellars and hot attics are not allowed.

Temperature and Humidity

For most things in your collection, most of the time, if the environment is comfortable for you, it will be good for your collection. Generally, that means temperatures should not exceed 68°F (20°C) and relative humidity should not exceed 50%–55%. A hygrometer is a tool that measures relative humidity (RH). You can purchase a small one at any archival supply store. I found a great one on eBay that includes a temperature gauge. The best thing about the hygrometer I bought is that it tells the temperature and humidity highs and lows within the last twenty-four-hour period.

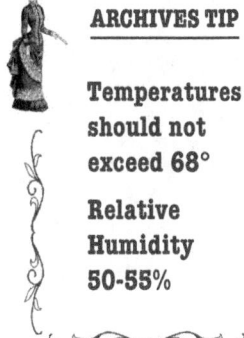

ARCHIVES TIP

Temperatures should not exceed 68°

Relative Humidity 50-55%

Keeping the environment stable is another important consideration. Changes in temperature or humidity cause materials to expand and contract. The water content in your materials increases and decreases on a microscopic level when the humidity in the air rises or falls. Constant expansion and contraction accelerate degradation. Slow changes over a longer time span, like the changing of the seasons, are not as damaging. If your power goes out and your air conditioner is off for a day or two, don't panic. This will not completely destroy all your artifacts. The point is to provide as much stability in temperature and RH as possible. Temperature and RH levels should not fluctuate more than ten degrees or ten percent in a twenty-four-hour period.

Without intervention, most home environments will be cooler in the morning, hotter in the middle of the day, and back to cool in the evening and at night. These daily fluctuations can increase the humidity levels 10% or more, especially during the warmer months. Fluctuation of 10% or more stresses your materials and increases the degradation process. If you do not have central air conditioning, you may want to put a free-standing unit in the room where you are going to store your materials. Keep the hygrometer in the area as well, and check it daily to make sure the temperature and RH remain stable. Storing your materials in a dry, stable environment reduces risks from pests, mold, and chemical deterioration.

Light

Light is the other great source of destruction for archival collections. We are all aware of the fading that occurs to curtains, rugs, and furniture when they are exposed to periods of daily sunlight. The storage area for your collection should not be exposed to sunlight. A closet is a perfect location, but if the closet door is bathed in sunlight for a portion of the day, it will not be ideal. Keep curtains and blinds down during these hours, or at all times if possible, or find another place that will not be subject to this kind of environmental concern. Generally, the north side of houses experience less exposure to light.

Our historical artifacts, like vampires, hate sunlight and sunlight hates them.

The speckles on this photograph caused by dust, and the fingerprint smudge have become permanently embedded.

Ultraviolet (UV) light rays are most damaging. This holds true for the artwork you value. Naturally, you want pictures of ancestors and artwork to be displayed where everyone can enjoy them. It is important to keep in mind that every minute those photographs and paintings are exposed to sunlight they are deteriorating and fading. UV curtains and UV framing materials can provide some protection from infrared rays. Look to archival stores to find special materials that offer UV protection for framing. Carefully choosing the best place to hang your precious paintings is essential for ensuring they have the longest life.

While we are talking about UV damage, incandescent light bulbs are more damaging than LED light. Incandescent light bulbs create more heat, which can make a difference under certain circumstances. This will not be a problem unless the bulbs are close to an archival item or enclosed in a small space such as a display case.

Dirt and Dust

Dirt and dust are a regular part of our daily lives, leading us to diminish how damaging they can be to archival collections. Textiles are particularly vulnerable, but documents, photographs, books, and other materials can also sustain permanent damage from dirt and dust. On a microscopic level, dirt can scratch surfaces or cut delicate fibers. Dust attracts pests that can cause further damage. Since much of this damage is irreversible or expensive to correct, you want to minimize the damage as much as possible. At the same time, overzealous or improper cleaning can do as much, if not more, damage.

The best preventative measure against the dreaded dirt and dust demons is to house items in the proper archival enclosures. Boxes, plastic sleeves, and acid-free tissue paper form a protective layer against a damaging environment. Items such as books that will be stored open on a shelf require regular GENTLE cleaning with a microfiber cloth. Do not use any chemicals or commercial dust sprays and use water sparingly, if ever. Use a soft artist brush to remove dirt and dust from photographs and from silver or gold artifacts. Textiles require special care. (See Chapter 8 for more information on cleaning textiles.) HEPA vacuums are a better choice for both your health and the health of your collections. They retain 99.7% of vacuumed dust. Other measures you can take are making sure the heating system in your home is properly filtered and ensuring screens are on all windows.

Environmental Pollutants

Archival collections housed in cities show more accelerated levels of deterioration than collections stored in more rural settings. Sulfur dioxides from automobiles and industrial wastes can damage your archival materials. Most people are aware of air pollution outside their homes, but few are aware of how many pollutants are within their homes and can be damaging to their collections. These include gases, acids, and alkalis. Dyed fabrics, wooden cabinets, plastics, glues, and products with formaldehyde can all emit harmful gases, corrosive acids, and damaging alkalis that accelerate the deterioration of your collections. Cigarette smoke causes silver and copper alloys to discolor or corrode. Rubber products can give off gas pollutants that cause discoloration of metals, paper, and photographs. Salts, oils, acids, and other chemicals can also cause damage if they come in direct contact with archival materials.

The best preventative method for deterring the damaging effects of indoor and outdoor environmental pollutants is housing items in proper archival storage enclosures. Awareness is the key. Keeping harmful gases and pollutants away from your collections is helpful. Though you have some control over your internal environment, you have little control over the pollution outside your home. Several layers of protective housing will form a shell that extends the lifespan of your collections. For example, storing a photograph in a plastic sleeve, in an enclosed photo album, inside a box, inside a closet, inside a room offers several layers of protection against the exterior world.

LOCATION, LOCATION, LOCATION

The area in your home where you choose to store your collection makes a significant difference. Some of these choices are obvious, but others are not. Unlike bats, spiders, and vampires, archival collections do not like attics or basements. Attics are known to have high temperatures, and while basements tend to be cool, they also tend to have high humidity. Items stored in basements can be exposed to flooding above from overhead pipes and flooding below from cracks in the foundation. The temperature of the inside walls of your house will fluctuate with outside temperatures, so closets bordering outside walls are not the best places for storing archival collections. Neither are areas with fireplaces, heating vents, or other localized heat sources that can create higher temperatures in a small, contained area. It's important to think of the plumbing in your house. Will your storage space be at risk of water damage from a burst pipe?

If you live in a flood zone, you might want to consider storing photographs and documents as high up as possible, perhaps on the second floor. Waterproof containers may also be a wise choice. You should have an emergency response plan in place before the flood comes. (See Chapter 14 for more information on how to deal with floods.)

Never store anything directly on the floor. Try to keep items at least four inches off the ground. This will help in the event of a minor flood caused by a dripping pipe or a spilled glass of soda and will also guard against mold or pests. Having good circulation is the key. Regular dusting and vacuuming also reduces the risk of mold and pests.

ENCLOSURES

Storing items in the proper enclosures not only provides ascetic value but also protects documents for the long-term. Proper enclosures provide structural support and prevent further deterioration. Making sure objects lie flat or stand up straight and do not overlap is also important. The right enclosures will protect documents from airborne pollutants, fingerprints, and light, and will help maintain temperature and humidity stability. Replacing acidic paper and plastic or vinyl enclosures with archival-quality boxes, folders, and polyester sheets will increase long-term preservation.

Most items will end up in a box, folder, or chemically inert plastic sheet. For paper boxes and folders, look for **acid-free, lignin-free, buffered** materials. Acid is the single most damaging chemical that accelerates the destruction of paper. Lignin is a component of paper that forms acid that causes brittleness and discoloration. Buffered materials contain an agent that reduces the harmful effects of the acid in paper; the most common buffering agent is calcium carbonate. Though buffered materials are safe for most paper materials, blueprints and certain inks, paints, metals, textiles, and photographs are sensitive to alkaline buffering. These items require storage in either unbuffered enclosures or unbuffered tissue paper. I will explain when to use unbuffered materials when

Clamshell boxes can hold photographs, documents, or artifacts.

Hollinger Metal Edge

1: ARCHIVAL BASICS

speaking of specific items as we go along. Enclosures labeled acid-free but not buffered have some protection, but they will not protect against long-term acidic damage.

Plastic enclosures are typically used for photographs and certain paper documents. In professional archives, papers might be put into plastic enclosures if they are heavily damaged or will be frequently used. I do not think it is necessary to put all paper documents in plastic enclosures, but I have seen family collections that use this method. Depending on the age and level of deterioration of the document, you might consider this option. Otherwise, most papers will be perfectly safe in acid-free, lignin-free, buffered folders.

ARCHIVES TIP

For paper boxes and folders, look for acid-free, lignin-free, buffered materials.

Safe plastic enclosures are polyester, polypropylene, or polyethylene. These plastics are considered inert, which means they will not cause further damage. Stay away from polyvinyl or polyvinyl chloride (PVC) plastic. Polyvinyl is a cheaper grade of plastic found in most loose-leaf binders and non-archival photo albums. Enclosures made from PVC release harmful elements that can affect the stability and appearance of photographs or papers. When traditional plastic begins to deteriorate, especially in hot conditions, it gets soft and sticks to pages. Over time, plastic sheets and binders will turn to goop, damaging the very items they were meant to protect. Preservation-quality polyester is the most stable, but polyethylene or polypropylene are also safe if they do not contain plasticizers.

In the archives, we look for photographic enclosures that have passed the Photographic Activity Test (PAT©). Documents that have passed this test will say "Passed PAT" somewhere in the description. PAT is a test developed by the Image Permanence Institute (IPI) that guarantees the enclosure will not react chemically with the photographs. Professional archivists turn to and rely on the IPI as the trusted resource in the field. The institute tests specific products and adds its seal of approval only if the products meet certain standards. The institute does not guarantee that a product is the best or will last the longest, it guarantees that the product will not do further damage to an item.

ARCHIVES TIP

Look for photographic enclosures that have passed the Photographic Activity Test (PAT©).

Many modern commercial manufacturers now sell photographic storage supplies that are made from good plastics. The scrapbooking craze of recent years created awareness and resulted in positive changes in the industry. This means that many items sold today in office supply and craft stores will be archivally sound. But items housed in the old magnetic albums or with PVC plastic will still need to be rehoused.

Other Handy Supplies

Other supplies to purchase before you begin your archival project include a good pencil and eraser. Archivists always use pencil. Not because it is easy to erase (although we are grateful for that!), but because it is the one writing implement that lasts the longest. Ink fades fairly quickly. Forget gel pens; they will be gone within a few years. Magic markers fade. Pencil fades over time too, but as of today it still lasts longer than the others.

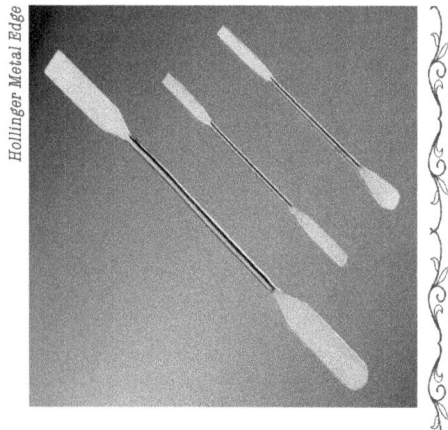

Microspatulas

A good eraser is like a good editor. They clean up your mistakes and no one is the wiser for it. Do not rely on the eraser at the end of a pencil. Typically, these are only good for erasing small areas. A good eraser is cheap enough and worth the price. In the archives, I have labeled folders in a section only to realize as the project unfolded that I needed to change all or most of the folder titles. When faced with having to erase twenty-five folders, I was very happy to have a good eraser that made the job simple and easy and the final product clean and ready for the new title.

As discussed earlier, a good temperature/humidity gauge, or hygrometer, is essential for monitoring the area where your documents will be stored.

Tissue paper has many uses in the archives. Glassine is also a common archival supply. Glassine can be used to interleaf photographs, documents, or other items. Tissue paper and glassine come in buffered and unbuffered varieties. Glassine is familiar to many of us who used to send film out to be developed. The film that came with our developed pictures was housed in glassine envelopes.

> "I could have saved myself a lot of time and money. Rather than doing therapy I should have been doing genealogy. Now knowing my ancestors, I understand a lot more about myself."
> —Ruby Wax.
> WDYTYA-UK.14.10

Boxes come in full size cartons, half size flip-top boxes, or quarter size flip-top boxes. Full size cartons can house *either* legal- or letter-size folders, but the smaller flip-top boxes come in legal- *or* letter-size. Clamshell boxes come in many different sizes and are good for housing items that need to lie flat. For oversized documents, you can purchase larger boxes up to 36" x 48" with folders to match. You can also find special boxes to house artifacts.

At library lectures, I pass around a catalog from one of the archival supply houses. I give away one catalog at each lecture. I recommend that you visit the archival supply houses online and request a free catalog (see Suggested Resources for a list of archival supply stores). Flip through the catalog and look at what is available for your particular collection. It is a good idea to do this before beginning your processing project. Becoming familiar with the wide array of archival enclosures will help you decide how best to store items in your collection.

Folder supports found in archival supply catalogs are a must. It is important to keep documents upright. After spending the time and money to properly rehouse your documents, you do not want them to be ruined because of slumping. I often hand-make folder supports with empty folder boxes, but unless you are going through many boxes of folders, this is not a practical solution. If you decide to make your own folder supports, make sure the paper is acid-free.

A clean workspace is important to the success of your project.

CREATING A WORKSPACE

Creating the proper workspace is an important next step. I do not recommend working on your archives at your kitchen table. If this is sensitive, valuable material that you want to have last for a few hundred years, you want to make sure that you work in such a way that nothing is destroyed or damaged while you are working. With that in mind, please find a place in your home where your materials will not be exposed to potential hazards. If you can designate a room in your house, that would be perfect. If not, if it must be the kitchen table, then put everything in a box (or boxes) and put it away when you are done working.

When you work on your archive, make sure your pets are in a separate room and young children are either sleeping or are out of the house. You do not want cats walking across your great-grandfather's war letters or a dog running off with his medal of honor. Small sticky fingers should not come within miles of your grandmother's handmade doilies.

You should have no food or drinks in the area where you are working. Maybe you want to work on your project at night when you come home from work and relax in front of the television (entirely possible). Perhaps you like to have a cup of tea in the evening or a small snack when you watch television. Is it okay to do that when you are archiving your photographs? No. If you were archiving Ernest Hemmingway's materials, would you have a cup of tea and a greasy cookie nearby? No, you would not. So do not do it when working on your own collection.

I can assure you that you will not die from not eating or drinking for a few hours while you work in the vicinity of your photographs and memorabilia. Archivists do it all day, all the time—no food or drinks in the archives. We leave our water bottles outside the work area. I will not even bring my lunch bag into the area just in case there are fruit fly eggs buried in the bottom. We have no plants in the archives either. As we say, nothing lives in the archives except the archivist. If you are dying of thirst, go outside and take a few sips of water, but otherwise, no food or drink in the work area. Smoking should go without saying. You do not want ashes dropping on your mother's 1940 prom invitation or burn marks in your father's military discharge papers.

Archivists also do not use pens, highlighters, markers, or anything else that can damage materials. Think about your workspace before you begin, and be respectful of your artifacts.

Always wash your hands before you begin. It is not necessary to wear white gloves as is often seen on television, but your hands should be clean. Wearing gloves is a little bit of a controversial issue in the archives field today. Some archivists prefer that their patrons wear gloves when they look at certain documents. It has been found, however, that the bulkiness and clumsiness of cotton gloves sometimes creates more damage to objects than the oil from your hands. Gloves dull the tactile sensation that guides us when handling sensitive documents. Without the tactile feel of an object, it is easy to tear brittle edges. Cotton gloves easily become dirty, making it likely that dirt will transfer from one document to the other. I will leave it to your best judgment whether to use gloves generally.

The exceptions to this rule are photographs, films, metals, and textiles. You might want to wear gloves while working with these types of objects. Nitrile examination gloves are preferred over white cotton gloves for photographs. I never wear gloves when I work, but I always wash my hands before working and am careful not to put fingerprints on photographs. Although I am going to be touching this document now, it may not be touched again for another hundred years. If you think there is going to be more traffic with your documents, you might want to use gloves.

Think about how you would handle the documents of Thomas Jefferson or Susan B. Anthony. Think of your favorite rock star, movie star, political figure, or historical person of note. If you were going to preserve their documents, how would you handle them? That is how you should handle your things. In other words, you should handle these documents with care. It is easy to toss around the pictures we have looked at a thousand times and not treat them like the historical documents they truly are. But if you were given the archives of Martin Luther King, wouldn't you wash your hands before you touched the clothing he wore, make sure there was nothing that could spill on them, and refrain from smoking or eating anything when working on these materials? Treat your own documents with the same respect.

PROCESSING BASICS CHECKLIST

- Either lay it flat or keep it upright.
- Avoid bending, folding, curling, or slumping documents.
- Use a folder support.
- Remove
  - paper clips
  - binder clips
  - rubber bands
  - rusted staples
- Copy bad paper such as newsprint, thermal paper, or old copy machine pages onto acid-free paper.
- Place smaller items on top of larger items.
- Lay oversized items flat.
- Roll paper only if necessary.

Description

- Describing photographs and other items:
  - Who – is in the picture?
  - What – is happening?
  - Where – is it taking place?
  - Why – is this important?
  - When – did it happen?
- Only use pencil.
- Do not write on documents.
- If you must write on documents, write in small letters in pencil on the back. Use for reference to a longer description kept elsewhere.

Creative Ideas

- ✓ To describe photographs in a photo album, insert a sheet of acid-free paper behind the photograph with a handwritten description of the image on it written in pencil. This allows for a longer description than a caption permits.

- ✓ For artifacts placed in a box, such as jewelry or ceramic pieces, place a separate sheet of paper that describes the item(s) in the box with the artifact(s). This can also be done with a folder; insert a piece of paper in the folder that describes what is in the folder.

- ✓ Folder titles should describe what is inside, such as "Purchase and Sales Agreement York Avenue, 1/27/1917."

- ✓ Documents should be stored in such a way that if the box was thrown off the shelf, it could be put back together—not by you, by Baby 2135.

- ✓ Do not use glued labels; they will fall off. If you do use a label, write in pencil underneath so that when the label falls off there is still a description. Writing on the inside cover will also let someone know what is in the box. Archival supply stores sell archival quality "permanent" labels you can use that will last much longer than other kinds of labels.

- ✓ Do not use any type of pen or magic marker. The ink will fade over time and become unreadable. Pencil is best.

CHAPTER 2

ORGANIZATION

We are family
I got all my sisters with me
We are family
Get up everybody and sing

—**Sisters Sledge**, *We Are Family*

Before beginning the creation of your family archive, we need to discuss organization. When I teach the "Organizing Your Materials" lecture, participants get overwhelmed very quickly. Organizational skills are very intuitive and easy for some people, but for others they are difficult and arduous. It depends on whether you are more right-brained or left-brained. Chances are, if you bought this book and love doing this type of work, you are left-brained and will take to this easily. But if you are a more abstract thinker and this is overwhelming, do not get scared. Just start thinking about the organizational structure of your materials at this point.

Having the principles of organization in mind while doing an appraisal and a survey will help you begin to conceptualize how the final archive will be organized. The two archival principles that form the basis of the organizational structure of all collections are *Respect du Fonds* and *Original Order*.

RESPECT DU FONDS

Respect du Fonds is the principle in archival theory that states collections should be organized according to their creator. In other words, do not mush everybody's stuff together. It makes it confusing. The idea in archival principle is that ordering records by their creatorship provides authenticity and context to the records

> **ARCHIVES TIP**
>
> *Respect du Fonds* is the principle in archival theory that states collections should be organized according to their creator.

and reveals relationships between creators and their environments. This theory developed after trial and error.

As an example, Charlotte Perkins Gilman (1860–1935), was an author who wrote many books and articles, most famously the short story "The Yellow Wallpaper," which explores medical theories and the oppression of women. Today she is considered an early feminist, having developed ideas about the status of women, the role of housework, and women's dress reform. The Charlotte Perkins Gilman Collection is housed at the Schlesinger Library at the Radcliffe Institute in Boston, MA. Perkins Gilman lived in Rhode Island for ten years in her youth and continued a correspondence with her childhood friend, Martha Luther Lane. Thirty-two letters written by Charlotte to Martha are housed at the Rhode Island Historical Society. It is tempting to think that the letters at the Rhode Island Historical Society should be included in the larger collection on Perkins Gilman at the Schlesinger Library. In the early days of archival collecting, archivists did exactly that. They mushed everything together. Soon they realized that this was not a good idea. What should they do if there was a letter in the Martha Luther Lane collection that discussed Kate Chopin, another famous author and a contemporary of Charlotte and Martha? Should they take that one letter and put it with Kate Chopin's collection? It becomes too confusing. Archivists in the 19th century quickly realized that keeping documents with their creator made the best sense.

I know what you might be thinking—Charlotte Perkins Gilman was the creator of the letters sent to Martha Luther Lane; therefore, they should be kept with the other documents that Perkins Gilman created. Yes, it's true that Perkins Gilman created the letters, but Luther Lane created the archive that turned those letters into a collection. See the difference? Keep this in mind when you go through your family's documents and materials. Many of the genealogists who come to my lectures ask questions about how to organize materials. When you are gathering all your materials to do an assessment and an appraisal, do not mix things up. Keep your father's stuff together, your mother's stuff in another pile, your aunt's materials somewhere else, and your great-grandfather's in another place.

Charlotte Perkins Gilman

How does this relate to a family archive? Have you seen the movie *Love Actually*? One of the opening vignettes is of the wedding of a young couple. The groom's best friend films the wedding. He is very cold to the bride, which leads her to believe he is jealous of her for taking his best friend away. When the pictures from her videographer are delayed, she asks to see his video. He makes excuses as to why she cannot see it, but through a series of missteps and her determination, she finds his video and pops it into his cassette player. She watches with dawning amazement while he cringes in the background—the entire video is of her; only her. It is obvious that, rather than despising her, the best friend is actually in love with her.

This is an extreme example, but it shows that the pictures and videos taken by one person could be very different from those taken by someone else. The shots, angles, and subjects one chooses when taking a picture say something about the photographer as well as what is photographed. We can assume the pictures you take at cousin Carol's wedding might be distinctly different from the pictures your brother takes. I know in my family my mother was notorious for cutting people's heads off in pictures. We want Baby 2135 to be able to make some inferences based on who the creator of the collection is as well as who is in them. I would not want Baby 2135 to think all those pictures with the chopped-off heads were mine. Just saying.

To clarify, you may organize all the materials of your spouse, children, siblings, cousins, and grandparents, but you should consider each one a separate collection and treat it as such.

ORIGINAL ORDER

The other primary archival principle that archivists keep in mind when dealing with collections is the principle of Original Order. Sometimes there is no original order and you are free to create one, but often the creators of documents, photo albums, scrapbooks, stamp collections, and other collectibles had an order in mind when they created them. You should respect this order. You may decide that the old magnetic photo album with browned pages and plastic covers stuck to the photographs needs to be dismantled and the contents placed in an archival-safe photo album. This is a great idea, but keeping the original order should be essential. When I dismantled one of my mother's magnetic photo albums, I took digital photographs of the pages before I took them apart. When putting the photographs in an archival-safe photo album, I kept them in the same order that she had them in the magnetic album as much as possible. Because the format of the original photo album and the rehoused one were quite different, I was not able to replicate exactly what my mother had. That was why I took photographs of each page before I took it apart and put a copy of the original pages at the front of the rehoused photo album. Now Baby 2135 can see how it originally looked.

In instances where the original order cannot be determined, you can create your own. A friend of mine received a box of early-19th century letters between her third great-grandfather and his wife, her third great-grandmother. The letters were still folded in their envelopes. To archive them, they should be removed from the envelopes and opened to lie flat, but the envelopes should be kept with the letters. After over 100 years of being looked at by various family members, if there ever was an original order, it had been long lost to time. The logical order for such letters would be chronological. Use your common sense and do what you think is best.

I highlight these two archival principles before you begin your appraisal and survey so that you will not alter the materials in your collection. Once the context and authenticity are lost, they cannot be recreated.

INTELLECTUAL VS. PHYSICAL ORDER

The principles of *Respect du Fonds* and Original Order refer to the **physical** order of your items. Archivists use other tools to organize materials **intellectually.** These are primarily the Series List and the Finding Aid. The following material gets a little confusing. Feel free to read through it several times until it sinks in and makes sense, especially if you are right-brained.

When I first started giving library lectures, I did not include information about how to organize materials. Many genealogists came to the lectures, and I quickly realized that they were overwhelmed with the amount of information they had gathered and were at a loss as to how to organize it. So, I started teaching the principles we use in the archives to organize materials both intellectually and physically.

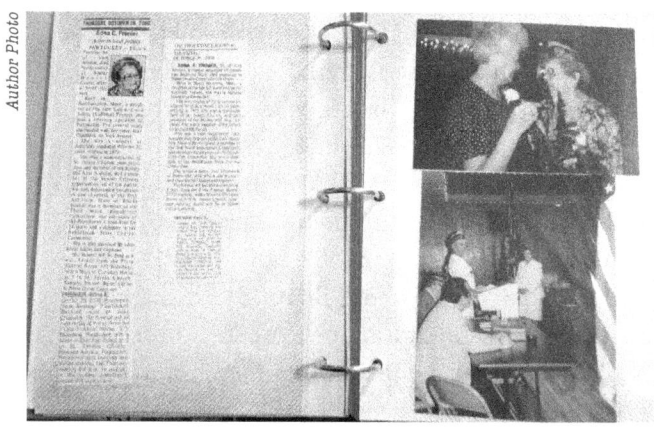

Taking photographs of photo albums before they are pulled apart for archival processing will show the original order the creator had in mind.

For a smaller collection, creating a Series List and Finding Aid may not be practical and realistic. Do not feel compelled to take this step if you are organizing a few photo albums or have just a few family heirlooms and artifacts. I offer this information to genealogists and others who have amassed massive amounts of information.

A few years ago, a gentleman attended one of my library lectures. He was part-owner of a family home that had been left to several children over 100 years ago. At the time the man attended my lecture, the ownership of the home had been extended to over 200 people, all descendants of the original children. They all had joint ownership of a vacation home that was in a scenic area. He and a small group of cousins were putting together an archive of pictures, stories, and other memorabilia that had been collected over the life of the house. Many of the actual documents and artifacts were housed at the vacation cottage. Their goal was to inform all family members about what was there and what it meant and make it available to the entire family. A Series List and Finding Aid would help this group organize the material and disseminate it to a large group.

Creating a Series List

The Series List forms the foundation of the Finding Aid. The Society of American Archivists defines a Series Lists as:

> *A group of similar records that are arranged according to a filing system and that are related as the result of being created, received, or used in the same activity; a file group; a record series. - 2. Bibliography · A group of items, each with its own title, also bearing a collective title for the group as a whole.*[3]

The Series List is a global structure that will be used throughout your collection, whereas the Finding Aid is particular to a specific collection based on what is actually in the collection. One of the archives I worked at collected the documents of feminist theorists. All the donors were college professors. When I was hired, there were only about twenty-three collections that had been fully processed. I put all the Finding Aids into an Excel spreadsheet to conduct an analysis of what was contained in the records. Cumulatively, the documents fell into six broad categories. Professors teach, write, attend conferences, speak at conferences, are on committees, and have personal lives. I created the following Series List that could be applied to all the collections:

    Series I – Teaching

    Series II – Writing

    Series III – Conference Attendance

    Series IV – Speaking Engagements

    Series V – Committees, Groups, Organizations

    Series VI – Personal Documents

Some professors had more teaching documents than writing documents. Some did not have personal documents or did not include documents from committees or organizations they belonged to. My goal in creating the Series List was to have all the collections that came into the archives follow the same structure. When I arrived, some of the collections listed Writing as the first series, others had Teaching as the first series. My objective was to have consistency and a structure that I, my students, and other archivists could follow when processing the collections.

When I arrived at the American Textile History Museum (ATHM), the staff provided me with a ten-page Series List that had been devised twenty years earlier by the then head of archives and a volunteer from Harvard Business School. Most of the collections at the ATHM were of textile manufacturers and other businesses associated with the textile industry. The Series List provided a structure all archivists could use to organize the materials in each collection. My collection had 683 boxes and over 100 ledgers. I was most appreciative to have a structure in place that I could organize my particular collection around.

A Series List is logical, somewhat intuitive, and makes common sense. Having a good sense of the materials in your collection allows you to devise your Series List before beginning to touch your material items. Throughout this chapter, I give samples of how to devise a Series List. You can follow this structure or create your own. Try searching for family collections in libraries, special collections, and archives. Type "family" in the search terms, narrow it down by "family" in the title, and see what comes up. Spend some time exploring how archivists structure family collections and see what makes sense for your collection.

According to the principles of a Series List, each branch of your family would form a different series within your family archive. These would be considered the major series with subseries below them, and it would look like this:

Family Archive
    Series I – Chapman Family Documents
    Series II – O'Malley Family Documents
    Series III – Lafond Family Documents
    Series IV – Proulx Family Documents

In this family, Chapman and O'Malley are on the father's side, and Lafond and Proulx are on the mothers' side. When passing this information on to descendants, structuring archival materials' organization by the different branches of the family makes sense. Separating the families along genealogical lines helps facilitate passing information down to cousins on either side.

Family Archive – Chapman

    Series I – Chapman Family Documents

    Series II – O'Malley Family Documents

Family Archive – Lafond

    Series I – Lafond Family Documents

    Series II – Proulx Family Documents

Within each of these broad series, there will be subseries. A Series List should capture everything that MAY be in the collection even if those documents are not in ALL the collections. In other words, the Series List provides a consistent structure that can be used for all the series in the collection. The Finding Aid will determine what parts of the Series List are used based on the actual documents in the archive.

Let's start with one Series and consider the SubSeries and Sub-SubSeries that might form that archive. The Series is The Chapman family. The first level of SubSeries are the children or siblings in this family:

Series I – Chapman Family Documents

    SubSeries A – Stella (Bowen)

    SubSeries B – Robert

    SubSeries C – James

    SubSeries D – Theresa (Scotti)

    SubSeries E – Raymond

    SubSeries F – Hope

As an initial SubSeries, each person in the family is listed. The collection has materials from Stella, Theresa, Hope and Raymond.

The next SubSeries could follow the genealogical pattern and list their children. It might look like this:

Series I – Chapman Family Documents

    SubSeries A – Stella (Bowen)

        Subseries a: Chester

        Subseries b: Roberta

        Subseries c: Russell

        Subseries d: Agnes

SubSeries B – Robert

SubSeries C – James

SubSeries D – Theresa (Scotti)

SubSeries E – Raymond

    Subseries a: Dawn

    Subseries b: Diane

    Subseries c: Veronica

SubSeries F – Hope

We could add another level of family members such as this:

Series I – Chapman Family Documents

SubSeries A – Stella (Bowen)

    Subseries a: Chester

    Subseries b: Roberta

    Subseries c: Russell

    Subseries d: Agnes

SubSeries B – Robert

SubSeries C – James

SubSeries D – Theresa (Scotti)

SubSeries E – Raymond

    Subseries a: Dawn

        Subseries a: Michael

        Subseries b: Emily

    Subseries b: Diane

        Subseries a: Katiana

        Subseries b: Robert

    Subseries c: Veronica

SubSeries F – Hope

This should make sense, especially to genealogists. Keep in mind that the Finding Aid will only list the family members whose documents are contained in the collection. Also, the Finding Aid will not contain the words "Subseries." This word has been added for demonstration purposes only.

Once the documents are in order by the family line, the next things to consider are **subject areas.** These should also be consistent. You could create a Subject Guide as follows:

- ✓ Legal Documents
  - ✓ Deeds
  - ✓ Wills
  - ✓ Lawsuits
  - ✓ Other Legal Documents
- ✓ Events
  - ✓ Births
  - ✓ Birthdays
  - ✓ Weddings
  - ✓ Deaths
  - ✓ Religious Holidays
- ✓ Work Papers
- ✓ Business Documents
- ✓ Sports
  - ✓ Baseball
  - ✓ Football
  - ✓ Soccer
- ✓ Hobbies
  - ✓ Stamp Collecting
  - ✓ Photography
  - ✓ Swing Dancing
- ✓ Art
  - ✓ Quilts
  - ✓ Drawings
  - ✓ Paintings
  - ✓ Sculpture

This list could potentially appear under each person's Subseries depending on what is contained in the collection. The documents in this collection might appear like this:

Series I – Chapman Family Documents
    SubSeries E – Raymond
        Subseries c: Veronica
            Legal Documents
            Photographs
            Events
                Births
                Birthdays
                Weddings
                Deaths
                Religious Holidays
            Work Papers
            Business Documents
            Hobbies
                Knitting
                Photography
                Historical Re-enactment

Cousin Charlie

Once this basic structure is in place, Subject Guides can be compiled that help organize materials in other ways. Libraries do this regularly. Most library websites have a section that lists Subject Guides in specialized areas. Again, this may be overblown for a small family collection, but in other cases, or for certain events, you might want to bring together the information from several collections into one collection.

My cousin Charlie was a Vietnam Vet and a paratrooper. Many family members attended a skydiving event he participated in shortly after he returned from the war. Each skydiver jumped from a moving airplane with the goal of landing on a circle in a field behind the airstrip of a small local airport. The challenge was to be closest to the circle, if not right on it. Potentially, several family collections could contain photographs of this event that might be interesting to look at together. Keeping the principles of *Respect du Fonds* and Original Order in mind, we would not want to take the photographs out of each collection and bring them together. But Subject Guides or Finding Aids could act as road maps to help someone find documents on that one specific event or person found in several different collections.

Creating a Finding Aid

A Finding Aid is the final document created by archivists. It contains information that is actually found in the collection and is based on the Series List. The Society of American Archivists defines Finding Aid as follows:

> *A Finding Aid is a tool that facilitates discovery of information within a collection of records. It provides a description of records that gives the repository physical and intellectual control over the materials and that assists users to gain access to and understand the materials.*[4]

Finding aids will help you have **intellectual control** over your documents. Original Order and *Respect du Fonds* help organize materials **physically**. Using those principles, you will keep your mother's items in one box, your father's in another, and your grandmother's in a third—theoretically. A Finding Aid will bring the information in all those different collections together in one resource.

Using the Series List as a guideline, you will now process a collection and create a Finding Aid based on the documents, artifacts, and materials you actually have. Above we saw the Series List of a sample family. Here is a sample Finding Aid for the father that follows the structure of their Series List:

Series I – Chapman Family Papers
    SubSeries I – Robert
        Artifacts
            Stained-glass lamp

    SubSeries II – Theresa (Scotti)
        Artifacts
            Glassware, china
            Ceramic milk vase
            Ceramic cookie jar
            Red china dishes
        Jewelry
            Jade necklace

SubSeries III – Raymond
- Photographs
  - Korean War
  - Childhood
  - Family
- Artifacts
  - Korean War items
  - Military documents
  - Military hat
  - Military pin
  - Dog tags
  - Tape recorder and reels

SubSeries IV – Hope
- Photographs
  - Childhood
  - Adulthood
- Artifacts
  - Furniture
    - Childhood desk

Comparing the Finding Aid to the Series List, you can see that the same basic structure is followed by all the collections. The photographs category comes before the artifacts category. In this collection there is nothing that belonged to Stella or James, so they are not listed. The names should be kept in the order found on the Series List regardless of their significance to the person creating the Finding Aid. You would not put your father ahead of an older sibling because he is more significant to you. His place on the Finding Aid is determined by his position in the family, not the significance to your life or the number of materials you have for him.

A spreadsheet such as Microsoft Excel is a great tool for creating Finding Aids. See my website at https://lenasalina.com/secrets-from-the-stacks-guides/ for further explanation on how to create a Finding Aid in an Excel spreadsheet.

Next to each line above should be a description of where the item can be found. In a family archive, unlike a repository, all items might not be stored away; we might have things on display that we want to keep on display, and we would want our heirs to know they are significant.

In my house, the ceramic pickle and olive trays given to me by my Aunt Thelma many years ago hang on the side of a cupboard in my kitchen. I have no intention of taking them off the wall. But when I pass, I want whoever is going to pack up my belongings to know that they were significant; they belonged to my Aunt Thelma and are not something I picked up at an antique store on a whim. A Finding Aid can act as a map to the items in our homes that are significant in terms of family history.

To apply this to our sample family, the section of Theresa's things on a Finding Aid might look like this:

    Theresa Chapman

        Artifacts

            Glassware, china – packed in boxes in cellar

            Ceramic milk vase – book case dining room

            Ceramic cookie jar – left side of kitchen sink on counter

            Red china dishes – box in cellar on gray metal shelves

Before leaving this section of the Finding Aid, I want to give you another example of creating special Subject Guides. I relayed above the idea of the entire family attending an event such as my cousin's paratrooper exhibition. Another more common scenario for most families is a wedding.

To demonstrate this, let's pretend that each person in your family archive has their own separate box. In reality, one person might have three boxes, and one box may contain the records of three different people. But for demonstration purposes, let's say your great-grandmother's materials are in Box #1, your father's are in Box #2, your mother's are in Box #3, your aunt's are in Box #4, and yours are in Box #5. Let's say everybody went to your wedding. A Subject Guide compiled from your Finding Aid might look something like this:

    I.   Family Archives

        a.   Special Occasions

            i.   Weddings

                1.   My Wedding (Your Name)

Under "My Wedding" would be this list of items and where to find them:

    a. Box #1 – Great-Grandmother – Photographs

    b. Box #2 – Father – Photo Album #3

    c. Box #3 – Mother – Photo Album #16

    d. Box #4 – Aunt – Photo Album #1

    e. Box #5 – My Stuff Box I

        i. Photo Album #2

        ii. Folder with invitations, thank you cards.

    f. Box #6 – My Items Box II

        i. Wedding Dress

In looking at this, you see that to find information relating to your wedding you must look in six boxes: two of yours and one each belonging to your great-grandmother, your father, your mother, and your aunt. This can be expanded as necessary, and keep in mind that the box numbers are probably not going to be this neat. Also, instead of the titles, Great-Grandmother, Father, Mother, etc., you would use the person's name. As stated earlier, there could be three collections all in one box. Included could be the photograph on the wall in your family room, the wine glasses used for the toast on the bookshelf in the living room, and the marriage certificate found in another box.

Remember, not every object in your house belongs in a family archive. You could include everything, but it is better to be discerning of what has enduring value or is considered a family heirloom and what are everyday items.

The Subject Guide could be expanded further by asking other family members what they have. This might be more relevant when compiling a list of items related to a specific person. I have my father's military items, but my sister has an antique phonograph and records that were his. When putting together a Subject Guide on my father, I might want to include what other family members have. Many items in our family archive and collection of family heirlooms are part of our living households today. They are not stored away in closets or attics or housed in boxes and drawers like they would be in a professional archive. It might not seem relevant now—everyone might know that you have the funeral flag from when your father died and that your brother has his army medals—but think again of Baby 2135. Will they know that? And who will those items have been passed down to over the generations?

Alternatively, think of your great-great-grandfather. You may own some of his items, but other belongings of his might be spread across the country in the homes of relatives you do not even know. Wouldn't it be great to discover that while you have his Civil War letters a distant cousin has his rifle and uniform?

Depending on your family values, the items in your possession, and your interest, you could compile Subject Guides on each person's wedding or on the military service of each person in the family who served. That would be pretty cool.

You do not have to nail anything down now. Sometimes Series Lists are organic. You might want to begin with one person's collection and see how it goes. Finding Aids are definitely organic because they cannot be formed until the materials are actually processed.

OTHER PARTS OF THE FINDING AID

Other parts of the Finding Aid, including the Historical Note, Scope and Content, Provenance, and Inventory, may not be necessary for a family archive. I leave it to you to decide. Creating a Historical Note will give some context and information about your family collection. The Scope and Content give Baby 2135 a basic overview of what is contained in the collection. Provenance gives an idea of the journey the materials you gathered for the archive took, and where they originated. An Inventory is just that; it describes piece by piece what is in the collection and where it can be found.

Historical Note

The Historical Note, or biographical background in an archival Finding Aid, provides researchers with basic information about the collection. In your family archive you can provide background information on the entire family and a section on each of the main people in the collection. I suggest you look at Finding Aids in any local archive or search online. You can get as detailed as you want. Typically, the Historical Note or the biographical background is found at the top of a Finding Aid. If you have accumulated a great deal of information, I suggest you give a summary of the family at the top of the Finding Aid and provide a biographical background of each family member in their section of the Finding Aid.

For example, the main Historical Note could read something like this:

> *The Olney Family Archive dates back to 1635 when Thomas Olney emigrated from England and settled in Providence, Rhode Island, with Roger Williams. Thomas had two sons when coming to America, Thomas and Obadiah. This branch of the family stems*

from Thomas Olney, born 1632, and traces the family through ten generations. The family owned the land where a national park is now found. The pond in the national park is named Olney Pond after the family. There is also a family graveyard on the property.

This basic note can continue adding any highlights Baby 2135 might be interested in knowing. This section of the Finding Aid can contain biographical information on all family members, or the individual biographical backgrounds can be placed with the person's name in the Finding Aid. It can also be in both places depending on your preference.

When processing the papers of the Troy Mills Collection, I included Historical Notes on Trade Union Papers, the Environmental Records, and one on Presidents of the Corporation. I included brief descriptions in the historical background at the top of the Finding Aid but put more extensive histories in the different sections.

Scope and Content

The Scope and Content section of the Finding Aid provides summary information on what kind of documents are found in the collection. Here is what the Rhode Island Historical Society has for the papers of Granville Olney:

These records were all apparently kept by Granville S. W. Olney for his various business concerns and partnerships. Determining which business each volume relates to has proven unusually difficult in this case, as none of the volumes are labeled, many volumes were put to multiple uses, and the dates overlap to a great extent. The records have been organized by first date, and the few direct connections between the volumes have been noted in the inventory. Many of the records name individual workers. Wool carding piecework is shown in great detail in some of the ledger and daybook accounts. Other books show daily attendance by workers, and some volumes also track board bills due to Olney or his companies by the workers. Some of these records may relate to the Smithfield Cotton and Woolen Manufacturing Company, popularly known as "Sinking Fund Mill," which George Olney was a founding partner of in 1809, and sole proprietor in 1825. An 1825 labor book attributed to that mill survives in the Greene Family Papers (MSS 1043) but does not seem to correspond to the account books in this collection.[5]

As you can see, the Scope and Content tells not only what the collection has but also what is missing and where other information relating to this collection might be found. It is not unusual for a Scope and Content note to say that the collection contains Board of Directors Meetings from 1878–1932 with the years 1925–1926 missing.

Your family archive might read:

> *All documents for the O'Malley family prior to 1932 were lost in a fire in the family home.*

Or you might add where other documents can be found:

> *Photographs of Simmons, Diane (Chapman) can be found in the collections of Hockney, Diane (Chapman), and Chapman, Veronica.*

Provenance

I think of Provenance as the story of the collection. The true definition of provenance is considered the place of origin of an object or the earliest known history of something. Often in the archives, Provenance tells not just where the documents or objects originated, but also how the records came to be in the archive. The story of the records of Gorham Manufacturing, for example, are fascinating. Most of the Gorham collection was donated to the archives when Textron, who acquired the collection in the late 1960s, sold their interest in the company in 1982. The remainder of the documents were rescued from a dumpster when the company finally closed in 2003.

I love hearing the story of objects and how they find their way into an archive or museum. A recent museum exhibit told the story of how a group of glass plate negatives found their way to the museum. When the photographer died, his brother inherited them. The brother's daughter inherited them upon her father's death. She sold them to a college professor, who sold them to another college professor, who sold them yet again. The final recipient of the collection donated it to the museum, but not before she figured out the cataloging system the photographer had devised. The museum was able to connect photographs to names and families that still lived in the neighborhood a hundred years later, and were descendants of the photographer's subjects.

Since your family archive is not being donated to an archive or museum, you might want to say something like this:

> *Items in this collection were handed down through the generations. I acquired the collections of my mother JE Chadwick, my father, RE Chadwick, my Aunt H Chadwick, and Aunt E Frenier upon*

their deaths. Aunt T game me her hats and jewelry when she went into assisted living in 2002. Items belonging to Salina Frenier, my maternal great-grandmother, were given to me by my mother in her lifetime. The official family archive was put together in 20XX upon my retirement.

Inventory

Typically, the Inventory forms the main part of the Finding Aid and indicates exactly what is in the collection and where it can be found. This is where the Series List and the Finding Aid come together. In the archives, finding aids might be by box, by folder, or by item, depending on the importance of the collection and the resources of the staff. Since your collection is relatively small compared to some of the collections found in an archive, you can foreseeably create an item level or folder level finding aid. Refer to my website at https://lenasalina.com/secrets-from-the-stacks-guides/ for a few samples of finding aids.

APPRAISAL

Identifying What You Have

Now that you have a good concept of the organizational structure of your documents, the next step to creating a family archive is identifying what you have. This portion of the project is called an appraisal. Your goal is to identify what you have, decide what to keep, and decide what should be part of your family archive. Go through your house and locate where everything that will be part of the family archive is. I don't know about you, but I have memorabilia in several places in my home. A closet in my living room contains the photo albums I took from my mother's house when she died. A box of photographs from my aunt is in a buffet in the dining room. My personal photographs are in the bottom drawer of a hutch in a hallway. Ephemera (cards, concert tickets, movie stubs) are in the bottom left-hand drawer of my bureau. In my den are plastic boxes with more items such as photographs, old letters, and old artifacts. My more recent photographs are digitally stored on my computer and an external hard drive.

Look for all items such as photo albums, Uncle Joe's stamp collection, Aunt Harriet's silver tea service, your wedding dress, the christening gown that has been handed down for generations, your great-great-grandfather's love letters, your great-grandmother's Hanukkah candelabra, and the genealogical documents your third cousin sent you. You may want to bring everything together in a secure, safe workspace. See the section, "Creating a Workspace" in Chapter 1.

It is not necessary at this point to take your wedding dress out of storage or your grandfather's rifle off the wall in the living room, just make a list of what you have. You can do this with a pencil and paper or type up a word document. It might look like this:

ITEM	BELONGING TO	LOCATION
Photo Album – Family Photos early 20th c.	Edna Frenier (aunt)	Dining Room Closet
Photo Album – Trip to Italy	Rhonda Chadwick	Dining Room Closet
Photo Album – 1980s	JE Chadwick (mother)	Living Room Coffee Table
Ceramic Puppy	JE Chadwick (mother)	Shelf in Kitchen
Wedding Dress	Lena Provost (maternal grandmother)	Off-Site Storage (ABC Storage Co.)
Land Deed and Other Legal Documents	Rhonda Chadwick	Safety Deposit Box at Bank
Cut Glass Fruit Bowl	Salina Frenier (maternal gr-grandmother)	Kitchen Cupboard

You are going to use this information in a survey, so you might want to skip this step and begin directly with the survey spreadsheet so you do not have to write it twice. You decide. It should be easy enough to take a pencil and paper and walk around your house and write down the above information, then later type it into a spreadsheet as part of the survey. See the next section for information on doing a survey.

Keep it, Toss it, Put it in the Family Archive

In her book *The Life-Changing Magic of Tidying Up*, Marie Kondo suggests that when decluttering your home, the best thing to do is bring everything together in one spot, then pick up each item and decide whether it is useful or if it sparks joy. If it does neither, she suggests that you get rid of the item. I suggest that you do something similar, but instead of asking whether it sparks joy or is useful, ask how each item helps tell the story of an individual or the family as a whole. Always think of Baby 2135 and others beyond that. What do they need to have or know about the family to understand their roots and where they come from?

My Auntie Edna was forty-four years old when I was born. I only knew her as a middle-aged or elderly woman. The pictures of her as an awkward teenager and sexy-ish twenty-something reveal a part of her life I did not directly experience. They completely change my perception about who she was and what her life was like.

On the other hand, I have a boxful of pictures from my father's military service in Korea. Most of the pictures are of the army base where he was stationed or are of men I do not know. I will keep the pictures of my father. I will keep one or two shots of the army base. I will keep the picture of the dog he adopted while he was there because it says so much about who he was. But I will throw away the other pictures. I have no idea who the men are. I do not need to keep twenty-five photographs of the same wide expanse of an army base in Korea. I do not even know where it was. My father never told stories about his service in Korea, so the photographs are not relevant. The Veterans History Project at the Library of Congress may be interested in these photographs, but otherwise they serve no value to my family archive.

Elderly aunts Edna & Mabel as teenagers at the beach

Review the types of documents that make up a family archive. When going through items you might want to put them in three different categories:

1. Items that will be included in the family archive

2. Items that will not be included in the family archive, but that you want to keep for yourself

3. Items that can be tossed

My sister is the "Declutter Queen." After reading Marie Kondo's book, she handed it to me saying, "I thought you might want to read this," a not-so-subtle hint. I easily admit that I am a bit of a pack rat. My sister keeps purging her house saying that she does not want her kids to have to deal with her stuff after she dies. I certainly understand that sentiment. However, first, I think we both have quite a few years left before our inevitable passing. Second, I believe there are certain things we need to have with us while we are here. Naturally, daily clothing is not going to end up in the family archive, and yet I need to have clothes to wear while I am still living.

Other items may fit into the same category. Over my lifetime I have built a nice little library. After getting out of library school, I cataloged my books, putting them all into an app on my phone that organizes them and is easily searchable. I placed them on the shelves by subject, in alphabetical order by author last name. I weeded a little bit, but most of the books I kept. Many of the books are unread, but as a friend once said to me, unread books are like friends I have not met yet. I love that when I watch a movie, attend a lecture, or read something online about a certain subject or a particular author, I can go into my library and start pulling books off the shelf that are related to that subject area. Many of the books are signed by the authors. I cherish my books and am not willing to part with them before I depart this green earth. Once I go, my nieces and nephews can toss them all if they want. But while I am here, I want access to them.

My bookshelf

Many pictures also fall into this category. They are not relevant to the family archive, but you may want them near you while you are here. The trip to France I took in 2006 was the first time I brought a digital camera on a major trip. My favorite joke on that trip was to look at how many photographs I had left to shoot and say, "Aw, I can only take 1,275 more photographs." I was used to film that would only allow maybe 72 to 106 pictures (depending on how many rolls of thirty-six frames I brought), so it was amazing to think I could take that many photographs and not have to pay to develop them! What luxury. I went hog wild! I think I took 1,500 shots. I had nothing to lose, so I shot away. When I got home, I made an hour-long, thematically-produced video with music. I love that video and all those pictures, but really, no one else is going to be interested. I make my videos for myself. If my family members want them after I go, they can keep them, but they are not relevant to the family history.

THE SURVEY

When approaching a project in the archives, it is best to begin by doing a survey. In the archives, we conduct surveys because we do not know what kinds of materials are in the collection. It could be photographs, blueprints, artifacts, drawings, cassette tapes, DVDs, etc. We are also trying to get a sense of what the collection is about. A larger collection needs to be separated by subject. For example, I worked on the collection of a large textile mill at the ATHM in Lowell, MA. Before I was hired, the staff had separated the 683 boxes into five broad sections: administrative, personnel, sales, production, and accounting. When I surveyed the boxes, I also made note of other subject areas that would be important to researchers such as union records and environmental records.

Having identified everything in the appraisal portion of your project, you do not need to survey your entire collection. You can survey all your photographs first, or just survey the older ones you got when your parents died or the ones from high school stored in your bedroom closet. You decide.

The survey should prepare you for what comes next, which is that you will be rehousing items for permanent storage. You are going to need to purchase items in which to store everything. The survey will help you determine how much you need. Using a spreadsheet is helpful when doing a survey. A six-column pad or a notebook could be used instead. I like to use a spreadsheet because I can sort and organize it any way I want later on. It is easy to add columns or reword things in a spreadsheet. If I structure it properly, a spreadsheet will also automatically total columns and let me know how much I am spending.

Depending on how things are stored, each item should have a line. For example, photo album 1, which has been stored on shelf 2 of the dining room closet, belonged to Auntie Edna and contains 120 photographs of the Frenier family. Of those 120 photographs, there are five 8" x 10"s, ten 5" x 7"s, and the rest are 4" x 6" or less. The subject matter could be broken down as Frenier Family, Grandma's Wedding, and Family Outing. Refer to p.42 to see how this would look on a spreadsheet.

As each item is added to the survey, the collective information will become important. It not only provides a history of how the items were originally stored but is a rich resource for determining what you have and remembering what you later disposed of. Also, adding up the number of pieces will help you decide what to purchase. Shipping costs for archival materials can be expensive. Most likely you will need to order these online since they are not sold at Staples or Office Depot. Placing fewer orders will help cut down on shipping costs.

The information on the spreadsheet will also help you work out how to organize the materials when the time comes. As you can see, since I own the records of several family members, I have indicated whose collections each item comes from. The survey indicates how old the materials are and how fragile they may be. This gives you a hint as to where to begin the archival process. You always want to start with the oldest and most fragile items and with the materials that will deteriorate more quickly than others.

Adding columns for "Description" and "Preservation" is important. When working on collections in the archives, it can take years to complete a project. Your home project may also take years to complete, depending on how much time you have to devote to the project and how much life gets in your way and slows you down. Write down your impressions of any special considerations you need to be mindful of when doing the survey. This will help you down the road when you get to the point of actually processing the material.

I have expanded my spreadsheet to include different types of materials. As you are doing your survey, you will be making decisions based on the information I am providing you in this book regarding how to house items properly for long-term storage. You will also decide whether something is worth keeping or whether you should dispose of it. If you don't know this information right now, don't worry. You will by the end of the book, before you start your survey. Read on.

> **It's such a terrible pain to be cut off from your family and to be cut off from what *really* is your home.**
>
> MARGARET CHO
> *Finding Your Roots*
> S1.E8

You do not have to do the survey, but it will help you organize your materials, purchase the right materials needed to complete your project, and prepare for digitization. Whenever we start any home project, the preparation work is the least fun but often the most important. I know every time I paint a room, I cannot wait to put the color on the walls. But I have learned the importance of preparing the surface of the room first. I hate removing furniture, sanding, wiping down surfaces, putting tape along the edges, and placing drop cloths down to protect rugs and floors. Yet these are necessary steps for making the project run more smoothly and completing the job with the least amount of mess. Still, they are not nearly as much fun as adding fresh paint to walls and woodwork.

Item	Collection	Dates	Qty.	Material	Description
Photo Rolodex	JE Chadwick	1980–1990	120	Photographs	Photos taken by Mom of family; kids when they were little; some of her friends; travel w/friends; several weddings
Photo Album	Edna Frenier	Early-20th Century	250	Photographs	Photographs of Lena Provost's extended family; Lafond and Frenier cousins; a wedding; a day at an outdoor event, perhaps a fair.
Ceramic Puppy	JE Chadwick	Ca. 1950	1	Artifact	Blue puppy planter
Quilt	Rhonda Chadwick (made by sister Donna)	Ca. 1988	1	Textile	4' x 4' quilt
Binder with College Reports	Rhonda Chadwick	1989–1994	25	Letter Paper	Graded college reports stapled together and bound in large loose-leaf 3-ring binder
File Folder	Edna Frenier	1920	1	Legal Paper	House Purchase and Sales Agreement for house on York Avenue

2: ORGANIZATION

Preservation Needs	Processing Instructions	Folders	Photo Sheets 4 x 6	Photo Sheets 3 x 5	Telescoping box 16 x 20	Artifact Box 3 x 6
In good condition	Digitize. Leave in Rolodex for time being.	12				
Some photographs are stuck to pages	Digitize. Place in poly sleeves.	25				
In perfect condition	Photograph. Leave on sill. Put in small box at some point.					
A few minor tears, via cats	Wrap in tissue paper and place in a box.					
Some pages are browned	Digitize. Place reports in acid free folders and place in acid free box. Remove staples. Copy browned pages.	25				
Pages are folded	Unfold pages. Place in legal-size folder and acid-free box. Remove any staples.	1				

Perhaps now that you have seen the expanded view of the spreadsheet, you will understand why I like to do it this way rather than writing it down. I find as I move through a collection that I often need to add columns for items I have not anticipated.

After the Survey

When the survey is complete, you now know how big your collection is and can anticipate how much work will be involved in completing the project. You should also know which items are in most need of preservation activities. In the archives, we usually begin with the oldest documents and the ones that are in most need of preservation attention. A project in an archive or museum could take anywhere from one to three years depending on the size of the collection and the types of materials involved. Your collection may only take a couple of months to complete. However, if you are doing it when you can while you are also taking care of a million other things, it could very well take a year or two to finish. We all know how life can throw us curve balls that push us off track for a while. With that in mind, I suggest you begin in the same place a professional archivist would—take care of the oldest things and the ones with the most sensitivity and instability first. Typically, the most sensitive items are media such as photographs, film, and audio/video files. This category may include textiles or metal objects. Start with the most fragile items, then move onto the sturdier and more modern ones. Once the material items are completely re-housed in good enclosures and are organized, you can start the digital part of your project.

CHAPTER 3

PHOTOGRAPHS

The fundamental belief in the authenticity of photographs explains why photographs of people no longer living and of vanished architecture are so melancholy. Neither words nor the most detailed painting can evoke a moment of vanished time as powerfully and as completely as a good photograph.[6]

—Beaumont Newhall, *The History of Photography*

Photographs contain some of our most treasured family memories. It is true that a picture is worth a thousand words. Images of important family events and loved ones who have passed trigger memories and emotions that are strong and enduring. We love to pore over photographs to recapture the memories, feelings, and happiness of our family's important days. As we age, photographs harbor the only images of our parents, grandparents, partners, and friends. This makes their preservation all that much more important. As we try to build a family legacy, photographs are the easiest and most pleasurable way to prompt memories, introduce loved ones to the next generation, and tell stories. Both children and adults love to look at photographs together as the stories, dramas, personalities, and legacies of family members are told and retold. Preserving print photographs will be at the top of any good family historian's list of items to preserve.

One of my favorite family photographs is from my grandmother's 90th birthday party. Everyone who lived locally went to the party. At the end of the day, all the direct descendants of Lena posed around her smiling, beaming face. To her left sat her only surviving sibling, her youngest sister Edna. Behind her stood her three remaining children and behind them were all the grandchildren. (For some reason the great-grandchildren were left out of the picture, although six of them were there that day.) Looking at that picture not only reminds me of that one day but leads me to notice how many family members are no longer with us. I am glad that moment in time was captured on film.

Lucky for us, my cousin Michael recorded the day and later made a video that he generously shared with the entire family. I have since had it digitized and have shared it with other family members. Long after my grandmother passed away, my cousin Charlie, who lived out of town and was not at the 90th birthday party, visited me. I boldly teased him saying, "I can make you cry." "Yeah?" he laughed nervously. "Yes," I said and popped the video into a DVD player. Within seconds this Vietnam veteran paratrooper was reduced to a puddle of tears. As was I.

This chapter provides a basic overview of preservation concerns and processing instructions for photographs. The following three chapters provide in-depth information and discuss in detail 19th-century photographs, 20th-century photographs, and film.

THE TECHNICAL STUFF

Photographs consist of three basic parts: a support layer, an imaging medium, and something that binds them together. The support layer can be paper, glass, metal, or plastic film. The image medium is typically made up of finely divided particles of silver or platinum in a black-and-white photograph, or organic dyes for color photographs. The binding element for most modern 20th-century photographs is gelatin, although early-20th-century photographs may have used cellulose nitrate as a binding agent. In 19th-century photographs, albumen or collodion was used as a binding agent.

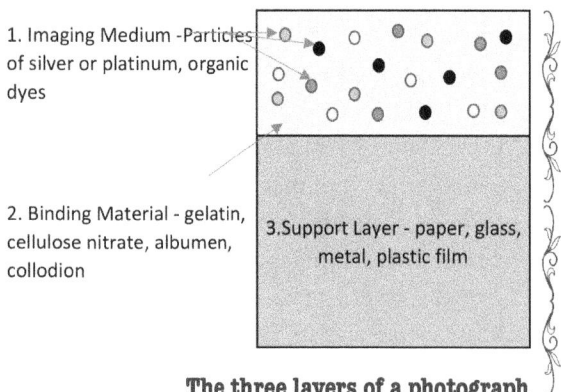

The three layers of a photograph

Chemicals are used when the picture is taken, when the image is transferred from film to paper, and when the image is fixed and stabilized. No wonder photographs fade and deteriorate! With that said, black-and-white photographs can easily last for a century or more. Color photographs tend to fade quicker, and Polaroid "instant" photographs tend to be the most unstable and fade the quickest. You have probably noticed this in your own personal collections.

When working on records in the archives, I always begin with the most sensitive materials. Typically, photographs are at the top of the list. Heat, light, and humidity are enemies of photographs. High humidity, high heat, and pollutants cause the silver image-forming particles in black-and-white photographs to fade and discolor. Sometimes an iridescent metallic sheen called "mirroring" is formed on black-and-white prints. The dyes in color photographs are particularly sensitive to light. Some fading can occur even when photographs are kept in the dark. The support layer of photographs is also vulnerable to deterioration over time. Paper and cardboard become brittle, causing pieces (usually the edges) to crumble and are sensitive to touch. Heat and humidity cause the edges of photographs to curl into the center. Nineteenth-century, metal-based photographs can rust, and glass photographs can corrode or, worse, break.

Chemicals and oils from our fingers can discolor and accelerate the deterioration of photographs. Have you ever seen an old photograph with a fingerprint embedded in the image? As much as possible, you want to avoid your fingerprints, and those of curious onlookers, touching photographs. The many opportunities for deterioration demonstrate the sensitivity of photographs and the necessity of good preservation care.

The Environment

The single most important thing you can do for your photographs is store them in a good environment. Current ANSI/ISO[7] standards state that temperatures should not exceed 65°F for prints. Humidity levels should be between 30% and 50% for black-and-white photographs and between 30% and 40% for color prints. If you keep all your processed photographs in one place, the temperature should not exceed 65°F and the humidity level should be between 30% and 40%.

ARCHIVES TIP

Current ANSI/ISO standards state that temperatures should not exceed 65° for *prints*. Humidity levels should be 30% to 50% for *black and white* photographs and 30% to 40% for *color prints*.

Film has greater requirements. Acetate film can last about fifty years at room temperature with moderate relative humidity (RH). After that, film will begin to seriously degrade. Those negatives and reel-to-reels that were created in your lifetime might still be in good condition, but they will not last into the future unless you take corrective measures today.

The best thing to do with reel-to-reel films that are in good condition is digitize them as soon as possible. This is discussed in greater detail in Chapter 6. (Also refer to Chapter 11 for more specific details.) Once they are digitized, the original is less important. At this point in time, a DVD will provide greater life storage than an old, already deteriorating film. This type of digital storage may extend the life of a film, but this should not be considered a permanent storage mechanism.

The standard for black-and-white films is that they should not be stored in a place where the temperature will exceed 70°F. That makes them easy to store with your photographs, but the humidity level needs to be lower—between 20% and 30%. Color film has even higher standards, with a maximum temperature of 40°F and no more than 20% to 30% RH.

This probably sounds confusing, so let me break it down for you. If you have a place in your home where a temperature of 65°F and an RH of 30% to 40% can be maintained, your photographs can be stored there. If you have several films that you need to store, have them digitized and store them along with the photographs. Archives housing many films use special refrigerators for storing them. Using refrigeration for film storage is specialized and requires particular storage materials. Defrosting film is difficult and requires considerable care. Unless you are a professional photographer or a prolific hobbyist, this is an extreme measure. Services are available today that will digitize all your photographs and film at once. If you do choose to use refrigeration, good file storage is cold: 40°F with 30%–50% RH. Frozen is even better: 32°F with 30%–50% RH.

The Fun Part

Okay, I admit it, when I am working on a collection in the archives I like to start with the photographs because they are fun. I am glad I can use the excuse that they are one of the more sensitive media in the collection and need immediate attention. I like looking at the pictures, and I find that no other part of the collection tells a story quite like images do.

ARCHIVES TIP

Keep It Simple

If you have a place in your home where a temperature of 65° and a relative humidity of 30% to 40% can be maintained, your photographs can be stored there.

One of the collections I worked on was of a factory that was in business for over 150 years and was run by five generations of a single family. During the 1970s and 1990s, two labor union strikes occurred. Because I did an initial survey of the records, I was aware there had been at least one strike. Other documents in the collection, including newspaper articles, told of the incidents that had occurred. However, unlike the other documents, the photographs powerfully portrayed both the peacefulness and pedestrian quality of the demonstrations, as well as the drama and violence that erupted as a bitter dispute escalated. As I looked through the lens of that long-ago camera, I wondered who the photographer was and considered his situation as he took photographs of angry protesters who were stopping a delivery truck from entering the gate. Was he at risk? Did he know the protesters? Did he feel threatened? Photographs of the destruction after a night raid carried the danger of the situation over the years. Broken glass on the rug beside an office desk portrayed the fear and violation management must have felt. Large holes in the sign outside the factory with the company's name and logo revealed the contempt of the protesters.

Other photographs in the collection showed baseball games, team photographs, annual company picnics, and Christmas celebrations for employees' children. An endless number of photographs revealed the business owner's tradition of passing out gifts to employees who had reached the milestone of working at the company for five, ten, fifteen, twenty-five, and even fifty years. These photographs created a feeling of the factory as a community, a fun place to work, and a family. As I looked at photograph after photograph, certain faces stood out. I was able to connect the people in the photographs with some of the leading executives in the corporation. By the time I had finished processing all the photographs, I almost felt as though I had worked at the factory myself and had known some of the people.

PROCESSING PHOTOGRAPHS

For most photographs, storage in polyester or polypropylene sheets is the most common and effective means of storage. As discussed earlier, make sure any plastic materials have passed the PAT and that all paper materials are acid-free, lignin-free, and buffered. Archival supply houses have a variety of plastic sheet sizes for all your pictures. Since these materials tend to be expensive and are sold in groups, try to buy ones that can house several sizes of photographs. When doing your survey, you will determine how many photographs of each size you need. Yes, you need to count every photograph in order to know. In a collection with many sizes, you could buy two sizes: 8 ½" x 11" and 4" x 6". These will generally hold most of the photographs in your collection. When you are deciding what to order, keep in mind that 3" x 5" photographs will fit in 4" x 6" enclosures, but the reverse is not true; a 4" x 6" photo will not fit into a 3" x 5" enclosure.

Large Prints

Chances are, the large prints you have in your collection are items currently hanging on the walls of your home or ones that hung on the walls in the past. If you want to continue housing large prints on the walls, consider which room of the house might be better suited for them. Does direct sunlight hit the prints at any time of the day? Items on walls are better off in a northwest facing room, which has diffused light, rather than a southeast facing room, which gets direct sunlight. Closing the blinds during the day is helpful. Even moving the prints to another wall so that they have their back to a window is an easy solution for extending the life of photographs.

Another option is to digitize the original and put a copy on the wall. Even without printing a copy, digitizing a print provides the opportunity for reprinting another copy in the future. Modern technology is sophisticated enough to make a photograph look like a painting. At a historic home where I volunteer, photographs of family heirloom paintings going back over 150 years were digitized and printed to look like the original paintings. Our guests are never the wiser that the originals are safely stored in an archive.

Large prints

Prints can be reframed using UV-blocking glass or acrylic and acid-free framing materials. Reframing can be expensive. If you choose to go this route, reframing one large print per year could help manage the expense. Another option is to be like a museum and hang pictures for short periods of time, perhaps around the holidays when company visits. Otherwise, keep them stored in a cold, dark, and dry environment.

If you think you will not hang a particular picture on the wall any longer, such as your grandmother's wedding picture that you want to keep but no longer want to have on the wall, you can store it in the frame or without the frame. If you think you will not hang a picture on the wall again, it is better to de-frame it. Framing materials contain varnish, metals, and other materials that may deteriorate or damage photographs. In the archives, when we are placing an image in long-term storage, we de-frame the print. Be sure to also remove all cardboard, mats, and other housing materials.

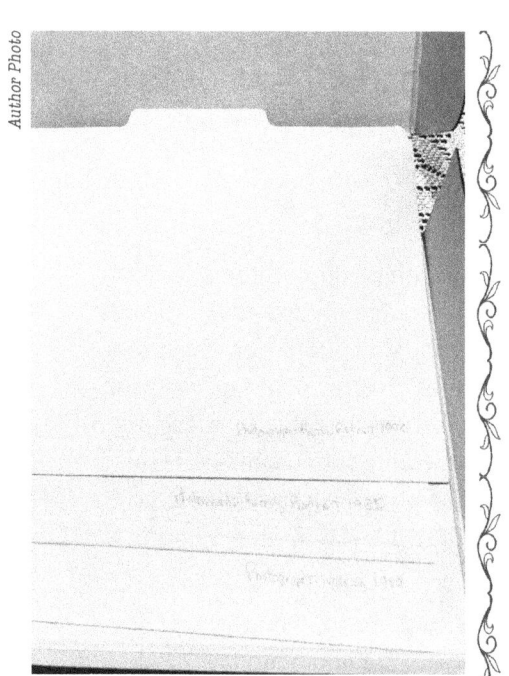

Labeling large prints

Large photographs should be laid flat in acid-free boxes. They can also be put into acid-free folders, but this is not necessary. Here again is a place where measuring everything will come in handy. Obviously, depending on how many prints you have, you want to buy a box that will house the largest size. You can purchase folders to match the boxes and use them to separate groups of photographs. Place acid-free, lignin-free, buffered tissue paper or glassine paper between each photograph within a folder or within the box.

To be more specific, let's say you have twenty-five large photographs ranging in size from 10" x 12" to 16" x 20". Five of the photographs are from your wedding. Six are of your children at various ages. Seven are family portraits taken by a professional photographer. Seven are from trips you have taken. All the photographs can fit in one 16" x 20" box. They can be separated into four different folders, and each folder will house a different category of photographs. Separate each photograph within each folder with acid-free tissue paper.

When placing the folders in the box, label them in pencil in the lower right- or left-hand corner (depending on your preference) at the folded side of the folder. This way, if you want to pull out just the children's photographs, you can easily lift the other folders without having the contents inside spill.

You will want to include information that tells your descendants who is in the picture, the year it was taken, and the reason or occasion. Writing lightly on the back in pencil would be one way of doing this. Another way would be to include a sheet of paper tucked behind the photograph that provides this information. A third option would be to write a number in the lower left-hand corner on the back of the photograph. Then on the front of the folder you could write out the information. For example:

> *Emily Karen Jones; David Stephen Jones; Stephanie Susan Jones, 1985, ages 12, 13, 10. Family photograph taken at Mills Studio, Providence, RI.*
>
> *David Stephen Jones; Emily Karen Jones; Michael David Jones; Stephanie Susan Jones, 1987; ages 15, 14, 18 months, 12. Family photograph taken at Mills Studio, Providence, RI.*

You get the picture.

When placing items of different sizes in the same box or the same folder, make sure that smaller items are placed on top of larger items. This will prevent larger items from buckling or bending if placed on top of smaller objects. The difference in size between a few photographs may seem minuscule, but over time, incorrect storage can result in warped or misshapen photographs.

Snapshots, Small Photos

For most people, the bulk of their photographic collection is small, snapshot size photos. These are generally 3" x 5", 4" x 6", or Polaroid pictures that are 4" x 5".

Plastic enclosures

Archival supply houses provide many types of storage options for photographs. Look through their catalogs online or order a free catalog and decide what you think will be best for you. Here are some recommendations:

1. If you decide to buy some kind of loose-leaf binder, make sure it is not overstuffed. When the binder is closed, it should lie completely flat. The archival supply houses sell great loose-leaf binders that turn into boxes when they are closed. I love them!

2. Each photograph should have its own enclosure. Do not put more than one photograph in each sleeve. You know how typically you put one photograph on one side and the other on the side behind it? Do not do that.

3. Do not overlap photos on top of each other.

4. Write identifying information lightly in pencil on the back of the photograph.

5. Better yet, write identifying information in pencil on a sheet of acid-free paper and slip it into the back of the same sleeve as the photograph. Most copy/print paper is acid-free these days. Keep it simple.
You can use the same paper found in your printer. (See Chapter 7, which explains why modern, inexpensive paper is "good" paper.)

> *"Learning about past generations makes them real. You see that there's a real foundation underneath you."*
>
> **—Stephen King.**
> Finding Your Roots S2.E1

In the archives, we do not typically use any of the binder types of enclosures like loose-leaf ring binders. We place photographs in polyester or polypropylene sheets, place them in acid-free folders, and then place those folders in acid-free boxes. If you have an abundant number of photographs, this might be the better option for you. The boxes we most often use in the archives are called flip-top boxes, which are 12 ¼" W x 10 ¼" H x 2 ½" D. The boxes should be filled enough so that the contents are not slumped. If there is not enough material to keep the folders standing upright, put a piece of cardboard in the back. You can purchase cardboard designed for this purpose from the archival supply houses, or you can make an insert yourself. I usually fold up one of the acid-free boxes that the acid-free folders are shipped in. Be creative, but make sure the material you use is acid-free and is not off-gassing anything strange that would damage your photographs.

Century boxes, or SafeCoat® boxes, are sold by Hollinger Metal Edge and are a good alternative. The polypropylene sheets lie flat in these boxes, and they are decorative and easy to handle. These boxes are on the pricey side, but depending on how many you need, you might want to consider this option.

Clamshell boxes are another nice alternative. They are inexpensive and come in a variety of sizes. If you are going to use these, you might want to purchase folders to go with them and label them as indicated for the larger pictures—on the outside of the folder near the fold. Polypropylene sheets tend to be slippery. If the box is not the exact same size as the photographic sheets, they will slide around and quickly become disorganized.

In a recent project I worked on, I put all the 4" x 6" and smaller photos in four-on-a-page sheets. I cut the section of the page off where the holes for a binder were. I did this because otherwise that section of the sheet would have extended over the top of the 8 ½" x 11" folder. I then put the sheets in acid-free folders, around five to ten sheets per folder. I labeled the folders, then put them in an acid-free flip-top box.

In the archives, we only use pencils. Pens, markers, and gel pens all eventually fade and become unreadable. Professional archivists have found that pencils are the one writing instrument that will last into the future. Go figure, a simple pencil is the best. Personally, I like mechanical pencils, but any kind will work. Pencil will not bleed through papers or photographs. But remember to write lightly. You do not want the pressure of your pencil to alter the image on the other side.

Another option for storing photographs is mounting them on acid-free scrapbook-style pages. Though this is great for short-term storage, it is not recommended for long-term storage because the paper will not last into the future. If you choose this method, be sure to use mounting corners that hold the photograph in place. Do not glue photographs to pages! Glue will eventually turn brown and can damage your photographs. I have seen many scrapbooks in the archives that were once beautiful creations turned into a mess because of large streaks of browned glue-covered pages. It is heartbreaking to see the careful handiwork of the creator destroyed by time and bad materials. Wet glue can also buckle the pages and create wavy textures on your photographs.

Using mounting corners is the safer alternative, but mounting photographs to archival-quality pages is also not recommended. All glue will eventually dry up. While it looks great today, one hundred years from now when those mounting corners have dried up and fallen off, it could be very messy. Photographs that have detached from their descriptions can be impossible to identify. You do not want your future descendants to pick up a scrapbook and have all the photographs fall out onto their laps.

If you do choose this method, however, archival supply houses sell special white pencils that you can use to write on black background mounting paper. Used properly, black archival paper can add a classy, rich look and feel to your photographs. Archival supply houses also sell graphite pencils that you can use to write on the back of photographs. Many photographs are coated on both sides with polyethylene laminate, a form of plastic, making writing on the backs difficult. Graphite pencils can help with this and can also be used to write on glass, plastic, metal, leather, and rubber.

Photo Albums

Photo albums often document a specific event such as a wedding, trip, or particular time period—the summer of 1962, for example. Sometimes the creator of a photo album took great care to arrange the photographs in a specific order and, with any luck, explained who or what was in the photographs and why they were important. Perhaps the photographs tell the story of a special trip or show the building of the family home. Maybe they document the opening of a new business or capture that crazy summer you spent at the beach. The stories contained in the photo album are important. But often the mechanism in which they are housed is not ideal, resulting in damaged photographs, poor long-term preservation, and challenging viewing.

Photograph Storage

Hollinger Metal Edge

Showcasing your photographs and telling stories with pictures is an essential process. The trend today is to digitize photographs that are not already born digital and to create coffee table books, family history books, or memory books.

Photo albums can be very challenging for archivists. They come in different sizes, shapes, and mediums, which make them hard to preserve. If photographs are mounted on construction paper using corner tabs from which photographs can be easily pulled out without damage, this type of photobook is easier to handle and store.

Let's get specific. The plastic in most commercially sold photo albums, whether it is the page covers or the sleeves, is usually not archivally sound. Many more modern photo albums produced today are employing archival methods, but albums from the 20th century used polyvinyl or PVC plastic. This kind of plastic turns into goop over time, especially in warm temperatures or high humidity conditions. It also has a bad habit of sticking to photographs. Not good. When the plastic is removed, part of the image goes with it.

Then there is the dreaded glue. Most people have "magnetic" photo albums in their collection that were sold in the 1960s and 1970s. These albums are not actually magnetic. They use heavy glue to hold photographs to pages that are covered with PVC plastic. Now, over forty years later, the photographs are stuck to the pages and cannot be removed without damage. While these albums may have looked great when they were created, they have discolored over the years to a rust or yellow. In truth, magnets would have been preferable in "magnetic" photo albums since they would be easy to detach. But on the plus side, the photographs in these deteriorated messes are often still in good condition.

In the archives, we pull photo albums apart, put the photographs in polypropylene sheets, put those sheets in acid-free folders, and then place those in acid-free boxes. Part of the reason we do this is because the archives have limited space. Other times we put an intact scrapbook or photo album in a box. What could be easier? I am going to give you the information you need to make your own decision on how you want to process your photo albums. You  will need to use your judgment based on the age and condition of the albums. Spoiler alert: in the end I am going to recommend that you digitize every print photograph you have. We will discuss this in Chapter 11, but for now let me say this—by digitizing your photographs, you can use them in your storytelling process. Digitization is also how you will preserve your photographs if disaster strikes. I do not recommend that you throw everything away after digitizing, but with a digital copy as insurance, you may opt to keep and store your photo albums intact.

ARCHIVES TIP

Don't over stuff binders!

If you do pull apart your photo albums, you can still keep the photographs together in folders and polypropylene sheets. You can still tell the story that the photo album was designed to tell. All will not be lost. On the contrary, more will be saved. Archival supply stores sell newer, safer photo albums you can transfer your photographs into. Please do not overstuff them, though. You want to make sure the first page and the last page are not folded, bent, or creased. The album itself should lie flat.

If photographs are stuck to the pages and you cannot get them off without damaging them, do this: keep them stuck. Eventually the glue will dry up and the photographs will come off on their own. You may not live to see that day, but it will happen eventually. I suggest removing the individual sheets from the photo album and either placing them in a folder and a box or just laying them flat in a box. You can pull apart an entire photo album and place the individual sheets in a flat box with acid-free tissue paper between them. Enclosing each sheet in a separate folder will keep them from getting mixed up with the other photographs when the day comes that the glue dries up. This is a great idea, and you may choose to do it, but it is not necessary. Keeping the sheets separate with tissue paper will be just as good. You will probably want to have a separate box for each photo album if you have several of this type.

The same is true of plastic sheets that are stuck to photographs. You can gently try to separate them. Archival supply stores sell little spatula-like pieces of equipment called micro spatulas. Use these to help separate photographs from the plastic. The rule to remember when doing this is: go slow and be gentle!Let's say you have a wedding album with mostly 8" x 10" prints. The album itself is in perfect condition. Maybe the outside is a little discolored, but the photographs are in perfect condition. However, a piece of plastic is in between each photograph. You could keep the photo album intact, remove the bad plastic by gently and carefully using a razor blade, then place a piece of tissue paper between each page or you could place a sheet of good polyester or polypropylene between.

My mother had a Rolodex photo album she kept on her fireplace that I took after she passed away. The Rolodex itself has memories and is meaningful to me and my family. I hate to take it apart. But I know the plastic sleeves in the Rolodex will eventually turn to goop and the pictures will be damaged and possibly unviewable. I will digitize them and probably keep them in the Rolodex photo album with instructions to rehouse them in acid-free folders after my death. Or maybe I will do it myself later in life. My nieces and nephews also remember the Rolodex sitting on Grandma's fireplace mantle, and I know it brings fond memories for them too. If I do not have confidence that whoever takes the family archives after my passing will make the effort to transfer them to acid-free folders, I may decide to take a photograph of the Rolodex and put that with the pictures, explaining that this is how they were originally housed.

A method that can be used to remove photographs from the "magnetic" pages of photo albums is using dental floss. First put on nitrile gloves so that when the photograph is detached you will not touch it. Use dental floss that is not wax coated or flavored; choose one that is as bland as possible. Slide the floss underneath the photograph. You may have to use a micro-spatula to lift one end. Once the floss is underneath the photograph, use a back-and-forth sawing motion to gently detach the photograph from the page. If it begins to rip the face of the picture, STOP! You could try coming from a different angle at that point, but if the face of the picture continues to tear, leave it alone. As mentioned earlier, the glue will eventually dry up and the photograph will detach.

A student working at the Smithsonian Institution created a video demonstrating this process. You can watch this video at: https://www.youtube.com/watch?v=sCguXhNaLXs.[8] There is also a link to this in the Resources section of my website.

DAMAGE TO PHOTOGRAPHS

Damage to photographs happens for many reasons. Storing photographs in high heat and high humidity can cause flaking, curling, and spotting. Dirt, dust, and soot can accumulate on photographs that are stored in attics and basements or are exposed to outside elements. Mold can discolor and eat away at prints. Aging or prolonged exposure to light will fade photographs.

Most of this damage can be adjusted and fixed in the digital world. Color and light can be increased and balanced. Rips and tears can be removed through "smudging." Spots can be "erased." Flaking or curled photographs can be digitized and reprinted. Most family archives are small enough to be completely digitized. Once a digital copy is produced, photographs can be enhanced and corrected using many different software programs designed for this purpose.

Digitizing

Digitizing photographs at their current stage of deterioration will preserve the image as it is at that time. Programs such as Adobe Photoshop or iPhoto have features that can balance contrast, lighten darkened areas, and remove imperfections. Discussion of these technologies is beyond the scope of this book, but many resources on the internet are available that can assist you in learning these programs. Many computers come preloaded with one of these programs. If you digitize photographs and retain the original, playing around with the features of a photo-enhancing program can be a fun and creative process. You can save multiple versions of the photograph after trying different image-altering selections. Once you have it the way you want, print it out on photographic paper or use an online service such as Shutterfly.

The instructions below refer to the actual photographs and discuss what to do to correct damage done to the original.

Basic Deterioration – Fading, Spotting, Flaking

Fading is most commonly caused by overexposure to light. However, the organic dyes in color photographs will fade even if photos are kept in a dark, cool environment. This is called "dark fading." Since dyes fade at different rates, photographs can end up looking distorted and uneven. **Spotting** occurs on black and white images and usually

Fading

looks like red or orange blemishes or measles. Spotting of this type is caused by localized oxidation of the photographic layers. **Flaking** occurs when the layers of a photograph detach, causing small pieces to separate and "flake" off.

You cannot fix fading, spotting, and flaking damage. The best you can do is stop the deterioration. Place fading black-and-white images in polyester or polypropylene inert plastic sheets purchased from a good archival supply store. Color photographs should also be placed in inert plastic sheets that have passed the PAT. Placing color photographs in plastic sheets and keeping them in a cool, dark environment will slow the deterioration, but keep in mind that "dark fading" will continue to occur.

Photographs that show signs of flaking or spotting should not be put in plastic sheets. Even plastic sheets that have passed the PAT will produce a static charge that can cause further damage to photographs. Archival supply stores sell paper envelopes or folders that can be used for photographs that are flaking. As discussed previously, choose papers that are acid-free and lignin-free. Normally you should choose buffered paper products, but this is one of those cases when you should choose unbuffered to avoid discoloration. Write on the outside of the envelopes what is in them, and store them vertically in shoeboxes or lay them flat in a clamshell box. Place only one photograph in each envelope or folder. Make sure the photographs do not rub against the envelopes upon removal. Another option is to place a heavily damaged photograph in a four-fold flap envelope in which photographs lie flat and are not slid into place. Each section of the four-fold flap adds an extra layer of protection that will reduce the possibility of further damage occurring to flaking edges or torn images.

Curled Photographs

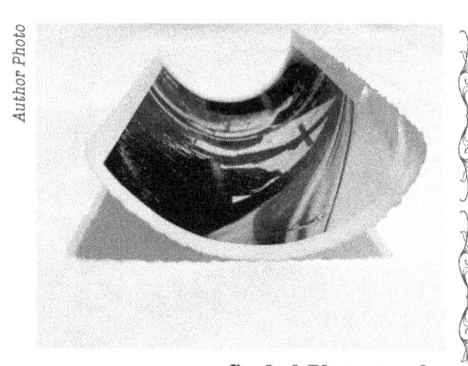

Curled Photographs

I have a suitcase full of photographs my father took while he was stationed in Korea during the Korean conflict in the early 1950s. They are all severely curled. I have not attempted to uncurl them as of this date, but at some point I will. The most common reasons photographs curl are because they have been stored in high heat or humidity or have been exposed to water.

The National Archives does not recommend correcting the damage from curled photographs. Depending on the age, value, and level of damage a photograph has sustained, much care needs to be taken. You do not want to do further damage in your attempt to correct the original problem. Because photographs use so many different types of base, imaging, and binding materials, it is impossible to list a "one size fits all" method for correction. With that in mind, please use caution when referring to the methods below. Use judgment when determining whether your photograph is fixable. If you have any doubts about whether a photograph can be fixed or whether you are equipped to do it, STOP, and contact a conservator. I offer the information below knowing that many people are artists or photographers who can benefit from the information. Know yourself. If you are not someone who tends to have great success in home repair projects, you are better off calling a conservator. I do not consider my father's Korean pictures of high value; therefore, I might play around with them a bit and try different methods. But my parents' wedding pictures, I would not hesitate to take to a conservator. Use your best judgment.

The image of a severely curled photograph can crack when pressure is used to uncurl it. Once the image pulls away from the support layer, it may be impossible to reattach it. Sections can fall off, leaving gaping holes in the image.

The method used to remedy curled photographs will depend on the type of photograph it is. To identify what type of photograph it is, refer to Chapters 4 and 5.

Before proceeding any further, if possible, make a digital copy of the original photograph. This can be done either by placing it on a flatbed scanner (if doing so will not crack or damage the photo) or by taking a digital photograph of it. Always test a less desirable photograph first to be sure your chosen method will work. If in doubt, call a conservator.

Photographs that have a slight curl on one edge can be placed in polyester or polypropylene archival sleeves. If placed in an archival photo album, the pressure of the sleeve and the weight of the other photographs should be enough to eventually relax the photograph so it lies flat.

Placing more severely curled photographs under a heavy weight of uniform pressure can assist in getting them to lie flat. Be sure to protect both the image side and the backside of the photographs by placing blotting paper or another protective layer on both sides. You can do this by putting them in polyester or polypropylene sheets first, or by placing a piece of acid-free tissue paper between them and the weight. Placing the photograph in an acid-free, lignin-free file folder would add even more protection. You can also use a piece of glass from a frame. You may have to let it sit for a week or more for the effects of years of curling to relax.

Moisture is what most likely caused the photographs to curl in the first place. It can assist in uncurling them as well, but be very careful! You can try brushing the back side of the photograph very lightly with a clean, wet artist brush. Be sure to test this method first on a less important photograph in the collection. Once it is slightly damp, use pressure to lay it flat as described in the method above. This method can be used with some success for inkjet prints on microporous paper, but not for those on swellable paper.

Creating moisture in the atmosphere can also work. Use a room vaporizer or place photographs in a mold-free bathroom with the shower on. See my website (https://lenasalina.com/secrets-from-the-stacks-guides/) for instructions on how to create a DIY humidity chamber to uncurl photographs and documents.

Dirt on Photographs

Having dirt and dust on photographs is not the same as having dirt and dust on your furniture. It is not so easy to just wipe photographs clean and go; you must use care and caution. Photographs that have a gelatin or laminate topcoat can be gently wiped with a soft, clean cloth. Beware of any damage already on the surface. Flaking, spotting, marks, cracks, rips, and tears can be further damaged if you rub the photographs in any way. Do not attempt to wipe damaged photographs, and do not use chemical solvents or cleaning agents. Avoid using a rough cloth or paper towel that can scratch the surface. Do not use liquid air, such as the kind we use on computer equipment; it contains chemicals that can damage photographs. Wipe gently with a soft, dry cloth or a soft artist brush.

Ripped photograph

Rips and Tears

Rips and tears pose special problems. Correcting them is a real art and takes specialized knowledge and materials. I am not a conservator and would not attempt to repair a photograph on my own. If I were to take that on, I would first digitize it and print it to make sure the reprint comes out okay before I start potentially damaging the original. Programs such as Photoshop can create miracles with torn photographs. I was able to remove the tear in a picture of my great-great-grandfather. It looks great in the digital world, but when I printed it out, the smudging method I used was obvious. I am not a graphic artist, so my talents are limited. However, this kind of correction can be done skillfully in the digital world and a reprint can be made. Never use tape or glue to repair a tear on an original photograph. If you have an important photograph with a large tear in it, contact a conservator for advice on getting it repaired.

Stuck Photographs

See the previous section in this chapter titled "Photo Albums" for a discussion on photographs that are stuck to photo albums.

At one of the library lectures I presented, a woman approached me afterward and said she had a photograph that was stuck to the glass frame it was in. When I got home, I did a little research on what to do in this situation. There is a method, but in truth I would not attempt it, especially not with a photograph I considered important and precious. This is another time to call a conservator. The method involved submerging the photograph stuck to the glass into a pan of water and leaving it to soak for an hour or longer. This is a specialized procedure that I do not recommend non-professionals attempt.

Water Damage

We have discussed using water to hydrate paper and photographs and to remove strongly stuck photographs from glass enclosures. On the other hand, water can be very damaging to photographs. If yours have been caught in a flood, whether it is of historic proportions or just from a burst pipe within your home, much care needs to be taken to restore your photographs to their previous dry condition. If your home has experienced a major flood, please refer to the American Red Cross publication, *Repairing Your Flooded Home.* You can also refer to the IPI's, *A Consumer Guide for the Recovery of Water-Damaged Traditional and Digital Prints*. These documents can be found on my website at https://lenasalina.com/secrets-from-the-stacks-guides/.

Keep in mind that digital prints that were printed on home computers or by commercial photo finishers have different needs than traditional prints. These instructions are general. Please refer to the documents mentioned above for more specific instructions. If you read them now before disaster strikes, you will be more prepared and less panicked when an actual disaster occurs.

Consumer Guide

The best defense is a good offense. Before catastrophe strikes, make sure photographs are housed in good archival materials. These materials may not be flood resistant, but they will not do further damage to your photographs such as bleeding, sticking, and chemically reacting. The IPI recommends using journaling pens and colored papers that are made with waterproof pigment colorants and will not bleed onto prints.[9] You can purchase journaling pens from archival supply houses and colored papers with pigment colorants wherever photo papers are sold. Digitize photographs and make sure to have backups in a separate location and in the cloud. Refer to Chapter 14, "Disaster Preparedness and Disaster Recovery" for more specific instructions.

CHAPTER 4

19TH-CENTURY PHOTOGRAPHS:

Daguerreotype, Calotype, Ambrotype, Tintype, Carte des Visite

Photography is a way of feeling, of touching, of loving. What you have caught on film is captured forever... It remembers little things, long after you have forgotten everything.[10]

—**Aaron Siskind**

If you are lucky enough to have photographs old enough to be in this category, it is your moral responsibility as the family historian to do all you can to preserve them properly. Again, environment is going to be the most important factor. Keeping the temperature between 40° and 68°F (4° and 20°C) and the RH between 30% and 40% for all types of 19th-century photographs will ensure their longest life.[11] Humidity, as we will see, is the greatest enemy of these types of photographs.

A photographic preservationist I heard speak at a conference likened the photographic development in the 19th century to the development of computers in the 20th century. Those of us who lived through the rise of the computer age are familiar with the constant need to upgrade computer software and hardware as the industry improved processes and equipment. In a similar way, inventors experimented with different base materials, imaging materials, and binding agents

Kodak Camera ad November 1889

throughout the 19th century. As each invention improved upon the last, photographers changed from one medium to the next. Like the development of computers, after years of constant flux, a level of stability was attained when George Eastman used gelatin-based rolled transparent plastic film in the Kodak camera. Eastman's greatest contribution to photography was that he developed the film for his customers after the pictures were taken, a practice we are all familiar with due to its great success. An early *Harper's Magazine* ad for Kodak declared, "You press the button, we do the rest."[12]

To satisfy your curiosity, and so you can be educated and sound smart when showing off your pictures to family, friends, and relatives, below is a little background information on each of these different photographic processes. But as the family archivist, you can treat all these different types of photographs similarly. If you want to start archiving immediately without the historical background, skip to the individual sections about processing for each type of photograph listed below.

DAGUERREOTYPES

Louis-Jacques-Mandé Daguerre publicized the invention that came to bear his name, the daguerreotype, in the *Gazette de France* in 1839. Daguerre had partnered with Joseph Nicéphore Niépce, a French inventor whose early development of photography laid the foundation for all future advances. Soon after Daguerre publicized their work, the French government gave Daguerre and Niépce's heir (unfortunately, Niépce did not live to see his invention introduced to the public) a commission for life for the right to publish their inventions. Many other inventors were experimenting with photography at the same time, but the daguerreotype provided a clearer image and, more importantly, a way to "fix" the image. Daguerre published a seventy-nine-page booklet that explained his method and, along with his brother-in-law, began manufacturing cameras and distributing them around the world. The process quickly caught on because of its ability to create a "truthful likeness" and because the French government made the process available to all who wanted to use it.

> "There's this energy in your ancestry. It's more than just facts and who was born where."
>
> Gwyneth Paltrow. WDYTYA US.2.7

Americans in particular embraced the daguerreotype like no other nation. As the Wild West was being settled, professional photographers used daguerreotypes to document westward expansion. Families leaving home for the West brought photographs of loved ones left behind, at the same time leaving images of themselves with their families in the East. Daguerreotype studios opened across America in all major cities. Photographers exhibited prints of celebrities and political figures in their display windows to entice the public into their museum-like studios and invite them to be photographed. To demonstrate the popularity of daguerreotypes, an 1855 statistic indicates that 403,626 daguerreotypes were taken in Massachusetts alone.[13] That is a lot of pictures!

Enclosure for daguerreotypes

Daguerreotypes were most popular between 1839 and 1860. Their popularity waned after the invention of the ambrotype photograph in 1851, which was faster and less expensive. Although ambrotypes did not create a clearer image, for most people speed and price were more important than image quality. Daguerreotypes used a silver-plated copper base, which was cleaned and polished until the surface looked black when held up in a darkened room. Plates were sensitized with iodine before being exposed to light for three to fifteen minutes to create the photograph. Mercury was used in the developing process and sodium thiosulfate was used to fix the image. Daguerreotypes were placed in a special hinged frame designed to keep air away from the silver plate that would easily tarnish. The frames are typically made of wood covered with leather, paper, cloth, or mother of pearl. Often silk or velvet lines the interior.

Processing Daguerreotypes

Daguerreotypes are highly sensitive and are easily at risk of tarnishing and abrasion. Do not remove daguerreotypes from their original cases. Do not expose daguerreotypes to intense light. If you have these types of photographs, you might want to work with them at night under a subdued light. It is not recommended that daguerreotype photographs be put on display. I have several friends who have daguerreotypes on the walls of their homes, on bookshelves, and in other photographic display areas. This is not advised. Instead, it would be better to reproduce the image by taking a digital photograph of it and placing it in a similar frame. With that said, daguerreotypes can very resilient. If housed properly, they can last for a long time. Consider that the daguerreotypes you have in your collection are well over one hundred years old. But, to keep the photographs for the longest possible time so that future generations may enjoy them too, they should be taken off the wall and stored in the proper enclosures out of the light.

Daguerreotypes come in standard sizes:

- ✓ Full plate: 6 ½" x 8 ½"
- ✓ Half plate: 4 ¼" x 5 ½"
- ✓ Quarter plate: 3 ¼" x 4 ¼"
- ✓ Ninth plate: 2" x 2 ½"
- ✓ Sixteenth plate: 1 ⅜" x 1 ⅝"

The standard sizing of daguerreotypes makes purchasing housing materials for them simple. Archival supply houses have boxes specifically made for daguerreotypes, allowing those processing a collection to simply place original daguerreotypes in an acid-free box. You can buy either photographic boxes or book boxes from the archival supply houses. If you are the creative type, you can make your own boxes. Do not use glue! Wrap the daguerreotype in acid-free tissue paper or put crushed pieces around the photograph to keep it from moving in the box. Be careful not to break the glass frame. Boxes should be stored vertically or horizontally together in a larger box. Include in the box a notation of who is in the picture, the year it was taken, and any other information you may know about it. You may want to include information to let your descendants know how to handle this type of photograph (e.g., do not take it out of the case, do not expose it to intense light, and do not display it for long periods). If you do not know the exact year the daguerreotype was taken, writing "ca. 1839–1860" will provide at least some information. It is possible a daguerreotype was taken after 1860, but it is unlikely.

If your daguerreotype photograph has a damaged glass covering or a damaged frame that allows air to get inside, you should consult a professional conservator. They can make a new frame enclosure that allows the original photograph to be preserved. In any case, take a digital picture of it right away. Once exposed to air, daguerreotypes will tarnish and fade quickly.

CALOTYPES

William Henry Fox Talbot of Great Britain found that if photographic images were captured on chemically treated paper rather than on silver or glass plates, exposure time could be shortened, and the development process could be continued after the image was removed from the camera. This process was called the "developing out process" and is still used today on non-digital images. Talbot named his process *calotype* from the Greek word meaning "beautiful picture." A shortened exposure time made calotypes an attractive advance over daguerreotypes because the paper could be treated the night before, and multiple images could be made from one single negative.

Chances are you do not have calotype images in your collection. Two circumstances prevented the calotype from surpassing the daguerreotype as the preferred method of photography, especially in the United States. First, the images created on paper tended to be fuzzier than those created on silver or glass plates, making calotypes less appealing for portraiture photography. Second, Talbot patented the calotype process in Britain on February 8, 1841. At the time Louis Daguerre announced his photographic process in 1839, Talbot had already invented a similar form of photogenic transfer. Because Talbot didn't publish or patent his pre-1839 invention, and because the French government paid Daguerre and Niépce a lifetime commission for theirs and made the process freely available to the world, Talbot was not able to profit from his invention. Feeling left out of the race, he patented his new invention, the calotype, two years later in Great Britain. By patenting his invention, no one could use it unless they paid a fee to Talbot. He patented the process in France but did not seem to enforce it there. The calotype was used extensively in France and the French even improved on the process.

Calotype

In the United States, the story was a little different. Two American photographers paid Talbot for the exclusive rights to use calotype negatives in the United States. When they tried to sell the idea to American daguerreotype photographers, the savvy Americans did not see the point in paying for a photographic method that produced less detailed images. Like software licensing a century later, Talbot wanted photographers to pay an annual fee for the use of his method. In the end, calotypes were used primarily to capture landscapes and architecture by specialized photographers, travelers, and archaeologists, but most common professional photographers stayed away from using them. If you do have a calotype in your collection, treat it the same way you would a daguerreotype. The chemicals used in the photographic process are similar.

AMBROTYPES

Unlike the calotype, the ambrotype, also known as collodion positive, was immensely popular in America between 1851 and 1880. The ambrotype photograph supplanted the daguerreotype with its use of the wet plate collodion process. Developed by Frederick Scott Archer, an English sculptor, the collodion process revolutionized photography. Collodion is a sticky solution that is a mix of nitrocellulose in alcohol, ether, and potassium iodide. After brushing this substance onto a glass plate (rather than a silver plate used in daguerreotypes), the glass was dipped in a solution of silver nitrate. The glass plate needed to be wet when exposed in the camera, and the photograph had to be developed immediately after exposure while keeping the plate wet until the process was complete. The ambrotype process required the photographer to always have easy access to a darkroom; hence, the photographic wagons that are familiar throughout the Civil War and out West.

Ambrotype

Ambrotype photographs are glass negatives backed with black cloth, paint, or varnish to produce a positive image. Ambrotypes became popular in the United States because they were easier to produce than daguerreotypes. Portrait photographers preferred them even though daguerreotypes produced a more detailed, sharper image. The most attractive feature of the ambrotype for the professional portraiture photographer was that they were easier to produce and could be finished and delivered at the time of the sitting. Portraiture was the most common use of ambrotype photography. Images were sometimes colored by hand.

Like daguerreotypes, ambrotypes are typically housed in hinged cases made of wood covered with leather, paper, cloth, or mother of pearl. Deterioration is typically caused by high humidity and high temperatures and will show up as flaking and cracking. Breakage is the other most common form of damage to ambrotypes since glass is used as the support layer.

Processing Ambrotypes

To protect ambrotypes from abrasion, light, and pollutants, process them the same way you would daguerreotypes. Do not remove them from their original frames. Do not touch the surface image as oxidation can occur if they are exposed to air. Place the entire photograph in the frame in an acid-free box, one per box, and then put acid-free tissue paper around them to keep them from moving, if necessary. Your best option for ambrotypes is to use four-flap negative enclosures sold by archival supply companies. If signs of flaking are visible, store ambrotypes flat. Otherwise, they can be stored vertically in envelopes or four-flap boxes. If you have many ambrotypes, they can be filed standing vertically in shoeboxes.

Environment is critical to all 19th-century photographs, but especially to ambrotypes and tintypes. Make sure they are kept at 40°F to 68°F and 30% to 40% RH. Do not store them in wooden cabinets. If you will be keeping them in a file cabinet, use one made of enameled steel, stainless steel, or anodized aluminum.

Similar to the daguerreotype and calotype, put a description of the photograph—answering the who, what, where, when, and why—written in pencil on a piece of acid-free paper and insert it into the envelope or enclosure. You can also write in pencil on the outside of the four-fold box.

TINTYPES

Tintypes use the same wet plate collodion process as the ambrotype, the difference being that a thin sheet of iron is used as the support layer instead of glass. Hamilton I. Smith patented this process in 1856. The advantage of the tintype was that it was not fragile like the glass ambrotypes. Tintypes, also known as ferrotypes or tin-o-types, could be sent through the mail or kept in the coat pocket of a son on the battlefield because of their sturdiness. Like ambrotypes, they were processed while the customer waited. Many tintypes could be produced cheaply and quickly. Photographers

Tintype

at social events made cheap portraits on the street, at public fairs, or at special family events and outings. Friendship photographs and local landscapes were also common. Because tintypes were cheap and easily accessible, many soldiers during the Civil War were photographed by using this method.

Tintypes were often used for cartes-de-visite, a photographic alternative to visiting cards or calling cards. They came in the small standard size of 4" x 2 ½". Tintypes were sometimes placed in hinged frames, as was the convention of the day with daguerreotypes and ambrotypes. More often, tintypes were inserted into folding cards or a type of window envelope made of paper or metal.

Tintypes are highly sensitive and at greater risk of water damage than any other 19th-century photograph. The greatest risk to tintypes is high humidity. Contact with water will lead to oxidation and rust. If your tintypes show signs of blistering, flaking, or loss of image, they were probably exposed to water most likely via high humidity or a leaky roof in the attic. Rust stains may also be seen on the paper support sleeves. Over time, the collodion binder in tintypes will yellow and delaminate. Tintypes are often damaged by scratches and dents.

Processing Tintypes

Do not expose tintypes to intense light. Store them in acid-free envelopes purchased from an archival supply store, one tintype per envelope. A piece of archival cardboard inside the envelope will prevent the photograph from becoming deformed in storage. If your tintypes already show signs of flaking, lay them flat for storage. Otherwise, file them vertically with dividers between each slide. You can also use sturdy four-flap enclosures for storage. Wrap the tintypes in acid-free tissue paper, if necessary, to keep them sturdy and from moving around in storage containers. Do not store tintypes in wooden cabinets as the off-gassing from paints and varnish can damage them.

Since humidity is the greatest enemy of tintypes, you want to ensure they are stored in an environment with temperatures between 40° and 68°F and RH between 30% and 40%. To offer them the longest life, you might want to keep these photographs in another location or donate them to a local library or archive, especially if you do not think you can keep your home within the necessary environmental conditions.

Do not forget to describe the photograph by answering who, what, where, when, and why, handwritten in pencil on a piece of acid-free paper inserted in the envelope or enclosure.

4: 19TH-CENTURY PHOTOGRAPHS

CARTES-DE-VISITE

Many collections contain these small photographs. Victorians loved cartes-de-visite. They were enormously popular and cheap to produce. Rather than using experienced professional photographers who were required for creating daguerreotypes, ambrotypes, and tintypes, unskilled laborers could create cartes-de-visite. They became a staple of Victorian life in the mid-19th century, replacing the common "visiting card" that was in vogue at the time.

The carte-de-visite process was patented by André Adolphe-Eugène Disdéri in France in 1854. Disdéri sought to make photographs more accessible to less affluent audiences. Cartes-de-visite used a wet plate process employing

Cartes-Des-Visite

a special camera with four lenses and a plate holder. The plateholder was slid back-and-forth from side to side, capturing four exposures on each side of the plate—eight exposures in quick succession. A single print on paper could be made from the eight exposures. The photographs were cut up into individual prints, then pasted on a mount measuring 4" x 2 ½".

The standard small size of cartes-de-visite led to the creation of photographic albums by 1860, in which people collected photographs of friends and family as well as current celebrities. Celebrity cartes were sold at stationary stores like postcards are today. Cartes-de-visite are not considered high art. They lack aesthetic value, and their small size often makes it difficult to make out facial features. But they were highly popular in the 19th century, and chances are high that you may have a few in your family collection.

Many cartes-de-visite were printed on albumen paper, the most common printing material used by photographers after 1850. Invented in Paris by Louis Désiré Blanquart-Evrard, the process used egg whites brushed on high-quality paper, with potassium bromide, acetic acid, and silver nitrate added to transfer images from glass plates to paper.

Processing Cartes-de-Visite

Cartes-de-visite should be processed the same way all other 19th-century photographs are processed. A description of the photographs answering the who, what, where, when, and why can be handwritten in pencil on a piece of acid-free paper and inserted in the envelope or enclosure. You can find special envelopes for cartes-de-visite in archival stores.

View-Master

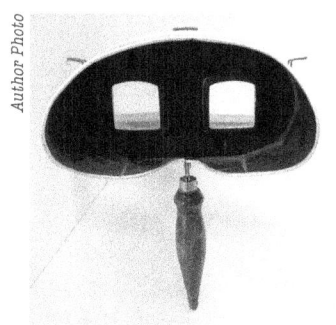

19th Century Stereoscopic Viewer

STEREOSCOPIC SLIDES

Did you have a View-Master when you were a kid? View-Masters are those little plastic binocular-looking gadgets that you slid a circular disc into. By depressing a lever, the disc advanced and all kinds of magical images presented themselves. I loved my View-Master. I have an artist friend who has a grown-up version. Whenever I go to his house, I love looking at the 3-D pictures he keeps nearby of exotic places, plants, flowers, foliage, and deep space. The View-Master is a modern adaptation of the original stereoscopic slides.

Stereoscopic photography was produced by using twin-lens cameras. The result was a 3-D image that was similar to human binocular vision. Experimentation began as early as the 1830s, but the use of these photographs did not become popular until 1849 when Sir David Brewster invented a device for easily viewing them.

The more significant result of stereoscopic images is that they provided the first vehicle for action photography. Stop-action photography of human and animal behavior was nothing short of revolutionary. For the first time, bipedal walking was recorded. Oliver Wendall Holmes Sr., a 19th-century American physician, found the images of people's stride startling, declaring that the images differed from conventions that had been used for centuries to describe how people walked.[14] His interest in analyzing walking techniques was aimed at designing artificial limbs for Civil War veterans.

Stereoscopic slides and the recording of motion was also the foundation of the eventual, but inevitable, development of motion pictures.

Chances are you do not have stereoscopic slides in your collection. If you do, they are very cool. You may have an old slide viewer. Shortly after Brewster invented his viewer, millions were sold. You might also have an antique stereoscopic camera that is most likely worth money.

Stereoscopic photograph

The good news is that archival supply stores sell polyester sleeves specifically made for stereoscopic photographs. Simply slide the photographs into the plastic sleeves and place in acid-free folders and acid-free boxes. As with all your other photographs, environmental conditions are the most important factor to consider. If your stereoscopic negatives are glass, you will naturally want to keep them in a four-flap enclosure or other small box. For larger sizes, look to book boxes. As with all your photographs, make sure to provide whatever information you can on a piece of acid-free paper, handwritten in pencil, with the photograph describing who, what, where, when, and why.

DETERMINING THE YEAR OF A PHOTOGRAPH

As a non-expert, you may not know whether the photograph you own is a daguerreotype, an ambrotype, or a tintype. Once you determine what kind of photograph you have, the year it was produced can be narrowed down. Daguerreotypes were popular between 1839 and 1853. Ambrotypes reigned supreme between 1851 and 1880, and tintypes prevailed between 1853 and 1930.

The obvious difference between the three most common forms of 19th-century photographs is that daguerreotypes use silver plates as a base, ambrotypes use glass as a base, and tintypes use iron as a base.

One way to determine whether your photograph is a daguerreotype or an ambrotype is to hold it up and look at it from different angles. The polished silver plates of daguerreotypes will look like a negative, positive, or a mirror, depending on which angle you view them from. The ambrotype will look like a positive image and will not change when held at different angles.

ARCHIVES TIP

19th Century Photographs Cheat Sheet

Daguerreotype (1839 – 1860s)
Tintype (c. 1853 – 1930s)
Ambrotype (c. 1854 – 1880s)
Cartes de visites (1850 – 1920s)

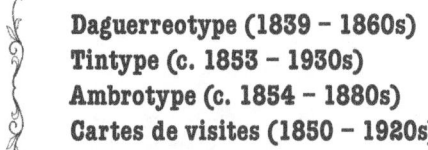

Since tintypes were made using iron, the easiest way to determine whether a photograph is a tintype is by using a magnet. If the magnet sticks, it is a tintype. Tintypes were also cheaply made, and the image quality tends to be dark and poor. Early tintypes were put in cases like daguerreotypes and ambrotypes, but later tintypes used papier-mâché or cardboard enclosures. Today, many are found loose with no accompanying enclosure. Another dead giveaway that your photograph is a tintype is rust. If you have rust spots on your photo, it is a tintype.

Cartes-de-visite are easy to determine by their standard size used throughout their history. The photographs themselves were 3 ½" x 2" and were pasted onto mounts 4" x 2 ½". Since they were used over such a long period (late 1850s through the 1920s), one way to determine the age of a carte is by the thickness of the mounting. The thinner the mount, the earlier the photography. Another clue is the shape of the mount corners. Earlier cartes have square corners. In the 1870s the mounds had rounded corners.

Another way to date old photographs is by looking at the clothing people are wearing, the hairstyles they have, and background architecture, furniture, lamps, and signs. It is beyond the scope of this book to outline the complexity of fashion conventions, styles, and architectural periods. An online search will bring up many articles and photographs that may help you narrow down your search. If you are a genealogist as well as the family historian and archivist, you are well aware of the need to be a sleuth in putting together your collection. Maureen Taylor, the Photo Detective, assists people in dating photographs and determining who is in them. Visit her website at https://maureentaylor.com.

CHAPTER 5

20TH-CENTURY PHOTOGRAPHS

In my mother's house
There's a photograph
Of a day gone past
Always makes me laugh

— **Corinne Bailey Rae,** *Butterfly*

Two advances toward the end of the 19th century resulted in the mass production of photographs. First, George Eastman invented rolled nitrate film, which allowed multiple exposures to be taken before removing it from the camera. He also developed the film into photographs at his factory, so people only needed to put it in an envelope and mail it to him.

Eastman Kodak Factory, Rochester, NY

Second, manufactured photosensitive paper was mass-produced. This meant that the photographic base, now evolved from glass or metal to paper, no longer needed to be sensitized by hand by a professional photographer immediately prior to taking the picture. In addition, photo papers that were chemically developed reduced exposure time in the developing process from minutes to less than a second, allowing photographs to be printed quickly and in large quantities.

The paper photographic base was further improved in the late 1960s when resin-coated papers called "RC" papers were used. These photo papers were manufactured with polyethylene laminate, a form of plastic, on both sides. Laminate helped to keep prints flat after wet processing and reduced the amount of processing time. RC print used to refer to wet-processed photographs only, but now RC papers are also used in the manufacture of dye-sub and many inkjet photo papers that replicate the look and feel of photos of years past.

The other major advance in the 20th century was the invention of color film and color photographs.

COLOR PRINTS AND FILM

All color film and photographs use three component dyes. Most of us have become familiar with these colors because they are the same colors used in our modern printers and copy machines. The colors are cyan, magenta, and yellow. As the family archivist, one of the most important things to know about color photographs is that the three different colors fade at different rates. Another thing to consider is that throughout the 20th century, manufacturers were constantly improving and changing photographic materials, often without announcing the changes to the public. This makes it difficult to pinpoint the different chemicals, organic materials, or processes that were used to create a specific photograph in a specific place at a specific time. The first use of color film was introduced in 1935 by Kodak and was called "Kodachrome" film. In 1942, a less stable version of Kodachrome film was used.

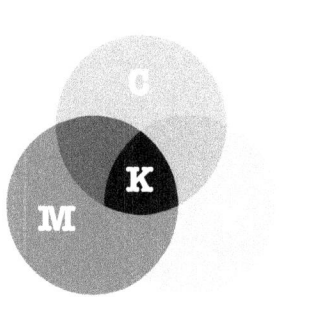

Basic color theory

Color photographs use what is called **chromogenic development**. This means that the color dyes in the final picture are formed during processing. All color photographs are made using this technology except for Polaroid, invented in 1963, which is non-chromogenic. Chromogenic dye photographs are inherently unstable and will fade when exposed to light. They are also subject to dark fading, so they sometimes fade to yellow in the dark. If possible, store color photographs at 20% to 50% humidity and 40°F. Excessive dampness from humidity is the most damaging condition for all color photographs.

Interestingly, color photographs are less sensitive to environmental pollutants than black-and-white silver images. The instability of dyes is the most common cause of fading for color photographs, not environmental pollution. However, pollution does affect color photographs over time. Paper enclosures are not sufficient to protect against pollution. Use plastic enclosures instead.

5: 20TH-CENTURY PHOTOGRAPHS

Temperature is the most significant environmental factor in determining how quickly dye fading will occur in photographs, more so than RH. Near-freezing conditions will allow color preservation indefinitely, but this is not practical for most of us and is not recommended since removing items from a frozen condition requires special care.

The chart below is a guideline that is used in archives. I present it to you so you can make your own determination in figuring out the best course of action for your color photographs. Because most of us will not be able to achieve temperatures below 60°F or RH under 50%, we must accept the fact that our photographs are not going to remain stable for more than fifty years. The truth is that wherever you have stored your photographs, they most likely have not met these environmental conditions. Therefore, most of your childhood photographs have faded a bit, and because the different dye components fade at different rates, the fading is not consistent.

Approximate Time in Years to Significant Dye Fading in Color Photographic Materials							
Temperature	20% RH	30% RH	40% RH	50% RH	60% RH	70% RH	80% RH
30 F/-1 C	8000	3500	1500	800	600	450	350
35 F/-2 C	4500	2000	1000	600	350	300	250
40 F/4 C	3000	1500	700	350	250	200	175
45 F/7 C	1750	900	450	250	175	125	100
50 F/10 C	1000	600	300	175	125	90	80
55 F/13 C	700	350	200	125	80	60	50
60 F/16 C	450	250	125	80	60	45	35
65 F/18 C	300	150	90	50	40	30	25
70 F/21 C	180	100	60	40	25	20	18
75 F/24 C	125	70	40	25	19	15	12
80 F/27 C	80	50	30	19	14	11	9
85 F/29 C	50	30	20	13	10	8	6
90 F/32 C	35	20	14	10	7	6	5
95 F/35 C	25	15	10	7	5	4	3
100 F/38 C	15	11	7	5	4	3	2
105 F/41 C	10	7	5	4	3	2	2
110 F/43 C	7	5	4	3	2	2	1
115 F/46 C	5	4	3	2	2	1	1
120 F/49 C	3	3	2	1	1	1	1

Credit: James M Reilly, *Storage Guide for Color Photographic Materials* (New York)

With this in mind, the best you can do is slow down the destruction. I doubt most of you will be able to completely stop the deterioration, and the fact is that most archives do not take special measures where photographs are concerned. Archives with the photographic works of famous, noteworthy photographers will strive to achieve the longest life for their photographic collections. I have worked in archives that had special freezers for certain film collections, but I have also worked in archives where everything was stored in the same place under the same environmental conditions. My point in conveying this information is not so that you can freak out over the fact that your photographs are fading. The point is for you to take measures to slow it down as much as possible knowing that fading and deterioration is inevitable.

The most practical step you can take to increase the life of your color photographs is to put them in plastic enclosures. As discussed earlier, plastic enclosures form a more protective barrier against environmental pollutants than paper enclosures. This does not mean everything has to be plastic. It is sufficient to put photographs in plastic sleeves within a paper photo album or a paper file folder and a paper box.

Loose-leaf photo album

Personally, I love the loose-leaf photo albums sold by archival supply stores. You can buy sheets that hold photographs of different sizes and put them together in the same photo album. All the plastic sleeves sold by archival supply stores have passed the PAT. Descriptions of photographs can be handwritten in pencil or printed from a computer on acid-free paper and inserted before or between the sheets describing the who, what, where, when, and why of the photograph. You can place the photo albums lying flat in a standard records box, which is 12" W x 10" H x 15" L.

If you want to add an extra layer of protection, especially from humidity or dampness, you can purchase polypropylene records boxes. These are more expensive, so unless you are storing items in a cellar or other areas that are at risk of flood or dampness, they are not necessary.

Another option for storage is putting items in polyester, polypropylene, or polyethylene sleeves and placing those in acid-free folders inside of flip-top boxes. Since we do not use photo albums in the archives, and space is of utmost concern, this is how we store photographs in the archives. This is also a cheaper method of storage that you may choose for some or all of your photographs. If you use this method, be sure the folders stand up straight and are not slumped. To help with this, you can purchase folder supports from archival stores.

5: 20TH-CENTURY PHOTOGRAPHS

Digitization offers a solution for faded color photographs. Many computers come loaded with some kind of photo editing software. Adobe Photoshop is the most widely used and common. The graphic designers I know all use the Adobe suite of graphic design programs in their businesses. These are powerful programs that do amazing things.

For us regular folk, less advanced versions of Adobe Photoshop offer a wide variety of fixes and enhancements that can restore and recapture much of the fading and damage that has been done to photographs. iPhoto and Google Photo are other popular software programs that offer several automatic and manual fixes.

> *I was unprepared for how protective I would feel of my ancestors. And you know family's family, dead or alive. Family is family."*
>
> **Sarah Millican**
> **WDYTYA-UK-S10.E08**

Photo editing software programs provide instructions on how to use them and often have forums where users can share their experiences. YouTube has videos that walk you through many of the features. After scanning your old photographs into your computer, they can be enhanced so that the color is restored to near the original using these photo editing applications. After they are restored, you can print them out yourself onto photographic paper or use a service such as Shutterfly to have reprints made.

Photo credit: David Cruz

In addition to fixing the damage from fading, you can also make multiple copies of a scanned photograph and change them in a variety of fun and creative ways. You can turn color photos into black-and-whites, add oval frames, or even turn them into cartoons. I say, upload your photographs and have a blast. Since you still have the original photograph, you need not worry about damaging the digital copy. If you overwrite the original scan in error, you can just rescan the original photograph. So, have a good time, play around with the features, and see what you can fix and create.

A word of caution about digitization: do not throw away the original photograph. As of today, the digital environment is not stable. Please refer to Chapter 11 for more information on digitization.

NON-CHROMOGENIC FILM

Polaroid film was introduced to the market in 1963.[15] Its self-developing film is non-chromogenic. A look in any of our collections quickly reveals that Polaroid photographs fade much faster than chromogenic photographs. When processing your collection, you might want to process the Polaroids first and give them the special care and attention they need.

Polaroid camera

Cibachrome or **Ilfochrome** photographs are non-chromogenic and are made of silver dye bleach rather than organic colors. These are rare, but if you have them in your collection, they are said to be able to last several hundred years. Cibachrome or Ilfochrome are typically used in large format cameras. The photographic base is polyester rather than paper. Standard commercial printers did not typically use these types of photographic bases. Unless you have the collection of a professional photographer or hobbyist who developed their own photographs, you most likely do not have photographs using Cibachrome or Ilfochrome. Ilfochrome was produced up until 2011.

20TH-CENTURY PAPER

As mentioned earlier, the invention of pre-sensitized photographic paper was a major development in photography. It led to the mass production of photographic paper, which in turn led to the mass use of photography by the public. In addition to mass-producing photo paper that could be sold and used by professional photographers, Eastman Kodak offered photographic processing services to the general public. After taking photographs on a roll of film stored inside the camera, the lay photographer could easily take the roll of film out of the camera and mail it to George Eastman's factory in Rochester, NY. Eastman Kodak processed the film and sent both the film and the processed photographs back to the photographer. What could be easier?

Most of us remember the days when we dropped film off in the mail or at a photographic kiosk or the drug store for development.

Many of us remember the days when we dropped film off in the mail, at a photographic kiosk, or at a drugstore for development. Like dropping clothes off at the dry cleaners, a few days later our photos were ready to be picked up and we had the joy of seeing how well our photographs came out (or if you are like me, the disappointment of seeing how bad the photographs came out).

Without a single-lens reflex (SLR) camera, most of us are guilty of chopping off a few heads in the photos. I went to a wedding and took a roll of thirty-six frames, only to find out when I got them back that the film had not properly mounted on the sprockets inside the camera and therefore never advanced. I received a roll of blank pictures.

The next advancement in photographic-based papers came in the late 1960s when resin-coated paper began to be used. This paper added polyethylene laminate to both sides of the sheet of paper, which helped keep print photographs flat and reduced the amount of processing time. Modern digital inkjet photo papers use this same technology so that printed digital photographs have the same look and feel of traditional photos.

PROCESSING MODERN PHOTOGRAPHS

The term "photo paper" previously referred to any light-sensitive paper used to create photographic prints. With the advent of computers, digital photographs, and modern printers, film is no longer needed and many types of paper can be used in the printing process. This has led to another revolution in photographic processing. Now, instead of sending film to a store to be developed at a factory using the traditional wet process, we can print photographs ourselves for a fraction of the cost. Regardless of the type of processing or paper you use today, however, all modern paper should be processed using the same protocols.

The IPI in Rochester, NY, recommends that all types of modern photographs be stored in photo albums. I think it is acceptable to house photographs in other types of archival-quality storage materials such as small boxes specifically designed to house 4" x 6" or 3" x 5" prints. Like most other photographs, you can also put modern photographs in plastic sheets and place them in acid-free folders

Photograph Enclosures

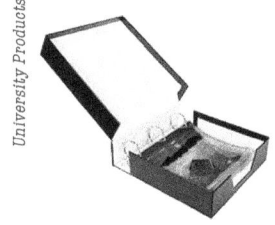

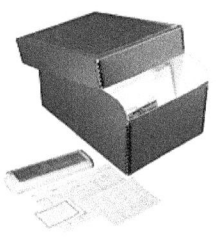

Photograph Enclosures

inside an acid-free flip-top box. Or, lay them flat in polyester sheets and acid-free folders and store them in clamshell boxes.

If using a photo album, make sure it is a high-quality one with materials that have passed the PAT. All papers in photo albums should be acid-free, lignin-free, and buffered (refer to Chapter 1 for a more detailed explanation of these terms). Photos should be stored in polyester, polypropylene, or polystyrene enclosures. Do not stack color prints. They can bleed onto adjacent sheets or stick together. And as with everything in your archival collection, make sure that the environment they are stored in meets the RH and temperature guidelines as best as possible.

Photographs printed at home should be allowed to dry for twenty-four hours before placing them in plastic sleeves, even if they are advertised as "instant dry." Any dampness remaining in the paper could cause the image to stick to the inside of the plastic sleeve. Sleeves that have passed the PAT are not immune to this problem.

Photographs bring to life family members, events, and important life passages in a way no other documents can. Take your time when processing photographs. Doing it in stages might be the best way. Transferring documents to archival-quality enclosures is step one. Organizing photographs into a visual story by describing the people, places, and events and adding dates is more time consuming and may take a little more forethought and attention. Remember who you are doing this for. On one hand it may be to delight your children and grandchildren. But remember Baby 2135. Put your photographs together in such a way that the stories of previous generations are told in a sensitive, revealing, and fun way that will instill a sense of knowing, a sense of pride, and the sense of family roots and history that we all long for.

CHAPTER 6

FILM

Photography is thus brought within reach of every human being who desires to preserve a record of what he sees. Such a photographic notebook is an enduring record of many things seen only once in a lifetime and enables the fortunate possessor to go back by the light of his own fireside to scenes which would otherwise fade from memory and be lost.[16]

—George Eastman

Film comes in three broad categories: cellulose nitrate, cellulose acetate, and polyester. Each category improves and advances the technology of the previous one. We will look at each type of film and discuss whether you would find this type of film in your collection, how to identify it, and what to do with it. Keep in mind that film comes in two forms: photographic negatives and motion pictures.

NITRATE FILM

George Eastman began producing nitrate film in August 1889.[17] At the time, it was a major advancement in the technology of a base support for photograph production. As discussed in Chapter 4, prior to the introduction of film, glass plate negatives and tin-o-types were the most popularly used photographic bases. Photographers experimented to find a support base that was flexible and lightweight. The formula for celluloid is cellulose nitrate combined with a plasticizer such as camphor. Cellulose nitrate was revolutionary because it could be cut into thin sheets and rolled for easy transport and use. George Eastman popularized the use of celluloid when he started producing it in his factory in Rochester, NY.

Another revolutionary aspect of rolled film is that it led to the creation of motion pictures—an extraordinary advancement in human development. Motion picture film allowed scientists to analyze the natural world in slow motion and to see things the naked eye could not see. Medical doctors marveled to see the human body in frame-by-frame motion, which resulted in the development of proper prosthetic limbs.

Photo credit: Lance Aram Rothstein

Kodak, Nitrate Film

With all its benefits, the greatest problem with cellulose nitrate film is that it is highly flammable. In the 19th century, several tragic fires prompted Eastman Kodak and other producers of nitrate film to further develop the technology so that film was less flammable. The result was acetate film, which is known as "safety film." Eastman Kodak last produced nitrate motion picture film in 1951. The last time anyone produced nitrate film packs was in 1949, and film rolls in 1950.

Nitrate film negatives in good condition are neutral black. Once the film has started to deteriorate, it turns to a yellow or brown tone. The film support can turn brittle and become sticky. It can off-gas highly corrosive materials that are harmful, have an acrid smell, and be very toxic. I have seen nitrate film rust the metal containers they are housed in and the metal shelves they are stored on. That is pretty corrosive.

The flammability of nitrate film is of concern. It is believed that nitrate film can auto-combust, although I have read articles that dispute this. Regardless, there is no question that nitrate film is highly flammable.

Most of the early motion picture films made using nitrate were produced on 35 mm film—typically, movies played in movie theaters. The National Film Preservation Foundation, a non-profit organization, is devoted to preserving America's film heritage. You may have been asked while attending a movie to donate to this cause. Much of their work involves the preservation of motion picture film produced for movie theaters on 35 mm nitrate film. The foundation has saved films such as *Gone with the Wind* and several films of Charlie Chaplin and Mary Pickford.

The greatest problem with cellulose nitrate film is that it is highly flammable

Home movies were not developed until the 1920s and typically used 8 mm and 16 mm film. By this time, safety film was the standard of the day, replacing nitrate film. Eastman Kodak never used nitrate film for 8 mm or 16 mm motion pictures. Chances are, if you have motion picture film, it is not cellulose nitrate. You will, however, want to check the rolled film of still photographs in your collection.

One way to tell if the film you have is nitrate is by looking on the edge of the film. If "Safety Film" is printed in black letters on the edge, you know it is not nitrate. Safety film is acetate film. After safety film was developed in the 1920s, nitrate film began to be labeled "Nitrate" on the film's edge. Obviously, if you find the word "Nitrate" on the edge of the film in your collection, you know it is nitrate.

If the film is not labeled at all, there are other things you can do to determine whether it is nitrate. First, acetate film was not developed until the early 1920s. If you have film that is older than 1920, you know it is nitrate. Still, do not assume that if the film was produced after 1920 it will be acetate. Unless it is specifically labeled, you need to do further research.

Safety Film

Another thing to look for is that nitrate film tends to roll into very tight scrolls. After 1903, a gelatin was applied to the reverse side of film to prevent this type of tight curling. Other edge markings can offer clues as well. A "V" notch code identifies Kodak sheet film prior to 1949 as nitrate.

If you are in doubt about rolled film in your collection, there are tests that can be performed to indicate whether it is nitrate film. These are not tests that can be done at home, so you will have to send the film to a conservator.

The question to ask yourself is, Does this film need to be saved? If there is a chance the film you have is nitrate, this is an important consideration. If the film is of a photograph in your collection, there is really no need to keep both the film and the negative. Negatives and photographs can be both digitized and reprinted if necessary. If you only have film and no picture, you can have the film developed. Contact a conservator or the IPI. Nitrate film can be transferred to a polyester support, which is safer and more stable.

If you do decide to keep the film, it should be kept in cold, dry storage at temperatures from 5° to 40°F (-15° to 4°C) and 30% to 40% RH. I do not recommend this. Keeping film frozen has its own considerations. Removing film from a frozen environment needs to be done slowly and with care. Cellulose nitrate film should also be stored in buffered paper sleeves, not plastic of any kind. Plastic enclosures will entrap harmful gases, which can accelerate deterioration.

My recommendation is to either dispose of nitrate film, transfer it to a more stable support such as polyester, or have it digitized and then print a photograph. Why take the risk and keep something so toxic and flammable in your home? If you think the film you have is valuable and of historical importance, you should consider contacting a local archive and donating the materials or contacting the National Archives or the Library of Congress. Large archives are better equipped to house delicate materials for long-term preservation. Libraries and archives will also purchase certain materials if they are of significant importance to our national heritage and have monetary value. Some historians think of film as an important historical document that should be preserved. But that does not mean you have to keep it in your home. Again, if you think the film in your collection has historical value, contact a local archive, the National Archives, or the Library of Congress. If you decide to dispose of silver nitrate film please check with your local waste disposal services. Nitrate film is considered a hazardous material and must be disposed of properly.

ACETATE FILM

In reaction to the high flammability of nitrate film, producers sought a better solution. Film called "acetate" fulfilled this directive. Beginning around 1923, different chemical compositions were developed that produced less flammable film. The details of this are rather complex. If you are interested, I refer you to the bibliography at the end of this book to learn more about this process and the different chemical compositions that were used.[18]

For our purposes, it is important to understand that there was more than one type of film that fell under the common heading, "acetate." Kodak, the producer of film used by most amateur photographers, distributed a form of acetate film between 1927 and 1949. In the 1950s, manufacturers switched over to triacetate, which uses methylene chloride. This film support is still being used today. Added to the mix was color film, which was first produced by Kodak in 1942 under the name Kodacolor. Shortly after, Agfacolor was produced by Agfa. Acetate film was used in the production of rolled film, sheet film, and motion picture film. In the 1970s, polyester started to be used for most film.

ARCHIVES TIP

Film in an active state of Vinegar Syndrome can be hazardous to your health!

Although acetate film corrected the flammability issue of nitrate film, it is still an unstable medium that is subject to deterioration under normal room temperature conditions found in most homes. Acetate film's deterioration process is called **vinegar syndrome**. Additionally, the chromogenic color dyes used in acetate film are not permanent. They fade over time, even under optimal conditions.

Acetate film can be identified by the words "safety film" on the edge of the film. Kodak also used a U-shaped notch on their acetate film. Note: this is a small cutout in the film, not the letter imprinted. V is for nitrate, U for acetate.

Vinegar Syndrome

Decomposing acetate smells like vinegar. If you open a box or canister of film and it smells like vinegar, beware! The vinegar odor is caused by decomposing acetate. Other problems caused by the degradation of cellulose acetate film may be distortion, shrinkage, and brittleness, but by far the most dangerous is vinegar syndrome.

Evidence of Vinegar Syndrome

Film in an active state of vinegar syndrome can be hazardous to your health! Touching or sniffing degraded acetate film can produce burns and skin irritation as well as dizziness, light-headedness, and mucous membrane irritation. The best way to deal with objects already in a state of decay is to use protective nitrile gloves. Work in a well-ventilated area (outside or on a porch would be ideal) and wear a facemask. If you are particularly sensitive to environmental chemicals, you may want to allocate this part of your project out to someone else. You can also hire a professional archivist or personal historian to assist with this part of the project.

Film and photographs should be checked periodically for deterioration and specifically for vinegar syndrome. How often they should be checked is based on the temperature and humidity ranges they are being stored at. Items kept at an average room temperature of 72°F need to be checked every two to five years. For spaces cooler than 72°F, recheck every five to ten years. In cold places (50°F or less), check every ten years. If film is stored in a freezer with temperatures less than 41°F, only check every twenty-five years.[19]

Prevention of vinegar syndrome is important because there is no known cure for it. Once photographs and film have reached this level of deterioration, the degradation process accelerates. Not only will film decompose at an increased pace, but the syndrome can also spread to surrounding materials. As film begins to deteriorate, the acetic acid migrates to the surface making small holes in film, reel-to-reel, audio tapes, and video. This causes shrinkage and film deformity and can lead to the formation of a sticky substance on the surface of the tape that can spread to nearby objects. What smells like vinegar is actually acid. After the onset of vinegar syndrome, deterioration can be extreme and quick. Within a matter of months, a great deal of damage can occur.

Storage

Acetate film uses the same storage requirements as nitrate film. Ideally, to slow deterioration, it should be stored in cold temperatures 5° to 40°F (-15° to 4°C) with an RH of 30% to 40%. Individual buffered paper sleeves should be used since plastic enclosures will entrap gases that may accelerate deterioration. Although you do not run the risk of setting your house on fire with acetate film, the question you still need to ask yourself is, Do I need to keep this film? If there is a good photograph of what is on the film, you do not need to keep both the film and the photograph. Acetate film can be transferred to polyester film, which is more stable. Digitization is also an option. Some organizations think that film is an important medium in and of itself. Instead of throwing your film in the trash, you might want to consider donating it to one of them. Start with the National Archives (NARA.org).

POLYESTER FILM

Introduced in the 1950s, polyester film gradually replaced acetate sheet film beginning in the 1960s and 1970s. Polyester film is non-flammable, not subject to vinegar syndrome, and in the right environment is predicted to last up to 500 years. Because polyester film is completely synthetic, it provides a more chemically stable base than either nitrate or acetate film. Unlike nitrate and acetate film, polyester film does not contain the solvents or plasticizers that cause shrinkage or other problems with age. Over fifty years of manufacturing, polyester film has proven to have exceptional chemical stability.

> "When you think about how many people's names history just never remembers and the people whose stories are never told. It's shameful, and I feel such a sense of shame over it. At the same time, it's the history of this country."
>
> **ANDERSON COOPER**
> Finding Your Roots S2.E3

One problem with polyester film is that chromogenic dyes used in color negatives are not permanent, so they are vulnerable to fading. Even at room temperature dye fading can be rapid. Black-and-white negatives can be kept at 65°F or lower with an RH of 30% to 40%, but color film requires cold storage for long-term preservation.

6: FILM

When assessing the condition of the polyester film in your collection, black and white polyester negatives in stable condition are black. Polyester color negatives have an orange-colored tint.

As with nitrate and acetate film, the questions to ask yourself are: Do I need this film? Should it be digitized? Should I throw it away, keep it, or donate it to a library or archive?

Since polyester film is not flammable like nitrate film and is not at risk of hazardous vinegar syndrome like acetate, you could keep black and white film with no problems. You could also keep color film negatives knowing that they will fade over time. If there is no printout of a black and white or color negative film, have it developed, and keep the film if you want. You can have one or both digitized.

To learn more about cold storage of polyester film, see the bibliography at the end of this book.[20]

STORAGE OF SLIDES AND NEGATIVE FILM

Polyester slides and negatives can be housed in polypropylene sheets and placed in acid-free folders and acid-free boxes. Archival supply stores have special sheets for both these purposes. Negatives and slides can be put in these sheets and then in three-ring binders. The binders can be stored on a shelf or can be placed in an acid-free box. Storage in a flat box is preferable since it will provide long-term storage and eliminate the risk of dust and other environmental particles that cause damage. Make sure binders are not overstuffed and that folders are not slumped in boxes. Use cardboard inserts (purchased at archival stores) to make sure folders stand up straight.

Slides

Modern digital scanners come with special attachments that allow light to pass through slides and negatives, making scanning these objects cheap and easy. See Chapter 11 for more detailed information on scanning film and slides. The primary reason for keeping negatives is for emergencies. In the event photographs need to be reprinted after a hurricane, wildfire, flood, or tornado, the negatives will provide a better copy from which to make the reprints. Housing negatives in a separate place from the photographs makes good sense. If you can keep them at the house of a relative, such as your sister who lives in a different state, that would be ideal. If you lose both the picture and the negative, but you have digital copies of both, the digital copy of the negative will provide the best reprint photograph. Otherwise, the truth is you do not need to keep the film and can dispose of it.

Small Rolls of Film can be stored in Artifact Boxes

You can purchase enclosures for motion picture film and videotape VHS at archival supply stores. Store original AV (audio/video) tapes with the tapes rewound, off the floor, with spines up, and in some kind of enclosure; plastic cases and containers are preferred. Stacking tapes horizontally can result in uneven or warped tapes or loss of information at the edges. Improper storage can result in cracks and breakage or twisted tape. Accumulated dirt and dust can interfere with proper playback. Ultraviolet light, particularly sunlight, is damaging to film and video tape. Paperboard enclosures tend to hold moisture, which can result in increased acidity over time. They can also create dust as they deteriorate. Use storage containers made from acceptable plastics such as polypropylene or polyethylene, preservation-quality cardboard, or non-corroding metals that pass the PAT.

Metadata for Slides and Negative Film

As with your photographs, you will want to be sure to provide metadata for your negatives and slides. Including a typed sheet of paper that indexes and describes what is on the film or in the slides will help Baby 2135 make sense of them. Here is an example:

Film stacked in archive

Row 1, Column 1 – Edna (Frenier), age 17, 1949, Rocky Point Park, Shore Dinner Hall, with Blackie. Blackie was a stray dog found two years earlier by her brother Ernest (Frenier). He took Blackie with him when he married two years after this picture was taken.

Row 1, Column 2 – Edna (Frenier) and Ernest (Frenier), siblings, ages 17 and 19, 1949, Rocky Point Park, Shore Dinner Hall.

CHAPTER 7

PAPER:
Documents, Cards, Letters, Diaries, Books

Will the wind ever remember?
The names it has blown in the past?
And with its crutch, its old age and its wisdom
It whispers "no, this will be the last."

—Jimi Hendrix, *The Wind Cries Mary*

Before we get into the particulars of storing individual items, let's begin with a brief discussion of the history of papermaking. You will have a better understanding of why some paper lasts long and why other paper deteriorates more quickly. In the end, you need to know what bad paper is, how to look out for it, and what to do with it.

A BRIEF HISTORY OF PAPER MAKING

The Chinese are credited with inventing paper around AD 100. Over the next 600 years, the technology spread to nearby Japan and central Asia, eventually making it all the way to Persia (current-day Iran). Papermaking would not reach Europe until the 12th century when a hand papermaking mill was established in Spain. The use of paper spread throughout the rest of Europe over the next 300 years.[21] Paper use increased after Johannes Gutenberg invented

Woodcut of making paper from the Ming Dynasty 105 AD

the printing press in 1440. Although Chinese, Japanese, and Korean versions of printing were invented earlier than Gutenberg's European model, the Asian technology did not catch on as quickly as Gutenberg's, most likely because of the difference in characters. The Asian alphabet employs thousands of characters in the writing process, whereas the European alphabet, as we all know, has twenty-six letters and ten numbers, making it much easier to standardize printing.

> **ARCHIVES TIP**
>
> **The material used in the papermaking process determines the stability and lifespan of the product and is the most important thing to consider as a preservationist or family archivist.**

Handmade paper uses either cotton or wood fibers that are boiled into a watery pulp. A screen is passed under the pulp to form a mat of fibers. The mat is dried between felted rolls and then sized with starch or gelatin to make the surface smooth for writing.

Machine paper making was invented in France in the early-18th century and further developed in England in the early-19th century. Modern papermaking fundamentally uses the same techniques as the ancient handmade method. Most paper today comes either from recycling or from trees that are specifically grown for the purpose of papermaking. In both cases, the original product (wood or paper) is boiled into a fibrous mass that is extracted down to a textured mat then covered with a sizing material to make it smooth.

The material used in the papermaking process determines the stability and lifespan of the product and is the most important thing to consider as a preservationist or family archivist. Some materials are very stable and will remain intact for centuries. Other materials deteriorate quickly and need to be replaced as soon as possible.

Early paper production used linen, cotton, and hemp. These materials are relatively stable and durable and will last a long time. As paper production increased during the 19th century, a shortage of linen, cotton, and hemp caused papermakers to look for raw materials that were cheaper and easier to work with. In the 1840s, papermakers began using groundwood pulp. This is a form of wood that has not been cooked or chemically treated, has a high lignin content, and is very acidic.[22] Acid is the single most common cause for the accelerated rate of deterioration in paper. Most commonly, newspapers use this cheap form of paper, which is why they yellow and brown so quickly. When acid is exposed to light, heat, and humidity, it yellows and browns and weakens the paper, causing it to become brittle and break off. Paper made with inferior materials is said to have **inherent vice**. The term *inherent vice* refers to deterioration caused by the materials that comprise an item (in this case paper) as opposed to deterioration caused by outside influences such as high humidity, water, or light.[23] The "vice" is inherent, meaning it is part of the product.

Sizing materials used in the manufacturing process are another factor that influences paper quality. Alum-rosin sizing agent, which began to be used in the United States in the 1850s, needs an acidic environment to be produced. Alum-rosin leaves a sulfuric acid byproduct that causes paper to become brittle, which then leads to browning and quick deterioration. In the 1870s, a machine process for making alum-rosin sizing resulted in even higher acidic content, further accelerating "brittle book syndrome."

Poor quality paper not only deteriorates more quickly, but it also contaminates any materials it comes in contact with.

ARCHIVES TIP

The term *inherent vice* refers to deterioration caused by the materials that comprise an item (in this case paper) as opposed to deterioration caused by outside influences such as high humidity, water, or light

As early as 1898, the Committee on the Deterioration of Paper in London was formed as a result of librarians' concern over the deterioration of books in their charge. By the 1930s, it was well known that acid was at the root of the problem causing brittle, browned, and yellowed books in large library collections. At this time the search for "permanent paper" began. Preservationists define *permanent paper* as "Paper which during long-term storage in libraries, archives, and other protected environments will undergo little or no change in properties that affect use."[24] Not until 1984 was the first American National Standards Institute (ANSI) standard for permanent paper issued. Today, the ordinary copy/printing paper we use in our printers and copy machines passes ANSI standards. Librarians and archivists routinely copy old deteriorating paper onto the current acid-free paper. As an archivist, I have spent many an hour at the copy machine doing just this. As a family historian, you may do the same.

> As early as 1898, the Committee on the Deterioration of Paper in London was formed as a result of librarians' concern over the deterioration of books in their charge.

PAPER

Newspaper

As discussed earlier, newspapers have a high acidic content, are sensitive to light, and deteriorate at a faster rate than other papers because of the inferior products used to create them. The simple solution to archiving newspaper print is to copy it onto modern acid-free paper. In the archives, the theory is that the content of the news article is what is important, not the paper it is on. Cut out the article that is relevant, copy it, and throw away the original.

If newspaper is pasted to a scrapbook, remove the entire page and copy it. If you are going to take apart the scrapbook anyway, feel free to cut the entire page,

> **ARCHIVES TIP**
>
> The content of the news article is what is important, not the paper it is on.

assuming nothing is on the backside. For smaller articles, such as obituaries, engagement and wedding announcements, sports news, and other accomplishments, make a copy and throw out the original. Newspaper will stain anything next to it. The acid is contagious and easily creates brown stains on whatever it touches. If you want to keep a small original article of newsprint, encapsulate it in good, inert plastic sheets. I often come across a random newspaper article in a folder with other documents. Usually, I make a copy and throw out the original. But there have been times when I have decided to keep the original. In those cases, I put it in a polypropylene sheet purchased from an archival supply store.

If a newspaper article you want to keep is damaged so much that it is unreadable, most libraries carry microfilms of newspaper articles. It is easy enough to go to the library and get a copy. Many newspapers also have articles that can be purchased online.

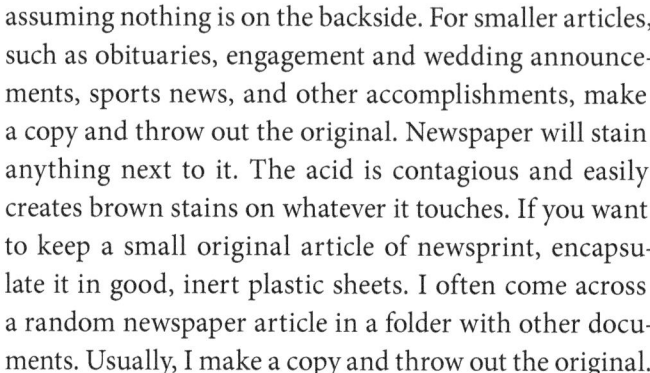

Browned Newspaper

Perhaps you have kept an entire special newspaper, such as an anniversary issue or a special event issue. I have a copy of *The Providence Journal*'s special edition of The Great Blizzard of 1978. You can make tabloid-size copies at most office supply stores. Decide how you want to store large pieces like this before you spend money on copies. Ideally everything in your archive should be laid flat. Creases or folds in paper add a level of stress and over time will weaken the paper at the fold line. Discoloration also occurs more often at the crease or fold in paper. With that being said, if you do not want to lay a tabloid-size document flat, it can be folded in half and placed in a legal-size folder. When folding the document, have the print facing out. In the event the paper becomes brittle in a couple of hundred years and cannot be opened, it can still be read if the information is folded out. Another option is to copy the pages in sections on legal- or letter-size paper. Again, the content is what is typically the most important, not the newspaper itself.

Archival supply stores sell boxes that will hold an entire newspaper. Placing the whole newspaper in an acid-free box and storing it in a cool, dry, dark place will slow the deterioration. We think of archives as storing one-of-a-kind materials, newspapers are not one-of-a-kind. If they deteriorate beyond recognition, thanks to the National Endowment for the Humanities Newspaper Program that began in 1982, most newspapers have been microfilmed and can be accessed in local libraries. I say if you want to keep that whole special newspaper, do so. If in a hundred years your ancestors cannot fully read it, they can look it up online. I think it would be cool to have a newspaper that my relative kept from the Civil War when Lincoln was shot or when the Titanic sank. It may be browned and brittle, but it would still be cool to have. I could go online or to the library to see a microfilm version of it too.

Newspaper Storage

Thermal Paper

Just when we thought we were rid of the crappy 19th-century paper, thermal paper was introduced in the 1950s when the development of copy machines began. Thermal paper is a special thin, fine paper that is used in high-heat environments to produce an image. It is coated with chemicals that change color when exposed to heat. Thermal paper was originally used in the first copy machines and fax machines. It is commonly found in archival collections beginning in the late 1950s through the early 1980s. Today it continues to be used in cash registers and credit card terminals. Most people are familiar with thermal paper because retailers use it to print receipts.

The problem with thermal paper is that it deteriorates very quickly—much more quickly than papers with high acidic content such as newspapers. It is extremely sensitive to light. Images copied onto thermal paper fade and become unreadable in a very short amount of time. The paper itself turns gray and sometimes shows silver particles. Thermal paper often has a slightly rubbery feel to it. One way to determine whether a document is on thermal paper is by the backside. According to the National Archives, 3M Company originally produced all thermal paper. Some thermal paper from the late 1960s has a blue-colored logo resembling three fanned-out leaves printed in a regular pattern on the backside.[25]

If you have thermal paper in your collection, copy it as soon as possible. The original can be thrown out afterward. If for some reason you need to keep the original, still make a copy and place the original in an acid-free folder in an environment with stable heat and humidity (not exceeding 68°F or 50% RH). If you find thermal paper that is completely illegible, don't panic, all may not be lost. Copy it anyway. On many occasions I have copied thermal paper that was so faded the lettering was like a ghost on the page. I put that baby on the copy machine, pushed a few buttons, and voila! A readable copy came out. Sometimes you have to tweak the contrast and darkness levels a bit to get a good copy. Be patient and persistent. Very few pages of thermal paper I have copied have continued to be unreadable. Sometimes copying in color works. Play around until you find the right setting.

Journals and Diaries

Diaries are kept for many different reasons. Some people journal on a regular basis about their daily lives. Other journals document a specific time period such as a trip to a foreign land, the birth of a child, or perhaps a spiritual retreat. The type and condition of the paper will determine what you should do with a bound diary. If the paper is in good condition, the pages are not stuck together, and the binding of the book is in good condition, simply place the book in an acid-free box. Now that you know how to keep it in an optimal environment, it should last into the future.

Old journals, diaries, letters.

If you notice a diary has browning and yellowing pages, or if the ink is fading and becoming unreadable, copy the pages onto acid-free paper as soon as possible. Be careful not to damage the binding when making copies on a copy machine (see the section titled "Books" below). Digitization is another option. If the binding is fragile or coming apart, you can either place the diary face down on a scanner or take digital photographs of the pages. Making digital copies will allow many people to access the document and its contents without causing further damage to the diary. After taking preservation measures, you probably still want to keep the original document. Diaries are unusual, very cool to have, and may bring joy to future generations. Unless it is unreadable beyond repair, a diary should stay safe in an acid-free book box. Since cursive handwriting is becoming outdated, transcribing the journal may be a fun project to take on and may make the content of the journal more accessible to younger family members.

Letters, Important Papers, Reports

When my friend Penny called me to look at the old letters her father had given her from the early 19th century, they were all folded in tight little bundles inside their original envelopes. The first thing Penny needed to do with these bundled missives was to open them up, carefully unfold them, and lay them flat in an acid-free folder.

Archivists have a number of tricks to get papers to lie flat. The simplest and the easiest thing to do is fold back on the crease in the opposite direction. Use your discretion when doing this, the paper needs to be sturdy enough to take the pressure. If the paper seems too fragile, do not attempt it.

Another trick is to gently lay the letter flat on a table and place something heavy on top of it. Some archives have a heavy iron press that acts like a vise and is used to lay papers flat. A heavy book (or several) that covers the document completely will do. Let it sit this way for a week to a month and check it periodically to see how it is doing. It does not need to be completely flat to be put in a folder and filed away. Over time it will continue to flatten if it is stored properly. Naturally, you want to make sure the table is clean and in a place where the letter can sit undisturbed. It is best to put a piece of acid-free tissue paper or glassine on top and below the letter. I have not always had success with this method; sometimes it works, but other times it does not.

A third trick is to add a *little* bit of moisture to post-1984 documents. Always go online and research the type of ink used on the paper before doing this to make sure it will not run. An ideal situation is putting the letter in your bathroom on a table or shelf that will not run the risk of staining the letter. Make sure your bathroom is clean and free from mold and to not expose the document to harsh chemicals. You might want to wait a day after cleaning the bathroom to bring your document in. Let the shower run so that steam fills up the room. The document will begin to relax as the moisture from the steam absorbs into it. Wait until the document is completely dry before handling it. If the paper is too moist, it could tear or the ink could smudge.

Beware that highly acidic papers that are already browning will stain if any moisture is added. If pages are highly curled and will not lie flat, copying them onto new pages might provide a final solution. If the document you have is pre-1984, and especially if it is from the 19th century, I do not recommend adding moisture to it. Contact a conservator for advice or to ask them for help with laying the document flat.

I once brought home a duplicate copy of a report that was highly curled from the archives so I could experiment and teach patrons who come to my library lectures. The document was on acid-free

Curled reports from archive that flattened due to high humidity in my home.

copy paper post-1984. I put the curled documents in an empty box and placed the box in my living room. It was summertime, and I do not have central air conditioning. Later that fall, as I was preparing for a workshop, I opened the box to discover that the document had uncurled and laid flat on its own because of the humidity in my house. I learned that a natural environment can be the best solution for flattening papers. A natural rise in humidity is slow, and less risky than putting documents in a shower or other wet environment where they might get damaged. Another option is creating a humid environment in a plastic box. Please see my website at https://lenasalina.com/secrets-from-the-stacks-guides/ for instructions on making a DIY Moisture Chamber.

Archival supply stores sell different types of enclosures for paper documents. A fragile birth certificate might be best housed in an archival envelope with a polyester window on one side allowing it to be viewed without touching it.

An attendee of one of my workshops arrived with a tabloid-size (11" x 17") birth certificate that was torn in three places. I suggested that she purchase an acid-free envelope with a clear cover on one side. The envelope would provide sturdiness and strength, and the certificate could lie flat in the envelope and be viewed without anyone having to touch it. In addition to housing it in the envelope, she could also purchase a tabloid-size box to give it added protection.

Legal Documents

Unfold and put legal documents into legal-size folders. When doing your survey, you will determine whether you have legal-size documents and how many of them you have. If you have both legal-size and letter-size documents, purchasing legal-size folders and boxes for your collection will allow you to store both sizes easily. Documents discolor, fade, or tear at the point where a crease or fold is present. Always unfold documents if possible. Logically, 8½" x 11" documents can be stored in legal-size folders, but the opposite is not true; legal-size documents cannot be stored in letter-size folders. If you must make a choice, go for the bigger size. If you only have a few legal documents and want to purchase letter-size boxes and folders for them, be mindful of where you fold the legal-size pages. Think of the effect the crease will have in that specific place if it is kept that way for one hundred years. Most papers have areas free from writing, for example between paragraphs. Often the bottom portion of a legal document is blank. Make sure not to put a crease where important information is, such as addresses, dates, names, or signatures.

Greeting Cards

Are you like me? Do you save birthday, anniversary, and Christmas cards? I have gotten better over the years; I do not save them all. But certain ones, especially those with a personal note inside, I still keep. I am glad now that I can look back at the cards my aunts and uncles who are no longer with us sent me. It brings back warm memories of the days when I had a big family around me. Now when I receive a card that I want to save, I write on the back the year and who it is from. Often the card signature found inside the card does not adequately describe who the sender is, especially to others in my family.

Like the other paper items in your collection, you will want to open cards so they are not folded. It is not necessary to have a folder for each card, but certain cards that have sparkles, buttons, ribbons, or other decorations may be put in separate folders so they do not damage the other items around them. Alternatively, you could place them in polyester sheets.

In terms of organization, it is your choice. You could organize them by person, by year, or by event. Do what makes the most sense to you. I organized my cards by person. I like the idea of opening one folder and seeing all the cards that one person sent me over the years.

Transcription

Handwritten letters and journals may be difficult to read. Studies have determined that millennials, the generation brought up after the advent of computers, have a particularly hard time reading cursive. We can assume this trend will continue. You may want to spend the time transcribing letters and documents. In a later chapter I discuss digitizing your materials. If you decide to transcribe certain materials, I suggest that you digitize them first, then work with the digital versions rather than the originals. Transcription is a slow process that requires frequent handling of the papers. Working with digital documents will prevent the originals from being damaged. If possible, work with dual screens. You can have the digital version of the document open on one screen while you use the other screen to type.

> *"Now I will be able to speak so much more confidently about who I am as a person knowing where I'm from. So now there's not any guessing game anymore. Now I can speak very concretely with a lot of pride about my ancestry, my lineage, and it's very interesting because now as I hear their stories, I understand where elements of my personality come from now, and that's another insightful part of this."*
>
> **CHEF AARON SANCHEZ**
> Finding Your Roots S2.E4

Transcription centers are located all across the country. After digitizing your documents and turning them into PDFs, you can email them to a transcription center and pay someone else to do it.

Another alternative is to read the letter into a recorder, then transcribe from the audio file. The audio file could then become part of the collection and family members who would rather listen to the audio than read the text can have access to it. You can also upload snippets of the audio file to a family history web page, Facebook page, or other resource.

Reports

Reports can include school reports from high school, college, and grad school; a master's thesis; or a doctoral dissertation. Perhaps you have saved the reports you have produced at work that garnered you particularly glowing feedback about your abilities. Your descendants may learn more about you through these written documents than by any other materials in the collection. Herein lies your thoughts, your rationale, or the products of your hard labor.

Like the other materials in the collection we have discussed, you will want to remove all fasteners from reports. If they are in standard plastic or cardboard three-ring binders, remove them from the binders. The best thing for reports of this type is to put them in acid-free folders. You should also remove the plastic report binders with the plastic edging. Work report covers produced for companies often have the company logo and colors. If these report covers are made of paper, you can keep them. But, if they are made of any kind of plastic, even the one-sheet interweaving leaf type, remove your documents from them. Plastic turns to goop eventually, unless it is inert archival polyester (a.k.a. Mylar) or polypropylene.

It is important not to overstuff file folders with big, thick reports. Notice at the bottom of archival folders there are four score marks. These allow folders to be easily folded so that thicker materials can fit inside. If folders are overstuffed, they will damage the pages, especially the first few and the last few. Overstuffed, heavy folders are prone to slumping in the box and will curve the papers and make them hard to read. A slumped folder can also damage the materials in nearby folders. Generally, archival folders will hold up to one inch worth of documents. After that, separate reports into multiple folders. You can label them (1 of 2) and (2 of 2) so that future researchers will understand that the two folders belong together.

MAPS, BLUEPRINTS, DRAWINGS, OVERSIZE ITEMS

All oversize documents should lie flat if at all possible. Archival supply houses have boxes and folders as large as 48.5" x 36.5". However, finding a place to store a box this big could pose a problem. If your collection contains many oversized documents of an artist, architect, builder, or scholar, you can buy large storage drawers to hold the folders and boxes.

Archivists try to avoid rolling documents because removing them from tubes and laying them flat can be problematic. If you must roll, be sure to use archival tissue paper and acid-free tubes purchased from archival supply houses. Blueprints are particularly fragile and should be housed using unbuffered tissue paper in unbuffered boxes, folders, or rolled tubes. Note that this is one of the times when unbuffered materials are preferred over buffered materials. Blueprints react to the alkaline in buffering agents.

Oversized Documents should lay flat

Glassine should also not be used with blueprints. Do not roll objects that are fragile, brittle, or torn. The tube should be longer than the object being rolled. Lay the object open on a flat surface. If using tissue paper, sandwich the item between two pieces of tissue paper. Starting at one end, carefully roll the object, making sure it rolls straight and does not start to roll unevenly. Tie white cotton twill loosely around the rolled item and place it in a rounded or squared acid-free storage tube. Tubes should be stored lying horizontally to alleviate pressure on one end. When unrolling a rolled document, proceed slowly and carefully.

PROCESSING PAPER DOCUMENTS

Keep Things Straight

Keeping paper documents standing straight is an important consideration. When documents are first put into new folders and new boxes, everything looks nice and pretty. Do not be deceived by all that newness and prettiness. Over time folders and documents slump if they are not kept straight. This is true of partially filled boxes, but it is also true of filled boxes. Archival supply houses sell acid-free folder supports that help documents stand straight, and they can be adjusted as

Keep items straight

you fill the box with more items. Without these supports, paper documents get curls that are permanent or hard to remove.

If housing large folders and smaller folders in the same box, always place the smaller folders in front or on top. Do not interfile them, even if that makes sense alphabetically or chronologically. Larger items placed on top of smaller items will overhang and bend. It may not seem important when they are first put in the box, but over time it will make a big difference. Oversized items such as tabloid-size marriage certificates should lie flat.

Fasteners

All fasteners should be removed from paper documents, including paper clips, staples, straight pins, rubber bands, and string ties. These items frequently damage documents and will continue to do so if they are not removed.

Paper Clips: If the paper is in good condition and the paper clip is not rusted, gently pry open and remove the paper clip using your fingernail or a micro-spatula. It is best to have the long side of the paper clip against a hard surface (the table) and the short end facing you. If the paper is particularly fragile or the paper clip is very rusted, placing a piece of Mylar between the paper and the clip will help minimize damage to the document. Working slowly and gently are the watchwords to use.

Rusted paper fastener

Staples: Over the past fifteen years, archivists have started keeping staples in documents because removing them slowed processing down to the point where there is now a twenty-year backlog in most archives. The logic to keeping staples in is that once the documents are in the archives, they are in a climatically controlled environment and are at minimal risk of forming rust on the metal. Since your family archive does not have the same space or time limitations as an official archive, and because your environment is not guaranteed to maintain stable temperature and RH ranges, I recommend removing all staples.

Be careful when removing staples; you do not want to tear the paper in the process. If staples are not rusted and the paper is in good condition, a staple remover will work sufficiently on more modern documents. When removing staples, begin from the backside and open the two curved ends. Once they are opened, turn the document over and gently pull from the flat end of the staple. Removing staples this way minimizes any damage to documents.

7: PAPER

If the paper you want to remove staples from is fragile or the staples are rusted, you need to use even more care. Use a micro-spatula to gently lift the two curved edges of the staple on the back side of the document. Turn the page over, insert the micro-spatula underneath the straight side of the staple, and gently lift each side of the staple until it is completely removed. In cases where the paper is particularly fragile or the staple is severely rusted, insert a tiny piece of stiff Mylar underneath the straight portion and the curved side of the staple and gently lift.[26]

Straight Pins: I know it is cool to see the straight pins people used to use to fasten documents before staples became popular, but keeping them in the paper will only further damage the document, especially if the pin is rusted or at risk of rusting. It must be removed for posterity. A sacrifice to coolness, I know.

You could take a picture of the pin before removing it. You could even save it in a little inert polyester bag and put it with the letter so future generations can appreciate the coolness of it. The holes will show how the pin was originally fastened to the paper.

Like paper clips and staples, if the paper and the pin are in good condition, gentle tugging should do the trick. If the pin is rusted or the paper is particularly fragile, however, place pieces of Mylar underneath the pin before removing it. This should reduce or eliminate any damage done to the document during removal.

Rubber Bands: Oh, the dreaded rubber bands. Depending on the age and condition of rubber bands, they can either be dried up browned strings that disintegrate upon touch or a goopy mess that is difficult to remove. If the rubber bands are dried but still stuck to a piece of paper, you can usually gently push them with a fingernail to remove them completely. If you do not want to use your fingernail, your handy micro-spatula should do the trick. Just be careful not to tear the page when you are working.

If the rubber band is goopier and less dry, try putting the micro-spatula underneath it and lifting. Do not use harsh chemicals, solvents, or any other means of removal. If you cannot get it off, just leave it. Time will take care of it; eventually it will fall off on its own. If the paper is left with a sticky residue, place it in a polypropylene sheet so that it will not damage other documents next to it.

String Ties: In the 19th century it was common to tie bundles in brown cord made of cotton or leather. Cut and remove all strings and ties. Similar to rubber band removal, do not use chemicals or solvents. Instead, gently push the strings with your fingernail or a micro-spatula. It is better to leave the string in place than to damage the document. If you decide to re-tie items, use archival-sound white cotton string. Be sure to tie the string loosely so you do not subject the documents to any further damage.

Binding Documents

If for some reason you need to keep documents clipped together, there are a number of methods you can use. First, you can purchase stainless steel staples and paper clips from archival supply stores. They are expensive, so be prepared, but they are guaranteed not to rust. Keep in mind, however, that staples and especially paper clips can damage a document by the depression they make in the page. If at all possible, it is better to go without.

The easiest way to keep a group of letters together is by putting them in the same folder. Another method is making an enclosure from a piece of acid-free paper by simply folding it around the documents you want kept together. If you have a large number of letters that you want to lay flat in a box without using folders, you could tie them together with white cotton cloth tying tape. You can also use this tape to ensure delicate books with loose pages are kept intact. Be sure to tie them loosely so that the papers are not folded under and the tie is not making a depression mark on the paper.

If the pages of paper documents are torn or brittle, or if you think they will be handled often, you may want to put them in an inert polyester or polypropylene sheet. If you are going to put them in a ring binder, make sure the binder is not overstuffed and that the letters lie flat. Think of what the binder will look like in a hundred years. If the pages are curved from overstuffing today, in a hundred years they will be curved permanently. File folders and boxes are perfectly sound enclosures for these types of documents.

I do not recommend attempting to fix tears with adhesives. Conservators are trained to make these types of repairs. The materials they use can be purchased from archival warehouses, but I do not recommend that untrained individuals attempt this. There is an art and a skill to document repair, and it is best left to the experts. If you have a highly valuable document you want repaired, contact one of the conservation places listed at the back of this book.

If someone before you tried to repair a page or letter with adhesive tape, do not attempt to remove it. It has no doubt discolored the paper and left a big brown stain where it adhered to the page. Trying to remove the tape will only cause more damage. If you leave it alone, it will eventually come off by itself.

Tape and Glue

Never use tape or glue to bind your documents. Depending on what is in your collection, you may notice that any papers with tape or glue are now browned at the point of contact. In particular, scrapbooks that have been glued can be nothing but a browned mess. What was invisible when applied, in time becomes streaks of overbearing brushstrokes. There is nothing that can be done to remove the brown stains. The lesson is to not do the same thing now for future generations to find. If you make scrapbooks or attach photos to pages, use corner tabs. These will eventually fall off, but they will not damage the items they hold.

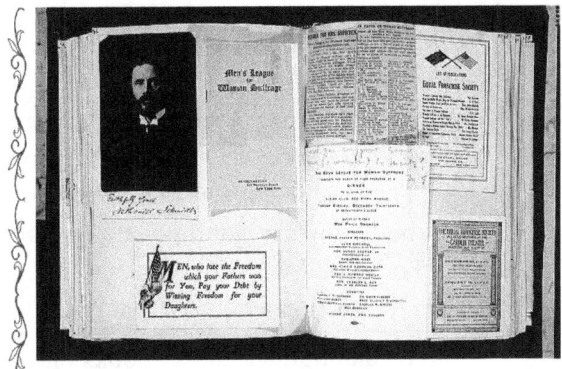
Damage from tape and glue

If there is something in your collection that is stuck together and you want it unstuck, the good news is that all glue and tape will eventually dry up on its own. If you cannot get an item unstuck yourself, leave it alone. Eventually it will become unstuck. Keep this in mind when you go for the tape dispenser or the glue stick.

If a document is ripped, you can place it in a special envelope with a clear side so it can be viewed without removing it. The envelope can be placed in the same folder with other related documents. Your future family member can figure out that the documents belong together, but you could always leave a note explaining to your future descendants that the sheets belong together.

BOOKS

Books enrich our lives in many ways. Our relationships with our books can be deep, heartfelt, and long-lasting. The right book can literally change our lives. Other books bring us hours and hours of pleasure. It can be that one line that made you finally understand your relationship, or the advice book that helped you understand your teenage daughter. Or it could be the group of like-minded people who live "out there" but understand why you are mad about a particular social issue in society. Perhaps it is the 16th-century poet who speaks the truth of your conviction with astounding clarity or the poem you read to your husband on the day you were married. Or maybe it is the book that is teaching you how to preserve your family legacy.

Bookcase with old books

My friends regularly give me bags and boxes of books. Many times I have come home from work to find a bag or box of books on my porch with a note from a friend who is moving out of the area and must downsize. I think they feel better giving their precious books to someone they know will value and treasure them. I have sat in conversation with two different friends, on two separate occasions, both of whom got rid of all their books before moving across the country. They both cried when they started telling me about a book they had, only to realize they no longer owned that book. I understood their pain.

True bibliophiles collect books on many different topics. For many, some books are works of art in their own right. For others, the most important book in their collection is the family Bible that may contain birth and death dates going back generations. Some books we write in and have a "conversation" with in the margins. Others we highlight like crazy such as our college textbooks. Some books have author signatures, and first-edition books can be rare and valuable. If you are like me, you may have a bit of all of the above.

Book Making

Books have complex structures. They can be crafted with covers made of paperboard covered with leather, cloth, or vellum; pages made from parchment, rag paper, paperboard, or wood pulp; inks made of different compounds, such as highly acidic iron gall ink used from the 8th century through the early-20th century; and bindings made from various glues and adhesives, hemp cord, thread, or metal staples.

Leather, parchment, and vellum are made from animal skins. It would be rare for a 20th-century American to have something written on parchment or vellum, but having books covered in leather is quite common. Parchment and vellum may also be found in book bindings or as the basis for artwork. The term *parchment* refers to any animal skin prepared for use in writing. It typically refers to sheepskin. Vellum refers to calfskin.

Books are bound (meaning sewn) or glued together. The cover is connected to the binding and the binding is connected to the pages.

Appraisal

I cherish my personal library and have no intention of weeding or downsizing—EVER. My books are one collective item I need to have with me while I walk this earth. When I die, my nieces and nephews can get rid of most of my books. But I will want them to know which books are important to keep, which ones may be valuable and could be sold, which ones are signed by the author, which ones

7: PAPER

could go to a library of rare books, and which ones (the majority) they can chuck.

To make these distinctions, let me explain how things work in the library world. The difference between archival materials and library books is that archival materials are one-of-a-kind, whereas library books can be found in hundreds of thousands of libraries and homes around the world. Rare books had a limited distribution, are first editions, or are signed by the author. Older books usually fall into this category and include books that are out of print and/or do not have many copies left in the world—think, *Uncle Tom's Cabin*.

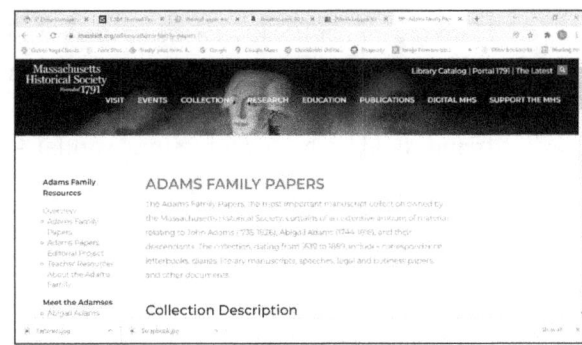

Website showing Archival Collection

To demonstrate the difference between archival materials, library materials, and rare books, consider information on John Adams as an example. The Massachusetts Historical Society houses the original love letters written by John and Abigail during their many years apart as well as other original documents written by John Adams. Those letters are considered **archival materials** because they are one-of-a-kind. In 1856, John Adams' grandson, Charles Francis Adams, produced a ten-volume set of books titled *The Works of John Adams*. These books contain all the writings of John Adams and are considered **rare books** because they were written over one hundred years ago with a limited publication, and there are few of the originals left. David McCullough published a book about John Adams in 2002. His book would be considered a **library book** because there are many copies of them found in libraries around the world and owned by individuals personally. See the difference?

Rare Book

When appraising your own collection, you might want to separate your books into different categories. The first step might be to make a list of all your books. While I was doing an internship at the Sophia Smith Collection at Smith College, the archives obtained the records of Mary Daly, a feminist theologian. We received Daly's work papers, original manuscripts, research materials, and other original documents. She had a small library in her home of books that informed her thoughts and theories. Instead

Library Book

of taking all her books, a list was made and included with her archival materials. A researcher could easily find a copy of any one of the books in many libraries around the world. When my friend's father who was a history teacher died, my friend could have done something similar—make a list; dispose of the book.

I have an app on my phone that lets me scan the barcodes on books and automatically imports all the data about it. Sweet! If the book precedes barcoding, I can enter the title and/or author and it searches and imports data from Google Books. I can also add all the data myself if necessary and can add my own categories for each book and make notes. I have added a category called "Gift from…." for books that were given to me as a gift. I have a different category for each person who gave me a book, because some of them have given me several books over the years. The books I receive from people who drop books off on my porch, or the ones I have taken from a relative who has passed, I categorize as "From the Library of…." The app will automatically assign a subject category, but I have added my own because I do not want as many categories as found in a library, and books are meaningful to me in ways other than how they might be found in the library. I sometimes add information about when I read the book and what I thought about it. I will indicate whether I have "disposed" of a book, read it in full or partially, or loaned it out to someone (useful in getting it back). I will also note whether the author signed it and where the book is found in my library (L1S2 is Library bookcase 1, Shelf 2). I am a librarian; I can't help it! If I want to, I can export the list into an Excel spreadsheet and easily share, print, or add to it.

I do not expect you all to be bibliophile nerds like me, but I know many of you are. I know you are out there! You could simply separate the rare books, make a list of them, and put that with your important papers so your descendants will know what to do after you have passed. If you have an idea of a good home for your books after you pass, you might want to indicate that as well. Someone who has a library of astronomy books might want to donate their books to a local observatory, for example.

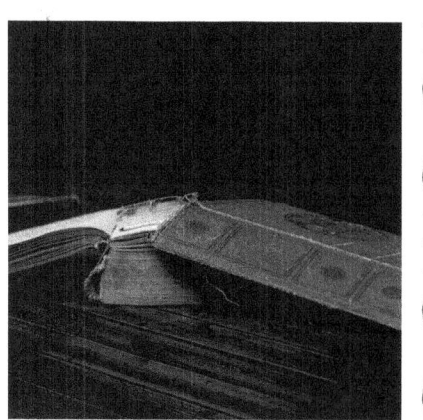
Damaged cover and spine

Caring For and Handling Books

Damage comes to our books in many ways. Covers fall off, pages fall out or become torn, pests feed on pages or starch-based glue, mold stains and causes unpleasant odors, or dog ears create creases. With that said, all "damage" is not destructive or undesirable. In the archives we keep the books that are marked up. People converse with their books in the form of margin notes, bookmarks, dog ears, underlines, and "notes to self." If we had a book of Herman Melville's that was marked up like this, it would be considered much more valuable than a pristine edition of *Moby Dick*. Consider if it was a copy of *The Scarlet Letter*, a book written by Melville's acquaintance Nathaniel Hawthorn. That would be so cool. Similarly, if your grandmother marked up her books, you and Baby 2135 would most likely treasure it dearly. It would tell you what was meaningful to her, what moved her, or what taught her a lesson in life. Perhaps she agreed with the author, or perhaps she saw a flaw in their theory. A person's books can reveal little pieces of their knowledge and philosophy in a way nothing else will. Having such books in our charge requires special care and attention.

Our books can be a little like Goldilocks needing it "just right" when it comes to temperature and humidity. On one hand, high temperature and high RH encourage mold growth. On the other hand, extremely low RH can cause brittleness. Storing books in basements and attics increases the risk of mold and warping, while storing them in unheated buildings encourages brittleness. Heat vents, radiators, hot lights, or fireplaces will raise localized temperatures and raise RH. Try to keep temperatures no higher than 75°F and RH at 50%.

Sunlight, especially direct sunlight, causes book covers to fade and pages to discolor. If possible, keep books in a closed-off room on the north side of the house. At the very least, keep the blinds drawn during the day in an empty room.

Air circulation is crucial. Do not pack books too tightly. Leave a little room behind books if possible. Dust frequently with a soft cloth, a soft artist brush, or a vacuum on low suction with a brush attachment covered by cheesecloth. Never store books directly on the floor.

Sunlight on books

Many critters can damage books. My cat, Willow, was fond of spraying the books on the lower bookshelves until I covered them with plastic. Puppies like to chew everything. Small children think all books are coloring books. Books are a pleasing dinner for mice and other vermin. Silverfish in particular are prone to eating book pages, and cockroaches go for the glue in book spines.

Next to poor storage, poor handling is the second greatest cause of damage to books. Handling books properly prevents damage that can be expensive to correct and lowers the value of rare books. Here is list of dos and don'ts:

- ✓ Stand books up straight. Slumping causes bindings to break and can warp pages. Bookends were created for a reason. Use them.
- ✓ Do not overstuff books on shelves. Like you, they like to breathe. A little room reduces the threat of mold and prevents damage when books are removed from the shelf.
- ✓ Shelve books of similar sizes together. Keep small books separate so that the weight of heavier books does not crush them.
- ✓ Lay oversized books flat. Do not store more than three on top of each other.
- ✓ Never store a book with the spine side up. The weight of the pages will cause them to pull away from the binding and become loose. If a book is too tall to stand upright, always store books spine side down facing up.
- ✓ Do not pull books off the shelf by the end cap. Instead, create a little space on either side of the book, grasp the book with your thumb and forefinger, and pull by the sides of the book. As an alternative, grab books by the fore-edge.
- ✓ Do not use a flatbed copier. If you feel compelled to copy a page from a book, some libraries have a copy machine with book supports on one side. If you must use a flatbed copier, do not press the book down or use the cover. Be gentle. A gentle alternative is to take a picture with your phone and print it out or read it on a tablet or Kindle.
- ✓ In the archives, cradles made of foam wedges, padded blocks, or Plexiglas are used to support the spine of old books when looking at them. In similar fashion, create supports for books when opening them at home using towels, soft sheets, boxes, or other books. The goal is to keep the book from opening fully and breaking the spine or dislodging the pages from fragile bindings.
- ✓ Place fragile or rare books in a four-fold book box or clamshell box. Use acid-free tissue paper to keep the book from moving or slumping.
- ✓ Do not force an old book open.
- ✓ Do not stuff papers inside a book. If someone wrote notes from a book, place them in a separate acid-free envelope or folder and place those next to the book on the shelf or loosely tie them together with white cotton twill outside the binding.
- ✓ Remove Post-it notes or arrows. Over time, the glue will discolor and dry up and the

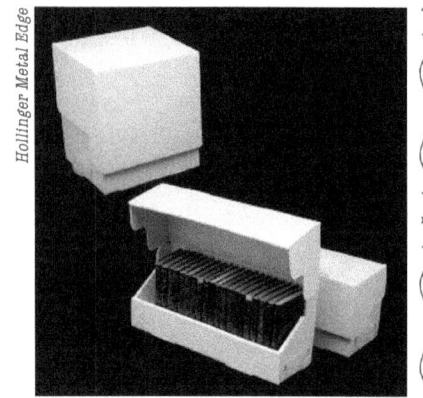

Archival book storage boxes

Hollinger Metal Edge

note will fall off. If you want to remember where a Post-it or arrow was, write the page number and section on it, place it in an envelope, and place the envelope next to the book on the shelf or loosely tie the note to the book with white cotton twill. Alternatively, handwrite or type out a page describing where all Post-it notes were and include it with the book.

- ✓ Remove paperclips, rubber bands, flowers, newspaper clippings, and bookmarks; they will all discolor, rip, or cause chemical damage to pages.
- ✓ Keep dust jackets. They can add to the value of a book and protect the covers.
- ✓ Never tape or glue a book. Ever. Did I need to say that? Glue turns brown over time.

Shelving

Unfortunately, most of us have wooden bookcases where we store our books. Wood is highly acidic and can be damaging to books and other materials. Most of my books are on painted pressed wood shelves. Other books are on varnished cherry wood shelves. Since most of my books will be tossed after I go, I have no intention of doing anything different with my books. They will be fine for my lifetime. After identifying which books in your collection are potentially valuable to a collector or determining which ones will be included in the family archive, you may want to set them aside in a better location so that acidic wood does not cause damage.

Four-fold cover for fragile books

The best shelves to store books on are glass, powder-coated, or baked enamel-coated. Glass bookcases will protect books from dust. Otherwise, line wood shelves with polyester film or heavy, acid-free paperboard to form a buffer between the book and the acidic shelf or store books in acid-free book boxes. Book boxes and acid-free paperboard linings stored on acidic wooden shelves will still need to be checked every five years or so. The acid from the shelves can eventually damage the cardboard and seep through to the book.

Protection

Fragile, rare, and old books can be placed in a book box. Book boxes provide structural support and protect valuable books from environmental damage. Archival supply stores sell four-fold boxes that can be custom made to size if necessary. Using a four-fold box can prevent damage from occurring when the book is put into or taken out of the box. Clamshell boxes are another option, especially for large or oversized books. Clamshell boxes come in many different sizes. If necessary, wrap the book in acid-free tissue paper and put crunched up sheets of tissue paper around the book to prevent it from moving around in the box, slumping, or warping. Books in four-fold boxes can be stored upright on shelves, but books in clamshell boxes should be laid flat.

To protect more modern, less fragile books that you nevertheless want to keep safe from dust and other environmental pollutants, make a book cover with acid-free tissue paper or inert polyester sheets. Polypropylene or Polyurethane sheets are also acceptable, and you can purchase any of these from an archival supply store. Remember how you covered books in elementary school? Yeah, like that. This is not a good choice for rare or fragile books, however, because placing the cover on it can cause damage. Only use this method on sturdy books in good condition.

Repairing Damage

Most of the damage done to books will need to be corrected by a conservator. You can call a conservator for problems with acidity, embrittlement, flaking pigments, discoloration, distorted boards, red rot, broken bindings, the presence of tape and poor-quality adhesives, and water damage. The following are some temporary or home remedies along with some corrective measures a conservator can take:

> **Browning, Flaking, Embrittlement:** Place the book in a book box as soon as possible. A box will not stop the deterioration, but it will protect the book from the environment and slow down the rate of destruction.

Book with broken spine and damaged cover

> **Broken Spine:** A book box can be a temporary home remedy for a broken spine, but a conservator can provide a permanent solution. Another home remedy to use is white cotton twill to keep the book together. Do not bind it too tight and never use elastic. When the spine on my father's Bible broke and detached, I did not have it fixed for many years because I was afraid a poor job would be a worse solution. Eventually I found a good, reputable bookbinder who did an

amazing job. I am so happy I took the risk and had it fixed. It came out beautiful and I now have something valuable of my father's to pass on.

Torn Pages: A home remedy for torn pages is to encapsulate the page with a piece of polyester sheeting. Polyester sheets can be cut to size and slipped over the page, remaining open on three sides. A conservator can provide a more permanent fix using wheat starch paste, methyl cellulose, or Japanese paper.

Pencil Marks: You can erase pencil marks using a clean, soft vinyl eraser and a little patience. Do not use harsh erasers that can rip or discolor pages. Test an area first and proceed gently. Remember, some markings are not considered "damage." Do not erase the poem your aunt wrote in the margin.

Leather Covers: Do not use leather dressings or oiling. This was a common practice in the past that has since been found to do more damage. If you have a leather-covered book that is damaged, a conservator is the way to go. They will provide the best solution to the particular damage your book has sustained.

Red Rot: Red rot is found in leather book covers from the late-19th to early-20th centuries. It is a result of the decaying of sulfuric acid used in the tanning process. Red rot displays as a red powder. It is very messy and can get on your hands, clothing, and nearby books. Books with red rot should be encapsulated in acid-free buffered tissue paper, polyester film covers, or acid-free book boxes right away. This helps prevent damage to other books, the shelves they are housed on, and anything else they touch. Though there is no cure or reversal for red rot, a conservator can apply a solution that seals it. Not all conservators support this treatment, but you might find it is appropriate for the books in your care.

Red Rot

Odor: Books that smell musty contain microscopic active mold. Dehumidification will eliminate the odor. If the books have been stored in a container, remove them from the container and place them in an area with a dehumidifier. Open or fan the pages if possible. It may take a few days or weeks for the odor to completely disappear. Another option is to place the books open in the sun. Sun exposure lowers humidity and dries out the mold spores. Be aware that sun exposure will fade books, however, so use caution if choosing this method. Drying should occur quickly. Check every fifteen minutes. For a method recommended by Cornell University, see my website at https://lenasalina.com/secrets-from-the-stacks-guides/.

CHAPTER 8

TEXTILES

And your heart beats so slow
Through the rain and fallen snow
Across the fields of mourning
Lights in the distance

Oh don't sorrow, no don't weep
For tonight, at last
I am coming home
I am coming home

—**U2, *A Sort of Homecoming***

I did not realize my Uncle Charlie was a war hero until the day of his funeral. During World War II, Uncle Charlie was a paratrooper who was part of a group of soldiers that landed on the French shores of Normandy the day before D-Day. Their mission was to prepare the area for the ground soldiers who would land the next day. I always knew Uncle Charlie was a paratrooper in World War II. I knew that he was what they used to call "shell-shocked," which is now known as PTSD. I did not really know what that meant except that I knew every now and then Uncle Charlie would "lose it" and think he was back in the war. He would be hospitalized for a few days or weeks until he was better, then they would send him home again. Uncle Charlie could not work a regular job like the other men in his generation. The family lived across the street from a racetrack, and Uncle Charlie would clean the stalls when he was feeling okay, in between episodes as it were.

Paratroopers landing before D-Day

Uncle Charlie was married to my mother's sister, and they had five children. To me he always seemed weak and nervous. Years after he died, I found out from my cousin that Uncle Charlie had five brothers. They were all well over six feet tall and were all state troopers. Uncle Charlie's father had been the head of the state police department for years. I was familiar with the colonel who headed the state police since his name was in the newspaper all the time. I did not realize he was my Uncle Charlie's father.

Uncle Charlie was buried in the Veteran's Cemetery with a six-gun salute. Anyone who has attended one of these ceremonies knows how deeply moving they are. As the bugler played Taps and the soldiers folded the American flag that had covered his casket, they thanked Uncle Charlie on behalf of the president of the United States and all the Armed Services for his duty as a soldier. I realized for the first time that Uncle Charlie had given his life for his country. He had not died on the battlefield as so many other soldiers had on D-Day, throughout World War II, and in the many wars our nation has fought, but nevertheless, he had given his life for his country. He came back from that war so emotionally crippled and damaged that he was never able to live up to his full potential. While he brought five children into the world who loved him and carried on his legacy, the pain and sorrow of his sacrifice was forever a presence in each of their lives.

I know many people have loved ones who served in the military and have the flags that are given at the funeral. They may have soldier's uniforms, soldier's hats, white gloves, medals, and certificates. Photographs of our loved ones have special meaning because we can see their faces, their smiles, and remember a day, a moment, and an occasion. But the clothing that our loved ones wore has a different sensory appeal.

Textiles surround our lives

Textiles surround our lives in other ways. Many of us keep our wedding dresses in the hopes our daughters will wear them one day. Christening outfits are often passed down from one generation to the next. Quilts made by great-grandmothers we never met can keep us warm on a cold winter night or add to the décor of a bedroom or living room. We live our lives in clothing, some homemade. Many of us make textiles including quilts, knitted scarves, mittens and hats, draperies, and costumes. From heavy tapestries to delicate lace, upholstered furniture, doll clothing, and fans, textiles are functional and aesthetic at the same time. In my collection, I have afghans and crocheted coat hangers made by my grandmother, quilts made by both my great-grandmother and my sister, cross-stitched artwork made by my sister and me, tatted doilies made by my great-Aunt Mabel, hats worn by my Aunt Thelma in the 1940s, and my Auntie Edna's fur coat. Other textiles include tapestries, carpets, curtains, tablecloths, and napkins, as well as objects composed of textiles such as dolls, parasols, or artwork.

Doing an inventory and appraisal of the textiles in your collection is important. Textiles that you are currently using will not be archived. To demonstrate this point, I have a quilt my sister made for me on the back of my couch. I love the way it creates an ambiance of hominess in my living room. I am not going to archive this, ever; I am using it. However, the 100-year-old quilt my great-grandmother made is archived. When I die, if the quilt my sister made me ends up in the hands of my great grandniece, she may want to archive it at some point.

Silk wedding dress

In thinking of archival preservation, we must consider that textiles are created in different ways including weaving, knotting, braiding, felting, or knitting. They can be decorated with beads, pins, embroidery, feathers, or buttons. In bygone days, clothing was finished with starch to keep it stiff and wrinkle free. Sugar was added to clothing to give it a shiny sheen. Metal threads were woven into fabric, and bone stays were sewn into garments to help keep their shape. Dyes using iron, and silk finishes using metallic salts, pose special problems for modern conservators. Textiles are some of the most beautiful objects in our homes, but they can also be the most fragile, the most prone to dirt, the most attractive to pests, and the most expensive to clean.

Many of the textiles in our collections we display on the walls of our homes—quilts, cross-stitched items, or military flags, for example. These need to be preserved in a special way to ensure their longest life. Other items will be stored away and used either periodically (such as a christening gown) or will be kept for sentimental reasons. Keep in mind that every time a textile item is used, it adds wear and tear to the fabric. All textile items will most likely become too fragile for use. However, this does not mean you should not keep them. It may seem silly, extravagant, or maybe even useless to save a wedding dress or army uniform. But think back, wouldn't you relish a Civil War uniform or the wedding dress of your forebear who married in 1794? You would not want to wear it, but it would be amazing to have.

This chapter discusses the different types of fabrics used in the construction of textiles; the enemies of fabrics; how to handle, clean, and maintain textiles; and the best way to store and display them. If you have any doubt about how best to preserve your textiles, by all means contact a conservator. We will go over the basics and then provide more specific information for special cases.

FIBER TYPES

Natural

Most fabrics, especially older ones, are made from natural fibers such as cotton, wool, linen, and silk. Wool and silk are made from animal products, while cotton and linen are made from plants. These different sources have different needs and deteriorate under different circumstances.

Wool and Silk

Wool and silk made from sheep and silkworms, respectively, are composed primarily of proteins. Protein-based fibers are susceptible to deterioration from strong alkalis that can be found in certain soils or from cleaning solutions that use alkali salt bases. The buffering agent used in archival boxes and tissue paper is typically alkaline-based calcium carbonate. Keep this in mind when purchasing supplies to store textile materials. *Always use unbuffered boxes or tissue paper when storing silk or wool.*

Silkworms

Another consideration with wool and silk is that their fibers tend to be highly absorbent. In humid conditions they can absorb twenty percent of their weight in water. That excess water weight will render materials heavy, causing the fibers to lose strength or alter their original shape. Water mixed with dust or dirt can cause staining that may be permanent.

Cotton bolls

Cotton and Linen

Plant-based fibers are at risk of deterioration by acids. Linen, made from flax, is highly absorbent and will change shape and strength in high humidity environments. *Use acid-free, lignin-free, buffered boxes and tissue paper when storing cotton and linen materials.* The buffering agents will help absorb the naturally acidic quality of plant-based fibers and slow the deterioration process.

SYNTHETIC

The term "synthetic" refers to any manufactured fiber made from chemical synthesis. First produced in the 20th century, synthetics were made to replace and replicate natural fibers by maintaining the desirable qualities of natural fibers while eliminating the undesirable ones. Synthetic fibers were developed to be resistant to oil, mold, mildew, and moths. Many synthetics are wrinkle-free, quick-drying, and easier to wash and dry than natural fibers. Synthetic fibers tend to be stronger and more resilient than natural fibers and deteriorate at a slower rate.

Rayon

First produced in the 1880s, rayon is regenerated cellulose fiber. Since it is made from wood pulp, it is considered semi-synthetic. Some rayon retains lignin while others are lignin-free. Although it was often called artificial silk, it can imitate the look and feel of silk, wool, cotton, and linen. Rayon is easily dyed. The fibers are soft, smooth, comfortable, and highly absorbent. Rayon fibers do not insulate body heat, which makes clothing made from rayon ideal for hot and humid climates. Most rayon needs to be dry-cleaned. Trade names are Viscose, Bemberg, Modal, Tencel, Accordis, and Lyocell.

Nylon

The first "true" synthetic fiber to be manufactured was nylon in 1931. It is the second most used synthetic fiber in the United States after polyester. Nylon's first use was to replace women's silk stockings in 1939. During World War II, nylon was used by the military for tents, parachutes, and ropes. After the war, nylon was and continues to be used in blouses,

Nylon fabric

lingerie, swimwear, ski clothes, and raincoats. It can be found under the trade names Antron Durasoft and Supplex. In terms of preservation, be aware that nylon yellows with age.

Polyester

Polyester started to be commercially produced in 1953. During the 1960s and 1970s, its introduction as "wash and wear" and "wrinkle-free" heralded a new age of reduced household duties for women. Imagine having to iron every piece of clothing that is washed in your home every week, and you can appreciate

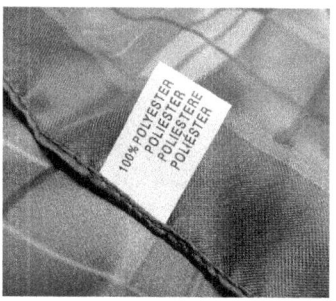

Manufacturers' tags show the types of fibers used

what a revolution this product was to daily life. Polyester can resemble cotton, silk, or wool. It is often blended with natural fibers, so detection of polyester in a fabric can be difficult. The best way to determine the type of fibers used in an article of clothing is to check the manufacturers tag. Trade names for polyester include Dacron, Fortrel, Thermoloft, and Microloft. Be aware that oil stains in a polyester garment are difficult to remove.

Acrylic

Acrylic fibers began to be commercially produced in the United States in 1950. Acrylic fibers resemble wool and are known for their softness and warmth. Acrylic improves upon wool by being quick-drying and resistant to moths, sunlight, oil, and chemicals. It can also be machine-washed—another luxury of the modern age. As a wool replacement, acrylic is found in sweaters, socks, blankets, and sportswear. It comes under the trade names Orlon, Acrilan, and Cresian. The problem with acrylic fibers is that they have an uneven surface, making them pile and be at risk of abrasion problems. When working with these fibers, be careful that jewelry, belt buckles, ragged fingernails, and other objects do not catch the fibers and pull them out of shape. Wear clean cotton gloves or nitrile gloves when working with these materials.

Polyurethane

Like acrylic and polyester, polyurethane began to be commercially used in the early 1950s. Polyurethane products are quite diverse and include spandex, fake suede, fake leather, and water-repellent materials. Polyurethane was popular in the 1960s and 1970s in "wet-look" fabrics used for belts, shoes, purses, and jackets. From a preservation perspective, polyurethane is the most difficult of all the synthetic fabrics. It is extremely sensitive to light, heat, and atmospheric chemicals. Discoloration is one of the main forms of deterioration. Problems with the plastic layers can also occur in the form of cracking, delamination, or bubbling. Do not dry-clean polyurethane; the fibers can soften or become sticky. Plasticizers in polyurethane can stain other materials in a garment or corrode metal snaps, buttons, and decorations. Polyurethane is also highly susceptible to mold and mildew. Bonded polyurethane, used to make synthetic leather, suede, fleece, and spandex, can yellow or separate from the base fabric. Polyurethane foam yellows, becomes brittle, and will eventually crumble.

Spandex is a common form of polyurethane that became popular in the 1960s as a replacement for natural rubber. Because of its stretchability, it was used primarily in swimwear and undergarments, but it has also been used in jackets, skiwear, and exercise clothing. It is manufactured under the names Lycra, Cleerspan, Dorlastan, and Glospan.

CARING FOR TEXTILES

The environment is almost always the main reason for decay in textiles. As with other parts of archival collections, the main culprits are light, temperature, and humidity. Pests are a particular problem for textiles. Chemicals and pollutants can also damage textiles and accelerate their decay.

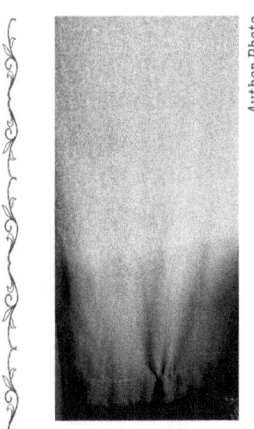

Sun damaged curtain

Light

Light is a great enemy of textiles as it is with most archival items. Light damage is cumulative and irreversible. Fading caused by UV radiation from sunlight or fluorescent light can occur quickly and is permanent. UV light will also cause fibers to become brittle, increasing the risk of tears or holes. Dyes fade when exposed to light. The only thing that will prevent light damage is total darkness. That may be practical for the wedding dress stored in a box in your closet, but not so practical for your grandmother's quilt hanging on the wall of the family room. There are some measures you can take to lessen the damage, if not eliminate it completely.

Most UV light comes from natural sunlight. Fabrics displayed on walls should be kept under UV protective glass or acrylic in archival-safe frames. Fluorescent and halogen-produced lights are a second major contributor to UV light. You can place UV filters over windows, fluorescent tubes, and incandescent light bulbs. Keep in mind that UV filters have a limited lifespan, so they need to be checked periodically and replaced every few years. Another problem with incandescent lights is that they produce a great deal of heat that can also be damaging to delicate antique fibers. If using incandescent lights, make sure they are far enough away from fabrics so that they are not affected by the heat.

Framed textile wall hanging.

These strategies will provide a measure of protection, but the best protection is to either keep sensitive materials out of the light altogether or limit the amount of light exposure as much as possible. As with other kinds of artwork, you can take simple steps to increase the lifespan of your textile wall hangings. First, consider the room you are keeping these artworks in. It is better to have them in a room on the north or west sides of the house that get diffused light rather than the south or east sides of the house that get more direct and sustained sunlight. Second, close the drapes during the main part of the day to keep the room dark. Blackout curtains provide more protection than light-colored or thin curtains that continue to let in sunlight. Third, be like a museum: change the artwork on your walls periodically so that each piece gets a rest from the constant strain of light exposure. Light damage is cumulative. Changing wall hangings and artwork seasonally is a good rule of thumb. Last, consider which wall in a room the artwork is hanging on. Having its back to a window or being outside the direct glare of a fluorescent light will bring your textile artwork much happiness and give it a longer life. Remember, textiles are like vampires; they prefer darkness and nighttime.[27] How much light is too much? The rule of thumb is that if you can take a photograph without using a flash, there is too much light in the room for an exposed textile.

Temperature and Relative Humidity

The single greatest measure you can take to ensure that your textile collection lasts into the future is making sure it is housed in the proper environment. This means ensuring temperatures remain in the 65° to 70°F range with an RH of about 50% to 55%. Keeping the environment stable is also vital. Temperature and RH levels should not fluctuate more than ten degrees or ten percent in a twenty-four-hour period. Textile fibers expand and contract as the humidity in the environment increases and decreases. Daily changes in the chemical makeup of fabric will speed its deterioration. Refer to Chapter 2 for instructions on how to maintain environmental stability; those rules apply to textiles as well. Too little humidity can cause textiles to become brittle and fragile. Humidity levels should not drop below 30%. A good hygrometer is necessary for measuring room humidity and ensuring that proper environmental stability is maintained. Be mindful of where you are placing textiles. Look for localized heat sources, dampness, and excessive cold from outside walls. Dehumidifiers, humidifiers, or air conditioners can help maintain a constant level of humidity in a room or storage facility.

Mold and Mildew

High temperatures and high RH pose special problems for fabrics and textiles. Mold and mildew are both fungi that thrive in wet, humid places. Mold and mildew usually appear dark blue or black and can stain textiles. Staining can sometimes be removed if it is caught early enough, but often the damage is irreparable. Mold will eat into fabric causing irreversible holes and tears.

If you find active mold growth on a textile object, the first thing to do is dry it out and put it in an area that has RH below 65%. According to the National Archives, mold cannot grow in environments with RH below 65%.

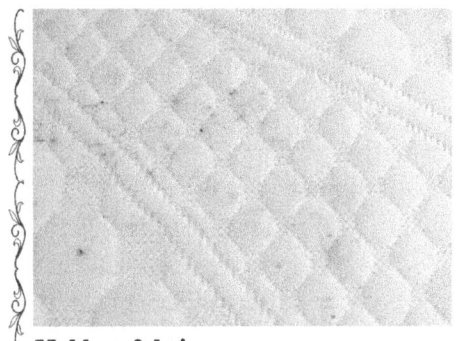
Mold on fabric

Since mold spores are prolific and can easily transfer from one garment to another, isolate moldy fabric from other textiles. If other textile items have been stored in the same environment, be sure to transfer all of them as quickly as possible to a less humid, cooler area. Let moldy items dry out on a clean, absorbent surface. Do not rub blue mold when it is wet; this will cause streaking and extend the damage to fabric. Do not brush mold when it is dry; the mold spores will get into the air and can spread. For musty smelling garments, a good airing out should fix the problem. Vacuuming afterward will help remove any dormant mold spores. Follow the instructions in the "Care and Maintenance" section below for vacuuming under a fiberglass screen. For items that are extensively damaged, or for fragile or very old antique items, call a conservator.

Remember that mold and mildew can be hazardous to your health. If you have asthma or other health concerns, or if the mold and mildew is extensive, contact a conservator. Ventilation is essential.

Mold and mildew are environmental problems. If you find mold or mildew in your collection, you must make the proper corrections to ensure they do not continue growing. Find the heat or water source. It could be high humidity, a leaking pipe, a leaky window, or something else. Air conditioners and dehumidifiers will help keep moisture and temperatures down. Use fans to increase circulation in the short term. Make sure the filters in air conditioners and dehumidifiers are clean and changed regularly. Air flow is important. Do not seal items in plastic or other airtight casings unless instructed by a conservator as part of a cleaning process or other specialized treatment. Fabric needs to breathe. Good air circulation is a must for keeping humidity, mold, and mildew in check.

Pests

Clothes moths, carpet beetles, silverfish, firebrats, and rodents can all wreak havoc with the natural fibers found in our delicate textiles. Be on the lookout for spiders too. Spiders will not eat textiles, but they may be a sign that other insects are present. High temperatures and high humidity increase the likelihood of having problems from pests. Stated another way, keeping temperatures and humidity low will reduce the risk of pests. Even in cool, dry environments pests can accumulate, which is why periodic inspection of textiles is essential.

Silks and wool made from animals that are high in protein are attractive to clothes moths and carpet beetles. Silverfish and firebrats will eat starches and sugars applied to fabrics and tend toward cotton and linen materials. Collectors who regularly purchase textiles from outside vendors, antique stores, or other homeowners will want to take certain measures when bringing new items into the collection. Keep in mind that pests are also attracted to fur, feathers, hair, and horn that may be attached to or part of a garment.

Clothes Moths: Clothes moths are attracted to protein and therefore feed on animal-based materials such as wool, silk, fur, and leather. They may also attack blended wool containing rayon or polyester, especially if the articles are stained with food or body oils. Since clothes moths prefer dark areas, they are more likely to be found in areas that are undisturbed such as closets and attics.

Damage from clothes moths

The larval stage of clothes moths lasts between two and six months depending on the environment. Clothes moths larvae are small cream-colored caterpillars with brown heads. Look for white cocoons or evidence of them on textiles, or look for the moths themselves, which are white and about half an inch in size. The cocoons they create either look like a webbing tube, or they have a more refined smooth case.

Clothes moths do not like light. If you see a moth flying around a light source, do not worry. They are not clothes moths and will not damage fabrics. Clothes moths prefer darkness and enclosed areas. They like to get into the folds of clothing and nest there. Adult clothes moths do not damage fabrics because they do not eat. However, they lay eggs on clothes and the larvae that hatch from them do eat fabric.

Dry-cleaning will get rid of larvae and mothproofing will give some protection, but neither will prevent a group of hungry insects from at least attempting to eat textiles. Be aware that not all materials should be dry-cleaned. Anything fragile should be sent to a conservator. For stronger and more modern materials, try to find a dry cleaner that specializes in vintage clothing or consult a conservator.

Good housekeeping is essential for reducing the risk of damage from vermin. Clothes moths will not eat cleaned wool. Make sure your textiles are cleaned before they are put in storage. In the past, people used moth balls to prevent damage from clothes moths. Moth balls can be toxic—to us, our children, our pets, and our clothing. They may help reduce clothes moths, but it is not guaranteed. *This is an old-fashioned method and is not recommended.* Moth balls or moth crystals use naphthalene or paradichlorobenzene to fight against pests. Naphthalene repels adult insects, and paradichlorobenzene kills both adults and eggs. If you decide to use moth balls, make sure they do not touch any fabric. Place them in a vented container inside the storage box. If you can smell moth balls when you open a closet door or enter a storage room, you have either put too many moth balls in the container or not properly sealed the box.

Carpet Beetles: Adult carpet beetles are one tenth of an inch long (about the size of a ladybug) and have white and brown stripes. Some of the older adult beetles are solid black or solid brown. Carpet beetles go outside before or after laying their eggs, so they are often found in doorways or windowsills. The larvae look like small, red-brown cocoons with many bristles or can look like small, pale worm-like insects. The larval period of carpet beetles lasts at least four months, at which time they molt several times before reaching adulthood. Evidence of molten carcasses may alert you to an infestation problem. Carpet beetles are attracted to proteins, so they will attack wool, silk, and leather products. They can feed on other materials besides your carpet, so look for them around pet food, fruit left on tables, or garbage areas.

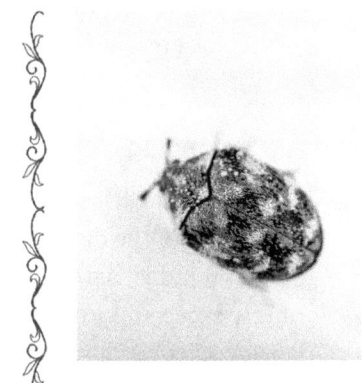
Carpet Beetle

If you have a major infestation of any of these pests, consult a conservator or exterminator. If just one or two items are affected, seal them in plastic bags. In the case of larger species, secure the items under plastic sheeting sealed with tape. Once you properly seal the items, freeze them to kill the insects and larvae. You can use a residential freezer if it is not too full. Obviously for larger items such as rugs, this is not practical. You will probably need to contact a conservator. The rapid drop in temperature should kill anything. Let the object(s) stay in the freezer for three to five days. Allow it to slowly return to room temperature by placing it in the refrigerator for a day, then bringing it to room temperature. Once this process is complete, repeat it by refreezing the article for another three to five days and slowly bringing it back to room temperature. Afterward, vacuum the entire piece (see instructions below), ideally using HEPA vacuum bags. Throw away the filters when you are finished to ensure no residual larvae escape or are reintroduced into your home.

Now you know why we call them "pests." Be aware that freezing can be damaging to nontextile items that may be attached to a garment, such as beading, boning, or metal. It is worth making a quick phone call or sending an email to a conservator to make sure you will not damage other parts of the piece while you are saving it from pests.

After taking care of the textiles, be sure to thoroughly clean the area where you found the bugs with hot water and dishwashing liquid (not the textile itself). Include walls, floors, cabinets, drawers, and storage containers. If you found bugs in cardboard containers, dispose of the containers immediately. After removing infested articles and cleaning the area, be sure to wash the clothing you are wearing and take a shower.

Air Pollution

Dirt and dust within our homes and chemical pollutants outside our homes can contribute to the deterioration of fragile textiles. Sulfur dioxides from automobiles and industrial waste can affect some dyes. Dirt can become embedded in fibers, especially in environments with humidity fluctuations, and can stain fabrics. Dirt can also be gritty and razor-sharp on a microscopic level, tearing into fibers and weakening them. Harsh cleaning solutions within our homes can also damage delicate fabrics. Never use ammonia or turpentine in the vicinity of fragile textiles.

Inherent Vice

As discussed in Chapter 7, the term *inherent vice* means that an object can be destroyed by the materials that were used in the manufacturing process or during the construction of the object. In other words, instead of being destroyed by external factors, the object is self-destroyed by its internal properties. For example, in the 19th century, metallic salts were added to silk during the manufacturing process to make it heavier and stiff. Called "weighted" silk, this material is vulnerable to cracking and eventually turns to powder. Light exposure increases the damage, which is irreversible. Weighted silk can be found not only in clothing but also in Victorian "crazy" quilts. Black and brown dyes that previously used iron as a fixative can rust and rot, staining fabric or leaving holes. Often pre-20th century dyes were not properly fixed. These dyes can change color or bleed into surrounding fibers, especially when exposed to light or high heat and humidity. Even the slightest dampness can cause bleeding, making it nearly impossible to clean such items. Because inherent vice is part of the fabric or the object, little can be done to eliminate the damage. The best you can do is try to slow deterioration. To repeat: keeping items in the proper environment and proper storage containers will aid in this endeavor.

> *"And it is so fragile, once you're gone, you don't want to be forgotten."*
>
> **OLIVIA COLMAN**
> WDYTYA British S.15 E.2

HANDLING

Most textiles are produced under the assumption they will be used and eventually discarded. Preserving fabrics long-term goes against their natural tendency to break down and deteriorate, especially those made from natural fibers. If you want to preserve and pass down family heirlooms and works of art, you must employ great care and attention. Every time you interact with a piece of fabric, the risk of damage is ever-present. Therefore, handling with care is essential.

Whenever moving a textile object from one area to another, make sure the entire piece is supported. Do not let the bottom of a dress or quilt drag on the floor as you move it from one room to another. Laying items flat during transport will decrease the likelihood of damage. If you can fold it, do so. Do not fold items that are brittle or ones that will be damaged by folding. During transport, place items on a piece of archival cardboard or in a box. Check the area they will be transported to before you begin to make the journey (from living room to bedroom, for example) to be sure there is someplace safe to set the items down when you get there. Keep pets and small children out of the work area when you are exposing fragile fabrics and while moving or working on an object.

Do not wear jewelry, belts, or pins that can snag a piece of fabric and cause irreparable damage. Wear either white cotton or nitrile gloves, or wash your hands to reduce the oils, soils, salts, and acids on them before handling a fabric object. Do not use hand sanitizers or other chemicals on your hands before you touch an old piece of clothing, including hand creams and lotions that contain oils and damaging chemicals. If possible, set up a work area in your home. When working with textiles you will need a clean table. Adding a clean pad or archival tissue paper to the table will give the object a soft place to lie on and provide a layer of buffering between the fabric and the hard surface. Never eat, drink, or smoke around archival fabrics. Periodically check archival textiles that are stored or on display for damage including mold and mildew, pests, or strain. If you have hung an object on the wall and it has become misshapen after a few weeks or months, you might consider taking it off the wall and laying it flat.

Do not wear antique or historic clothing (except a wedding dress or christening gown that is properly fitted to the new owner). Remember, before the modern age clothing was fitted to a specific individual. Old clothing is easily torn at the seams, and even the fabric itself can tear. This is why historical reenactors and guides at historic homes have new costumes made in the image of the old.

CLEANING AND MAINTENANCE

The daily lives of our textiles can be as hard-working and as rugged as our own. Think of what a military uniform may have experienced. Rugs on our floors have been walked on, have had furniture dragged over them and food and drinks spilled on them, and may even have been exposed to flooding, leaking pipes, hurricanes, blizzards, and all sorts of hazardous life events. After years of snuggling, even the hardiest quilt can show wear and look tired. Table linens are lucky to survive the life of their owner. One can imagine the cigars and cigarettes that have been smoked in their presence with ashes dropping here and there, not to mention hot plates and pans placed on top of them and all the many dinners, drinks, and grubby cake-filled hands that have touched them. Brides are beautiful, to be sure, and wedding dresses are often very delicate, but beautiful brides are often not very delicate, especially after a few drinks. Wine spills, dirty trains, misshapen bustles, ripped lace, missing beads, chocolate cake—you get the picture. From a historic perspective, these textile scars are the evidence of lives lived in them and may be the most interesting part of garment.

Textiles are completely intertwined in our daily lives. Caring for them is part of our regular routine of chores. We do laundry weekly, we make frequent trips to the dry cleaners, we regularly vacuum rugs and carpets, we sew hems, replace lost buttons, and perhaps we even make clothing on sewing machines or by knitting or crocheting. These activities and our familiarity with textiles may delude us into thinking we are experienced and equipped to deal with the antique objects in our care or the family heirlooms we want to pass down. This could not be further from the truth. For historic or heirloom objects, our goal should be to clean it once, then store it properly. Each time we attempt to clean an object, the risk of doing damage increases. Proper storage and maintenance can eliminate the need for future exposure to washing and drying.

Vacuuming

Vacuuming can remove accumulated dirt and dust. The difference made by removing dirt using this method can be amazing. If you are lucky, vacuuming will be the only cleaning action you will need to take for historic and heirloom items. For some objects, it may be the only cleaning method that is safe. On the other hand, be aware that for garments and materials that are in a state of high embrittlement and deterioration and have begun to turn to dust, vacuuming can cause more damage. This is especially true for silk. Great care needs to be taken when considering vacuuming a garment. Consult a conservator if you have any doubt vacuuming could cause more damage. Letting them do the work is best since they have experience and expertise in doing so.

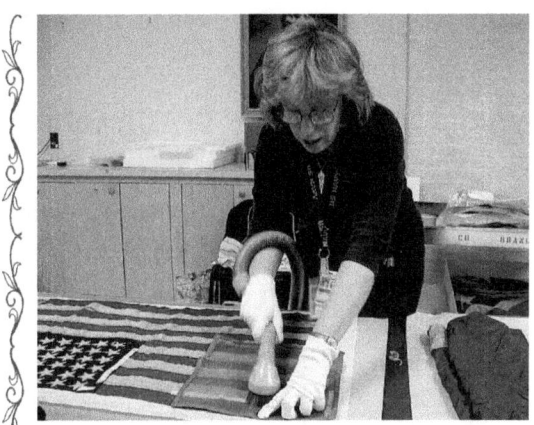
Vacuuming textiles through a screen

Objects that hang on walls or are in open living spaces will need regular vacuuming to help prevent infestation of pests, especially for wool and silk. Use a low-power, handheld vacuum if possible, or use a nozzle attachment on an upright vacuum. Velvets or pile rugs that have a nap should be vacuumed in the direction of the nap. This means the rug should not change color when you vacuum it. Do not go against the fibers.

Delicate or fragile textiles can be vacuumed using a fiberglass screen. Dirt and debris will filter up to the hose through suction while delicate or loose fibers will remain intact. To vacuum an item using a screen, place the object on a padded flat surface. To prepare a fiberglass window screen, tape the metal edges of the screen to ensure that rust will not get on the fabric or rough edges will not damage the material. Do not use a metal screen, because even the slightest bit of rust can cause great harm to fiber materials. Place the fiberglass window screen on top of the textile, then place the vacuum over the screen. Set the vacuum

> **ARCHIVES TIP**
>
> **The reason conservators are hesitant to offer guidance on cleaning is that if a textile is damaged during the cleaning process, it is irreversible. You cannot un-wet something.**

Gentle cleaning detergents

on its lowest speed and hold it over the screen for a few seconds. Do not rub! Be gentle. Move to the next spot and repeat. It is tedious, but a little care, attention, and mindfulness will go a long way. Alternatively, the safer way to go is to contact a conservator and let the professionals do what they do best.

Dry Cleaning and Wet Cleaning

Dry-cleaning an antique wedding dress could absolutely destroy it. Submerging older fabrics or those made in other parts of the world without using modern fixing techniques could cause all the colors to run. This will ruin the expensive piece of art you brought home from a foreign country or that your mother, grandmother, and great-grandmother preserved for generations, turning it into a big purple blob. Washing machines and dryers need to be reserved for the hardy items in a collection. A silk embroidered shawl does not fall into that category. When in doubt, call a conservator. Use your judgment. You do not want to create more harm in your effort to fix or make a piece better. Improper cleaning can cause shrinkage, color bleeding, color loss, or distortion of form.

Conservators are very tight-lipped when giving advice on cleaning. While I was writing this book, I asked one for advice and she said readers should call a conservator. The reason conservators are hesitant to offer guidance on cleaning is that if a textile is damaged during the cleaning process, it is irreversible. You cannot un-wet something.

When water contacts fabric pieces, it can cause more damage than it is worth and may not be safe. Items that have dirt on them could become permanently stained. Fabrics can shrink when wet, or the stitching can shrink and lead to puckering. Finishes like starches or sugars will be permanently lost during washing. Dye bleeding is also a common problem; if colors bleed when wet, the dyes can fade. Worse, the dyes can stain other parts of the article rendering it permanently damaged. The stain you were hoping to remove by cleaning might not be removed and could appear worse after being wet.

Commercial detergents use harsh chemicals that can be damaging to delicate fibers. Machine washing can be very hard on fabrics and in most cases is not safe. Over-wetting or machine agitating a woolen object can lead to felting. Heating woolen fibers causes the fibers to shrink, resulting in felting or matting. Never use bleach on old or delicate fabrics. Bleach can permanently destroy color and can create holes in delicate or deteriorating fabrics.

If you must, and if you are confident it will be safe, hand wash articles in cold distilled water using Woolite brand detergent, Ivory liquid dishwashing detergent, or products purchased from an archival supply company. You can check colorfastness prior to washing by placing the object on white blotting paper. Using an eyedropper, allow one drop of cleaning solution to penetrate the fabric in an inconspicuous spot. If the blotting paper remains white when the wet drop reaches it, try a few more drops to be sure the item is colorfast and can be submerged in water. Be aware that this test is not foolproof. All color fabrics are at risk of bleeding. Also, be aware that time is a significant factor in color bleeding. The longer something is submerged, the higher the likelihood of bleeding. Slowly increase the area of wetness as you work. Be quick, and do not soak the item. In-out, chop-chop. Use mesh netting or a fiberglass screen to lift an item out of the water. Remember, fabric will be heavier when wet and can easily be torn or distort its shape.

Once articles are wet, drying is the next challenge. Be sure to lay garments flat on a smooth surface. Since wool absorbs so much liquid, you might want to blot some of the excess water using clean towels. Never wring an item or twist its shape. Hanging items to dry may result in stretching and misshaping. If the garment is small enough, lay it on a sweater rack or absorbent clean towels. Cover items with clean cotton sheeting. It may take several days for an item to fully dry. Do not expose textiles to sunlight or hang them on a clothesline in the breeze. While the garments are wet, you can stuff them with soft netting to give them the proper shape, which will hopefully eliminate the need for ironing later. If soaked, replace the netting with fresh, dry materials. If you must iron, use extreme care! Always start with the lowest setting and move up if necessary. Use your best judgment, and when in doubt, call a conservator.

Textile conservation is a specialty. Textile conservators are educated and experienced in conservation methods for a variety of fabrics. While we all have intimate experience interacting with textiles and have all had our "red sock in the white clothes" moment, we do not have the specialized education and skills of a professional conservator. Depending on the age and condition of the garments in your care, the cost of having a professional assess and prepare your textiles for storage may be well worth the price.

Eliminating Infestations

Anyone who has experienced a flea infestation knows how quickly a flea-free home can become fully engulfed. Those with antique rugs and textiles at home will need to take extra care to protect their pets and home from fleas. Be sure to apply veterinarian approved flea medication to your pets monthly. If your home does have a flea infestation and you use an exterminator, make sure to let them know that your home contains delicate rugs, antique embroideries, or fragile 19th-century upholstered items. When I had a flea infestation in 2000, the only guaranteed way to get rid of the fleas and their eggs was to vacuum every day. I used powder on floors and rugs and vacuumed, vacuumed, vacuumed. I do not recommend using flea powder on antique objects, but it can be used on everything else in the area of antiques.

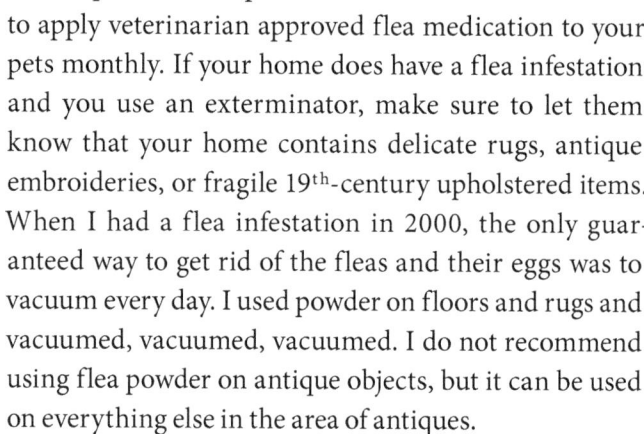

ARCHIVES TIP

Freezing bugs will kill them immediately. The problem with freezing your items, however, is unfreezing them

Isolate whatever objects you can in the event of a bug infestation. Objects that are small enough can be thrown into a freezer. For larger items, you will need to contact a conservator or dry-cleaner. Freezing bugs will kill them immediately. The problem with freezing your items, however, is unfreezing them. While quickly freezing your objects will not cause them damage, unfreezing them too quickly can. Remove items from the freezer and place them in the refrigerator. After they are fully unfrozen but are still cold, place them in an environmentally sound location. Then, vacuum the infested areas right away to make sure any residual larvae are caught before they cause further damage. Be sure to change the vacuum bags after each vacuuming session. When dealing with an infestation, wear synthetic clothing. Insects are not attracted to plastic. After handling infested items, remove your clothing and wash it thoroughly. Treating an infestation is a lot of work and is not fun, but it will potentially save your antiques and family heirlooms.

Carpets and Rugs

Carpets and rugs that are kept on the floor and are in continuous use in your home need proper, regular maintenance. Do not use vacuums with rolling bristles on expensive antique rugs or family heirlooms. Use a low-powered vacuum on the lowest speed. Rub only in the direction of the nap, never going against the fibers. The rug should be turned over periodically and vacuumed from the underside. This will help prevent insects from burrowing deep within the fibers. Clothing moths and carpet beetles are particularly prone to taking up residence in carpets and rugs. Send rugs to a dry cleaner that specializes in large objects.

Discuss the particulars of your objects with a reputable, experienced dry cleaner to ensure damage will not occur in the process.

Tapestries

Tapestries and other wall hangings that are exposed to sunlight and other elements will also need periodic maintenance. They should be removed from the wall and vacuumed on both sides. As instructed above, use a fiberglass mesh screen if these objects are at risk of being damaged by the suction power of the vacuum cleaner or contact a conservator.

How often to vacuum depends on the type of object, the condition of the object, and the state of your home. Homes with pets need extra care. While our cats and dogs bring great joy and pleasure into our lives and homes, their fur can wreak havoc on the textiles they come in direct and indirect contact with. See the "Eliminating Infestations" section above for information on how to deal with fleas.

Under normal conditions, carpets and rugs should be vacuumed once per week. Lifting rugs up to vacuum the undersides and removing wall hangings can be done once or twice a year. Conducting semi-annual inspections will tell you whether more maintenance is required.

Wool

Wet wool becomes very heavy and can lose its shape. If a woolen object in your care is dirty, vacuum it first using the method described above. To check if a woolen object is colorfast, place it on a white muslin cloth or white cardboard. Using an eyedropper, allow one drop of cleaning solution (distilled water and mild soap) to penetrate the fabric in an inconspicuous spot. If the muslin or cardboard remains white when the wet drop reaches it, the item is colorfast and can be submerged in water.

Machine washing and over-wetting a woolen object can lead to felting. Do not use commercial detergents as they use harsh chemicals that can be damaging to delicate fibers. Choose Woolite brand or Ivory liquid dishwashing detergent. Do not agitate or use heat with woolen fibers. This will cause the fibers to shrink, resulting in felting or matting. Wet wool needs to be laid flat to dry. Blotting wet wool with clean towels will remove some of the excess water and help reduce drying time. High twist yarns such as georgette, chiffon, or herringbone should not be wet cleaned.

Dry-cleaning modern woolens will remove stains, grease, oils, waxes, and resins and not harm the material. Historic fabrics should be hand dry-cleaned by a professional. Do not dry-clean at home with kits you can find at stores. Make sure colors are colorfast by using the method described above. Moths and other insects are attracted to residual foodstuffs, oils, and soils that accumulate in wool, which is why it is essential to make sure woolens are cleaned before being stored.

Silk

Silk is more delicate than wool and should be treated with extra care. Old silk is at risk of becoming brittle, especially at folds and creases. Be sure to remove creases by stuffing acid-free, unbuffered tissue paper in folds. Old silk should not hang freely; it should either be supported while hung, or better, laid flat. Many pests are attracted to silk.

STORAGE – GENERAL CONSIDERATIONS

When storing textiles, there are other things to consider beyond providing a good, stable environment (not too hot, not too cold, not too wet, not too dry).

> **ARCHIVES TIP**
>
> Wood is highly acidic. When fabric makes direct contact with it, the acid can transfer to fabrics and cause their natural fibers to become brittle, stained, yellowed, or darkened.

Some of our most cherished furniture is used for storing clothing, linen, and other textile materials. This furniture could be some of our favorite antiques. While linen stored carefully in a dining room buffet looks beautiful and may be convenient, storing fabric in wooden drawers or on wooden shelves in closets or cabinets may not be the best method. Direct exposure to wooden drawers, wooden boxes, wooden hope chests, or wooden shelves can damage sensitive textile materials. Wood is highly acidic. When fabric makes direct contact with it, the acid can transfer to fabrics and cause their natural fibers to become brittle, stained, yellowed, or darkened. The best shelving for textiles is rust-free metal shelving.

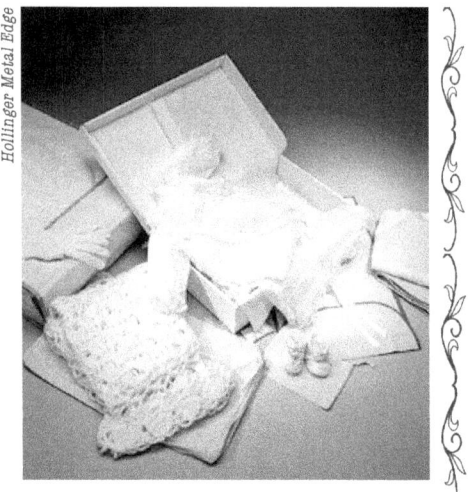

Archival storage boxes for textiles

You can use wooden shelves to store fabrics if you place a protective coating between the fabric and the wood. Though shellac or waterborne polyurethane varnish adds a layer of protection to the wood, the toxicity of this product could cause further problems to textiles. It is better to line drawers or shelves with white cotton sheeting or archival-quality cardboard or tissue paper. The lining will absorb the acid from the wood and protect the fabric. You should check the linings periodically and change them when they become discolored—once a year is a good rule of thumb.

Using archival-quality storage materials is your best option for antique and heirloom linens and garments. As discussed in Chapter 1, paper materials should be acid-free and lignin-free. It is better to store textiles in paper materials than plastic ones. Textiles, especially those made of natural fibers, need to breathe. Plastic containers do not allow enough breathability for most textiles. Also, the chemicals in plastic can contribute to yellowing of textiles. Stick to cardboard boxes purchased from a good archival supplier. If you do decide to use plastic containers, make sure they are made of inert polypropylene and purchased from a reputable archival supply store. Since plastic can accumulate condensation if exposed to high humidity, it is best to wrap textiles in acid-free *unbuffered* tissue paper before placing them inside the container. The tissue paper will absorb moisture and help keep the garments or articles dry. Be sure to check plastic containers periodically to make sure condensation has not accumulated. Change tissue paper that is damp or stained.

> **ARCHIVES TIP**
>
> **Protein-based natural fibers (wool and silk) are sensitive to alkaline. For these textiles, use unbuffered or non-buffered materials that are PH neutral or acid-free. For textiles made of plant fibers (cotton and linen), it is safe to use buffered materials.**

All paper-based storage materials should be acid-free and lignin-free. Whether to use buffered or unbuffered materials takes a little more know-how. Buffering in paper means that an agent is added to the paper during the manufacturing process that is designed to absorb the natural acidity of paper and slow down the deterioration process. Typically, the buffering agent is calcium carbonate, which is an alkaline-based product. Protein-based natural fibers (wool and silk) are sensitive to alkaline. For these textiles, use unbuffered or non-buffered materials that are PH neutral or acid-free. For textiles made of plant fibers (cotton and linen), it is safe to use buffered materials.

If possible, it is best to lay an object flat in a box rather than hanging it up. In some cases, if laying an object flat will cause more damage, hanging may be your only alternative. Do not stack textiles on top of each other. The ideal method is to store one item per box. In the case of large pieces such as rugs, carpets, tapestries, and quilts, rolling the item is the best option. Make sure garments or linens placed in a box or drawer are not folded, because fabrics discolor and deteriorate at the folds. Insert acid-free, lignin-free tissue paper in the folds so that the edges are rounded rather than creased.

It is of the utmost importance to store objects in a clean state. This will reduce the risk of pests taking up residence in your grandfather's military uniform or mildew forming on your aunt's wedding dress. Food stains and oils from hands are often not visible, but over time will attract unwanted guests or discolor with age. Perspiration is very acidic and will eventually form into alkaline ammonium compounds that will cause fabric to become brittle and easily torn.

For objects in current use (such as a wedding dress), be sure to have them professionally cleaned before storing them. For objects in your collection that are already dated and in a state of active deterioration, consult a conservator before taking it upon yourself to clean them. As stated earlier, some 19th-century dyes will run as soon as they contact even the smallest amount of water, brittle or fragile fabrics will not survive even a gentle handwashing, and many older or damaged materials would be harmed beyond repair by dry-cleaning. Use your judgment and err on the side of caution. Once the damage is done, it may be irreversible.

Cedar chests or cedar closets may deter moths, but they will not completely prevent them. And cedar has no effect on carpet beetles. Storing items in cedar chests is an antiquated idea, and this method provides little to no protection for textiles as cedar chests can harm fabrics. The lovely odor found in cedar chests comes from aromatic oils in the wood. Like other types of wood, direct contact between cedar and textiles can result in staining that is often permanent.

Metadata

As with other items in your collection, you should add information in the storage box that indicates what the garment is, who it belonged to, and a little bit of its history. Do not forget to add what type of material the garment is made of and the year it was made if you know this information. Never use ink, gel pens, or highlighters that can permanently stain fabrics. Do not pin anything onto a garment; all metal will eventually rust. Using a pencil, you can write the metadata on a tag and sew the tag inside a garment. Another option is to place written materials in a polypropylene or paper envelope and sew it to the garment, or you can just place the envelope in the box.

STORAGE – SPECIFIC ITEMS

Tapestry, Quilts, Display Rugs

Items that are too large to be stored in boxes will need to be rolled. Textiles should be stored with the design side out. Interleave the textiles with acid-free tissue paper. Make sure a rug, quilt, or tapestry is cleaned before storing. You can purchase acid-free inner tubes from archival supply houses. The tube should be about a foot wider than the piece to be rolled. Leave at least six inches on each side of the empty tube. Once the piece is rolled, place either more acid-free tissue paper or white cotton muslin cloth around the outside. This will protect it from dirt and grime that can accumulate in storage as well as protect it from light. The ends of the tissue paper or muslin can be tucked inside the inner tube. Use cotton twill ties to secure everything in place. Rolled items can be stored standing up or lying flat. Make sure wherever they are stored, the area is ventilated and has the proper heat and humidity controls. Remember, to an insect, fibers look like a meal. Depending on the size of the finished rolled product, the entire thing could be stored in acid-free boxes made for this purpose. Check the archival supply stores or make a box yourself. This is not necessary but will add a layer of protection.

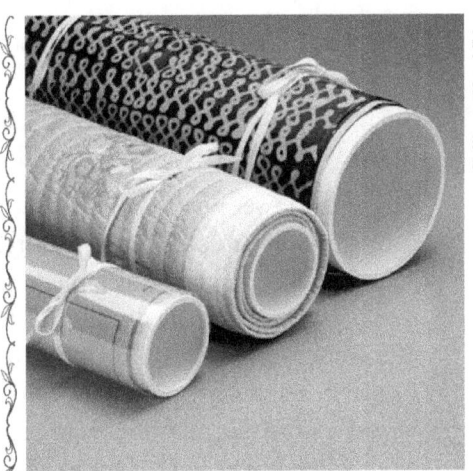

Rolling large textile articles

Wedding Dresses

Preparing wedding dresses for storage is a specialty, and you can easily find companies that provide this service. If you decide to take it upon yourself, or if you want to make sure you have hired the right company to do the job, here is how a wedding dress should be stored.

Gowns that are heavily beaded should be stored in acid-free, lignin-free boxes. If silk is used in the construction of the dress, choose unbuffered materials. You can purchase an 18" W x 60" L archival box for this purpose. When placing a wedding dress in an archival box, there will inevitably be places where it will need to be folded. The bottom edge may need to be folded under, the arms may be folded over, and any creases in the skirt part of the dress or the bustle will need attention. Fabric tends to discolor and deteriorate at the points where a crease exists, so you do not want any

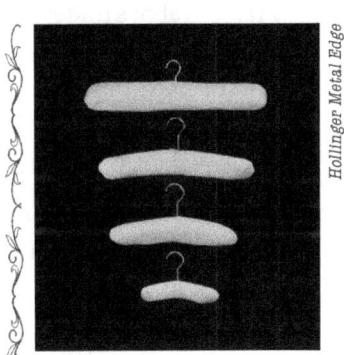

Padded hangers

creases anywhere. Using archival acid-free tissue paper, puff out the bodice, the sleeves, the fold where the bottom is folded under, and any other places where a crease or a fold may cause future damage. Take your time and be thorough. Your daughter will thank you if the day comes when she wants to wear it.

An alternative to storing a wedding dress in a box is hanging it on a plastic hanger covered in polyester quilt batting that is then covered with washed, undyed white cotton muslin. This method is acceptable only for lightweight gowns that are not heavily trimmed and beaded. When hanging a wedding dress or any article of clothing, choose a hanger that is the correct size and shape to support the weight of the item and will not create creases in stand-up collars. Do not use wooden hangers.

Use padded hangers so that the shoulders of the dress will be fully supported. You can get them from better clothing and department stores or online. Make sure they do not have polyurethane or latex foam in the batting. If you are creative and ambitious, you can make your own padded hangers.

If the lower portion of the dress is heavy, it can strain the upper part of the dress and eventually cause distortion and even tearing. To avoid this, museums create a support piece made of twill strips that reduces the strain of the downward pull of the dress. This is done by basting twill strips into the seam allowance of the waistline of the dress. This twill strip can then be attached to other strips that are placed over the hanger underneath the dress—like suspenders. A seamstress may be able to make this kind of support for you. Alternatively, contact a conservator for advice or lay the garment flat.

Do not use plastic dry cleaning bags or vinyl garment bags for storage. They are chemically unstable and unsuitable for long-term storage.

Hats, Gloves, Shoes, Purses

Dresses, uniforms (work or sporting), christening outfits, graduation gowns, aprons, and any other articles of clothing can use the same principles as those relayed above under the section "Wedding Dresses." Make sure the items are clean before storing. Lay them flat in a box if possible. Puff out creases with acid-free tissue paper, using unbuffered tissue paper for wool and silk clothing. If laying the clothing flat will cause more damage, hang the items on padded hangers. As always, keeping the items in a favorable and stable environment is essential.

Hats: Clean hats before storing. Stuff the crowns of hats with acid-free tissue paper and place them in acid-free boxes that are large enough not to crush any aspect of them. Archival supply houses sell boxes specifically made for hats. They come with see-through windows on one side or fully enclosed. Be sure to include a piece of acid-free paper with penciled notes indicating who the hat belonged to, how old it is, and why it is important.

Gloves: Gently stuff each finger of cleaned gloves with acid-free tissue paper. Do not overstuff them. You want to stuff them just enough so that there are not any creases, but they do not have to look like they are occupied. Wrap the gloves in acid-free tissue paper and place them in a box. Add metadata and keep the box in a stable environment.

Shoes: Cleaning shoes may pose more of a problem. Do not use harsh chemicals, cleaning solutions, shoe wax, or shoe polish. Stuff shoes with acid-free tissue paper or archival polyester batting so that the shoes will stay upright. Then wrap them in acid-free tissue paper and place them in a box that will not crush the edges of the shoes. Since shoes cannot be cleaned to the degree that other textiles can, and because many shoes are made with animal products (leather in particular), take extra care to ensure pests do not take up residence in antique shoes.

Purses: Depending on the material, clean the outside of purses with a bristle brush or a damp cloth. Gently vacuum the inside to remove all traces of crumbs, hair, and dust, and then gently wipe the purse with a damp cloth dipped in distilled water. Gently stuff the purse with polyester batting or acid-free tissue paper, wrap it in tissue paper, and place it in an acid-free archival box. As with shoes, if the purse is made of leather or other animal products, be on the lookout for pests.

Flags

Flags are made from all kinds of materials including natural fibers such as silk, wool, linen, and cotton as well as synthetic fibers such as nylon, rayon, and polyester. The age and type of material your flag is made of will determine how you care for it. If necessary, older flags should be brought to a textile conservator for cleaning and

Archival storage box for flags

repair. More modern flags can be hand-washed with a gentle detergent such as Woolite or Ivory Liquid. Be sure to check the color fastness before submerging a flag. Though most synthetic fibers can be hand-washed, a flag used in battle may contain stains that contribute to the story of the flag. In that case, you would not want to wash out significant gunpowder, blood, or dirt stains.

Use the same rules for storing flags that you would use for storing other textiles. Flags can be rolled instead of laid flat. Follow the directions for storing quilts. Otherwise, lay flags flat in a box after stuffing the creases with acid-free tissue paper. For preservation reasons, if a flag is stapled to a wooden pole, it is better to remove it from the post. Rust stains will most likely form where the flag is nailed to the post, and the wood, as we have learned, will also stain the fabric. Make sure not to do any damage to the flag while removing the post. If you want to keep the post because you think it is a significant part of the flag's story, you can still remove it from the flag and place it in a separate box. This will allow you to keep the post and keep the flag without causing further damage to either. Alternatively, wrap the wood in tissue paper or glassine so that it will not come in contact with the fabric of the flag. It should be checked periodically for bleeding. Contact a conservator if you have trouble removing the flag from the post.

DISPLAY

Fabric decorative arts fill our homes with warmth and comfort, bringing back memories of loved ones who perhaps knitted, crocheted, or hand-stitched items. Military families like my Uncle Charlie's are proud to display the American flags given in appreciation of their loved ones' service to their country. Tapestries, quilts, rugs, embroidery, and cross-stitch pictures add beauty to our homes. Hanging on a wall in the guest room of my house, I have eight black hats from the 1950s that belonged to my Aunt Thelma. On another wall in the same room hangs my Auntie Edna's costume jewelry, my Aunt Mabel's hand-tatted doily, and a small fur jacket I "rescued" from an antiques shop. My grandmother's afghan sits at the end of the guest bed, while in the living room the quilt my sister made for me many years ago rests on the back of my couch. Several cross-stitch pictures I was given as gifts and ones that I made hang on other walls of my home. While I want to enjoy the beauty and memories these pieces of fabric art bring to my life, I also want to do whatever I can to ensure their longest life.

A few small changes and mindful adjustments can make a big difference. You want to make sure that if you are using wooden frames, the wood does not come in direct contact with the fabric. As we have learned, wood is toxic to fabrics and will cause acid degradation, staining, and brittleness. Do not use iron nails that can rust, stain, or create holes in fabric. You also do not want to puncture the fabric anywhere at any time. Using UV-filtering glass or acrylic in framed art; acid-free, lignin-free mats and backboards; or UV filters on windows and fluorescent lights will help extend the life of your textile art. Other small measures you can take to extend the life of your collection are keeping rooms darkened during the day, placing artwork in a location where it will not be exposed to direct or indirect sunlight, and changing textile artwork seasonally.

Wall Hangings - Quilts, Tapestries, Rugs, Carpets

For heavy pieces that will be hung on a wall, you must ensure that the piece will not be damaged by hanging. If you have any doubts about your ability to do this on your own, call a conservator for specific advice. Museums and historical societies use VELCRO® brand fasteners[28] to hang quilts, tapestries, and rugs on walls. The "male" part of the strip is tacked or stapled to a varnished piece of wood that is affixed to the wall. The "female" part of the strip is machine sewn onto a piece of fabric that is then hand sewn to the article to be hung. The strips need to entirely cover the piece to be hung. When removing an item from the wall, be sure to slide your hand underneath the artwork and pull the strips apart directly. Tugging on the quilt or rug may result in the piece tearing before the strip gives way.

A method that museums use if objects are too heavy or delicate to use VELCRO® strips is building a frame that will hold the object on all sides. Mounting fabric is stretched over the entire frame, providing support for the quilt or tapestry. The display piece is then gently sewn to the mounting fabric on all sides. This is a somewhat specialized procedure that you might want a conservator to do.

Floor Carpets and Rugs

Textiles, probably more than any other items in our collections, create a dilemma. On one hand, we want to enjoy the beauty of the object and use it in our daily lives. But on the other hand, to give it the longest life possible, we do not want to use it. Carpets and rugs probably take the biggest beating of anything we have in our collections, and yet they can also be one of the most beautiful and valuable items we own. The dilemma is always present: Should I use it, enjoy it, make it part of my daily life knowing that doing so adds to its demise, or squirrel it away to be loved and appreciated intermittently for a longer period of time? No one can answer this question except the owner, but maybe there is some place between the two extremes where we can find happiness. Many of these considerations are common sense.

Storing carpets and rugs

Do not walk on it. If you can place an antique rug in an area that will get little or no traffic, do so. If this is not possible, perhaps covering it during times of high traffic will help. Use a heavy muslin or canvas cloth to cover a rug at times when you want to protect it. You may decide to protect it from the mishaps and damages of daily life and uncover it when entertaining. Or do the opposite—display it when your house is quiet and you and your partner can enjoy it, then cover it when having that wild party on New Year's. Keep in mind, stiletto heels can be very damaging to antique rugs.

Placing a good quality pad underneath a rug helps reduce wear to the underside. Be sure the padding is made of synthetic fibers rather than rubber or felt. Rubberized pads often contain sulfur, which disintegrates over time. You do not want rubber crumbs embedding themselves into your grandmother's antique Persian rug. The problem with felt padding is that it often contains wool, which tends to attract pests. Pads should be fitted to the individual carpet. They should be cut to within an inch of the carpet's outer edge and should be no more than a quarter of an inch thick.

It is better not to place furniture on top of antique rugs. If you must, do so gingerly. Using furniture coasters, also called caster cups, will offer some protection by providing even weight distribution and will help prevent dents in the rug. Caster cups with spikes facing into the carpet may be an option. Ideally, the spike will separate the fibers rather than push them down. Practicing a little bit of care when installing spiked caster cups will go a long way. Another option is placing square-cut carpet remnants underneath the furniture (obviously not squares cut from your antique rug). If you do not have remnants lying around from a previous carpet, you can probably get some from a local carpet company that might be more than happy to provide you with what you need in a color that will blend with your antique rug. Make sure you know the composition of the fibers and are certain they do not contain dyes that will bleed or cause other damage to your antique rug. Placing a piece of thin white cotton muslin between the rug and the remnants will offer a little protection. Periodically shifting furniture, even an inch or two, will help prevent permanent dents. Do not drag furniture as it can snag fibers and cause damage.

Many older Persian rugs are made from lanolin-rich wool and are amazingly stain resistant. If liquid is spilled on an antique rug, blot; do not rub. Clean from the outside of the spill to the center. If the rug is wool-based and a little soap is needed, try a mild hair shampoo. Use a drop or two at a time and be gentle. If wine is the culprit, blot immediately with clean, dry towels. Do this while you are still entertaining. The next morning, mix a quart of water with one or two drops of a mild liquid detergent such as Ivory soap. Add one to two teaspoons of plain white vinegar. Do not use apple cider vinegar. Moisten. Blot. Moisten. Blot. Repeat until the stain is removed. Then moisten and blot with plain water to rinse out the soap and vinegar. To dry, lift the rug from the surface below and allow air to get to it. Do not leave a wet rug in place for a long time without circulation. Raising the wet area by placing a box under it may be helpful. Do not use home remedies or chemical stain removers. If clear water or a little hair shampoo does not remove the stain, call a conservator or rug specialist.

In the event of a flood, you can hang smaller carpets outside to dry. You will need to use a wet vac to remove the moisture from larger carpets. Do not rub when using the wet vac. Blot. After removing as much water from it as possible, have the rug professionally cleaned and completely dried before placing it back on the floor. Antique Persian rugs should not be dry-cleaned, steam-cleaned, or have moth balls near them. Consult a professional rug cleaner or a conservator.

Never place potted plants on top of antique rugs. Even with plastic basins, moisture can collect below the plant and cause staining or mold. Plants also invite pests that can then find their way into the carpet.

For regular maintenance, it is better to use a non-electric carpet sweeper rather than a vacuum cleaner if the pile of the rug is low enough. You can use a straw bristle broom on any pile rug. Be careful when cleaning hand-woven rugs; vacuum cleaners can pull out fibers, catch knotted fibers, and damage frayed edges. For younger, sturdier rugs, vacuum at the lowest setting in the direction of the pile. Go in one direction only. Do not go back-and-forth. If your vacuum cleaner only has a high setting, consider getting a lighter weight vacuum that has either a lower setting or a lower suction such as a floor sweeper model. Remember, your goal is to preserve the fiber while removing the dirt. Do not use a beater bar—ever.

Embroidery, Cross-Stitch, Lace Doilies

You will naturally want to display embroidery or cross-stitch works in picture frames, but you might also want to consider framing the lace doilies in your care. A friend of mine had a cache of antique doilies that had been in the family for years. One Christmas she framed the doilies and gave them away to her nieces, cousins, and siblings as Christmas gifts. What a great way to preserve a family treasure while at the same time displaying something beautiful in our homes.

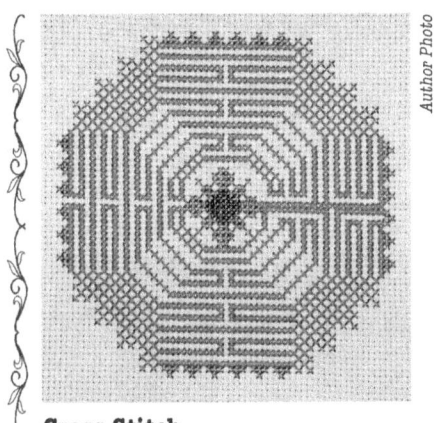
Cross Stitch

Please refer to earlier instructions about where to hang items in your home (away from heat sources, light sources, and with proper heat and humidity levels). When framing any works of art, including textiles, it is best to use UV-filtering acrylic or glass frames. Protective glass or acrylic will also protect the artwork from dirt and dust. Archival-quality framing materials made with acid-free, lignin-free mats and backings are recommended. Use unbuffered materials for silk and wool objects, otherwise choose buffered ones.

Typically, it is better to use acrylic than glass because it is more flexible, less at risk of breaking, and lighter in weight. On the other hand, acrylic tends to be electrostatic, meaning objects stick to it through static electricity. This can be a problem with objects that may already be in a state of deterioration and decay. Be aware that electrostatic properties can pull fragile fibers loose, causing holes or damaging delicate works. If the item you want to frame is in a fragile state, choose glass instead.

Keep in mind, however, that glass comes with its own problems. Mold can easily grow in areas where textiles and glass come in contact, especially in high humidity environments. Textiles should never come in direct contact with glass. An easy way to keep glass and textiles apart is to place an archival mat between them. The fabric will remain securely along the edges underneath the mat, and the mat will provide a small buffering zone between the glass and the textile in the center of the piece. Another method used by museums is mounting small pieces of acrylic in the corners of the piece which raises the glass frame just enough to not touch the fabric. While acrylic is less damaging to framed fabrics, it should not touch the piece directly either. Use the same methods described above to keep the fabric away from the outside frame.

Here are a few other things to keep in mind: Never glue fabric to mounting boards. If I catch you doing this, I will take the piece away. Traditionally, samplers were hung in this way. Glue that was once white or clear turns brown or orange over time, staining anything it comes in contact with. Many once beautiful samplers have been extensively damaged by this traditional framing practice. On top of that, old samplers were glued to highly acidic mounting boards that added their own level of damage to a piece and caused staining, browning, and accelerated deterioration. Once glued, fabric pieces are impossible to remove, and the stains are usually permanent. So sad. When needed, conservators today use special adhesives to repair or restore pieces. I do not recommend using these. If you have a piece that is highly damaged, contact a conservator and let them do what they were trained to do.

> "There's an undeniable connection with all these people. I am connected to them somehow, and these are people that are a part of me as a human."
>
> **AZIZ ANSARI**
> Finding Your Roots, S4.E10

If you have a particularly old piece of embroidery or needlework that is in its original mount, you might want to contact a conservator. Historians and conservators have begun to recognize the historical and monetary value of pieces that are in their original mount. They are looking for ways to conserve the piece whole and are developing new methods all the time.

Flags

When September 11th occurred, many of us displayed flags from our homes and cars in an act of patriotism and unity. I was no exception. I displayed my father's eight-year-old military funeral flag from the front of my house. My Korean War veteran neighbor helped me put it up. It is the only time my father's flag has not been stored away. I was proud to display it at this time of great despair and national pride in our nation's history. While I was happy to add my voice to the mix, I worried the entire time the flag was outside. Fortunately, it never rained during the days I had it up and I was able to put it away with no damage done to it. With that said, you should never display a historical, fragile, or delicate flag outside, ever. The risk of damage from wind, rain, falling leaves, or passing birds is too great.

The best way to display a flag is to lay it flat under glass with a sheet of clean muslin cloth below it. To display a flag upright, follow the directions for hanging quilts and rugs. I know many people display military flags in wooden triangle boxes made for this purpose. As you now know, wood is damaging to textiles. If you have a flag in a wooden box, you should probably rehouse it as soon as possible. Archival supply houses sell acid-free cardboard boxes that are safer for flags. If you want to keep the flag in the wooden box, you should line the interior with acid-free cardboard or white muslin and check and change it regularly—at least once a year. The other thing to consider with the triangular wooden display boxes is that the glass or acrylic covering should have UV filtering. If this is not the case, you can move the flag to an area of your home where it will not receive as much sunlight or direct light from fluorescent bulbs.

Upholstery

Do not sit on furniture that is old and creaky. Keep pets off and do not eat on it. Do not smoke on or around it. Do not place antique furniture in direct sunlight and keep furniture covered when not in use or on display. When entertaining, remove the item from the living area if that is possible. If not, either put a cord over the front edge of a chair or sofa or put a slipcover or sheet over the chair. You could make little "Please don't sit on me" signs and place them strategically on the furniture. If food or

Antique Tapestry Chair

drink is spilled, blot it up as soon as possible. Do not rub the spill; pat it with a clean sponge or cotton cloth. Sometimes it is better to let a food item dry first, then vacuum it through a mesh screen. If antique upholstery is stained, contact a dry cleaner that specializes in antiques or a conservator. If the fabric is torn or ripped, contact a textile conservator for repair. As discussed earlier, we interact with textiles so frequently and regularly, it is easy to be fooled into thinking we can fix anything. But even expert tailors or seamstresses should contact a conservator if their antique fabric is torn. Antique fabrics have special needs that textile conservators are specifically trained to address.

Vacuum regularly to keep dust and minor residue from building. Follow the instructions above on how to vacuum through a mesh screen.

You should keep the original upholstery intact if possible. The piece of furniture will retain its highest value with the upholstery still intact. If this is not possible, keep the upholstery and either store it as you would any other textile, or consider donating it to the appropriate museum or archive that may be interested in such a piece.

SECTION TWO

THE DIGITAL WORLD

CHAPTER 9

DIGITAL BASICS

I'm climbing
Higher mountains
Trying to get home
I'm going up the Side of the mountain
On my way home (meet my people)
Trying to get home
Climbing the rough side of the mountain
On my way home

—**Aretha Franklin,** *Climbing Higher Mountains*

As I write this chapter, Hurricane Harvey recently devastated the Houston area of Texas, Hurricane Irma is bearing down on Florida, and Hurricane Jose is out at sea posing another potential threat. Meanwhile out west, twenty-seven wildfires are destroying homes and properties in several states. I can imagine that while you are reading this, other weather disasters are taking place somewhere in the world. It is part of daily life in the age of global warming.

Damage from a Natural Disaster

Faced with these life-altering events, victims' first concerns are that they and their loved ones, including pets, have weathered the event safely. Television interviews show that once people determine all family members have survived, their next concern is not for their houses, their cars, or their clothing. Standing in the devastation of their burned down homes, victims cry over the loss of their photographs and memorabilia. The pain is particularly hard when losing memories of loved ones who are no longer with us. I watch the devastation today knowing that entire family legacies have drowned in the Texas floods and burned in the California wildfires. Taking preliminary steps well before a disaster occurs can ensure that our memories will live on regardless of the catastrophes we may have to endure.

Natural disasters are not the only cause for alarm of the potential loss of precious memories. The only childhood picture my friend has of herself shows her feeding a carrot to a horse when she was about five years old. Otherwise, there are no baby pictures of her at all. A fire in her parent's first apartment burned all the memories of her early years. While not as catastrophic as losing generations of photographs, not having any pictures from infancy is sad and difficult. A house fire, a burst pipe, backed-up sewage, and any number of personal misfortunes can quickly and permanently destroy our family memories.

Today you do not need to experience such catastrophic losses. You can digitize your entire collection, and if a wildfire, hurricane, tornado, flood, burst pipe, or house fire happens, you can print everything out again and recapture your family history. I wonder how many of the thousands of families who experienced these disastrous events this summer have secured their families' legacies in this way. I would venture to guess not many. Most of the recent pictures you have taken with digital cameras or cell phones will be preserved. But the photographs of grandparents as children, great-grandparents, and baby pictures of older generations could be lost forever.

The information in this chapter is technical, and in some cases, difficult to digest. I know some of you are more tech savvy than others, so I provide as much information as possible for the techies. If you are tech shy and the information seems overwhelming, don't panic. Read through the information, take what makes sense, and leave the rest. Or, skip over it and go right to Chapter 12 to learn which file formats to use for the best practices in digital preservation.

THE DIGITAL WORLD

Before we begin, let's consider the digital world. What is it exactly? Most of us spend a great deal of time in the digital world and we basically, kind of, sort of know what it is. A little specific knowledge of what happens inside your computer may help make the following discussion a little clearer.

Computers operate on a binary system. Binary systems relate to, are composed of, or involve two things. The two "things" inside a computer are categorized as 0s and 1s. This is the binary system of the computer world and the World Wide Web. But really, there are not a bunch of zeros and ones floating around inside the computer. The zeros and ones represent on and off switches that signify either low electrical frequencies or high electrical frequencies. Ones represent "on," and zeros represent "off." In a sense it is like standing in your bedroom and flashing the light switch on and off very quickly. The on and off switches happen in micro-milliseconds based on what a human programmer tells it to do.

Even though we do not always think about it, we are aware that what we see on the computer screen are electrical impulses. We understand the difference between a painting made up of paper and oil paints and a digital image of a painting that is an electrical vibrating light display that disappears once we close the browser or image.

The Binary System

Let's go back to the light switch analogy. Flicking on and off in patterns will create different things. As an example, we are all familiar with the first four notes of Beethoven's 5th Symphony: Da-da-da-daaaaa. Imagine that those four notes translate to the color red in computer impulses. A programmer would enter those four notes of code each time they wanted something to appear red. Apply this concept to every color, letter, sound, image, motion, and everything else that appears on our computer screens. That is what is basically happening inside our computers—patterns of flickering light programmed to display different things.

While we see a red balloon on our computer screen, the computer is translating reams of code to display a million pixels of different shades of red color, tone, shading, hue, and contrast. While we hear a beautiful melody on our iPods, the computer is reading hundreds of tiny sound bites all put together to emit what sounds like one complete piece of music. These tiny pixels all come together to display an image, make a moving image, or create sound that is seamless to the human eye and ear. Understanding that the computer is only reading code and creating electrical impulses based on that code helps conceptualize what happens to our digital images and audio/video files when they are displayed and stored. Seeing our digital data from the computer's perspective helps determine the best long-term storage options for our digital content.

BORN DIGITAL VS. DIGITIZED

The term "born digital" refers to documents, photographs, audio files, video files, and other items that begin life in digital format. Archivists distinguish born digital items from items that begin life in the material or non-digital world by using the term "analog." This is not the proper use of the word, but it is rooted in the difference between tape recordings made with an analog tape recorder and the digital audio files that replaced them. It became a sort of shorthand in the archives field that was eventually expanded to include other non-digital, material items as well.

ARCHIVES TIP

Archivists make a distinction between *digital archiving*, which is the preservation of born digital information, and *digital preservation*, which is the preservation of print materials through digitization.

Archivists also make a distinction between *digital archiving*, which is the preservation of born digital information, and *digital preservation*, which is the preservation of print materials through digitization. In this section, we will first discuss digital preservation and learn how to digitize print materials and audio/video recordings. Later in the section, we will discuss digital archiving and how to obtain long-term preservation for born digital documents and digitized analog documents.

If we digitize our entire collection, our born digital and born analog items will ultimately end up in the same place on our hard drives and in our backup storage drives. Our future descendants might have a hard time distinguishing between born digital and digitized documents. A digitized handwritten document will be obviously digitized, but photographs and other materials might be harder to tell apart. We have a responsibility to inform Baby 2135 what is what.

If you have taken the steps outlined in the earlier chapters to process the material portion of your collection, deciding what to digitize will be easier. When surveying and processing your material items you should have done some weeding and gotten rid of duplicate photographs and unnecessary papers. If everything is nice and organized in archival boxes, polyester sheets, and archival photo albums, the digitization process will be much easier. It is not critical to have the processing portion of your project complete first, but it will avoid duplication and might save you from unnecessarily digitizing certain items. Also, when striving to create a comprehensive organizational system, processing and organizing the analog materials first will make the digital organization process smoother and easier.

Ultimately, the challenge is to organize, store, and make available digital documents for periods longer than a human lifetime. When thinking of long-term digital preservation, consider the different components that comprise digital access.

Preservation of the Medium

What are the lifespans of different media? How long will a CD, DVD, hard drive, thumb drive, or computer last? CDs are determined to not reliably last more than fifteen to twenty years. If air gets through the plastic coating, the metal reflective layer corrodes. Gold CDs could possibly last up to 100 years, but as of today this has not been tested because gold CDs were developed less than 100 years ago. Magnetic tapes have a lifespan of thirty years at best. The lifespan of flash drives is no more than ten years or up to 100,000 erase-rewrite cycles. Hard drives are determined to last no longer than three to five years while in active use and possibly up to thirty years in an archival setting. It is difficult to know how long most media will last because the technology is new and has not yet been tested.

Technology Preservation

Technology preservation refers primarily to the software programs that allow digital information to be read. As software is upgraded and changed, our digital documents must be refreshed, migrated, copied, upgraded, or imported into the new technology; otherwise, they will not work. This can be the most challenging aspect of digital preservation. However, certain file formats provide better options for long-term storage. Programming languages (unlike programs or applications) are unlikely to disappear and can be used as alternative mechanisms for long-term preservation.

> *"You base who you are on your immediate lineage and so if there are gaps in that and mysteries in that, there are mysteries in you." "*
>
> **ALAN CUMMINGS**
> WDYTYA-UK.7.9

Intellectual Preservation

Intellectual preservation refers to keeping the integrity and authenticity of the information as it was originally recorded. This is particularly true of photographs and video. Digital photographs and media can be copied quickly and easily. You might assume that they are being copied exactly. But while copying is easy and simple, undetectable changes may also be made that, over time, will alter the integrity of the original. Eventually, you don't know whether you are looking at an original or a copy, or whether the dress was bright red or deep red in the original. This is similar to copying a document repeatedly on a copy machine. Over time the integrity of the original is lost becoming fuzzier and fuzzier and probably speckled and eventually unreadable. Your goal as a family archivist is to keep things as unaltered as possible in perpetuity.

TERMS

It will be helpful to understand a few terms before we proceed. The first few terms describe different types of file formats. The next few terms describe compression types.

- ✓ **File Formats:** a standard way information is encoded for storage in a computer file.
- ✓ **Extension:** the three or four letters after a file name, preceded by a dot, which are automatically added and identify the type of file. Examples are .docx, .pdf, .jpeg, and .mov.
- ✓ **Proprietary:** a file format that is developed and owned by a software company, organization, or individual that keeps secret its properties and structure.
- ✓ **Non-Proprietary or Free:** a published specification usually maintained by a standards organization which can be used and implemented by anyone.
- ✓ **Open:** a file format that is freely available online.
- ✓ **Unpublished:** a file format code that is kept by the developer.
- ✓ **Compression:** a term used to describe the reduction in file size created when saving a digital document, image, audio, or video file. When a file is compressed, two actions occur. First, it is compressed upon saving. Second, it is decompressed when opened or during playback. Types of compression include the following:
    - ✓ **Lossy:** compression that results in permanent loss of data usually associated with image, audio, and video files. The decompressed data will not be identical to the original. Typically, the lost data is imperceptible to the human eye or ear. If it is perceptible, it may appear as jagged edges, pixelated areas, a watery sound in audio files, or blurred video images. The tradeoff between using lossy or lossless is file size over image quality.
    - ✓ **Lossless:** compression that is mathematically reversible and results in no loss of quality. It allows the decompressed data to be exactly the same, bit for bit. The disadvantage is larger file size.
        - ✓ **Visually lossless:** essentially the same as lossy compression. Loss of data occurs but not enough to be visible to the naked eye.
        - ✓ **Mathematically lossless:** no data is lost during compression and decompression.
- ✓ **CoDec:** short for "coder-decoder." In media files, encoded data must be decoded to be played back. CoDec is different from compression/decompression, but most CoDecs do compress the original data and reduce the original file size. CoDecs can be lossless, meaning the quality of the original medium is not reduced, or lossy, meaning some data is lost and can result in reduced quality.

- ✓ **Metadata:** means "data about data." There are two types of metadata. The first describes the technical and structural data that is automatically created by a file format. Technical metadata may include the file format (docx, jpg), the size of the document in pixels, and who it was created by. The second type of metadata is the information we add to describe a computer file as a document, an image, an audio file, or a video file. You can find technical file metadata by right-clicking on the file name and selecting Properties.

- ✓ **ISO Standard:** International Standards Organization. This is an independent, non-governmental international organization with a membership of 161 national standards bodies. It brings together experts to share knowledge and develop voluntary, consensus-based, and market-relevant international standards.[29] ISO provides specifications for products, services, and systems to ensure quality, safety, and efficiency to facilitate international trade.

File Formats

A file format is a standard way that information is encoded for storage in a computer file. It specifies how bits are used to encode information in a digital storage medium (e.g., computer, CD, DVD, flash drive). File formats may be either **proprietary** or **free** and can be either **unpublished** (meaning the code is kept by the developer) or **open source** (meaning it is freely available online). Examples of open formats include PNG for images, FLAC for lossless audio CoDec, WebM for a video/audio container format, or HTML as a markup language used to create web pages. Examples of closed proprietary formats are PSD by Adobe Photoshop, used for its native image format, and WMA owned by Microsoft. Many of us are familiar with DOC or XLS, the file extensions for Microsoft Word and Microsoft Excel. These were formerly closed/undocumented but are now part of the Microsoft Open Specification Promise. This is a promise to not sue people who use their specifications, although it does not confer any rights.

File formats are identified by their extensions, which are the three or four letters at the end of a file that are automatically added to the name we give it. For example, you may save a Microsoft Word document as "MyGreatAmericanNovel." When you look at the file, you notice it has either .doc or .docx at the end of it. The extension tells the computer how to read that particular file. For our purposes, we want to use file formats that have a higher likelihood of long-term digital storage and long-term digital preservation. We will be limiting the file formats to a few types based on ISO standards and Library of Congress recommendations.

Refer to Chapters 11 and 12 to learn about the best file formats to use for long-term preservation. Those chapters indicate which file formats are either ***best practice*** or ***good practice*** for each type of digital object you may have. If you are only interested in knowing how to store items for long-term preservation, you can skip to those chapters. Because I know you probably have many different types of file formats on your computer, and you may possibly have documents in file formats that will not open and are not accessible, I want to help you understand the different file formats and their history and provide the information you need to extrapolate the data and preserve it for future use. This section provides that understanding.

Caroline Arms and Carl Fleischhauer of the Office of Strategic Initiatives at the Library of Congress list seven general rules for libraries to use when selecting file formats. These are good rules of thumb for anybody, and you should incorporate these rules when creating your digital family archive:

- ✓ **Avoid Using Proprietary Formats.** Use open-source, non-proprietary formats whenever possible.

- ✓ **Use Popular Formats.** Popular formats are less likely to become obsolete quickly, and tools for migration are more likely to be developed by the industry. In the list below, some non-proprietary formats supersede proprietary ones for archival purposes due to their open-source status. However, certain popular formats are acceptable even though they are proprietary, based on their popularity and commonality of use.

- ✓ **Ensure Transparency.** Formats should use standard character encodings written in plain language with no encryption.

- ✓ **Incorporate Self-Documentation.** Basic descriptive metadata should be embedded in the object. This is the metadata that is a part of a picture indicating the size, the ratio, and other information about the file itself, not the metadata you will add that describes what is in the picture.

- ✓ **Understand External Dependencies.** The more a format relies on one particular software program, the less desirable it is as an archival tool.

- ✓ **Know About Patents.** Patents are less of an issue for individuals who are using proprietary software or file formats for personal use. However, an awareness of what is patented and what is not is good knowledge to have.

9: DIGITAL BASICS

- ✓ **Avoid Encryption.** Encryption potentially renders files useless if the file cannot be opened, migrated, or replicated. This means do not password protect an archival document.

Armed with the basics, let's move on and look at the file formats that are available for the different types of documents and files we may have in our care. Organized by types of media, this list is a basic overview. Determining which type of file formats are ***best practice*** and which are ***good practice*** is discussed in more depth in Chapter 11.

Text Formats

- ✓ **TXT** (Plain Text) format can be opened by any word processor. It is *non-proprietary*. The drawback is that it has limited formatting capabilities. Font styles such as bold, underline, and italics as well as font sizes, tables, images, and multimedia will not translate into a TXT file. The text will be available, but the original look and feel of a document may be lost. The program Notepad creates TXT files by default.

- ✓ **RTF** (Rich Text Format) is a *proprietary* program developed by Microsoft from 1987 to 2008. RTF documents can be opened in a variety of programs. They have some formatting such as font style, size, and color. The program WordPad creates RTF files by default. Not every program will open files in this format and the formatting is limited.

- ✓ **ODF** (Open Document Format) is an umbrella term used to encompass several other specific file formats. As of 2006, ODF is an ISO international standard, *non-proprietary,* and *open-source* format. Apache Open Office is a freely available open-source software program that creates this file format by default. ODF is one of the file formats preferred by the Library of Congress.
    - ✓ **ODT** format is used for text documents.
    - ✓ **ODS** format is used for spreadsheets.
    - ✓ **ODP** format is used for presentations (similar to PowerPoint).

- ✓ **PDF** (Portable Document Format) was created and is maintained by Adobe. Originally proprietary, PDF has been non-propriety and open since July 1, 2008, when control was passed to an ISO Committee. Text and multimedia are supported in PDF. Images, video, or audio files will be saved with a PDF document and transported with it in the event it is moved. PDF also has searchable text, bookmarks, highlighting, and hypertext links. PDF is an acceptable format approved by the Library of Congress.

- ✓ **PDF-A** (Portable Document Format/Archives) is a preferred format by the Library of Congress. It is an approved ISO standard that is *open-source* and *non-proprietary*. The ISO standard requires this format to be backward compatible, meaning that newer versions can read older versions. The limitations of PDF-A are that it does not allow audio or video embedding, the use of executable files like JavaScript, or encryption. These limitations are to ensure the file will always be displayed as the original. To read them, video and audio files are dependent on other programs external to PDF. When possible, use PDF-A, but if you have documents with audio or video clips, use PDF instead.

- ✓ **DOC or DOCX** format was developed by Microsoft Word. It is *proprietary* and must be opened with Microsoft Word. Complicating things further, earlier versions of Word files may not open or function properly in newer versions of the same program. Microsoft documents including Word, Excel, and PowerPoint can easily be saved in other file formats. Follow the path File\Save As\Other Formats and scroll through the list until you find the format you want.

Text documents

- ✓ **HTML** (HyperText Markup Language) is a language, not a file format. It is used to create web pages and for sharing information online. As a language it is not dependent on any software company, search engine, or web browser. A document created in HTML can be read by any number of browsers. It is created in a word processing program (typically Notepad), saved as a TXT file or WordPad, saved as an RTF file. HTML documents look like plain text. Any special fonts, colors, images, or audio files are encoded in the language. The language itself uses standard terms. For example, the HTML text will **bold** the word text.

To view HTML coding, go to any web page, right-click, and select View Source. (Okay, if that just scared you, move on. You do not need to know this to archive your family records. I share this for people who did not get scared.) HTML files can host image files and audio or video files; however, the files are separate and are kept in separate folders. The HTML document directs the browser to look in a specific place for the specific file. The advantage of using HTML is that documents created using this language can be displayed online. HTML documents are stored in TXT or RTF format and are therefore very small files that can be easily transmitted online. Documents that contain images, audio clips, or video clips can be retained as long as the linked files are kept with the HTML file. HTML is a great tool if you want to link multiple files.

9: DIGITAL BASICS

Coding in HTML might be a great option for those who are tech savvy and want to create a family or personal archive. While the language evolves and some instructions become obsolete, chances are a descendant could clean up an HTML file and replace the old terms with new ones. A disadvantage is that different browsers interpret the information differently. Also, it is difficult to keep the links that point to stored pictures and video/audio files unbroken. They should all be put in one folder, but even then, a descendant would have to relink them to have them reattached and working properly. Relinking can be done at any time as long as the files are kept together. It is not difficult; it just needs to be done.

HTML Code

Images/Photographs

- ✓ **BMP** (Bitmap) is an older file format that opens with many but not all programs. It cannot be compressed and cannot be transmitted over the internet.

- ✓ **TIFF** (Tagged Image File Format) can be either lossless or lossy. TIFF files are usually not compressed and are usually large file sizes. TIFFS are considered best practices for digital image preservation by the Library of Congress. However, due to their large file size, other methods might be preferable. See Chapter 11 for further discussion on best practices versus good practices.

- ✓ **GIF** (Graphics Interchange Format) limits images to 256 colors (from sixteen million possible choices), which requires fewer bits per pixel and results in smaller file sizes. GIFs can be easily compressed to even smaller sizes. GIFs work best with and are often used for images with few colors, such as line art, logos, or grayscale images. GIFs can be animated, but they do not replicate full-color photographs well.

- ✓ **PNG** (Portable Network Graphics) format improves on GIFs by using more colors with higher lossless compression and smaller file sizes. PNGs are designed to be used on the internet and cannot be animated. PNGs are not supported in many software programs.

- ✓ **JPEG or JPG** (Joint Photographic Experts Group) format can be highly compressed using lossy compression. Because information is lost with each compression and decompression, JPGs can become corrupted over time. However, it is a good choice for photographs and complex images, is commonly used, and is recommended by the Library of Congress for general public use.

Digital photographs can be formatted as BMP, TIFF, GIF, PN, JPEG, SVG or others

- ✓ **SVG** (Scalable Vector Graphics) format saves images by their shape rather than by individual pixels. The greatest benefit of SVG files is that they can be enlarged or reduced without losing image integrity.

- ✓ **Native Formats.** The formats listed above are general and can be read by many different software programs. File formats that are created in certain software programs are native to that software and can only be read by that specific software program. For example, the extension .psd is created by Photoshop and can only be read by that program. If you have photographs or other files in formats you do not recognize, the best thing to do is search online. There are many smart people out there with great advice on how to open these files and possibly convert them to better file formats. It is beyond the scope of this book to list each possible file format and the instructions for transferring them to better file formats.

Audio Data Formats

- ✓ **AIFF** (Audio Interchange File Format) is a *proprietary* format developed by Apple and is similar to and interchangeable with WAV files.
- ✓ **BWF** (Broadcast Wave Format) is a *proprietary* type of WAV file that allows for adding metadata in the header. It is used primarily by television and radio stations.
- ✓ **FLAC** (Free Format Lossless Audio CoDec) is a *non-proprietary* lossless file format similar to MP3 that is unlicensed and free. FLAC is compatible with most operating systems, including Microsoft Windows, OS/2, Unix, and Linux. Playback on portable audio devices is limited.

- ✓ **MIDI** (Musical Instrument Digital Interface) files create synthesized music and are not recordings of real music. MIDI files are instructions for a synthesizer to play a sound, piece of music, or particular instrument. MIDI files are used by the music industry and are common in video games.

- ✓ **MP3** is short for MPEG-1: Audio Layer 3. MPEG stands for Moving Pictures Experts Group, an alliance that developed the standards for video compression. It is an ISO standard. The coding for MP3 was patented, resulting in several lawsuits. As of 2017, the patent has expired in all countries, so this should no longer be an issue. Also, in most cases, using patented items for personal, non-commercial use is not prosecutable. Most of us are familiar with MP3s. They are very popular and most likely you have them somewhere on your computer, if only in the form of purchased music files. MP3 is an audio file format considered acceptable by the Library of Congress for archival purposes. MP3s are highly efficient at compressing audio files using the lossy method. During compression, the file removes or reduces sounds not detectable to the human ear. The files are reduced in size, so they take up less storage space on hard drives.

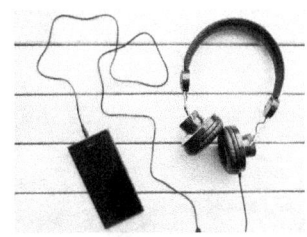

Digital Audio Files can be formatted as AIFF, BWF, FLAC, MIDI, MP3, QT, RA, WAV, or WMA

- ✓ **QT** (QuickTime) was developed by Apple and is *proprietary*.

- ✓ **RA** (Real Audio) requires a Real Audio player, so this format is not practical for archival purposes.

- ✓ **WAV** (Waveform Audio File) format is *proprietary*. It was originally created by Microsoft and IBM and is commonly used. WAV is the main file format used in Microsoft Windows. It is compatible with Windows, Macintosh, and Linux operating systems and can be compressed, but it is typically uncompressed. WAV files can be tagged with metadata, making them suitable for archiving. WAV stores both mono and stereo sound. Because WAV files are usually uncompressed, they are often large.

- ✓ **WMA** (Windows Media Audio) is part of the Advanced Systems Format, which is a Microsoft *proprietary* digital audio format primarily meant for streaming media. This file format is licensed, is not distributable, and is not compatible with open-source licenses.

Video Data Formats

- ✓ **MPEG,** as we just learned, is an alliance that developed standards for audio/video files. MP3 audio files are part of this group. MPEG-4 is used for transmitting video data online. MPEG-2 is for general use with video data and can create highly compressed lossy video files. Similar to the way MP3s condense data by removing sound files undetectable to the human ear, MPEG-2 removes video frames that have no detectable change from one frame to the next in a video stream. Typically, video files have thirty frames per second, so losing a few per second does not alter the visual end-product but reduces the file size and saves space on hard drives. Since MPEG-2 uses lossy compression, it is less preferable, although it is an acceptable format for archival purposes.

Video files can be formatted as JPEG2000, MOV, WMV, AVI or others

- ✓ **Motion JPEG 2000** is preferred by archivists, is an open ISO standard with a lossless CoDec, and results in very little loss of information during compression. Rather than losing frames as with lossy compression, in Motion JPEG 2000 format each frame is individually compressed.

- ✓ **MOV, WMV, AVI.** A **MOV** is a type of video format used in Apple's QuickTime program. **WMV** stands for Windows Media File and **AVI** stands for Audio Video Interleaved file, both of which were created by Microsoft. All three formats are *proprietary.* They are very common, and many software applications will run them. They are not desirable as an archival standard, however, due to their proprietary status.

- ✓ **Flash** format was developed by Micromedia and is now owned by Adobe. Flash files have the extensions FLA or FLV. Flash animations are often used online or as part of web pages.

DATA STORAGE

Our digital data is stored on many different types of devices, from computer hard drives to CDs, thumb drives, and magnetic media. These devices are made up of different materials that are all at risk of deterioration and have limited lifespans. While obsolescence causes problems as more advanced

9: DIGITAL BASICS   163

systems are developed, it is plain ol' deterioration that leads to the loss or inaccessibility of data. A brief look at the types of media on which we store digital documents and the ways they deteriorate will help you make decisions about where to store and where to back up your data. It will also provide a deeper understanding of the importance of using the "3-2-1 Rule" described in Chapter 10.

All methods of computer memory storage use some form of binary encoding. As discussed earlier, all data is encoded as either on/off or light/dark that computers read as zeros and ones. The only requirement needed for an effective encoding of binary data is some kind of either/or condition. As you will learn, each method of memory storage uses a different mechanism that ultimately translates to the same thing in computer-speak.

Optical Storage – CDs, DVDs, Blu-Ray

CD stands for compact disc. Compact discs are a form of optical media that are read by a laser. CDs do not require a magnetic charge, which means that they are less likely to lose data and have a longer shelf life. Some estimates indicate that the shelf life of a CD could be seven times longer than a magnetic medium form such as a computer hard drive.[30] CDs are cheap to produce, making them a desirable form of backup storage. All basic CDs record data on one side of a single disc. Many types of compact discs are available and in use today:

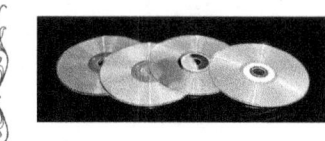

Compact Discs

- ✓ **CD-ROM** (Compact Disc Read-Only-Memory) discs can only be read by computers. The information on a CD-ROM cannot be altered by computers, which makes them a great backup storage mechanism for archival purposes.

- ✓ **CD-DA** (Compact Disc Digital Audio) discs are used for commercially produced music and can be played in any CD player including a computer, an automobile media player, or a dedicated CD player. When transferring music to a CD, you can usually choose to create it as a CD-ROM, which limits its use to a computer, or a CD-DA, which allows it to be played in any media player.

- ✓ **CD-R** (Compact Disc Recordable) discs are blank CDs with no information encoded until the user "burns" the information onto them. If CDs are one of the backup media choices you have made, CD-Rs are what you want to use. The information can be recorded but not written over.

- ✓ **CD-RW** (Compact Disc Rewritable) discs, as the name suggests, can be used repeatedly to overwrite information. A rewritable CD is convenient to use in your daily life because you continually change information and want to make sure the most updated version is saved. For archival purposes, however, CD-RW is not the best choice. Once you have established the information as part of your archive, you want to ensure that others cannot overwrite the data.
- ✓ **DVDs** (Digital Versatile Discs) are large-capacity compact discs that can hold multiple layers of data. DVDs can have two layers of information on one disc, and those can both be double sided. This essentially quadruples the information capacity of a regular CD. In DVDs, the aluminum layer found in CDs is replaced with semi-reflective silicon, gold, or silver. Storage capacity of a DVD is 17GB.
- ✓ **Blu-ray** is the largest capacity optical storage medium, having multiple layers that allow up to 128 GB of storage.[31] It requires a specialized reader that uses a blue laser instead of a red laser to read it. The blue laser allows more information to be stored and read. Blu-ray discs come in BD-ROM, for use with computers, BD-R, which are recordable, and BD-RE, which are rewritable.

Archival Storage of Optical Media

Like any other objects stored in our family archives, we have to consider the material needs and problems associated with optical media. CDs are readily available at any office supply store or archival supplier and through our favorite online stores. The life span of optical media depends on many factors, including the environment and the materials they are made from. Disks using gold as the reflective metal layer is the optimal storage material since gold is a noble metal and not subject to corrosion. Silver is a second alternative, and silver alloy is a third option. The cost of purchasing these materials may be prohibitive for the average consumer. Gold CD-Rs can cost hundreds of dollars. It is often hard to find them in smaller quantities that would be more practical for the average user.

Archival Storage for Optical Media

Some manufacturers claim gold CD's will last up to 300 years. This would be under ideal conditions with little use and a perfect environment. It is hard to know the life expectancy of gold CDs because they have not been tested yet. Under good conditions, it is highly probable that they will last up to 100 years.

- ✓ **Temperature** – It is essential that discs are stored in a good environment. Disks are highly sensitive to both heat and cold. The optimal temperature range is between 39° and 68°F.[32]

- ✓ **Light** – Sunlight is obviously damaging to CDs. They must be kept away from windows and direct sunlight and should always be stored in jewel cases. Ideally, they should also be stored in cardboard cases that will reduce the exposure to the environment and sunlight. Remember, our archival materials are like vampires; they like it cool and dark.

- ✓ **Humidity** – Moisture can be absorbed through the polycarbonate base of a CD and penetrate to the metallic center layer. Depending on the type of metal used in the metallic layer, this can be catastrophic. As we have already learned, the greatest cause of moisture in our collection is humidity. Optical discs need to be stored at RH levels between 20% and 50%.[33]

- ✓ **Handling** – Back in the old days when we listened to vinyl music on record players, there was nothing worse than a scratch right at the favorite part of our favorite song. As a result, we learned to handle our albums and 45s with great care. Those lessons will serve us well in knowing how to handle CDs, DVDs, and Blu-ray discs.

    Like you did with your albums, always pick up discs by the edges. Never touch the shiny writable surface area of a CD, and handle CDs as little as possible. When working with many at once, wear soft cotton archival gloves to keep skin oils and dirt off CDs and to reduce the likelihood of scratches. Disks should be stored vertically like books. Do not lay them flat or stack them on top of each other. Keep optical discs inside plastic jewel cases or protective sleeves. I recommend an additional storage casing that will keep out sunlight and add an additional layer of protection. This can be Tyvek or polypropylene sleeves, CD bulk storage boxes, CD bins, or CD albums.

- ✓ **Labeling** – Although the top lacquer layer on optical media can withstand more handling than the shiny bottom layer, archival materials that we want to have last for a hundred years or more should use different standards than the media we employ for everyday use. It is common for people to add paper labels to the outside of CDs or scrawl on CDs with magic marker, but these practices are not sound for archival materials.

Do not stick anything on the outside of a CD. Ball-point pens and pencils can damage CDs; if you press down too hard, they can distort the information on the disc. Felt-tip pens are preferable, but those that are solvent-based rather than water-based can be damaging. Since we do not know the long-term consequences of writing directly onto discs, do not take any chances. Writing directly on the disc is riskier for DVDs and Blu-ray discs that have writing on both sides of the inner metallic center.

When labeling optical media, write in small letters on the inner circle where no data is below. This may limit what you write, but as you have learned by labeling your photographs, you can develop a reference system if necessary.

- ✓ **Cleaning and Maintenance** – Because optical discs require a laser beam to shine through the base layer to the metallic inner layer, fingerprints, smudges, and scratches can compromise performance. If you store and handle discs properly, you may never need to clean them. But if your discs become dusty or dirty, you can blow the dirt off using the same photographic air blaster described in the section called "Canned Air" in Chapter 11. (Note: this is not the canned air purchased in most office supply or computer supply stores.) Another option is using a soft, lint-free, clean, dry cotton cloth. If the disc is still dirty, try a commercial optical disc-cleaning solution or common isopropyl alcohol. When cleaning, move left and right over the area containing data. Do not clean in a circular motion.

Like all digital media, we cannot "store and ignore." Make a date with yourself to periodically check the condition of your CDs. This means pulling them out of archival storage, popping them into a CD player, and making sure the information is still accessible. Since you will be using the 3-2-1 backup method described in Chapter 10, the data on these discs should not be your only storage mechanism.

The following are a few problems to consider when storing optical discs:

- ✓ **Laser Rot** – This term describes optical media discs on which the shiny metallic layer has become damaged in some way through corrosion, discoloration, or pitting, rendering the information unreadable. Laser rot often occurs when the lacquer

- ✓ or polycarbonate protective layers have been compromised in some way and atmospheric conditions penetrate to the metallic layer.
- ✓ **Dye Stability** – Dyes are used in CD-Rs, DVD-Rs, and BD-Rs to create the light and dark areas on the discs that produce the binary system necessary for the computer to read them. This makes them highly sensitive to heat and light. Some dyes are more stable than others. Phthalocyanine tends to be the most stable dye, cyanine is moderately stable, and azo is the least stable. Without standardization and regulation, you may not be aware of what kind of dye was used in the manufacture of the disc.
- ✓ **Storage** – Because of the limited space on optical media, and depending on the amount of material you need to store on them, the number of discs you need to back up your entire family archive may be prohibitive. For most people this will not be a problem, but I know of several professional and amateur photographers who use huge amounts of data storage with the images they have amassed over many years. The number of CDs needed to back up their entire collection may be too great, especially considering that other mechanisms can store greater quantities of data more efficiently.
- ✓ **CD Readers** – Another thing to consider is that CD readers are no longer standard in many computers and laptops. Today it is easy to purchase an external CD player, but it is possible that CD players will be unavailable or hard to come by in a hundred years.

Magnetic Tapes

Our most familiar association with magnetic media is music cassette and 8-track tapes. Floppy disks are another form of magnetic media that stores data on round film enclosed in a square casing of soft or hard material. The construction of all these types of tapes is the same.

Magnetic tapes can store enormous amounts of data. Magnetic media is one of the oldest methods of data storage and has been used for decades. Originally invented in 1898, magnetic tape was used to record sound by 1928. Before the advent of computers, magnetic media was used to record speeches and radio programs. Today, while the medium is not commonly used with personal computers, many small businesses still use it. The lifespan of magnetic tapes is typically ten to thirty years, although the oldest known is sixty years old.

Data Storage – Magnetic Tapes

When data is backed up onto a magnetic tape, the computer decides where the data will end up on the tape. In other words, cassette tapes that store music are read sequentially from one end to another logically—as our brain thinks. Magnetic computer data is stored using a term called "direct access." The reader head for a magnetic tape is on an arm that can move up and down. The tape itself can move back-and-forth. When recording data on a magnetic tape, the reader is able to access it by using its moving arm that reads across nine rows of magnetized dust. The reader head moves forward and backward to find the exact spot for storing the data. Direct access is quicker than sequential access because the reader can hop to the right location immediately rather than needing to sequentially fast forward or reverse through all the data on the tape.

Magnetic Tapes

Tape storage may seem a bit old-fashioned, but it is a medium that continues to be improved upon and updated.[34] Magnetic tapes tend to be inexpensive, especially for the amount of storage space they offer. Tapes come in standard sizes, which is important for compatibility with other tapes produced by different manufacturers. Typical size ranges for magnetic tapes are between 20GB and 800GB of compressed data, but you can purchase some tapes that can hold up to thirty-five terabytes (TB) of information. Compare that to CDs that hold about 700 MB of information. Depending on the size and type of materials in your archive, tape might be a good option. Another advantage of tape is that it has been around for a long time and its limitations are well understood, unlike some of the more modern storage mechanisms such as CDs and flash memory. Tapes require special equipment to read them. This has both advantages and disadvantages. The advantage is that a thief is highly unlikely to steal magnetic media and discover the sensitive data within. The disadvantage is that unless Baby 2135 has a tape player, they are also not going to be able to access the information.

Magnetic tapes are best used if you need to store large amounts of information. If your archive is on the small or average size, another medium might be preferable. To use magnetic tapes, you will need to buy a tape drive with the right software and hook it up to your computer to read and write data. Magnetic tape can also be on the delicate side, needing proper temperature and humidity controls. Dust or dirt on the tape can hinder its ability to be read properly, and the plastic bottom layer can warp or stick. Writing and reading data on magnetic tape is slower than other forms of data storage. Overplaying or reading the tape can also wear it out, so magnetic media are best as long-term storage options. There is also the possibility that the equipment needed to read a magnetic tape could become obsolete.

Archival Storage of Magnetic Tapes

Temperature

Store tapes at 68°F (20°C). Storing them in higher temperatures can result in warped plastic and increased degradation rates. Be mindful of localized heat sources such as radiators or heating units. Temperatures that are too low can also be a problem. Make sure tapes do not freeze; if they do, do not play them until they have had at least twenty-four hours to acclimate to room temperature.

Archival Tape Storage

Humidity

Keep tapes at 40% to 65 % RH. Going over 65% is dangerous to tape and can result in many problems. The polymer that binds the magnetizable substance to the polyester substrate can degrade and fail when exposed to too much moisture. This can result in a brittle, soft, or sticky and unplayable tape. The magnetic powders can also come off, oxidize, or rust when exposed to too much moisture. High humidity encourages fungal growth, which can render tapes damaged and unreadable.

Light

Keep tapes out of direct sunlight and away from glass windows.

Pollutants

Even a small amount of dirt or dust can obscure the data on magnetic tapes. Additionally, dirt on a tape can transfer to the read/write heads causing further problems. Magnetic tapes are sensitive to airborne pollutants such as smog or chemical toxins. Storing magnetic tapes in their cases inside another box will help keep them pollution free.

Magnetic Fields

Magnetic tapes are highly sensitive to magnetic fields that may be in our homes. Be sure to store magnetic tapes away from power sources that can create a magnetic field, such as microphone, headset, computer, or television equipment.

Storage and Maintenance

Do not store magnetic tapes flat. Like books and CDs, store them upright. Flat storage can cause warping. Regularly check tapes to make sure the information is still accessible. Remember to care for the recording/reading equipment. The read/write heads may need to be cleaned periodically.

Although they are older storage mechanisms, magnetic media have not lost their place in the world of computer data storage. If you already have a system for this medium and it is your preferred mechanism, consider this a viable alternative. Be sure to care for magnetic tapes properly; they may serve you well for the long haul.

Hard Drives

Most computers have internal hard drives to store permanent data. This is different from the RAM chips that are used to temporarily store data while they are being used. It is possible to purchase additional internal hard drives and install them into a computer. External hard drives are another option for data storage, either as a backup or as a storage mechanism for archival materials. External hard drives plug into a main computer or laptop through a port, usually a USB port. External hard drives are typically "plug 'n play" meaning you plug them in and they do the rest. There is no software to install or applications to set up. Installing a second internal hard drive requires opening the computer and setting it up manually. Unless you are computer savvy enough to pull this off, it is not recommended.

Computer Hard Drive

After my computer crashed suddenly in 2012, I purchased an external hard drive that I now keep plugged into my laptop at all times. I save everything to the external hard drive first, then periodically backup the data onto the internal hard drive inside my computer. Accessing the internal hard drive is dependent on many moving parts, making it more vulnerable to failure. The external hard drive is simpler in structure, which makes it less vulnerable to failure. It is also easy to move around and is convenient for traveling or using it with a second computer in your house. And in the event of an emergency, the external hard drive is easy to grab and go if necessary.

Another advantage of using an external hard drive as a storage medium is its capability of storing large quantities of information in one place. Unlike magnetic media, external hard drives require no special equipment to read them. External hard drives can be programmed to access and share information from both PCs and Macs. If you have both types of computers in your home, external hard drives could be an easy way of sharing information without needing to install a formal network. The caveat is that you must indicate this when you first use the external hard drive; otherwise, it will select either one or the other type of operating system.

Hard drives are made up of a number of disks, typically one to four, called platters. The platters are stacked one on top of the other. These circular disks are made from aluminum, glass, or ceramic. The platters are coated with magnetizable material used to encode data. Platters are lined up like a spindle, one over the other, not unlike the spindles used to play 45 records back in the olden days. The read/write head has an arm and reads the platters similar to the way a needle attached to an arm to read our favorite record albums. One difference is that the read/write head must not come in contact with the platters. If it does it can scratch the surface and the information will be unreadable.

One disadvantage of hard drives is that they are highly mechanical. Internal hard drives are dependent on the rest of the computer working. However, you can take out an internal hard drive and extrapolate the data if other parts of your computer fail, such as the motherboard. In addition to the platters and read/write head and arm, a hard drive has a motor, bearings, lubricants, and other materials, all of which can fail or cause failure. Hard drives are notorious for dying without warning—a good reason to make sure everything is backed up. Hard drives can also be rather delicate, they do not withstand falls or bangs very well. If the internal platters bump into each other, it can cause the drive to fail. If the read/write arm hits the platters, this can also cause failure or data loss. It is difficult to monitor and assess the condition of a hard drive because the platters are hidden from view, unlike compact discs that may reveal scratches or magnetic tapes that are torn or goopy.

One problem that can occur with hard drives is *bit rot*. This happens when tiny bits of magnetic encoding on a hard drive are erased by temperature fluctuations. Sectors can go bad for many reasons including dust particles on the platters, small writing errors in the data, or viruses.

Hard drives have been around for quite a while, but they have mostly been used as a mechanism for using data in the moment and not for archival purposes. They are not designed specifically for backup or long-term archival storage, and their function for this purpose has not been fully explored.

Archival Storage of Hard Drives

Temperature

Since high temperatures are one of the primary causes of bit rot, keeping temperatures in a good range is essential for long-term survival. Temperatures should be kept between 60° and 69°F (16° to 20°C). When hard drives are in use, their temperatures can rise up to 125°F (52°C). So be sure your computer is ventilated with good airflow and is not overheating.

Humidity

High humidity accounts for more disk controller and connectivity failures than high temperatures.[35] The 2.5" hard drives found in laptops are much more reliable for long-term archival storage than the 3.5" hard drives used in desktop computers. Research has shown that 2.5" hard drives used in an archival setting have a resting life expectancy of thirty years.[36] These experiments used accelerated conditions to simulate the effects of environmental conditions. As of this date, we cannot know the actual life expectancy of a resting hard drive. Regardless, it is important to keep humidity levels no higher than 30% to 45%. The lower the better within this range. Of utmost importance is not allowing condensation inside the hard drive casing. As temperatures increase, humidity levels need to decrease.

Magnetic Fields

Because they are encased, hard drives are more resistant to magnetic fields than magnetic tapes are. But to be on the safe side, take the same precautions recommended for magnetic tapes. Store them away from power sources that can create a magnetic field, such as microphones, headsets, computers, or television equipment.

Storage and Maintenance

Lay hard drives flat (horizontally), and do not stack one hard drive on top of another. Do not put anything heavy on top of a hard drive. Remember the internal platters are delicate and need to not touch each other. Never drop or shake a hard drive, keep static electricity away from them, and do not open their casing. Do not remove hard drives from a computer when they are still running. Go to the hard drive icon, right-click, and select "eject" before unplugging a hard drive.

Lifespan

Hard drives are meant to be actively used. A good one that is taken care of can last up to ten years (although typically our laptops die within five to seven years). Hard drives used for archival storage that are kept in good environmental conditions can last up to thirty years. It is thought that because hard drives are meant to be written and rewritten over and over, leaving them untouched may result in the loss of bits or generate errors. A way to get around this is to do a wipe and a reload every five to seven years. This means transferring all the data to another storage mechanism, wiping the hard drive, then transferring the data back. Doing this will eliminate bit rot since bit rot is not etched into the platter but is a loss of magnetization of certain bits or sectors. A wipe and reload will refresh the bits and restore the data.

Flash Memory

People typically think of flash memory as thumb drives, memory sticks (or sticks), jump drives, and pen drives that all plug into our computers with USB ports and are generally used as backup devices. These are forms of flash memory, but the SD (secure digital) cards in our cell phones and the memory cards in our digital cameras, digital camcorders, digital audio players, synthesizers, and video games all use flash technology as well. Flash memory allows portability with computer technology and can withstand a bit of abuse from users. We are notorious for dropping our cell phones, and we routinely throw our cameras into our luggage, backpacks, or purses where they are bounced around and jostled. MP3 players join us on early morning runs where they are jogged and banged up, and stick drives can be found in our pockets, on chains around our necks, attached to a key chain, or buried deep in our pocketbooks. It is hard to imagine a heavy, delicate, whirling hard drive functioning properly in any of these situations; and it wouldn't, which is why flash memory is so great for use in our daily lives.

Flash Drives, SD Cards, SSDs

But how does flash memory stand up as an archival storage mechanism? Optical storage writes to plastic discs, magnetic media write to tapes, and hard drives write to magnetized aluminum, glass, or ceramic platters. But flash drives write to transistors using silicon. Though the materials and technology differ, each of these devices is doing the same thing to accomplish the same goal: storing our data. The term "flash" was coined when a colleague of the inventor commented that erasure using this technology occurred like the flash on a camera. Whoosh!

Types of Flash Memory

Flash memory comes in three basic formats: flash drives, solid-state devices or solid-state disks (SSD), and secure digital (SD) cards.

Flash Drives

Flash drives may be the type of flash memory you are most familiar with. These are the thumb drives (or sticks) used to backup information. When thumb drives first became popular, college students were known to wear them as necklaces or attach them to key chains because they were small and portable. These devices come designed to be put into a computer USB port to read or transfer data. They are small, lightweight, and easy to use on any computer because of the USB plug.

Solid-State Drives/Disks (SSDs)

SSDs are bigger than flash drives and a little less portable. They are also more delicate, although still rugged enough to be found in portable devices. They are faster than flash drives or SDs. Modern computers sometimes use SSDs instead of the traditional hard drives described earlier. For archival purposes, an external SSD drive can be a viable option for storing information.

Secure Digital (SD)

SDs are small, thin cards that are used in cameras for storage or extra storage. They can be purchased in several sizes including miniSD and microSD. The greatest disadvantage of SD cards is that not all computers have SD slots. Typically, when we attach a camera to a computer using a USB port, the computer automatically reads the camera's SD card and any additional cards that are added to the camera. You can purchase separate SD card readers that connect to a computer using a USB port. Without the special cord to connect the camera to the computer, or without the separate SD reader, an SD card found among an archival collection will be of little use to the finder.

The advantage of using flash technology is that there are no moving parts inside the device. This makes flash memory very durable. You can drop a flash drive and still read the information. With no moving parts, there are fewer things to break. Flash memory devices can withstand a lot of abuse and keep functioning. Like the old motto for Timex watches used to say, they can "take a licking and keep on ticking." Flash drives can, however, be corrupted if they are removed from a computer while information is still being written to the drive. Make sure to click on "eject disc" before disconnecting it from a computer.

Archival Storage of Flash Memory

I have told you that the most important consideration in keeping your archives intact is the environment in which it is kept. Flash memory with no moving parts is one item in your archive that may endure a bad environment and still function. In an extreme case, a couple on vacation dropped their camera overboard only to have it rescued by a fisherman who was able to track down the couple by posting online the pictures from the SD card which amazingly still worked![37] Do not try this at home, but this story illustrates the durability of these devices.

Environment

Flash memory has been used in environments with 80% RH and in places where temperatures exceeded 150°F below freezing.[38] Of all the devices we have discussed, flash memory has the greatest chance of surviving a natural disaster such as a flood, an earthquake, a tornado, or a hurricane. Some types of flash memory are designed to be fire retardant.[39] Do not allow this to give you a false

sense of security, however. Flash memory does still fail. I will be teaching you about the 3-2-1 Rule in the next chapter, and considering their durability, you might want to make one of your choices a flash memory stick.

The bigger concern with flash memory is static electricity. Ordinary static electricity generated by simply transporting a flash drive in your pocket can erase the drive completely. Anti-static storage bags can be purchased that will protect against this. Archival suppliers sell anti-static cases for CDs, DVDs, hard drives, and flash memory that look like mini safes. They protect computer media from dust, dirt, debris, and static electricity.

Disadvantages

Flash memory in the form of thumb and stick drives are simple to use because they easily plug into a computer USB port. However, they do fail, and when they do it is usually abrupt and without warning. Unlike magnetic media in which the tapes may show visible signs of wear, or CDs that may show visible scratches or chips, flash drives with no moving parts and no sound leave the user unaware of their imminent demise. Even hard drives will sometimes send audio cues that something is not right, although they are also known to fail abruptly.

Information such as pictures, audio files, and video should be downloaded off portable devices as soon as possible. While flash memory may be one choice of backup, you still want to use the 3-2-1 Rule described in Chapter 10. No form of computer device is completely safe and secure. Have backups! If a flash drive does fail, it may be impossible to retrieve the information (unlike with hard drives). A specialist *may* be able to extrapolate *some* information, but it will take finding a specialist first and may be expensive to do so.

Writing and rewriting on a flash drive will cause it to wear out. If you purchase one for archival purposes and write on it once and store it, you should be okay. But the ones you keep in your pockets or handbags that you use over and over will eventually wear out. As they begin to wear out, stored data may become corrupted and provide false readings. Manufacturers may indicate how many times a flash drive can be written to. Pay attention and heed the advice. Flash memory can store information for long periods, but it will need to be refreshed periodically. This means plugging it into a computer to allow electricity to run through it, waking up the teeny tiny transistors so-to-speak.

Another disadvantage with flash memory is that because the devices are so small, it is hard to label them. It has become customary to attach a rim tag traditionally used for labeling door keys or car keys. Their small size also makes them easy to lose or misplace. That can be scary in two ways. One is that you will lose your data, the second is that someone else might find it.

Users of flash memory must weigh the unpredictability of sudden erasure and the small size against its ability to withstand less than ideal environmental conditions and its potential to withstand natural disasters. As family archivists, the ability to maintain an ideal environment is often challenging. We do not have the huge HVAC systems found in libraries or archives. On the other hand, though a flash drive may withstand a natural disaster, where will it end up? Also, survivability is not guaranteed. Because the technology is relatively new, it is uncertain how far into the future it will last. Periodic technological refreshing may pose problems for family historians.

Cloud Storage

The basic concept of cloud storage is that the information is stored on a highly powerful remote computer not in your control, and the information is accessed through the internet. With cloud computing you, as the user, agree to allow a company to store your data. Usually, though not always, there is a fee for this service. While cloud storage may be a backup system for you, the company storing the data typically has backups of their own. So, in terms of loss of data, cloud computing is pretty secure.

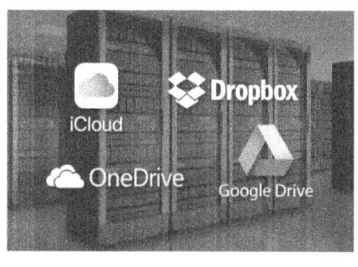

Cloud Storage Services

One of the greatest advantages of storing your data in the cloud is that in the event of a personal, local, or national disaster, your information will not be lost. This is why I highly recommend cloud storage as one of the backups we make using the 3-2-1 Rule.

Another great benefit of cloud storage is that the information can be accessed from multiple places. I love that I can be at work, on a bus, at a friend's house, or pretty much anywhere and go into my online storage to show someone a picture, get a stored recipe, or retrieve an itinerary for a trip. However, if the internet is not working, or if I do not have access to it, I cannot look at anything. If the electricity or the internet are out for any reason, or if you are in a secure area that does not allow access to Wi-Fi, you cannot get to your information. People who have lived through a natural disaster know the heartache of this type of scenario, and who among us has not lost electricity and internet for a while, even for short periods during a snowstorm or a summer heat wave? We all have. Other electronic devices will not work during an electrical outage, but cloud storage requires working electricity AND internet in order to be accessible. My experience is that losing access to the internet is much more common than losing electricity.

Many software companies no longer send discs for programs to be downloaded on hard drives. Instead, the trend is for users to pay a monthly fee to use the program through the internet. The information created in these software programs will be stored on the company's hard drives. You may be able to make a backup and download it to your hard drives, but the programs remain in the control of the company.

All cloud backup media are similar in that your information is out of your control to varying degrees. The greatest threat to your data with cloud storage is the rights and ownership of your data. This can be complicated. You need to consider what happens to your data if the company you are storing it with goes out of business. Will you be able to retrieve your materials? Even a lawsuit may not protect you in this case. I lost several slide show videos when a company whose website I stored them on was bought out by another company. They contacted me to let me know a transition was taking place, but by the time I realized their emails referred to the buyout and was not just another daily advertisement, it was too late.

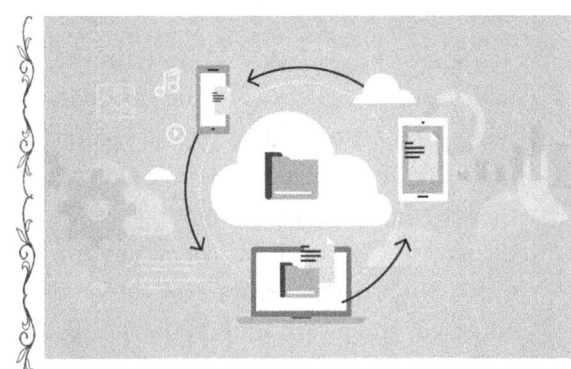

How Cloud Storage Works

The level of security offered by different companies varies. Information passing through the internet is always at risk of being hacked. Information stored on remote computers can be hacked or at risk of viruses, just as your own computers are. Some services use programs that browse our data for the purpose of finding marketing strategies that can be shared with interested parties. Cloud storage companies may look for and may delete illegal or pornographic data. The FBI shut down an entire storage facility after finding that many of the users were storing pirated programs, movies, and music on it. When the site went dead, even those with legal information lost access to everything.[40] Dropbox suddenly changed the terms of their service in 2011, giving them ownership to all data clients had stored on their servers. They rescinded after a public outcry, but smaller or lesser-known companies may go unnoticed when making such a claim.

These types of scenarios may make you shake in your boots. They should definitely drive home the idea that you need to be very careful with whom you choose to use as a cloud storage service. You should also come away with the undisputed knowledge that having data stored in one place is dangerous—even if it is in the cloud.

You also might want to consider the sensitivity of the data you choose to store in the cloud. Maybe you want to store your pictures and some data, but you might not want to store copies of your tax returns, your journals, or those romantic videos you made on your honeymoon. You can use data encryption for sensitive files or folders, but be sure to keep the passwords in a secure location—NOT in the cloud.

Some companies are more secure than others. For a paid fee, there are reputable companies that will store your data; block any access to the information; provide highly protective security against hackers, trolls, and malware; and do not make any ownership claims. Do your research. We live at the beginning of the internet and cloud computing age. One would hope that, in time, rights and ownership issues will be ironed out and the unethical practices that are legal today will become illegal in the future. For now, you need to be self-protective, educated, and aware, and do the best you can to ensure your data will be safe and accessible.

What should you look for when choosing a cloud storage company? First, consider that with cloud storage you will not own anything like you do when you purchase a CD, hard drive, flash drive, or magnetic tape. With cloud storage you are essentially renting space on the company's hard drive. Here is a list of some of the other considerations you should be mindful of:

- ✓ **Subscriptions**

    What is the length of the subscription? How does the subscription end? Typically, companies have criteria that determine behaviors on your part or their part that could cause the subscription to end abruptly. What happens if you want to end the service yourself?

- ✓ **Renewals**

    How does the subscription renew? Will it renew automatically? What happens if the credit card you are using for renewal expires and you forget to update your profile? Will you lose access to your data, and what must you do to get it back?

- ✓ **Backups**

    Does the company make backups, and where are they located? Do they make one backup or multiple backups? It is important to know where the servers are located because different states and different countries have different rules, laws, rights, and regulations about data storage. Do not assume data or backups are stored in the United States.

✓ **Warranties**

What are the warranties and guarantees of the company?

✓ **Legacy Data**

What happens to your data after you die? Will your executors and heirs have access? If not, what happens to your data? Is it deleted? (See Chapter 13 for more information about estate planning.)

✓ **Deleting Data**

If you delete data, is it really deleted? As many of us are aware, deleting something in cyberspace does not necessarily mean it is truly deleted. Companies often retain copies of deleted files. Can we be sure that those honeymoon pictures cannot be found on any server anywhere? Or that our kids will not see them after we die? Also, if you end your subscription with a company, can you be sure all data on all computers will be double deleted, meaning completely deleted?

✓ **Security**

What kind of security does the company offer? How many layers of security does it use? Will anyone notify you if there is a security breach? If there is a security breach, hacking, malware, troll, etc. can the company be held liable?

✓ **Data Collection**

Does the company collect data or look through stored data? If so, what kind of data do they collect, for what purposes, and what do they do with it? Do they share or sell data about their clients to outside services?

✓ **Ownership**

What are your rights of ownership? Does the service claim any ownership rights? Have they ever?

I hope this chapter has made you aware of how complicated digital storage is. When I give library lectures, the one on digitization is often the most popular. Digital storage is appealing because it seems easier, more fun, and more interesting than analog or material storage; it is the modern "cool" thing to do. But from an archival, long-term preservation perspective, digital storage is complicated and difficult, especially for individuals. Archives and libraries use XML, a digital encoding language that is a subset of HTML, for long-term digital preservation and storage. They have staff to periodically wipe and reload computers and refresh stored digital files. The average person does not have access to these technologies, at least not today. As you will learn in the next chapter, we cannot "store and ignore" digital files. They must be maintained. The questions we need to consider are, Will they be maintained, and who in our family can we trust to maintain them?

CHAPTER 10

ORGANIZING, BACKING UP, AND STORAGE

Back when I was a child
Before life removed all the innocence
My father would lift me high
And dance with my mother and me and then
Spin me around till I fell asleep
Then up the stairs he would carry me
And I knew for sure I was loved

—**Luther Vandross,** *Dance With My Father*

This and the next chapter discuss how to digitize material items such as photographs, letters, and reports and how to archive born digital documents, photographs, and audio/video files. Chapter 12 specifically discusses the best file formats to use for different types of media for long-term storage and preservation. Before we hop into that discussion, let's look at how to organize digital documents. We will be using and replicating the principles outlined in Chapter 2, while adding and outlining several special concerns for digital documents.

Organizing both your born digital and analog-to-digital documents can be a great challenge. To keep your family archives separate from other digital materials, create a folder on your desktop called "Family Archives." The Library of Congress suggests creating subfolders inside this main folder, listed by file type. It would look something like this:

FAMILY ARCHIVE
  AUDIO
  DOCUMENTS
  PHOTOS
  VIDEO
  DIGITIZED DOCUMENTS

An alternative method is following the organizational principles outlined in Chapter 2, creating folders according to the structure of the Finding Aid and Series List. The digital folders should mirror the material folders. In other words, if you have a folder called "Obituaries" in a box called "Important Family Documents," then create a digital folder called "Obituaries" and put it in another digital folder called "Important Family Documents." This will help you to find things later. If audio, video, or image documents are included, they can either be segmented separately (if there are enough) or kept in the folder with other documents.

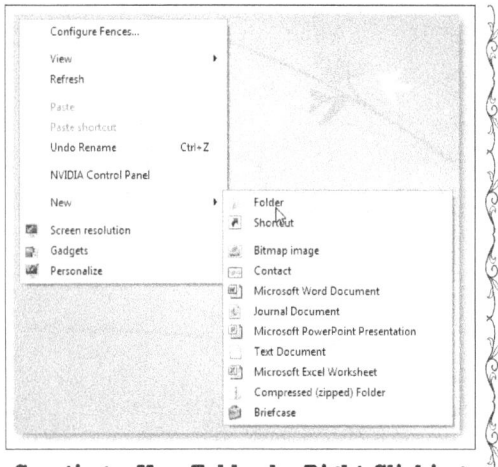
Creating a New Folder by Right Clicking

For example, let's say your mother's sister Mary died, and at the funeral her husband, children, grandchildren, neighbors, and friends all spoke about her at the ceremony. You recorded it all on your cell phone, imported it into video editing software, and created small videos of each speaker. Or you turned your phone on and off for each person as they went up to the altar and spoke. Either way, you have separate videos of each person sharing a memory of your aunt. The digital archive could look like this:

FAMILY ARCHIVE (folder)
  OBITUARIES (folder)
    SMITH, MARY (folder)
      Obituary.pdf (newspaper obituary)
      VIDEOS (folder)
        HusbandDan.voc
        DaughterSara.voc
        SonDonald.voc
        NeighborSally.voc

An easy way to create a folder is to place your mouse anywhere on your desktop or in any window or folder, and right-click. A submenu pops up that includes a section called New. Highlight the line New and another set of options appears. One will be called "Folder." Select this. To rename a folder, click the Name section once, wait a few seconds, and click it again. The Name will become highlighted, at which point you can enter a new name. On PCs, you can also right-click and select Rename.

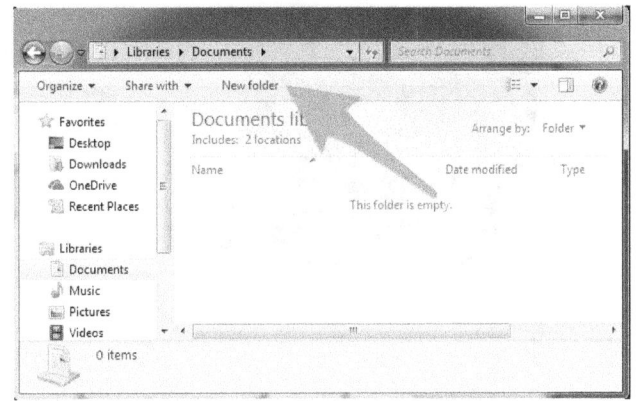

Alternatively, click the File Explorer folder on the task bar. Click a location, such as Desktop, then click the New Folder icon. Once inside the folder, you can easily create new folders by clicking the New Folder icon.

Creating a New Folder Using File Explorer

I recommend using a separate folder on your hard drive called "Family Archives" to distinguish between items that can be trashed after you pass away and those that should be saved in perpetuity. You can also easily upload this folder to a digital legacy cloud service (see Online Digital Estate Planning Services in Chapter 13).

BACKING UP – THE 3-2-1 RULE

Creating backups is an essential component of digital preservation. ***Best practice*** requires using the 3-2-1 Rule. This means we are going to make

> 3 copies, kept on
>
> 2 different storage devices, with
>
> 1 off-site storage facility.

The Library of Congress says that for most people, backing up files is like flossing. We know we should do it, but most of us never do. Or we think we are doing it often, when in reality we are doing it occasionally.

Copy 1

This is the place where the original copy is saved while you are working. I recommend purchasing a good external hard drive, but any of the storage methods already discussed in Chapter 9 will suffice (CDs, magnetic media, flash drives, etc.). Anyone who has had a computer crash, and I know there are many who have, has lived through the agony of losing documents. I tend to be meticulous about backing up, but the year 2012 was particularly busy, and apparently I never found the time to back up my documents. By December, I had a date and time in mind when I would back up all my 2012 files. However, a week before the blessed day arrived, my computer crashed and I lost everything for the year. Because the hard drive was corrupted, my computer guy was not able to retrieve anything. Ouch!

Laptop containing internal hard drive

I learned from that experience. I now back everything up to my external hard drive FIRST. Getting in the habit of saving documents to an external hard drive first increases your chances of retaining them. This is true more so than if you keep them on your computer's internal hard drive and periodically back them up to an external hard drive. Computer hard drives are somewhat fragile and die suddenly and unexpectedly. The lifespan of a laptop is three to five years. The lifespan of an external hard drive is about the same, but the chance of them both failing at the same exact time is slim to none. Right now, my external hard drive is about five years old, so I will be replacing it soon. But my laptop where Copy 2 resides is only a year old. The chance of both my internal and external hard drives crashing at the same time is highly unlikely.

Copy 2

Items from the external storage medium should regularly be copied onto the computer's hard drive or to a second local storage mechanism such as a flash drive, CD, or magnetic tape. Since we are creatures of habit, establishing a set day and time to do this is highly effective. Whenever you make changes to your family archive—whether it is uploading new information, adding digital photos and documents, or adding metadata—you should immediately drag the file folder to the second storage unit for backup purposes.

Copy 3

The third copy should be off-site. External media storage provides protection from computer crashes and viruses on the main hard drive. Backing up onto the computer's hard drive provides protection against the local backup file being corrupted or lost. But without cloud storage or another form of off-site storage, everything would still be lost in the event of a house fire, flood, or other natural disaster. There are many options for online storage; some are free and some are paid. Remember that some cloud services are more secure than others. Many email service providers provide storage space, so check with your local company.

Many people have automatic backup programs, and these are ideal. You can set your computer to back up to the cloud every night at 2:00 a.m., for example. The only requirement is that you leave your computer on, but that is a small price to pay for peace of mind. While automatic backups free us from having to do this task regularly, be sure to check periodically that they are working properly. I have known people who lived with the peace of mind that everything was being backed up every night, only to discover that the system had been down for months before the crash came. They lost everything.

An alternative to cloud storage is giving a copy of your digital backup to a relative or friend. Keep in mind, however, that this method comes with special considerations. For example, if you lived in Houston in 2017 and you gave a copy to your son who also lived in Houston, all your backups may still have been lost in the flood. If you lost your computer and backup copy, you would have also lost the third copy you gave to your son unless one of you grabbed it and took it with you before leaving the city. A second alternative is keeping a copy in a safe deposit box at the bank. Still, bank vaults are not waterproof and are at risk of flooding and often do not have temperature and humidity controls.

Use Flash Drives for backup

Having backups in three places should protect you from computer crashes, viruses, natural disasters, and other problems leading to the destruction of materials. Be sure to use the 3-2-1 Rule with all your digital documents. It is common today for many people, especially millennials, to create documents in the cloud and immediately save them there. Some people use notebooks that do not allow for much storage. Storing your documents only in the cloud presents the same issues as storing only on one computer hard drive. Security breaches, hackers, trolls, malware, spyware, and plain ol' human error could result in loss of data. Be safe and use the 3-2-1 Rule.

THE PROBLEMS OF LONG-TERM DIGITAL STORAGE AND ACCESS

People often tell me that they are going to digitize their documents and throw away the originals. A thousand archivists just fainted at the thought! Digitizing our documents provides insurance if a natural disaster occurs and we lose all our material documents. Digital documents are also easy to share online or through email. However, the digital environment is unstable and hard to maintain. Documents can be lost quickly and easily, sometimes without even trying. Do not be lulled into believing that digital is the end-all and be-all we have been told for decades it would be.

Sisters movie

Tina Fey and Amy Poehler's movie *Sisters* includes a scene in which Diane Wiest, who plays their mother, tells them that a neighbor's son digitized all their photographs and put them on thumb drives. She hands the two daughters their own sticks containing all the family photographs. They look at the stick drives in disbelief. Amy replies with hurt indignation, "You threw away our baby pictures?" Diane explains, "Of course not! We gave them to the nice man at the flea market. He turns them into greeting cards." Ouch. Please do not do this.

To use a term coined by the Library of Congress, you cannot "store and ignore," digital documents like you can with material objects. If you take the time to archive your material items by putting them in archival boxes and polyester sheets, and if you create a good stable environment for them, you really do not need to do anything else. You might want to check on things every now and then, but unless something serious happens, materials kept in a good storage environment will remain in good condition for a long time. Photographs, letters, and documents are sometimes found hidden in closets, attics, or barns after being stashed there for long periods of time, and they are often found in good condition.

This will not be so with digital documents. Digital documents are the high-maintenance children of your collection. They are dependent on hardware and software working properly. All those bits and bytes need periodic attention. Ignoring them will result in *obsolescence*, the watchword in digital storage. If either software or hardware fails, the digital documents become trapped like prisoners in cages of 0s and 1s, never to again see the light of day. Do not let this happen to your precious digital documents. All digital storage media have a limited life, and it is usually a short one. Digital preservation requires management. With software and hardware constantly changing, you need to migrate your documents to new hardware and regularly update your software. Have you ever tried to open an old Microsoft Word document from 1998 and ended up with scrambled eggs? I rest my case.

Hardware can also deteriorate and stop working. There are three main circumstances that cause digital documents to become inaccessible:

1. **Lack of Durability**

    All computer equipment has a lifespan. Typically, laptops need to be replaced every five years, whether we want to or not. Desktops tend to have a longer lifespan, but they will eventually break down and need to be replaced. Hard drives crash, motherboards die, and tiny computer components rust and stop working. Atrophy is a natural part of life. Computers are at risk of this too. The coatings on CDs can flake off, and external hard drives can stop working. Heat, light, and humidity—the enemies of our material collections—also adversely affect our media storage.

2. **Obsolescence**

    Technologies change swiftly. As new products are created, the old ones become obsolete. How do we access the information saved on a 5¼" or 3½" floppy disk today? Many new laptops do not have a CD-ROM drive. We have been using USB drives for a while, but the possibility that another technology will come along and replace it is high. The documents we have stored on an external hard drive with USB capability could be lost. Software also becomes obsolete. Those of us who live in a Windows environment are painfully aware of how upgrades to Windows create havoc and nightmares. With the introduction of a new Windows platform, our old programs stop working and our old documents will not open. Error messages replace photographs and Word documents.

    As digital archivists, we must consider these issues as we begin creating a family legacy. Even if you adequately maintain your digital documents during your lifetime, who will do it when you are gone? Today, you can find a bundle of letters buried in an attic hope chest, carefully open them, and see the information contained therein. This will not be true of the old Apple IIc that Baby 2135 finds stored in your basement. The information on those 5¼" floppies may be irretrievable, or the cost of extrapolating it might be greater than it is worth. The digital world requires us to be proactive. We must move information to new storage devices periodically and keep up on software upgrades.

3. Usage and Handling

The more things are used, the greater the chances they will fail. Each time a document is opened, a few bits are lost. This is one of the main reasons files, seemingly out of the blue, become corrupted and will not open. We know that constantly touching a paper document or a photograph will quicken its destruction and demise. But we may not be aware that the same principle applies to computer documents.

> **ARCHIVES TIP**
>
> The more things are used, the greater the chances they will fail. Each time a document is opened, a few bits are lost

Digital documents need to be migrated and refreshed periodically. Even though we think of digital documents as things that are floating in the ether world, in reality they are bits of information that live on hard drives and take up space (although infinitesimal compared to their material counterparts). People who leave their phones on all the time notice periodically that the phone is slow or apps do not open properly. The best thing to do in that situation is to shut the phone off completely and restart it. Restarting freshens everything and helps the phone work properly again. Your phone is a computer, and the same principle applies to our laptops, desktops, notepads, etc.

The dilemma family archivists face is that while opening objects can result in lost bits making them inaccessible, never opening them can result in software or hardware obsolescence that can also render the items inaccessible. You will need to be like Goldilocks and find the amount that is "just right."

In the archives, the digital objects that researchers and library patrons access are copies made specifically for that purpose. The original copies are kept in "cold storage." When the patron file copy becomes corrupted, another copy is made from the cold storage original. The digital archivist's job is to maintain the files in cold storage, moving them to upgraded equipment and periodi-

> *"I feel like I owe it to my relatives, and I owe it myself to just know our complete history."*
>
> **RASHIDA JONES**
> **WDYTYA US-S03E10**

cally checking to make sure they are functioning properly. As a family archivist, you have the same job—maintaining and upgrading objects. Using the best file formats, following the 3-2-1 Rule, and properly labeling digital documents will go a long way toward ensuring long-term preservation.

Like our precious documents, photographs, jewelry, and family heirlooms, our digital media need to be handled with "kid gloves." Tossing a USB stick drive on a dusty shelf that gets direct sunlight two hours a day is inviting trouble. Apply the same principles you have learned about protecting material documents to your digital materials: a clean, stable environment with moderate temperature and humidity levels; no exposure to direct sunlight, salt, or other harmful chemicals; and protection in good, safe enclosures. You should know the drill by now.

Be sure to label media that are important. Keep a copy in your family archive with instructions on what is on them and how to access them. Unlabeled media tossed in a drawer may inadvertently be thrown away.

THE PROBLEM WITH COMMERCIAL SERVICES

Cloud storage is the name of the game today. The trend is creating documents in the cloud and storing them there immediately. Many software programs that used to be installed on our computers now offer cloud-based programs for a monthly fee. Even hard drives are becoming obsolete; maybe not quite yet, but it appears to be the wave of the future. Cloud storage providers are many, with Google and iCloud being the largest and most familiar. The luxury of the cloud is that documents and programs can be accessed over the web anytime, anywhere. I agree it is a great innovation, and as noted, I recommend the cloud as one of your storage mechanisms.

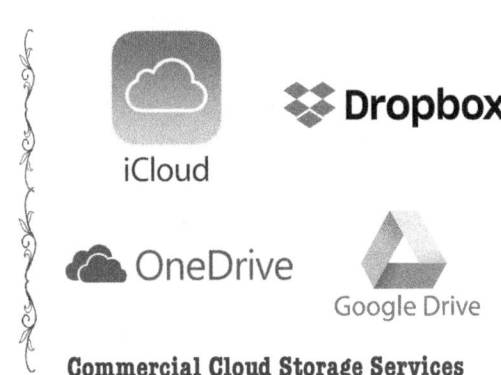

Commercial Cloud Storage Services

However, we need to remember that cloud service providers are businesses. If they are the only form of backup you are using, you could be in for a big surprise some day. Ensuring that your legacy remains intact for the next 100 years is not a cloud service provider's main purpose. Its purpose is making money. Period. It has no other purpose than that. Service providers have no obligation to you, and they do not care what you store in the cloud. It makes no difference to them whether it is a digital copy of the only photograph you have of your great-great-grandmother or the sales receipt from the earbuds you purchased last week. If they choose to, they can pull the plug at any time. Even if it is illegal to pull the plug, they still can. Either way, if you lose all your documents, would it make a difference? In his book *Digital Preservation,* Donald T. Hawkins states, "It is hard to envision a market between people who are dead and people who are not yet born...."[41] That it is.

Your parents and grandparents would have found it unbelievable that Sears Roebuck would go out of business. They could not have imagined life without F. W. Woolworths. These commercial enterprises were staples in their lives. Ask a millennial about F. W. Woolworth and they will probably tell you they have never heard of it. The generations living today might have a hard time imagining Google, Apple, or Microsoft going out of business and being defunct, but it could happen. Who knows who the new kid on the block will be in a hundred years?

The point is, do not rely completely on these institutions to care for your legacy items. Yes, by all means have a copy in the cloud. But do not upload the one photograph you have of your great-great-grandmother and throw out the original.

And lest we forget, these giants of the industry can also become the victims of hacking and data breaches. As I write this, Equifax just experienced a data breach. The federal government's records have been breached more than once. Large grocery and department stores' data have been compromised. Ransomware hackers steal individual and business information and hold it hostage until users pay a fee to get it back. As of today, federal authorities concede that the only way to get your data back is to *pay the fee*! Relying only on cloud storage could be catastrophic if it is your only storage mechanism.

With that said, some cloud storage services are more secure than others. Refer to the section called "Online Digital Estate Planning Services" in Chapter 13 for more information about secure cloud storage and distribution of digital information after you pass.

PRINTING DIGITAL DOCUMENTS

In the next chapter we discuss the best file formats for long-term preservation of digital content. While it is good practice to save documents in the best file format possible, if you really want to ensure something will last long enough for Baby 2135 to view it, print it out. I am not suggesting you print out all your digital photographs or every report you have ever written, but the items you want to be part of your family legacy should be printed. As you have done with other parts of your collection, you need to decide which documents should be printed and which are okay to leave in digital format. I cannot tell you how to make those decisions. It depends on the amount of money you want to spend having photographs and

Printing digital documents increases long-term preservation

10: ORGANIZING, BACKING UP, AND STORAGE

documents printed, how much physical storage space you are willing to provide for historical documents, and what you think is important.

In preparation for writing this book, I read a book on digital preservation and became familiar with the Library of Congress's recommendations. I listened to podcasts on digital preservation and consulted with the university archivist of a top university. By chance, I met a computer engineer and discussed digital preservation with him. They all said the same thing: the digital environment is still not stable. If you want something kept in perpetuity, print it out. This is especially true for families who do not have a paid staff that maintains digital files as large archives do. Family members may or may not provide stewardship of your digital archive.

Printing photographs can be accomplished in several ways. The easiest and probably the cheapest is to use an online service such as Shutterfly. These manufacturers print photographs using the traditional wet-processed, resin-coated photo paper. Because they print so many photographs at once, their prices are very reasonable. Special photo printers are also available. See Chapter 3 for a better understanding of photo processing methods and photo papers.

You can print paper documents on regular printer paper. You can also purchase archival-quality paper or paper with a higher bond rating, but it is not necessary. Higher weighted paper will provide a little bit more stability and reduce the potential for rips and tears, but all paper today is acid-free and has a likelihood of a long life.

CHAPTER 11

DIGITIZATION

These walls have eyes
Rows of photographs
With faces like mine
Who do we become,
Without knowing where
We started from?

Every day that will pass you by
Every name that you won't recall
Everything that you made by hand
Everything that you know by heart
And I will try to connect
All the pieces you left
I will carry it on
And let you forget.

—The Dixie Chicks, *Silent House*

In this chapter, you will learn how to turn analog items into digital items. Analog items are those that begin life as non-digital materials or items. These are items that you can touch with your hands such as paper documents, photographs, slides and negative film, and audio/video tapes. They are stored on the shelves of your home, in photo albums, and in file folders. The next chapter discusses what to do with items that begin life as digital objects—digital photographs, documents created in a computer program, and digital audio and video recordings—and the best file formats to use for long-term preservation. By the end of these two chapters, you will know what to do with all digital files, both those that have been digitized and those that are born digital. After digitizing your material objects, they will all end up in the same place as born digital objects: in your computer or in the digital world.

CHOOSING A SCANNER

When people find out I am an archivist, they are curious what kind of equipment is used in the archives to digitize documents. For the most part, we use the same kind of flatbed scanner used by nonprofessionals. Archives and libraries do have special scanners that allow books and oversized documents to lie flat so they do not have to be pressed down on scanner tables, and to keep fragile book bindings stable. Otherwise, we use the same flatbed scanners found in most homes.

Flatbed Scanner

Author Photo

Do Not Use a Top Feeder Scanner

Scanners do not have to be expensive or specialized. You can purchase a good flatbed scanner for about one hundred dollars. The main consideration is that the scanner allows documents to lie flat when being scanned. Do not purchase a scanner that requires documents to be fed through a top-loading feeder. Copy machines usually have both a top feeder and a flat glass scanner bed. Be sure to use the flatbed scanner when using an all-in-one copier. Passing fragile, delicate, or precious documents through a feeder poses great risk. Paper jams are common with feeder scanners. Our credo as archivists is to do no further harm. An old birth certificate can be irreparably harmed if it is jammed or torn when passing through a scanner feeder.

Scanner Apps

The latest technology in photo scanning are Apps that can be downloaded onto a phone or tablet. Many of these apps are free, others have additional features for a small fee. Given the arduous nature of scanning photographs, scanner apps are a great way to go. The program adjusts for slight hand movements or shakiness, and glare. Most come with automatic editing features that will adjust the color and tone. The digital photographs are stored with the other photographs on your phone or tablet that can be later downloaded to your computer as JPEGs. Scanner apps can be used on oversized items like maps, blueprints, posters, artwork, photographs, or books that are too fragile to go on a flatbed scanner. Scanner apps can also scan negatives and slides.

Portable Scanners

Portable scanners are handy and can be used in several ways. They typically come either with a feeder that documents are fed through, or as a fully detached unit that is used like a wand to scan documents. Do not use the type with a feeder on archival documents. Wand scanners come with software that will compensate for slight human movements, but overall, a portable scanner will not give as crisp a representation as a flatbed scanner. A portable scanner can also be used on oversized items.

Portable Scanner

Wand portable scanners are small and can easily fit in a purse or backpack. An SD card comes installed that can later be connected to a computer for easy download. A fully detached wand scanner can be used to scan documents or photographs owned by other family members by bringing the scanner to their homes and scanning them on the premises. The target audience for these scanners is academic researchers and students. Genealogists find them handy to bring to libraries and archives when doing research. The disadvantage of portable wand scanners is that without connecting them to a computer during the scanning process, you cannot review the scans until you are back home. If something came out blurry, you would not know until it was too late to rescan.

If you have a huge photographic collection or are a professional photographer, you can purchase a high-grade scanner specifically designed for photographs, film, and slides. If slides and negatives are part of your family archives, some regular scanners come with special attachments for those items.

Many family Bibles have handwritten sections that list the names and dates of birth of family members over generations. You must take great care when scanning books like these due to their fragile bindings. Archives and libraries sometimes have special scanners with an added section that allows one side of a book to rest gently to one side while the other side is scanned. At home, a foam wedge support or another book can provide this type of support. Be creative. The goal is to not overextend or break the binding. If you cannot rig something up at home, consider taking a digital photograph instead. If that fails, you may be able to find a specialized scanner at a local library or through a local service provider. Most libraries observe Preservation Week, an initiative started in 2005 to have libraries connect with the community and teach individuals about preservation. Preservation Week is usually in April or sometime in the spring. Many libraries sponsor digitization events where they teach digitization basics and sometimes provide equipment, including specialized equipment they may have on site. Contact your local library for more information.

All materials can be outsourced for digitization, but it may be more necessary for maps, drawings, artwork, blueprints, and other oversized documents. Another alternative is scanning the item in sections, then stitching them together with the software included with the scanner. Local libraries may have oversized scanners to do this and may make their equipment available during Preservation Week. Alternatively, preservation centers or paid service providers may offer this service.

Digital Camera on Tripod

Another option is using a digital camera. The trick is to hold it steady. A standard camera tripod will connect to most digital cameras providing more stability if necessary. I have successfully taken pictures of pictures and reprinted them. The quality is not as good as using a flatbed scanner, but it sometimes works. Also, when rehousing photo albums, I take pictures of the pages as they are before I begin to take the book apart so that the organizational layout is retained. Sometimes I cannot rehouse materials in the exact order, but I want Baby 2135 to know what the photo album looked like originally.

In addition to using cameras to take photographs of large objects that will not fit on a scanner, or to capture fragile items that could be damaged by being laid flat on a scanner, you can use cameras to take pictures of objects. This can work well for furniture, clocks, military paraphernalia, clothing, china, and silver tea sets.

If you plan to purchase a new scanner for your project, be sure to get one that meets your specific needs. You want one that can handle all the different types of materials you have in your collection including documents, photographs, slides, negatives, and oversize document stitching.

Scanning is simple and straightforward. Setting up the scanner may take a bit of effort, but even that should be relatively easy. Most scanners are pretty much "plug and play." Typically, once you press the Scan button, the necessary computer prompts will appear on your computer screen. Take time to learn each of the options your scanner provides. Read the instruction booklet. If you have misplaced yours, you can download most scanner instruction booklets from company websites. There are also many YouTube videos that explain how to scan and how to use the different features.

Push the Scan button, then follow the prompts on your scanner selecting the settings given below. To make scanning quicker and easier, you can scan everything into one folder now and transfer individual items to the proper folders later. Flatbed scanners tend to be slow, and the process is tedious and time consuming. Put on some good music and you will be fine. This is a perfect time to listen to a podcast or watch a movie. Just do not munch on potato chips and have a can of soda near your archival collection. And please, watch your edges! Make sure you do not cut off important parts of a photograph. Scanners typically have a preview pane that allows you to make sure you have not cut off a head or an arm or the birth date from a birth certificate.

PREPARING DOCUMENTS FOR SCANNING

The scanner settings discussed below for each type of scannable item are based on the Library of Congress's recommendations for personal archives. Note that there are instructions for **best practices** and **good practices**. Best practices are obviously the highest and best settings and file formats, but they will take up more disk space. Good practices are acceptable and are formats that provide stability, but they also allow for compression and will take up less disk space. Refer to Chapter 9 for a fuller discussion on file formats and compression.

Before scanning documents, make sure the scanner glass is clean. Even tiny specks of dust can show through on a finished scan. Never spray glass cleaner directly onto the surface of the glass when cleaning it. Instead, stand several feet away from the scanner, spray glass cleaner onto a soft cloth, then clean the glass with the moistened pad or lint-free cloth.

Prepare documents for scanning by removing all paper clips, staples, tape (if possible), elastics, and other items. Paper clips and staples can scratch the glass surface. If removing tape will cause more damage, leave it on. (All of these should have been removed during processing if you have taken that first step.) If you can, cautiously remove dust and smudges from documents. If removing dust and dirt will cause more damage, leave it. Also, be aware of any jewelry you are wearing; rings, dangling necklaces, and bracelets can scratch the delicate glass surface of a scanner.

DUST AND CANNED AIR

Do not, by any means, ever use canned air on your family archive photographs or documents. If I find out you have done this, I will personally come to your home and remove all family photographs from the premises. Canned air is not "air." Canned air contains gases that are compressed into liquids. Ever notice how the can gets cold after spraying for a while? That is because the can is filled with difluoroethane, trifluoroethane, or tetrafluoroethene. You do not want to spray your ancestral photographs with that!

Do not blow on photographs with your breath either. I know it is easy and tempting, but believe it or not, your breath contains spit that has lots of bad stuff in it that can damage photographs. A better option is an air blaster used by photographers. This simple device squeezes air into a rubber chamber and blows it out onto photographs. When using a device like this, keep in mind that when you blow the dust off the photograph it is going to go into the air and land somewhere else. Make sure it does not land on another photograph or your scanner. Take the photograph to the other side of the room to ensure the old dust does not adhere to something else equally important. Also, be aware of the condition of the photograph you are blowing air onto. If it is flaking or fraying, blowing air on it can cause more damage. Remember the archivist's credo, "Do No Harm." We can add to that, "Do No Further Harm."

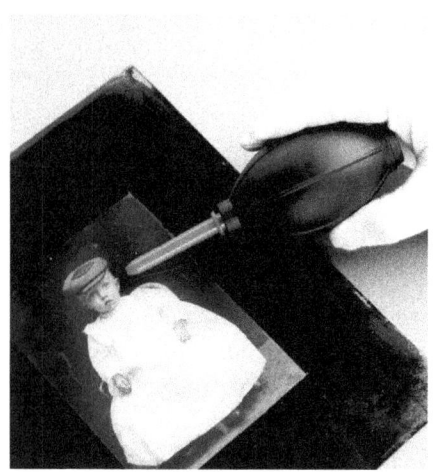

Hollinger Metal Edge

A safe way to remove dust

Many great YouTube videos and instructional booklets written or filmed by non-archival people are available online. I have looked at a few of them. Many of them offer great advice on how to scan, how to use different types of scanners, how to stitch oversized prints together, and what settings to use. However, several of them recommend using canned air to clean scanners, photographs, slides, or negatives. PLEASE DO NOT DO THIS! In truth, canned air is not even good for you, never mind your family archival items. With the dangerous chemicals it contains, I am not sure why it is still on the market. Regardless, it is meant to be used for electronic equipment, not archival photographs.

SCANNING DOCUMENTS

Family legacy documents include wills, house purchase and sales agreements, birth certificates, death certificates, awards, school reports, resumes, school or work presentations, military service documents, census records, insurance certificates, family tree printouts, documents from hobbies and special interests, and a host of other papers that tell the story of our lives and our families.

For scanning documents, the Library of Congress recommends using 300 PPI (pixels per inch) grayscale or bitonal. Saving paper documents as PDFs is **good practice** because this format uses some compression and takes up less room on your hard drive. Saving them as TXTs is ***best practice***; this format is uncompressed but will also take up more room on your hard drive. I recommend PDF-As because they are more practical. They are now an open source, non-proprietary ISO standard regulated by a committee, so their future survival is highly likely.

Family Legacy Documents to be Scanned

Another option to scan documents is an app called Adobe Scan. Using the camera on your phone or tablet, documents are automatically turned into PDFs. The app adjusts for slight hand movements, is able to stitch multiple pages together, and allows for editing so that the corners are correct. Documents scanned on a phone can later be transferred to your computer and turned into PDF-As.

SCANNING PHOTOGRAPHS

Some scanners allow you to place several photographs on the scanner bed and are able to distinguish them as separate documents after scanning. If you have that type of scanner, place photographs neatly in a row on the scanner bed. If photographs are curled, only place them flat if doing so will not cause cracking, peeling, or other kinds of damage.

4" x 6" or 5" x 7" Photographs

The Library of Congress recommends using 300 PPI for these sizes of photographs. To enlarge to 8" x 10" or greater, scan at 400 or 600 PPI. For family legacy photographs, save color and black and white photographs as high-quality JPEGs. (See Chapter 9 for further information on compression.) Saving as TIFF files is ***best practice,*** has no compression, and will take up more space on your hard drive. Saving as JPEGs is ***good practice***, has some compression, and will take up less space on your hard drive.

Save photographs to a folder you will be able to access later. You may want to create a folder within your family archive folder

Family Photographs to be Scanned

and name it "Scanned Photographs." Within this folder, you can further organize or add subfolders. For example, the scanned photographs from a photo album may all go in one folder called "Photo Album – Mom (Her full name: Smith, Mary), Date." Within this folder, the photographs can be labeled 1, 2, 3 with a title added. The computer will automatically sort photographs numerically or alphabetically, so placing a number before the photograph title will keep them in the order they were found in the paper (analog) photo album.

It may look like this:

FAMILY ARCHIVE (Folder)

    PHOTOGRAPHS (Folder)

        SCANNED PHOTOGRAPHS (Folder)

            SMITH, MARY–Photo Album 1975–1981 (Folder)

                01 – 1975-8-5-Birthday Party.jpeg

                02 – 1975-8-5-Birthday Party.jpeg

                03 – 1976-7-4-Fourth of July Party.jpeg

Some scanners have software that allows for some minor editing. Otherwise, the photographs may need to be imported into another software program such as Google Photos or Adobe Photoshop for editing, if necessary. Make sure the edited photograph is saved in the family archive folder and is not stored in the software program. See the section titled "Born Digital Photographs: Original Photographs vs. Photographs Stored in Photo Storage Software" in Chapter 12 for more information.

SCANNING SLIDES AND NEGATIVES

Slides and negatives require backlighting to come out right. Many modern scanners come equipped with a tray that holds slides and negative stripfilm. If you will be purchasing a new scanner for your project, be sure to get one with this feature. Follow the instructions that come with your scanner. Typically, the soft, white inside cover lid detaches and is replaced by the slides/negative attachment. The attachment places the slides or negatives under the scanning light. When the Scan button is depressed, the bright light scans the back of the slide/negative and makes the impression.

A simple homemade alternative is to place a piece of bright white glossy paper, such as film paper, on top of the slides after you place them on the scanner glass. This will act as a reflector. If you are more ambitious, you can build a backlighter. There are many creative people out there, and if you search "creating a backlighter for scanning slides," a bunch of videos come up that instruct how to do this. I found one that showed how to make a negative slider in a box that allowed digital photographs to be made of the negative.

Wear nitrile gloves or white archival gloves and use a photo air blower (described above) to ensure no dust is on the scanner or the slides/negatives. When I did my project, I found that the preview selection on the scanner was not always reflective of how the scan would come out. The negatives were pretty accurate, the photographs were very accurate, but the slides

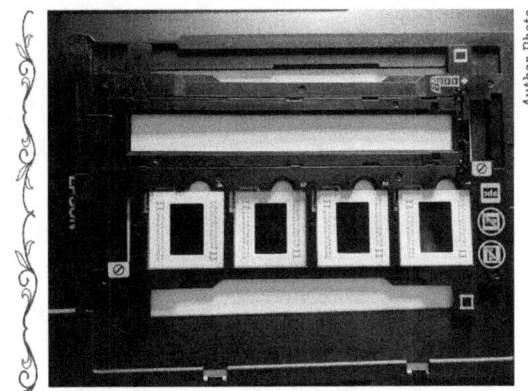

Attachment to scan slides and negatives

appeared grainier and lighter in the preview than they did when they came out after the official scan. Play with your scanner; learn its quirks and quarks.

The Library of Congress recommends using 1900 PPI for scanning slides and negatives. Either lay them flat on the scanner bed or use a slide tray. Save as individual JPEGs or TIFFs. Similar to photographs, saving as TIFFs is ***best practices***, has no compression, and will take up more space on your hard drive. Saving as JPEGs is ***good practice***, has some compression, and will take up less space on your hard drive.

Although the Library of Congress recommends 1900 PPI for slides and negatives, I scanned mine at 1200 PPI and was satisfied with the results. Scanning at 1200–1800 PPI or higher requires a bit of patience. My brand-new scanner protested and warned me that it would be a while. I made a pot of minestrone soup while I was waiting for the first four slides to scan. The porch got painted on the second set of scans. I read the entire *War and Remembrance* trilogy on the third scan, and *The Lord of the Rings* trilogy and *The Hobbit* on the fourth scan. For the fifth scan, I am planning to read all seven volumes of *Harry Potter*.

Okay, it is really not that bad, but it will take some time. However, the results are well worth the wait. When my mother passed away, I took a small box of slides from her nightstand drawer that were from the mid-1960s, taken at a summer resort we used to go to during my father's annual two-week vacation. I sent them to be scanned by a professional, which cost as much as purchasing a new scanner for myself. To say I was disappointed with the results is putting it mildly. They came back dark and grainy. I knew if I had scanned them myself and edited them, I could have had a much better result, and this has proven true. Some of the scans that I did myself were also dark and/or grainy, but I imported them into Adobe Photoshop and was able to lighten, sharpen, crop, de-speckle, and make other corrections that turned them into beautiful photographs of a bygone era. I treasure the images of my mother, my aunt, and my grandmother in the prime of their lives.

> *"I'll wait no more for you like a daughter, That part of our life together is over But I will wait for you, forever Like a river."*
>
> **CARLY SIMON**
> Like a River

Do not be afraid to play around with the settings on your scanner. Most computers today come with photo editing software. I encourage you to play around with this too. Be sure to save the original scan in JPEG or TIFF format, regardless of the settings you have chosen. Import the image into a photo editing software program or app. Immediately choose File, then Save As, and save it with the tagline, "Edited," "Cropped," "Copy," or any other tag you find relevant, as long as it distinguishes it from the original. This allows you to play and make all the changes you want while keeping the original scanned copy intact. Some photo editing programs will automatically save an image that has been altered as a "copy" but do not take the chance. Be proactive. Of course, if you totally mess up your original scan, you can always scan it again. But do you really want to wait for another scan to go through?

If you have photographs and negatives of the same pictures, it is not necessary to scan both. Typically, a negative will make a better scan than a photograph. You can test this out and see if it holds true with your scanner. It will depend on the condition of the photograph and the condition of the negative. I found that my negatives needed more adjustment after I scanned them, so in that sense, the photographs were easier. However, in the event of a catastrophe, if I need to print out my entire collection again, the scans from the negative will be the better choice.

SCANNING OBJECTS

So, you have scanned your important documents and digitized the family photographs, but there are many more items that make up your family legacy. These might include wedding dresses, jewelry, paintings, furniture, clocks, crystal, silverware, clothing, flags, and knick-knacks.

Many items including jewelry, medals, pins, and other small objects can be placed on a flatbed scanner and will come out as a scanned document. I advise extreme caution using this method, however, because if the glass on the flatbed scanner gets scratched it is difficult or impossible to replace.

An alternative is to take a digital photograph of the item. Better yet, make a video. Our smartphones make doing this easy and simple. You do not have to be a professional photographer to accomplish this. Obviously, the more care and attention you put into it the better it will be, but it is not always necessary.

When my mother passed away, my sisters and I each inherited one piece of antique furniture. My older sister took the mahogany bedroom set, my other sister took an antique curio cabinet, and I received the antique fireplace that had been in my mother's living room for over forty years. Imagine if Baby 2135 descends from my older sister's line. She or one of her siblings may have the mahogany bedroom set, but what about the fireplace and the curio cabinet? Where will they be? Perhaps a family moved across the country and the cousins do not know each other. I think Baby 2135 would be interested in knowing that the other pieces of furniture exist and were passed down to other relatives. If you take the time to scan a photograph of the items, at the very least your descendants will have a picture of them.

Photographing Objects with your Phone

Taking digital photographs of important objects, especially valuable antiques, can also be important for insurance purposes in the event of a theft, natural disaster, or home fire. Refer to Chapter 14 for further information about disaster preparedness.

PHOTOGRAPHING OBJECTS

Lighting is essential for ensuring the best quality pictures. Home lighting can create an orange hue. Fluorescent lights emit a bluish hue that tends to be better for indoor photography. You can invest in professional lighting, but it is not necessary. You could hire a professional photographer if you want to, but so many photographic mistakes can be corrected with digital software that this too is not necessary. Find a good spot in the house, have your daughter model the hats, hang the wedding dress on a free-standing coat rack … use your imagination. Just take the picture. Baby 2135 will thank you.

Taking several pictures of the same object will allow you to highlight certain details. You will want to take a large overview, but sometimes the real story is in the details. Take a close-up of the beading on a wedding dress, the artwork on a vase, the inscription on a wedding ring. You will bring to life parts of the object that may be overlooked with a standard photograph.

VIDEOTAPING OBJECTS

A great idea is to either have someone film you or use a "selfie stick" as you go through your house explaining to your future descendants what you have, where you got it, and why you love it. When telling your stories, the objects in your home are often the most overlooked—even though they may have been part of your daily life for decades and may have traveled very far with you along the road of life. How many times have you dusted and polished your dining room set? You probably know this piece of furniture intimately. You have established a relationship with it. It may be an inanimate object, yet it has hosted your family for Thanksgiving and Christmas for sixty years. Perhaps you and your husband purchased it together when you were newlyweds. You know exactly where the chip is from the time the movers banged it and how the dip in the center is barely perceptible. There is a story in that piece of furniture, a story of your family that is worth telling. Do not leave it out.

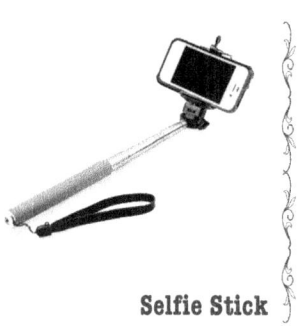

Selfie Stick

If you do not have a smartphone or a selfie stick, most laptops and tablets have video recording capability. This is why millennials are plastered all over the internet talking nonstop about their lives; video recording is the easiest thing in the world to do today. Do not be shy. Think of the service you are doing for your family. They may tease you today, but after you go they will be grateful you did not forget to tell the story of the special flowerpot you bought in France and why the painting of the Italian piazza is so important to you. In some ways, the objects we have around us say more about us than the photographs of special events. Often, we choose them with great thought and have lovingly cared for them for many years.

AUDIO/VIDEO

Magnetic audio and video tapes are very delicate. They are composed of plastic film, traditionally cellulose acetate, polystyrene, and more recently polyester. A thin polyurethane coat is added as a binder on one side. The sound waves are small magnetic particles on top of the tape. Polyurethane is hydroscopic, meaning it absorbs moisture from the air. If too much moisture is absorbed, it can result in *sticky-shed syndrome* (SSS). SSS occurs when excess moisture causes the binders in a magnetic tape to deteriorate, leaving a deposit of sticky residue. It is most often found in polyester-urethane binders from the 1970s onward and can be damaging to playback equipment. Deteriorating audiotape will sound wobbly; deteriorating videotape will be shaky. Both will sound and look fuzzy.

Unless video and audiotapes are kept in a low humidity environment, breakdown can occur in the binder material, or the magnetic oxide can separate from the polyester backing. The cellulose acetate is also subject to vinegar syndrome (refer to Chapter 6 for more information). Lubricants embodied in the tape can

evaporate and dry out, resulting in breakage. Mold and mildew eat tape. Partial erasure, particularly of the higher frequencies, occurs often and is usually the first thing to happen in the cycle of deterioration.

A much overlooked but potentially catastrophic problem for magnetic audio and video tapes is *stray magnetic fields*. Stray magnetic fields can demagnetize or erase the magnetic composition of a magnetic tape. They are produced by AC-powered motors or transformers. Typically, power lines inside and outside your home do not pose a problem. And the magnetic field of the earth is too weak to affect audiovisual tape. Of more concern is dynamic sound equipment such as microphones, headphones, loudspeakers, and moving coil instruments. Keep these objects at least six inches away from magnetic tapes. Ironically, we typically store our video and audiotapes in the same places we have our dynamic sound equipment such as televisions, tape players, and loudspeakers. This is potentially disastrous. Walls and cabinets do not shield magnetic fields, so you want to think about where you store your audiovisual tapes and what is on the other side of the wall.

If you have bulk erasure equipment, it must be kept far, far away from audiovisual tapes. This type of equipment, purchased with the purpose of erasing audio/video tapes for reuse, is extremely magnetic. Other seemingly benign but potentially fatal sources of magnetic threats include door shutters of cabinets and magnetic board stickers. The delicate nature of magnetic tapes makes them vulnerable even to lightning strikes, although this is rare. More commonly, electrostatic discharges can be created by walking over a well-insulated carpet or by the friction made when replaying a tape.

In addition to the breakdown of magnetic tapes, audiovisual materials are at risk of being inoperable due to the obsolescence of the machinery and equipment needed to play them. Baby 2135 is probably not going to have a cassette player, video player, or even a DVD player. The truth is your living grandchildren probably do not have these things.

Keep in mind that the video and audio tapes we are talking about are not your videotape collection of movies like the *Star Wars* saga that are readily available online, on YouTube, or in a million libraries all over the world. We are also not referring to the 8-track tape of Fleetwood Mac's *Rumors* that you wore out in high school or the Jane Fonda workout videos you used to lose baby fat after all your pregnancies. Those are "library" materials. Remember: the difference between library materials and archival materials is that archival materials are one-of-a-kind, whereas library materials can be found in hundreds of libraries around the world.

The video and audio tapes that belong in your family archive are the videos of your children's annual dance recitals, the video your cousin made of your grandmother's 90th birthday party, the original sound recording of your daughter's "garage" band, the video you shot of your son playing football, all the Christmas and Fourth of July videos your father shot when you were growing up, your wedding video, or the film your great-uncle shot of the Flood of 1936 when the bridge in town was washed out.

> **ARCHIVES TIP**
>
> By the end of the 20th century, IASA universally accepted that *preservation by digitization* was the preferred storage mechanism in archives for audiovisual materials.

Because of the high degree of vulnerability and instability of magnetic audio and video tapes, and because the content contained on them is some of your most precious memories, you will want to store them properly. I recommended that you digitize them. Digitizing audio/video is considered ***best practice*** by The International Association of Sound and Audiovisual Archives (IASA). By the end of the 20th century, it was obvious that audio and video tapes were not going to last for fifty or a hundred years. Rather than preserve audio and video tapes, IASA universally accepted that ***preservation by digitization*** was the preferred storage mechanism in archives for audiovisual materials. Long-term storage of audio and video tapes has its own problems, as will be discussed in Chapter 12. But it is still considered a better storage and preservation mechanism than simply storing audio and video tape.

After digitizing audio and video tapes, it is not necessary to keep the original analog tapes. However, if you do decide to keep them, general storage guidelines of the actual tapes are noted below. This list is provided in part to emphasize the fragility of magnetic tapes and to instill the necessity to get them digitized.

- ✓ Store in a cool, dry place out of direct sunlight.
- ✓ Strive for a stable temperature of 65°F with 38% to 42% RH.
- ✓ Ideally, keep your audio and video tapes in a cooler and drier environment than your other items.
- ✓ Provide a dust-free environment.
- ✓ Place tapes in a box inside a box to add a layer of protection from environmental heat, humidity, and pollutants.
- ✓ Keep tapes out of the range of stray magnetic fields.
- ✓ Keep bulk erasure equipment far away.
- ✓ Rewind video or audio tapes to the start position before storing them.
- ✓ Do not touch tape with bare hands. Skin oils can damage the binder and oxide materials.

✓ Store in acid-free, lignin-free, buffered cardboard boxes specifically made for these materials, purchased from archival supply houses. Plastic or metal containers are not recommended. Tapes benefit from a little ventilation. Degradation increases in tight enclosures such as metal or plastic. Open enclosures will slow decay but will not lower the acid content of an already degraded film.

CONVERTING AUDIO TAPE TO DIGITAL

The simplest way to digitize an audiotape is to send it out to a service. There are many good service providers today who will do this quickly and efficiently. Many musicians, wedding photographers, sound engineers, and others have the proper, good quality equipment and will provide this service at low cost. Some will require that you mail the tapes to them. If possible, look for a local vendor close enough that you can drop them off yourself. When working in the archives, I used a great local guy who digitized both audio and video files for the project I was working on. He charged $20 for a videotape, $10 for an audiotape, and $5 for an extra copy. It was well worth the cost.

Several years ago, I purchased an audio to digital recorder for the purpose of digitizing analog audiotapes. I received a cassette player with a USB port that plugged into a computer. The equipment allowed the cassette to be played while being recorded digitally at the same time. This sounds like a great idea; however, in addition to recording the music, it also recorded all other sounds in the room including the sound of the recorder. If you have a place where you can blast the sound without disturbing anyone else, this may work for you. Also, the machine recorded in real time, which meant the entire tape had to be played from end to end. Back in the day, I used to make copies of tapes in a dual tape boombox. It was easy to put one cassette on one side, and another on the other side and push the fast forward and record buttons. A new cassette was made in a minute or so. Not true with these recorders. If the tape is an hour, it will take an hour to digitize it.

> *"This whole thing gives you such an appreciation for people, who in the present understand that the future will want to know about the past. I feel like we live in a time when people are only focused on the present and they are not thinking about what the future is going to need. And the fact that somebody with this incredibly basic technology created a record that still lives...it's insane. It's a miracle."*
>
> **SETH MEYERS**
> Finding Your Roots, S5.E6

Best practice for saving audio files is to save them as WAV files. Saving them as MP3s is considered ***good practice***.

CONVERTING VIDEOTAPE TO DIGITAL

Video files that have been transferred from a device to a computer will show up on the device as **VOB** files, which stands for Video OBject. The videos we create on our phones or digital cameras will download as MOV files and will download at the same time our photographs download. The VOB files can also be found on DVDs that have been made on video recorders or directly on the video recording device. Make sure the information is not copyright protected before transferring it to your personal computer.

To digitize an analog video tape, I suggest contacting one of the many services online. Alternatively, if you have both a VHS player and a digital video camera, you can record an analog VHS video onto a digital camera by hooking the two together and recording the film. Put the VHS tape in a VHS player, hook the digital camera into the VCR player, then play the tape. The video will record onto the digital video camera and can then be transferred onto your hard drive and made into copies.

Another method would require purchasing a digital converter. A converter will interface between a VCR and a computer. It will create a digital video on the computer in real time as the video plays on the VCR.

If you have a VCR/DVD combo player, you may also be able to play the videotape while recording the DVD at the same time. Check your player for specifics.

CHAPTER 12

BORN DIGITAL

My life has been a tapestry
Of rich and royal hue
An everlasting vision
Of the ever-changing view
A wondrous woven magic
In bits of blue and gold
A tapestry to feel and see
Impossible to hold

—**Carole King**, ***Tapestry***

As was indicated in Chapter 9, born digital documents are items that were created in the digital world. This includes correspondence, reports, presentations, photographs, audio and video files, email, text, websites, and social media. When you stop and think about your entire digital footprint, it can be a bit overwhelming. In creating a family archive, you need to consider what is important enough to make it into the hallowed halls of your family archive. You do not need to save everything. Vetting is one of the biggest tasks you must do when creating a family archive. As discussed earlier, you need to determine what items have "enduring value."

Today, it is so easy to take pictures, record videos, and make audio files that you are likely to amass a lot of information that is not considered to be of enduring value. Many of your conversations today are done in the digital world through text, email, and Facebook messaging. Most of these conversations are not of enduring value. One of the reasons Snapchat is popular is because the images, texts, and messages are deleted by default after a few minutes. The born digital generation quickly learned the problem of long-term storage of useless, insignificant, or embarrassing information.

As an archivist, I learned the history of the collections in our archives and the harrowing stories of how they found their way into our stacks. Often documents are pulled from dumpsters, discovered in empty barns, or found hidden in the back of attics and basements. It is not unusual to hear of a valuable package of letters or a rolled-up piece of artwork discovered buried in an old suitcase or trunk. What will the digital version of this look like? It is not hard to imagine that a box of 3½" floppies will be found buried in the back of a closet. Will there also be data hanging out in a dead section of YouTube that is password protected and inaccessible? I imagine at some point YouTube, Facebook, Gmail, and other online services will get too big and will begin to delete old dead files. Think fifty or a hundred years in the future. Are they really going to keep all that data?

In truth, because of the fragility of digital files, the most likely scenario is that hard drives, thumb drives, and even cloud storage will be wiped clean and completely lost. If a thumb drive is in a damp and dusty attic for fifty years, will the data be accessible, or will the metal parts have rusted? The Library of Congress and the archival community worry that while our modern world has a glut of information, it will all be lost in the flick of a switch or by pressing the Delete button, and there will be a gap in the historical record as a result.

OBSOLESCENT MEDIA

The first step in archiving born digital materials is to gather everything in one place. This means bringing together all hard drives, computers, external hard drives, cloud storage, CDs, thumb drives, etc. Look at what is on all the media you have and determine where everything is. While you may want to bring all external hard drives into one place, you do not need to unplug and drag all your computers into one room. Also, much of your digital presence lives on the internet. It makes more sense to do an inventory by making a list of what is where and what is on everything. In many cases you will discover that the problem may not be that you have lost documents, it may be that you have multiple copies of the same photograph or document in multiple places. This should not be confused with the 3-2-1 method of purposefully making multiple copies for insurance purposes. We often end up with ten copies of the same photograph or file because we have moved it around and it got recopied over and over every time we did.

After identifying where everything is, you want to decide what items belong in your family archive. This requires identifying, sorting, organizing, and deleting duplicates.

Hopefully as you have upgraded your computers, information from older media types has been

Obsolescent Media: 3 1/2" Floppies.

migrated to newer computers, newer versions of software programs, and newer backup media. But what happens if the only copy you have of something is on obsolete formats such as 5¼" floppies, 3½" floppies, mini tapes, magnetic backup disks, and a host of formats that are no longer accessible? You may not even know what is on some of the old media you have stored in your basement. Archivists are faced with this dilemma when donors drop off stacks of 3½" floppies, old hard drives, and magnetic tapes. Digital archivists have developed ways of extrapolating the information off those old media, but what will you do? If you have important information in an old file format, but you no longer have the equipment to access it, there are a few basic methods you can use to capture the information.

Paid Services

A quick internet search reveals that there are many companies and individuals who provide this service for a fee. Do your homework. Make sure it is a reliable resource. Prices vary, so be sure to get the best deal. Send one or two disks to start and see how they do. If they are reliable and trustworthy, send the rest.

Purchase an External Hard Drive Reader

You can purchase brand-new modern versions or antique older versions of hard drive readers online. Make sure you have the right type of reader (for 5¼" or 3½" or other formats) and that it is compatible with your current operating system.

Libraries

Though not necessarily on purpose, sometimes libraries have older computers that still have ports for older disk formats. Call around. Some libraries may offer it as a service.

BORN DIGITAL DOCUMENTS

Letters, Spreadsheets, FileMaker Pro, Access, PowerPoint

PDF

Born digital documents such as Word documents, spreadsheets, and reports from financial, organizational, or presentation software can be turned into PDF, PDF-A, or TXT files. PDF stands for **portable document format** or **portable**

digital file. It is an "as printed" format that is portable between applications and systems. This means it can be opened on a PC, a Mac, a phone, a tablet, or online and it always looks the same. PDF is a more secure and reliable document format type than a Word document, and the Library of Congress recommends that individuals save documents as PDFs or PDF-As. PDFs create an image of a document, so the ability to edit or format a PDF, such as adding bold text, underlines, and italics, is limited or eliminated.

Adobe, the early innovator of PDF, made the format available free of charge in 1993. It was officially released as an open standard in 2008 under ISO 3200-1:2008 and is now controlled by the ISO committee. The basic version of Adobe Acrobat can be downloaded free of charge on Adobe's website. Adobe offers paid versions of PDF that allow for some editing, but not to the scale that is available in a Word document. For digital preservation purposes, it is recommended that all born digital Word documents or anything that can be printed as a report document be turned into PDFs or PDF-As. This includes spreadsheets, presentations (such as PowerPoint), reports from specialized software (such as QuickBooks financial software), and databases (such as FileMaker Pro or Microsoft Access) and genealogical programs.

PDF-A

PDF-A is a specialized format standard designed to be used for Archiving and long-term digital preservation of electronic documents. PDF-As prohibit features that are not suitable for long-term digital preservation and identify a profile for electronic documents that ensures they can be opened in multiple types of applications. The PDF-A standards are developed and maintained by a working group that has representatives in government, industry, and academia and is supported by Adobe Systems, Inc. Because PDF-As are an ISO standard, they are guaranteed the ability to be opened and rendered by future generations. The ISO standard requires that future PDF viewing applications must be **backward compatible**, meaning that they can read older versions of PDF-As. PDF-A files can be compressed into ZIP format using JPEG compres-

sion. Encryption, or password protection, is not allowed in PDF-A documents since the main mission of this format is to allow long-term accessibility. An alternative to encrypting an individual document is encrypting the file folder the sensitive document is in. However, when considering family archives, the information is meant to be shared. Why encrypt it at all? The first Adobe Acrobat Professional version that supports PDF-A is version 8.

Certain formatting in Microsoft Word documents may not be supported in PDF-A. Audio and video embedded content will not translate to PDF-A. JavaScript, hyperlinks, certain fonts, and certain colors may not transfer exactly. File sizes in PDF-As might be slightly larger than those of regular PDFs, but the increase in most instances is insignificant. Notes and annotations can be used in a PDF-A, allowing users to add explanations of documents.

Starting with Microsoft Word 2007, PDF-As can be created using the File-Save As function. You may need to download an add-in to get this option in Word 2007. If you have the option of saving a file as a PDF-A, then do so. If you do not, saving it as a regular PDF will suffice.

HTML

As an international standard, PDF is very secure, but another option is to save documents in HTML coding. HTML is a language, not a file format. In the event your documents live for 200 or 300 years, the chance that HTML coding will be completely obsolete is unlikely. Documents can be saved in HTML using the Save As feature in Word. Excel spreadsheets and PowerPoint presentations can be saved as XML, a language similar to HTML.

Open Document Format

Open document format (ODF) is a non-proprietary, open-source format that is available for text documents, spreadsheets, charts, and presentations. It was developed by the Organization for the Advancement of Structured Information Standards (OASIS) consortium as an XML-based file format that uses ZIP compression. In 2006, ODF became international standard ISO/IEC 26300. ODFs can be created and accessed using Apache Open Office, which is a freely available open-source software program. ODF is one of the file formats preferred by the Library of Congress. The extension for text documents is ODT, for spreadsheets is ODS, and for presentations like PowerPoint is ODP. Documents created in other programs can be saved in the ODF format using the File-Save As features.

Apache Open Office is a non-proprietary, open-source software.

Saving Documents in an Alternate File Format

- ✓ Open the document in the program in which it was created.
- ✓ Go to File.
- ✓ Select Save As.
- ✓ Select PDF, PDF-A, HTML, XPS, or ODF depending on the file format you have chosen to use.

The next screen that opens asks for a new file name. If you use the same name and save it in the same folder in which it was created, when you go back into the folder you will see both versions of the document next to each other. At this point you can drag the new version to the family archives folder and delete the original.

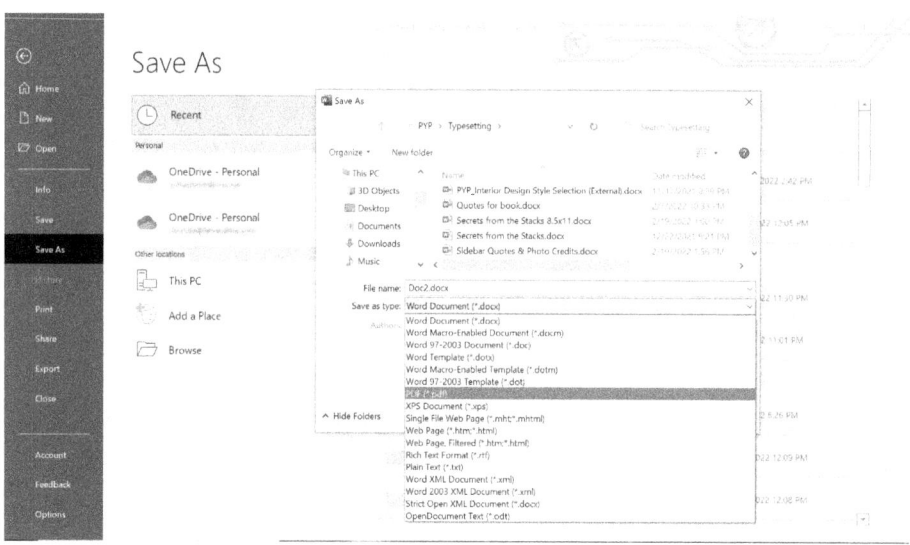

Screenshot of saving documents in a different file format

Saving Documents as PDFs Using the Print Function

Today, most computers come preloaded with an option for printing documents as PDFs. You can use this method to save documents from any program that can print a report, including spreadsheets, databases, financial software, or genealogical software.

BORN DIGITAL PHOTOGRAPHS

Original Photographs vs. Photographs Stored in Photo Storage Software

Chances are the photographs on your computer live in several different places. You may not be aware of this, but it is true. Digital photographs from your phone, camera, or scanner are typically stored as JPEGs. By default, PC computers save the JPEGs in the folder called "My Pictures." Mac uses a program called iPhoto, but the original photographs should be stored in a folder called "Pictures." This may be under your username on the Mac hard drive.

Notice that whenever you open a software program such as iPhoto, Google Photos (formerly Picasa), or Adobe Photoshop, the first thing the program asks you to do is import your photos. After you have done this once, the program will usually automatically import pictures every time you connect a camera or phone to the computer. Do not let this confuse you into thinking your pictures are only stored in the program. The original copy of your photographs is in the My Pictures folder on a PC or the Pictures folder on a Mac.

When setting up legacy folders, you want to store the original JPEGs of your digital photographs. This does not mean you cannot access them from Adobe or iPhoto. It means that the original lives in the folder you have given it.

When editing a photograph, never alter the original. Import it into the software editing program (Adobe), then save it with the same name and the tag "Edited." You might want to be more descriptive and

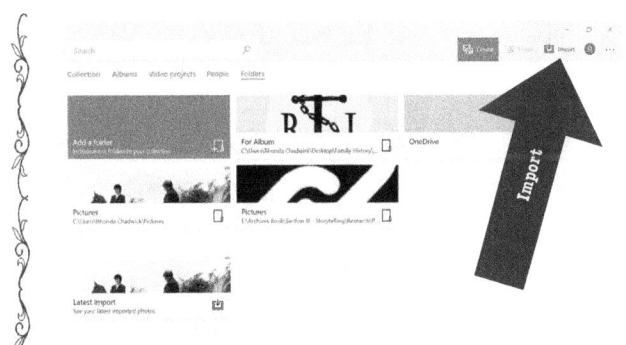

Beware the "Import" prompt!

write "Auto Edit" if you allowed the software program to make automatic edits, "BW" if you changed it from a color photo to a black and white, or "Cropped" if you ... you get the picture.

Location of Photographs

In addition to being in different places on your computer, your digital photographs can also live in many other places. You might have them on your phone, your digital camera, and in cloud storage. You may have uploaded them to websites, blogs, Facebook, LinkedIn, Twitter, Flickr, Snapchat, and Pinterest, to name some of the most popular social media sites. Online storage sites are available from Google, Shutterfly, and Dropbox as well as others.

The first thing you want to do is identify where your photographs are and bring them all together in one place; for example, one folder on your hard drive that can be backed up onto a second hard drive with a third copy in off-site storage. Begin by making a list of what you have. With so many photographs, you want to distinguish between photographs you want to keep for yourself and those that should become part of your family archive. It might be helpful to create two folders: one for yourself that can be disposed of after your death and one as part of the family archive. Think of Baby 2135 when creating the family archive folders. Which photographs are important for telling the story of your family? The pretty swans at a local lake may be a great photograph but will have little value for Baby 2135.

Since you most likely have an abundance of born digital photographs, you may prefer limiting the number that will go into the family archive. Devise rules such as allowing no more than 100 pictures per year or 100 pictures altogether. Maybe pick the five or ten best photographs of any event such as a wedding, family vacation, or holiday. You do not have to dispose of the photographs that are not in the family archive, but you may want to make a distinction between what will be important down the line and what is enjoyable for you within your lifetime.

TRANSFERRING PHOTOS FROM YOUR CAMERA OR PHONE TO YOUR COMPUTER

Many people keep photographs on their phones forever. It is not until they run out of space at the rock concert or on the bus tour that they find themselves frantically deleting items so they can free up space for their new adventures. A better option is to regularly download photographs, memos, and music to computers as soon as possible

If you have a digital camera, follow the instructions that came with your camera. Digital cameras come with software that must be downloaded onto your computer. Sometimes you need to update drivers for the software to work properly, especially if your camera is older. Once you properly set up the software, the computer will automatically begin downloading photographs when you plug the camera into the computer and turn it on. Today the connection is usually through a USB port. Other methods might require that an external SD card reader act as an intermediary between the camera and the computer.

Smartphones work the same as cameras. Their built-in cameras have an SD card that is installed inside the phone. Typically, you cannot remove these cards. Plugging the phone into the computer via a USB port usually automatically prompts the computer to begin downloading the pictures.

If the computer does not automatically begin downloading, you can drag the file containing the photographs onto the computer desktop. On

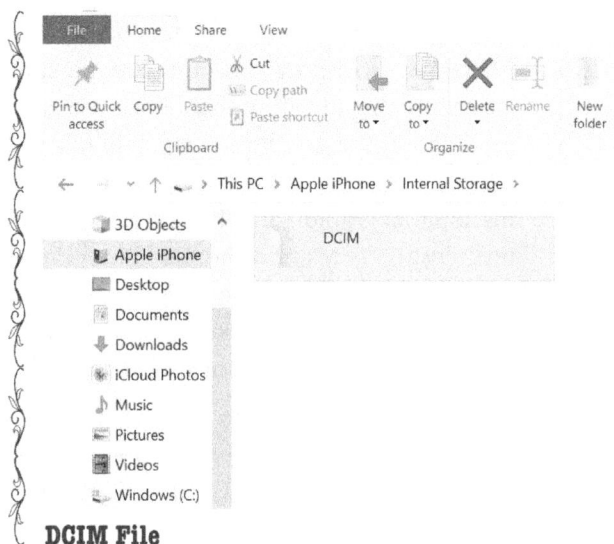

DCIM File

a Windows PC, open the File Explorer folder, usually found in the task bar at the bottom of the screen. On the left-hand side of the screen, look for your phone or camera device. Double-click to open it. If all your photographs have not been downloaded, you should see a DCIM folder. DCIM stands for Digital Camera IMages. This is the default directory that became the standard used by digital camera producers a long time ago. Drag the folder either to your desktop or into your My Pictures folder.

Mac users know that once you plug anything into a Mac an image automatically appears on the desktop. Open it up by double-clicking, and then drag the DCIM file onto your desktop or into a folder of your choice.

Digital photographs are taken in and stored on cameras in a format called RAW, but many computer or camera software programs will automatically import photographs in JPEG format. As of today, this is a good format that is relatively stable. The other common file format for photographs is TIFF. To import in TIFF format, you will most likely have to tell your camera to export in TIFF. Refer to Chapter 9 for an explanation of photographic file compression.

ORGANIZING PHOTOGRAPHS

Now that your photographs are on your hard drive, the next step is getting organized. There is no question that labeling and organizing all your photographs is an enormous undertaking. The Photo Managers is a professional group of photo organizers available to assist you with this endeavor. If you choose to pay someone to do this task for you, visit their website at thephotomangers.com to locate someone who can help.

At this point you will want to add metadata to your digital photographs. There are different types of metadata; some you add yourself and others are automatically added by the device you use to take a photograph. **Descriptive metadata** is the description you add to a photograph explaining the who, what, where, why, and when depicted in the photograph. **Structural metadata** is information that is automatically generated when you take the photograph. It usually includes the date and time the photograph was taken as well as the resolution and pixel size. It may also include the creator of the photograph, the GPS location, and the file format extension letters (JPEG, PNG, BMP, etc.). Most cameras will provide a file name that is automatically generated, such as "IMG_1112.JPG."

Most software allows you to title, tag, or add other metadata to a photograph. Beware that these descriptions are relevant only within that particular software program. As stated earlier, when you open one of these software programs, the first thing it prompts you to do is import your photos. After you have used the program once, it usually automatically imports photographs from your camera or phone when it is plugged into the computer. This practice can be deceptive, leading us to think our photographs are stored inside that program. They are not. Remember the original photographs are stored in the My Pictures folder (or the Pictures folder on a Mac). The photographs that are in the software program are a copy. Make sure when you are organizing your photographs for your family archive that you are working with the original photograph, not the imported copy in a software program. Working with the original picture is essential. If you work with software program copies, all the metadata you hand-typed into the program will be lost and inaccessible if the software program is discontinued.

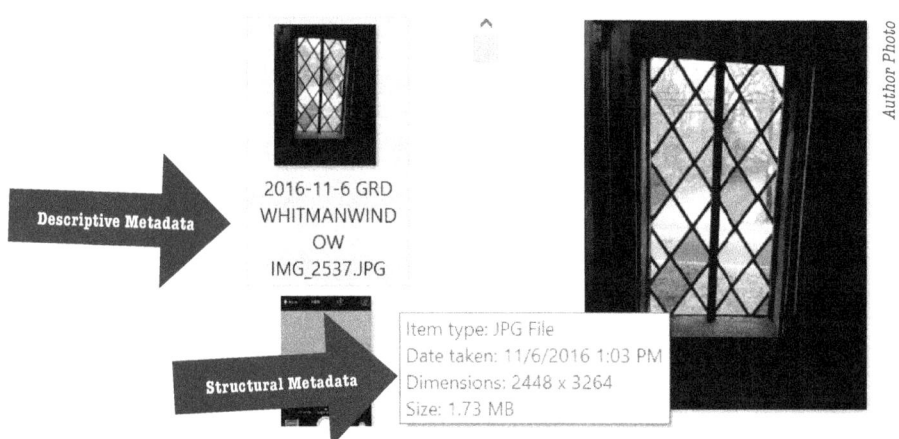

Structural and Descriptive Metadata.

In addition, photo editing programs that allow you to create metadata will strip the information when the photos are taken out of the program (Photoshop may be the one exception). Stripping occurs when photos are uploaded to the internet, emailed to a friend, or imported into another software program on your computer. When you purchase a new computer and upload all the old data onto the new one, all the metadata you created in the photo editing software may be lost. There is also no guarantee that the particular software program you are using will be available in the future. A better option is to title the original photographs and place them in folders on your computer's hard drive. You want to make sure that the metadata you add permanently attaches to the file and does not merely associate with it. By renaming the file, you can ensure this happens. The name or title of the photograph is permanently attached and will not be lost when transferring to a new computer, uploading to the internet, or moving the file within your computer.

A prime example of this potential hazard is Picasa, a popular photo storage software program that came preloaded on numerous computers for many years. Picasa was taken over by Google Photos in 2017, without warning their users. The metadata created in Picasa did not transfer seamlessly into Google Photos. Whatever software program is used to add metadata, there is no guarantee it will be around to be of use to Baby 2135. Considering the labor intensity of adding description and sorting mechanisms to photographs; it would be heartbreaking to have all that work disappear with the flick of a button.

A group of professionals recently formed a Family History Metadata Working Group (FHMWG) with the mission of ensuring that descriptive metadata is portable, interoperable, and consistent. Stay tuned. Retaining descriptive metadata across multiple platforms will most likely be a reality in the near future. For now, do not spend too much time in software programs that could become obsolete and result in total loss of all your hard work. See fhmwg.wordpress.com for updates.

Because digital photograph file names cannot be very long, one method of organizing them is storing them in folders that

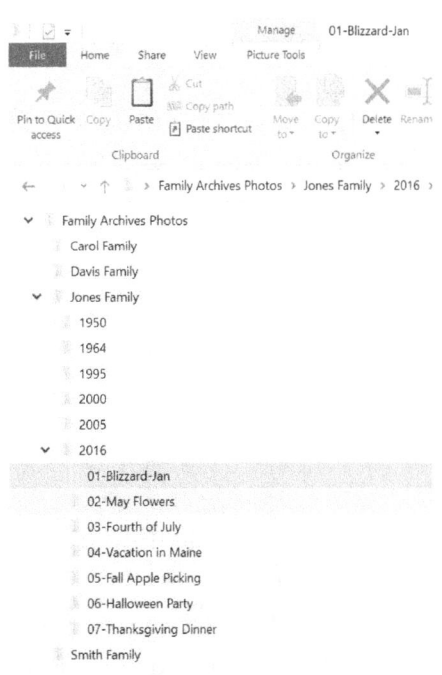

Organizing photographs using folders

group together images by date, event, place, or subject. When organizing photographs, you want to answer the questions who, what, where, why, and when. You also want to consider the automatic sorting features your computer uses. Many archivists suggest organizing by date. A typical folder title might look like this:

> 2010-May-Subject

A better option utilizing the computer's filing system is:

> 2010-05-Mother's Day

Within this folder individual photographs can be labeled:

> 2010-05-Mother's Day-Breakfast at IHOP-Jean, Dave, Steve, Susie-IMG-2340

The above photo title could be shortened to:

> 2010-05-MDB-JC, DC, SC, SD-IMG-2340

An explanation of the code would need to be stored somewhere else. The Finding Aid (refer to Chapter 2) of the family archive is the perfect place to link the photograph to the larger organizational structure of the collection. Within the Finding Aid will be a section for photographs. The line for the above photograph might read like this:

> 2010-05-MDB-JC, DC, SC, SD-IMG-2340 – Mother's Day Breakfast at IHOP. Pictured are Jean Collins, Dave Collins, Steve Collins, and Susie Darling.

Alternatively, since the folder tells us the when (2010-05) and the what (Mother's Day Breakfast), the individual photographs within the folder do not need the tag "2010-05-MDG." They could just list who is in the photograph: Jean Collins, Dave Collins, Steve Collins, and Susie Darling. Additionally, putting a number before the names will allow the computer to sort them in the order of your choosing:

> 1-Jean Collins, Dave Collins, Steve Collins, Susie Darling
>
> 2-Jean Collins
>
> 3-Stack of blueberry pancakes

Although the beginning tag "2010-05-MDB" and the ending tag "IMG2340" (which is the original photograph number) are not necessary, my instinct as an archivist is to add them. That way, if you later decide to move the photographs to another folder or want them to be identified in another way, the opening and closing tags will provide some helpful consistency.

Because computers tend to not like long descriptions, actual file names need to be as concise as possible. Folders can be used to segment many of your photographs. One suggestion is to include a PDF list of what is in the photographs in the digital folder. When organizing my own photographs, I create folders for each subject, keep the image structural file name, and include a PDF that I created in a word processing program.

To explain further, I took a trip in 2015 to three different countries. In each country I visited a large city and a "country" venue. The main folder for my trip is called "Budapest, Vienna, Prague 2015." I then created a subfolder inside this main folder for each city, such as "Vienna." Within each city I took several tours and did other things on my own. So, I created a folder for each of these activities:

> 1-Walking Tour City of Vienna
>
> 2-Schönbrunn Palace
>
> 3-Symphony Saturday Night

The photographs inside these folders are only for that one event. Included in the folder is a PDF that describes the event, my thoughts about it, and who is in each photograph. The end-product looks like this:

> Budapest, Vienna, Prague Trip 2015
>> 1-Budapest
>> 2-Vienna
>>> 1-Walking Tour, City of Vienna
>>> **LOG.PDF**
>>> IMG_1110.JPG
>>> IMG_1111.JPG
>>> IMG_1112.JPG
>>> IMG_1113.JPG
>>> IMG_1114.JPG
>>> IMG_1115.JPG
>>> IMG_1116.JPG
>>> 2-Schönbrunn Palace
>>> **LOG.PDF**
>>> IMG_1117.JPG
>>> IMG_1118.JPG
>>> IMG_1119.JPG
>>> IMG_1120.JPG
>>> IMG_1121.JPG

3-Symphony Saturday Night
LOG.PDF
IMG_1122.JPG
IMG_1123.JPG
IMG_1124.JPG
IMG_1125.JPG

3-Prague

LOG Description of Vienna Walking Tour

The tour took us to the oldest part of the city. We saw where an old tavern from the 16th century once existed and learned how the casks were rolled through the cobbled streets. While standing in a courtyard surrounded by old storefronts with apartments above, a Victorian horse and buggy passed through helping to create a vision of times long past. We stood near a stone monument while our tour guide told us the history of the area. Artur and I became aware of a haunting sound of people moaning. We looked at each other quizzically until we realized the sound was coming from the monument that we were standing next to. We walked around to the reverse side and saw that the monument was in memory of the Viennese Jews who were killed during the Holocaust. The artist did not hold back in depicting the horror of that sad chapter in Vienna's history. It was moving and memorable in its interpretation. One felt as though they were standing at the gates of hell seeing and hearing the moaning of the victims below.

This way of organizing your photographs is only a suggestion. Find a system and stay consistent with it. Scattering different systems will be confusing for you and for future researchers. Using keywords will allow for searching using the computer's Find or Explore functions. Your camera automatically assigns a number to a digital photograph. This number will stay with the photograph unless you remove it. Most professionals suggest that the number be kept with the image.

DIGITAL AUDIO

Audio files can include your favorite music, a recital of your children, an oral history with a great-uncle, your own musical recording, or memos you create with your smartphones. As mentioned in Chapter 11, it is not necessary to include commercial recordings in your family archive. You could include the song that was played at your wedding or other meaningful tunes, or you could let your future descendants know the songs and the musicians and they should be able to find them.

The first thing to do is identify which audio files are legacy items and need to be transferred to the family archive. If you have not already done this, you will need to transfer your audio files from the device you used to create them (typically a digital recorder or your smartphone) to your computer. The simplest way to do this is to import them into iTunes or another audio playing app or program. As with photos, when you plug your phone into your computer it will automatically download any music and audio files you have stored since the last time you plugged it in. The phone will automatically search for software that will import the records. If it does not happen automatically, open the software program of your choice, select File, then Import, and look for your device under My Computer.

As explained earlier, typical audio file formats are WAV and MP3. Popular music generally downloads as MP3 files. Because MP3s have lossy compression, they will have a reduction in sound quality. Since WAV files are uncompressed and take up more space on your hard drive, they will have the highest quality audio sound. Some recorders will automatically save and download in one or the other format. If possible, save the most important files in WAV format. Any oral histories should be saved as WAV files. Otherwise, MP3 is a good alternative.

The voice memo feature on smartphones can be used to record important events, conversations, or personal ruminations. When I have particularly important phone calls or personal visits with people that I want to remember, I record a voice memo right after the event because I know I will forget the details in a few days, if not hours. I purchased a high-quality digital recorder for doing oral histories, but I have used voice memos as a backup just in case something goes wrong. You may have recorded your oral histories right from your phone. If that is the case, you need to get them off the phone as soon as you are finished and get home.

One of the easiest ways to transfer files is emailing them right from your phone. Open the voice memo app, find the file you want to transfer to your computer, and click on the Upload icon. Then click on the email icon, enter your email address, and click Send. Once the file comes attached to your email, you can either drag it into your family archives/music folder, or you can copy and paste it into the folder (Ctrl+C, Ctrl+V). I like this method because it allows me to select the files I want to transfer without transferring all my useless shopping lists and reminders to myself.

To upload audio files to iTunes, plug your phone into your computer and open iTunes on your computer (you will have to download this free app if you have not already). When you open the file within iTunes, you should see a little icon of a phone at the top of the screen. Click that. Then, make sure the Music setting is selected on the left-hand side of the screen. Once that is selected, the screen on the right will change. Make sure the "include voice memos" radio box is checked. In the lower right-hand corner of the screen, select Sync. Let the upload run through its process. The voice memos will show up in the list under Unknown Artist.

Be aware that syncing will delete all the music on your phone and replace it with what is on your computer. If you have deleted music from your phone and do not want it re-added, do not use sync. Instead, download just the items you want without syncing by finding the files you want and dragging them from your phone to your computer. Syncing will also cause you to lose downloaded music from your phone if you have not downloaded it to your computer, so you will have to redownload it from iTunes. Backing up your music first will prevent loss of any tunes you want to keep.

Transcribing audio files is the final step. Audio files that contain music may not need transcription, but oral histories should be transcribed. As we have learned, the digital world is unstable. A transcription of an oral history or important audio file provides a good backup in the event the digital version becomes lost or corrupted.

Digital Video Recorder

DIGITAL VIDEO

Video preservation is complicated. At present, the archival community has no established definitive standards, protocols, or quantifiably proven methodologies. The application of hundreds of file formats, wrappers, and CoDecs used in the creation of multimedia files further complicates video preservation. Obsolescence is a major problem. It can occur quickly and permanently. If one component part of a digital video file becomes obsolete, the entire file is rendered obsolete. Complicating things further, new born digital video file formats are created with regularity. Hardware and software limitations produce constraints in developing standards and protocols. However, not doing anything may be far worse than digitizing without regulated standards. You will need to keep abreast of emerging developments to know how best to preserve digital video. I believe standards will be developed soon, not just for archives but for home collections as well. If possible, convert video files using the formats discussed in Chapter 9.

Because digital video is so complicated, and without regulated standards, a viable analog backup can provide an alternative option. What is the "analog" alternative? First, transcribe video content as you would audio content. Add narration to soundless sections such as, "Mary blows out candles on birthday cake" or "Uncle Joe enters the party escorted by son, Stephen, on the left and daughter, Sue, on the right." If music is playing in the background, identify it. Name everyone in the video. Print out pictures at regular intervals or of significant moments. Place everything in an acid-free folder, placing the pictures in plastic sleeves. Label the folder:

Recording Video Using SmartPhone

> Video: Uncle Joe's [Joseph Stephen Smith] 90th Birthday Party, September 19th, 1999.

Identify in the folder where the video file lives on the computer or external hard drive. Be sure to include the location of the video file and the metadata associated with it (those screenshots I told you to take earlier). With any luck, by the time Baby 2135 wants to access the materials, the technology will have advanced so that obsolete media types can be played. Even if the media files are still accessible, they might be wobbly or have missing pieces. Your transcription and snapshots may fill in the missing pieces for Baby 2135.

In the meantime, check video operability every three to five years. If a file becomes inaccessible, seek professional help. For more information, refer to the Federal Agency Digitization Guidelines Initiative which can be accessed at http://www.digitizationguidelines.gov/guidelines/FADGI_BDV_p1_20141202.pdf

EMAIL

Although emails are quite different from handwritten letters from the past, they are still written correspondence. Depending on the email system you use, email typically resides either in a software program on your hard drive or on a server on the internet. The basic process is to download it (if you can) and make a backup copy. You may, like me, have several email accounts including those at work.

The first step in email preservation is to organize it and remove any unnecessary email. You do not need to save every single email you write. Most of the conversational ones can be discarded. My sister and I get together every Sunday and either text or email the arrangements. They tend to look like this:

> HER: Do you want to get together this Sunday? There's a movie playing I want to see at this place and time.
>
> ME: I was thinking of seeing this movie? Is that okay?
>
> HER: Sure. Should I meet you there or come to your house?
>
> ME: Come to my house. I'll drive.
>
> HER: Okay. I'll be there at this time.
>
> ME: Okay. See you then.

Please do not torture Baby 2135 with reams and reams of uninteresting useless emails like those above. However, the emails you and your spouse sent to each other in the early stages of your romance might be memorable for you and interesting to Baby 2135, not to mention your children and grandchildren (if they are not too intimate, that is).

Like other parts of your archives, your first step may be to create a folder in your email programs called "Archive." Within that folder, create subfolders with the organization of your choice. I separate my emails by person. My sister and a few of my close friends have their own folders in my email account. Otherwise, they get dumped into a folder called "Friends" or "Family." I have business associates and clients who have their own folders that will not be kept for the family archive.

Deciding what to keep and what to get rid of is a good first step. As I have mentioned with other documents in our homes, there will be emails we want included in the family archives, ones that we will want to keep for ourselves (to be disposed of after our death), and others that can be trashed today.

Desktop

If your email is in a program (such as Microsoft Outlook) then the actual emails are located somewhere on your hard drive. Most desktop email programs offer the option of archiving or saving a copy of the email. You should back this up regularly. Check the backup procedures for your software program. Email software programs typically use the terms File/Save As, File/Archive, or File/Export. To back up in Microsoft Outlook, go to File then Import/Export and select Export to a File. At this point you have a few options. You can send the emails to an Access file, an Excel file, or a PST (personal storage table) file. The PST file is the true backup and will allow you to restore the documents to Microsoft Outlook if your computer crashes. Comma separated documents (CSV) will open in a spreadsheet, including Excel. You can also save individual emails as TXT files or print them as PDFs.

If you do not have Outlook and do not have one of the menu options listed above (File-Save As, etc.), search online to find out where the email lives in the program or on the computer directory. Search, "Where does [enter your program name] store my email files?" Some desktop email programs allow you to see the emails in a TEXT-reading program without opening the email program.

Online Services

Webmail is stored on hard drives owned by the webmail provider. Many webmail services offer the ability to turn emails into PDFs or download them to your hard drive. The best thing to do is search online or look within the webmail account for options in archiving. If nothing else works, most emails can be printed as PDFs. This can be time consuming and arduous. When searching how to save webmail, use words like "batch processing" or "entire file." Gmail used to allow automatic transfer of Gmail to a Google Doc, but that feature has since been disabled.

Larger service providers tend to allow you to download or back up your email. Smaller services may not provide this option. Also, you may have to pay for a premium service to have access to archiving/backup features.

If you have a desktop software program such as Outlook, you may be able to add the online email filter to the desktop program. Outlook will allow you to have multiple email accounts coming into the program. Once the emails are in the desktop software, you can backup and archive them.

Harvard University and Stanford University are working on a project to develop an open-source tool for archives to harvest and process emails and attachments. I am not sure if this tool will be practical or available for individuals, but it is important to know that this is being developed. Technologies that are developed for the archival community may eventually trickle down to individual use.

WEBSITES AND SOCIAL MEDIA

Websites and social media sites are records of activity just like the other documents in your personal archives. You may have a website for your business, a web page on your employer's website, or a personal website. Today, creating websites is easy, so you may have several. When I took an extended trip to Ireland several years ago, I created a blog that I could share with my family and friends as a group rather than sending individual emails about my trip. Even in a foreign country with limited access to the internet, I was able to easily create and sustain the blog and share it with family and friends.

Some websites and social media sites are free for the user, while others require an annual fee to be maintained. What do you think will happen to your business website or personal blog once you stop paying for the service? Most likely the host will take it down and it will be lost in the netherworld. If someone does not make a copy of it shortly after your death, it could be lost forever. Your family archive will most likely be filled with images and details of your personal life including weddings, holidays, vacations, sports, and hobbies. Your business web page is a window into a part of your life that is sometimes only vaguely known to your family.

My Aunt Hope was a single woman who lived with her family until they all passed away, at which time she lived alone. She started working at a major insurance company the year she graduated from high school and worked there until her retirement over forty years later. Although she had been retired for about ten years when she died, many of her coworkers came to her wake and told warm and interesting stories about the Hope they knew at work. It made us, her family, realize that she had had a rich, productive, and highly respected career that the family knew very little about. She did not have a website or even a page on the company's website (she retired before such things were in vogue). Had she worked in the 21st century, her web page may have illuminated her career in a way nothing else could have. In preserving her life story, it was sad to lose that part of her life. The best I could do was gather anecdotal information from strangers about that part of her life.

As with the other parts of your collection, the first thing you want to do is identify where you have content and what part of it you want to save. In addition to websites and blogs, you are probably using different popular social media sites. While it is beyond the scope of this book to explain how to archive every type of social media and website that exists today, I will give basic advice and provide specific instructions for some of the more popular sites. After that you can use the same principles to archive other platforms, or you can search their help sections to learn how to archive that information.

Websites

Websites are created using different platforms and content management systems. Even though they all use HTML coding, the software that is used to create them poses different problems when attempting to save a copy for archival purposes. Institutional archives use web crawlers to harvest websites. The Internet Archive found at www.archive.org is the largest internet archive in the world. It has a giant web crawler that harvests and saves websites to their Wayback Machine on a regular basis, sometimes daily, so that researchers can review the historical data of different relevant institutions, businesses, and organizations. These technologies are more sophisticated and complicated than is practical for a homeowner to use. There may be a time in the future when libraries will provide these kinds of services for individuals, but that day has not arrived yet. In the meantime, there are some simpler steps you can take to preserve the part of your legacy that lives on the internet.

Saving or Printing the Pages

If your web page can be saved by printing, lucky you. This is the simplest and easiest way to save a page. Sometimes not all the content prints properly, but most of it should come out looking just as it does on the internet. Print to a stable format such as PDF or PDF/A. You will need to save each web page separately and make one folder with a file for each web page. If all the pictures, logos, and content do not print, save the page as a Word document and then recreate it. Once it looks the way you want it to, save it as a PDF or PDF/A. Naturally, if your web page includes video, that poses special problems. Refer to the section on saving digital video earlier in this chapter.

Copy and Paste

All the pages on my website, created in WordPress, printed as a PDF with no problem. The pictures were retained, the content saved, and even the widgets looked right. The only page that would not print was the front page. Instead, I used the copy and paste function to save a copy. To do this, I opened the page in a web browser, selected everything by pressing Ctrl+A (All), and copied it into a Word document by pressing Ctrl+C (Copy) and then Ctrl+V (Paste). This pasted all the content into a Word document. It is not as pretty as it looks in real life, but it is close and will suffice. Once in the Word document, I saved it as a PDF.

Saving the Code

Another method of saving a website is saving all the code. In an HTML environment, the website could be recreated again, which would be very cool for your descendants. However, while this is valuable, the downside is that any JavaScripts, uploaded files (such as pictures), widgets, and other special coding will be lost.

Embedded in the code will be links to where these kinds of data are stored within the content management system. When you create a copy of the code, the links to other files will be broken in the saved document. The JPEGs and special coding can be saved in the same folder with the coding files. Keep in mind that this will require a future descendant to know how to code or create a website using coding or hire someone who will. Saving both the coding along with screenshots and saved pages will help a future descendant recreate the website in the future if they wanted to. To save the code of an HTML page, right-click anywhere on the web page and select View Page Source. Highlight all the code by first selecting Ctrl+A (All), then, Ctrl+C (Copy) then pasting it in a word processing document Ctrl+V(Paste).

HTML code

Backup

Most content management systems will allow a backup of the entire website to be made in the event the site crashes and needs to be restored. Backing up a website should be done on a regular basis for this type of insurance. For archival purposes, it will only be useful if your future descendant is able to import the data into the same content management system (such as WordPress or Squarespace) and if the content management system has the ability to read an older file. There is no guarantee in twenty, thirty, or a hundred years that it will. While it is good to have a backup for contemporary insurance purposes, it is less useful as an archival tool. I definitely think you should have a backup file, but I do not recommend it being your *only* archival tool.

Screenshots

Screenshots can be made using several tools including the "Print Screen" function found on most keyboards as well as Snip-it or Evernote. The beauty of a screenshot is that it captures the screen exactly as you see it. Screenshots are either saved automatically as JPEGs or saved to the computer's clipboard and need to be pasted into a Word document. On a Mac, a screenshot typically saves to your desktop. Once you take a screenshot, you can edit it using Photoshop or within Snip-it or Evernote. The problem with screenshots is that they will only capture what is on the screen, and many web pages extend far beyond a one-screen view.

12: BORN DIGITAL

To capture the entire page, you need to take multiple screenshots and stitch them together. This may be sufficient depending on what you are trying to capture.

If none of the above methods work to your satisfaction, contact your webmaster for assistance. They may be able to help you, or you may be the one to educate them. Most webmasters and program developers know how to preserve things for today. Many of them are not thinking far enough into the future to be of help in long-term preservation, but they may be able to provide feedback and tips.

Social Media

Facebook

My Facebook wall is an incredible window into my life. It reveals who my friends are; what I like; my political beliefs; the events I have attended or have been interested in attending; memes of silly cat videos, or words of wisdom I have reposted; trips I have taken; and many, many photographs of me with my family and friends. Altogether what emerges is a depiction of my values, my sense of humor, my interests, and my activities. Even the level of my activity reveals something about my life. During times when I was working long hours, attending grad school, or under pressure, I spent very little time on Facebook. Whereas periods of my life when I had flexibility with my time and less pressure, I spent more time on Facebook. Capturing these pages can create a great legacy for future generations.

ARCHIVES TIP

Who knows what will happen after Mark Zuckerberg passes or if a newer, shinier coin will toss Facebook out of the big pond of social media.

Facebook claims that it will never take a page down unless instructed. That will probably be true for the near future, but it is hard to say what will happen in a hundred or more years. Who knows what will happen after Mark Zuckerberg passes or if a newer, shinier coin will toss Facebook out of the big pond of social media. If you want to try saving your content outside of Facebook for the sake of insurance, I suggest doing so periodically. It will be important to share your username and password with loved ones before your death or make note of them in the family archive. Otherwise, they might not have access to your wall or your instant messages.

If requested by your heirs, Facebook will turn your wall into a legacy site after your death. Otherwise, the entire site can be deleted. Your wall can be edited so that individual posts, replies, and message conversations can be deleted. You can save them all, delete them all, print a copy in PDF or on paper, or do nothing and hope Facebook keeps its word and maintains your page forever. Just make sure your descendants have access to your account after you pass.

Facebook has a mechanism to create a downloadable archive of everything you have posted. Follow the instructions on Facebook. They may change from time to time.

> *"It changes the way I think about all history. I could never see myself before. But this information really allows me to know who I am. And if they didn't make it, none of us would have made it."*
>
> **KEENAN IVORY WAYANS**
> Finding Your Roots S3.E3

The files created by Facebook's archive contain the content from your Facebook page, but they do not display like they do online. The information is disassociated; one file contains pictures, while another file contains the status writing that accompanies each picture. The information is not without value, but it is not straightforward. The individual files will need some additional doctoring to make them understandable and relevant for Baby 2135. Photograph titles are long strings of numbers to Facebook. To make them understandable, you should re-label them. Most of these photographs are probably already in your digital photograph archive. If possible, it would be relevant to indicate when the photograph was uploaded and point it back to the original photograph. This will make a record of what was posted when. Most files come with HTM or HTML file extensions. When you click on them, they will open in a web browser. You can then keep them in this form or save them as PDF files.

I like my Friends List because it gives the date we became Facebook friends. Messages that are sent to individuals or groups of friends are captured by the name(s) of the person(people) you have corresponded with. Again, the title is given as a long string of numbers. Changing the title of the document to the person or group name is an easy metadata fix. These files are appealing because they show all the correspondence you have had with that one person or group. Some of the messages are in response to postings on Facebook. Since the response is disconnected from the original post, it is sometimes hard to know what you were responding to.

As with other parts of your collection, you want to assess whether the information is relevant to save. Some messages, especially those disconnected from the original post, can be deleted. Some of the message files written to one person can be copied and pasted into a Word document so that parts of the correspondence can be deleted before you save the document as a PDF. Use this tool if parts of the conversation are confidential.

Another option for saving Facebook pages is saving the pages on your wall as a PDF using the print function. Facebook only displays a little bit of data at a time, so for everything to print, you have to scroll down to the very beginning of time with Facebook, then select Print and Save as PDF. All the photographs, responses, things people posted to your timeline, and everything else will save just as it looks—as long as it is all loaded. I tried this and it would have printed 384 pages. It was too much for my little laptop, so it crashed before everything was saved. But if your computer can handle it, the beauty of this method is that it captures everything just as it looks on your wall. Photographs and content are together as they appeared originally. Doing this in sections or yearly is a better option than trying to do the entire thing at once.

Or you might want to save individual posts. My sister's husband's family owned a general store in their town for five generations. On the town's Facebook page a stream started where people shared their memories of the store and the family that owned it. It would be valuable to save just this conversation, which could be done through Copy and Paste, or by printing the pages.

Another option with Facebook is purchasing a hardcopy book of your memories. Facebook calls it a Past Book. It can be found at this link: http://www.pastbook.com/txt/facebook-photo-books/. Facebook will post it to your wall, if you want, or you can get a printed copy for about $20–$30. That is a pretty good deal. This is great if you upload many pictures since it is primarily a picture book. If you took the step of creating a family Facebook page, it might be nice to get a printed copy of everything that is posted on it. At the top of the order page, Facebook asks you to select the year you want to print. Be advised that lower down on the page, they allow you to select a date range, so you can select multiple years or specific dates.

As I write this section, I am reminded of a few family members and friends who are no longer with us. Perhaps your page is not the one you want to archive. Instead, you might want to save the Facebook page of a parent, a child, a friend, or a coworker. Every now and then, sometimes on their birthday, sometimes on the date of their death, I visit the legacy Facebook pages of family members and friends who have passed. Seeing the pictures, the posts, and the silly videos they enjoyed is a great way to reconnect and bring their memory back to life, if only briefly.

Twitter, Instagram, Flickr, MySpace, and Other Social Media Sites

It is beyond the scope of this book to provide specific instructions on how to archive every single web page, social media site, ezine, blogpost or other internet presence you have. I have provided the principles; the rest is up to you. Check

each social media site to see what sort of archiving options they provide, if any. Query your favorite search engine or computer magazine/ezine for advice. Try printing the pages as PDFs or copy and paste them into a word document for editing before saving as PDF.

Chances are new technology will continue to emerge that will provide digital legacy preservation. The Library of Congress has a goal to provide legacy preservation for families and individuals. When selecting a service, remember to keep the big picture in mind—you want to archive things for at least a hundred years, not just the next ten or twenty. Many web developers are not considering this, even as they develop software called "archives." Also, remember that a business's main goal is to make money, not to provide your family with a legacy. Hackers are real and will continue to threaten digital security. Having a backup copy of your social media content on a hard drive or in print version is always a good choice. Storing legacy content only in the cloud is not recommended.

TEXT MESSAGES

Many conversations take place today through text using our phone's messaging device or other apps such as WhatsApp. Depending on the service provider you use and the type of phone you have, the instructions will vary. iPhone will back up data to your hard drive through iTunes. iPhones also backs up to iCloud, and the data can then be downloaded onto your computer. Android uses G Cloud backup. There are also a number of apps you can download onto your computer. Some are free, others will cost a small fee. Some of the more popular ones include iExplorer, PhoneView (Mac only), CopyTrans Contacts (Windows only), and Wondershare TunesGo.

Some services will allow you to view text messages on your computer screen, but you will need to pay for the full service to be able to download the files. Most services download files in TXT, PDF, or CSV (comma separated values) format. Download in whatever format you prefer. You can open TXT files with Notepad and CSV files in a spreadsheet. For PDF files, you can copy and paste them into a Word document for editing purposes and then save as a PDF. If downloading is not as straightforward as all the apps and devices claim, see if you can find a SIMS file or SD file. These are small digital cards inside your phone that store digital content. You may need to click on either of those to open the messages. If you still cannot figure it out, go to your service provider (Verizon, Apple, T-Mobile, etc.) store and see if they can help you.

Figuring out how to download the text messages onto your computer is your first challenge. The second challenge is editing the messages so that you keep only the most important and poignant conversations. As with your other files, be sure to identify who is speaking. You may want to add why the files are important, such as "Last conversation I had with my father."

The organizational structure can vary based on the content. All conversations with one person could be stored in one place. But, if you won the annual golf league, and you received many texts of congratulations from friends and well-wishers, you could set up a separate folder and capture those texts in one place. Be creative but be wise.

And, as with all your digital content, be sure to use the 3-2-1 Rule—3 copies: 2 storage devices, 1 off-site.

The goals of an archive are to preserve things from the past and save things from the present for future generations. In that endeavor, you want to keep things in their original form as much as possible. Digital information is notoriously known for being changed, written over, or deleted, sometimes without prior thought to the impact this will have on the integrity of the work or how a future descendant will see it. As you are reading this book, you may be thinking of the emails you have deleted that you now think should have been saved. Or you may be thinking that it would be interesting and cool to see the unaltered original version of your LinkedIn account or how your website has changed from its original form. What does that say about how you, your business, or your hobby has changed?

In creating a digital archive, you want to be mindful of how you can ensure that documents are not overwritten, altered, or erased. You want to think about how to keep things in their original form as much as possible. This is not to say that when you get back from a trip you cannot edit your digital photographs, but you want to ensure important email is retained and word documents are changed to formats that will not allow further editing.

I hope this section has made you aware of the advantages and disadvantages of digital preservation and archiving. Transferring video and audio tapes to digital will most likely extend their lives. But the digital world requires software and hardware that is always changing, and you need to be aware of the pitfalls and dangers of this reality. Obsolescence is a real concern with digital documents. Even coding languages like HTML continually evolve and change so that codes that were used yesterday are updated and changed today. Digital documents can suffer from bit rot or data decay, hard drives and magnetic tapes can lose their magnetization, flash drives can lose their charge, and CDs can scratch, warp, fade, or melt. Because the digital world is so new, it is hard to predict how long these items will last.

Papyrus from ancient Egypt dates back almost 4,000 years. Is it possible for our digital legacy to extend so far into the future?

SECTION THREE

CREATING A LEGACY

CHAPTER 13

ESTATE PLANNING

Through autumns golden gown
We used to kick our way
You always loved this time of year
Those fallen leaves lay undisturbed now
'Cause you're not here

A gentle rain pours softly on my weary eyes
As if to hide a lonely tear
My life will be forever autumn
'Cause you're not here.

—The Moody Blues, *Forever Autumn*

Most people plan for their ultimate passing. Establishing a family archive simultaneously acknowledges that the time will come when you are no longer here and actively plans for the passing of the family legacy torch to the next generation. Many lawyers today who set up wills, trusts, and estates include digital legacy items, but many do not. And even if they do, their list may not be complete. If you set your will up many years ago, it might not include your digital legacy. My job is not to teach you how to create a will, a trust, or an estate. You will have to see a lawyer for that. My job is to make sure that your digital legacy is preserved for your descendants.

Think for a moment of your digital footprint. Do you use Facebook, Twitter, Instagram, or Pinterest? Do you store your photographs on Flickr or other photo service sites? What online services have you set up accounts with? What service do you use for email? Do you have storage with that company as well? What retail stores do you have accounts with? Did you use a service ten years ago that still has your data sitting on its server? Will the company destroy your content and, if so, when? These are the things you need to consider.

THE NON-DIGITAL AFTERLIFE

When preserving analog documents, you follow the same procedure that has been used for centuries. You allocate who gets what— that is it. When it comes to the items in your material family archive, think of the person who is most likely to take care of these items. You may decide the one with the most financial resources is the best suited to inherit the family archives. But more than that, think of the person who has the most interest in family history and has a love of genealogy. Some people do not have this sense of appreciation. To many people, the old stuff is just junk that should be trashed or dropped off at the nearest Salvation Army as soon as possible. Do not leave your archives to the person you think it "should" be left to simply based on their position in the family (e.g., the oldest child or the oldest son). Perhaps your youngest granddaughter is most interested in the family legacy. If that is the case, leave everything to her. Cement the responsibility by stating in your will why you chose this person and what your expectations are. Make it clear that the archive is in their hands, and they are now the "Keeper of Family Lore." Better yet, discuss it with them before you pass and have them sign "The Family Historian Legacy Promise" at the end of the book.

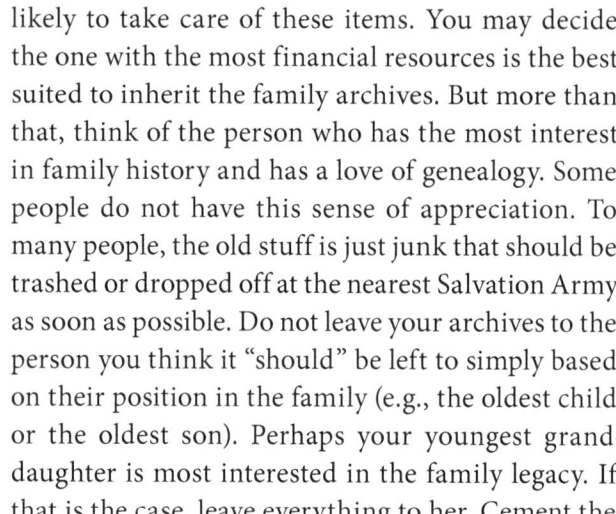

ARCHIVES TIP

When considering who to pass the family archive on to, think of the person who has the most interest in family history and has a love of genealogy.

Many parents strive to treat all their children equally. My mother always tried to make things even between her three daughters. At the holidays she would see something she knew one of us would love, so she would buy it but then realize she needed to get something for the other two to even it out. That is a nice sentiment for buying gifts, but it might not be the best strategy for the family archive. The archive should be a complete collection that is passed on as a unit to one person. Otherwise, everything will be scattered and most likely lost. With modern technology, it is easy to make a memory book or a digital archive with digital versions of all photographs and paper documents that all family members will have and can print out if they so desire. This is a great way to share the content of the family archive, but the physical documents should still be kept together as a unit and passed down to one person.

While it might be desirable to keep photographs, genealogical papers, and important documents together in one place, you may want to allocate artifacts such as jewelry, heirloom artwork, heirloom furniture, heirloom decorative pieces, military uniforms, wedding dresses, and christening gowns, to different children and grandchildren. If you do this, be sure to have photographs of these items in the paper and digital archives. The archived photographs will alert descendants to the existence of these items. A Last Will and Testament will indicate who they were left to.

THE DIGITAL AFTERLIFE

The digital afterlife for our parents or grandparents was much smaller than it will be for us. Before the internet, the digital afterlife consisted of perhaps a computer and some kind of backup device—often a CD or tape. In whatever manner it was stored, digital content was tangible. It was stored on a device and was considered part of all other tangible property when a forebear's estate was being settled. With the advent of the internet, social media, and cloud-based services, all that has changed. Now our digital footprint is in many places. Our information is stored on computer systems all over the world that are owned by services, not by us. Each service has different rules of how, when, and if content can be accessed by an heir. Our digital footprint can be so vast that we may not be aware how far it extends. Preparing our digital inheritance is another piece of the puzzle that must be in place for all our affairs to be in order. There are some basic things that you need to consider and plan for.

Identify

The first step in getting your digital assets in order is to identify where they are located. The biggest issue of digital inheritance is often awareness, not legality. If your heirs do not know what you have, where you have been on the internet, what accounts you have established, or what services you use, they cannot do anything about it. Additionally, if they lack your usernames and passwords, they may have trouble accessing the sites. Many companies will allow heirs to close accounts, but others do not. We will be discussing

ARCHIVES TIP

The biggest issue of digital inheritance is often awareness, not legality.

the bigger sites below. Most of us never think about what will happen to our accounts after our death, but without a plan in place our heirs will be faced with the challenge of figuring it out. They will be forced to piece together each bit of your digital legacy after you have passed on. You owe it to your heirs to get your things in order to make this job as simple and seamless as possible. Remember, in addition to needing to deal with your digital legacy, they will also be dealing with your material items—houses, clothing, furniture, tools, toys, etc.

Passwords

When compiling the list of companies and services that contain your digital content, think about the executors of your estate and what it might take for them to dismantle your digital assets. If they have access to your user IDs and passwords, their job will be much easier. With user IDs and passwords, they will be able to log in to different websites and close the accounts. Otherwise, they will have to contact each company separately and request that the account be closed. Normally this requires proof of who they are and their relationship to you and proof that you have passed, typically a death certificate. Access to your computer will make their life easier since your computer will have saved cookies allowing for automatic logins. Executors may also be able to see where you have visited based on your internet search history.

Knowing the User ID and Passwords is crucial at many sites

It is easy to create a master document containing passwords that you maintain during your lifetime and make available to your loved ones upon your death. A Word document with all your passwords can be password protected. I do this for myself so that when I go to a website that I have not visited in a while I can look up the password quickly and easily. Alternatively, you can create an Excel spreadsheet for easy sorting by company name. Using the Note app on your smartphone to list only those sites that might be needed when you are not at home is also helpful. This document can also be password protected; however, even though it is convenient, it is not as secure from hackers as a Word or Excel document on a computer. Entering password clues instead of the full password in the smartphone Note will hide sensitive data. I know the variations of my passwords so I write them with clues that I understand but no one else would, like A***B**c**1**2**#. That tells me some of the letters, where I may or may not have capitalized, and if I used symbols. Then I can fill in the blanks.

The value of having a password document is that it helps keep track of your digital footprint in the vast World Wide Web. Think of how often you visit sites that force you to set up usernames and passwords to access the information you want. You quickly set up this information in the moment without realizing you have just expanded your digital footprint. You might just want to look for red shoes, but the retailer requires that you set up a user ID and password first. You hurriedly enter your standard information and later forget that you even set it up. This is a very bad practice that I know many of us fall victim to. Keeping a Word document or a Note on your phone and entering the information right away helps you keep track of where you have been and what you have done. The list of passwords will also provide your executors with the specific accounts you have opened. These accounts can be deleted, but only if your executors know they exist.

For step-by-step instructions on how to set up a passwords document, visit my website at https://lenasalina.com/secrets-from-the-stacks-guides/.

Password Managers

Password managers automatically create long, hard-to-replicate password strings for you. These are online services that you may or may not have to pay for. According to Consumer Reports, the four largest are 1Password, Dashlane, KeePass, and LastPass.[42] In addition to creating passwords, they will store and protect PINs, credit card numbers, three-digit CVV codes, answers to security questions, and more. They will also sync between all your devices. Information can be stored locally on your own computer/devices or in the cloud on their servers. You can choose to store the information in either place or both places depending on your comfort level. I highly recommend reading the article, "Everything You Need to Know About Password Managers" from Consumer Reports. You can get a copy of this on my website at www.lenasalina.com/resources/digitization.

Access

Access is a legal issue. Armed with user IDs and passwords, the executor of an estate can go into each account and manage, archive, or delete the account on your behalf after your death. Without the user IDs and passwords, an executor can often reset passwords and gain access to many accounts if they have access to certain key information such as primary email accounts and answers to security questions. Having access to email accounts will make the executor's life much easier by allowing them to reset passwords. Using the email account, executors can also find what accounts you set up and used by scrolling through and identifying key emails that confirm account setups or purchases. They can then use any marketing emails to verify past activity by visiting the site and searching for an account.

Rights and Ownership

When it comes to rights and ownership, nothing is straightforward and simple. The rise of the internet created an abundance of issues surrounding copyrights that have not yet been fully resolved. A few Supreme Court decisions have been made, and no doubt there will be more on the horizon before everything is settled. We are living during the birth of the digital age and the growing pains continue to be worked out. The subject of rights and ownership is still a sticky one in the library world, although some things have been ironed out and there are current rules in place.

> **ARCHIVES TIP**
>
> When it comes to rights and ownership, nothing is straightforward and simple.

When people donate materials to an archive, they typically sign over ownership to the institution housing them, thereby giving up legal ownership. In the archives, this became an issue for documents that were received prior to the establishment of the internet. Was it legal to publish online content if the donor gave the collection before the internet existed? What about privacy? Even if it was legal, archivists had to ask whether it was ethical. I worked in an archive that had oral histories that were recorded in the early 1980s. The archive established an online digital archive in the 2010s. It was clear that the original tapes and the content on them were owned by the institution. However, at the time they were recorded it was understood that researchers would need to be on-site at the institution in order to hear them. On the internet, people all over the world have easy access to the entire content of the oral history, which is often very intimate. Was it legal or ethical to upload the interviews after they were digitized? What if the person giving the interview or donating the material, or a family member, wanted the content removed? These are some of the issues archivists have had to consider since the establishment of the internet.

> *"It makes me feel open now, open-minded. To really understand where it all comes from, where the family comes from, how they got here, when they got here, who's who... it changes a lot of things. This is a history lesson for me and for my family."*
>
> **CARMELO ANTHONY**
> Finding Your Roots S4.E7

Regarding your own personal digital archive, here are some things to consider:

✓ For any single object that exists in the digital world, there could be individuals, groups, and corporations that hold exclusive rights to possess that object.

✓ In the publishing industry, it has been long established that copyright ownership of published materials by an author (an individual) may extend rights to the publisher (a corporation).

✓ Authors who publish works, whether through an institution they work at or individually, have legal contracts with all parties involved that are established, agreed upon, and signed.

✓ When we create content online, including writings, photographs, and videos, we become the authors, photographers, and creators of that content.

The Terms of Use, which most of us ignore when we register for different online accounts, stipulate the rights and ownership of our digital content on that particular website. They are all different. The Terms of Use is a legally binding contract between the user (you) and the company offering the services (Facebook, Twitter, Pinterest, etc.). As is true of most contracts developed by a corporation, they are written and designed to extend the protections to the corporation and limit the protections for the user. Unlike contracts developed between publishers and authors, users of online services cannot negotiate a Terms of Use agreement. You either agree and use the services as-is, or you do not agree and do not use the services, period. As family archivists, our main concerns about the Terms of Use are ownership of uploaded content, the right to use that content, and who is authorized to access the accounts.

Many contracts prohibit the transference of an account from one party to another. They restrict users from allowing other individuals to use their usernames and passwords to access services. The main intent of the internet service providers is not to disallow an inheritor access to the account to dismantle it; their main concern is that multiple people will use their services through the same account. Whether paid for or not, they prefer that everyone have their own account. This means that giving an executor access to your account is problematic from a legal standpoint. Many attorneys think that a legal executor acting in the fiduciary role of a decedent without willful intent to use the service for personal gain can most likely access an account.

Digital assets include email, laptops, social media accounts, smartphones, cloud storage, ebooks, music subscriptions, and more

They can choose to close it, download the content, or otherwise determine the best course of action as part of settling the larger estate. Most lawyers believe these activities would hold up in a court of law.

Many companies are starting to consider what to do with accounts after a person has passed. No doubt protocols will continue to be established that will make this transition smoother in the future, but for now, it still presents significant problems. Some terms state that an account will be closed once it is determined (usually through a death certificate) that the person has died. If no action is taken, the information could remain on the internet indefinitely. Facebook still notifies me of a friend's birthday several years after her death, which is rather unsettling. An article on Facebook claimed that the platform will someday be the largest digital gravesite since it does not remove content unless instructed.[43] Your daily life could be on Facebook in a hundred years. Genealogists of the future may search for ancestors' Facebook pages like modern ones search for birth certificates and census records.

The laws governing the disposition of an individual's possessions are well-established, legally enforced, and socially acceptable. Lawyers increasingly include digital assets when establishing wills, trusts, and estate planning. The typical protocol is that an executor is appointed to handle all the affairs of the deceased until the estate is fully settled. Digital assets fall under the property included in a deceased's estate.

Blanket powers over digital assets can be established by placing a fiduciary in the role of taking care of all digital assets. A digital will can be set up to establish specific instructions for each digital asset that include a list of each item, the login information, and the decedent's wishes for it. This is a separate document from the main will but should be referenced in the will. A different executor of the digital will can be set up if necessary. Perhaps you want your son to be the legal executor of your estate, but your granddaughter is more tech savvy and you think she will be better able to take care of your digital assets.

If a will is not in place, estate laws governed by each individual state determine the rules for handling the deceased's possessions. Increasingly, states are addressing how digital assets should be handled. The Uniform Laws Commission (ULC) crafts well-drafted legislation that each state can use to bring clarity and stability to critical areas of state statutory law. They drafted an act in 2015 to address the digital assets of decedents. The act in part states the following:

> *This act extends the traditional power of a fiduciary to manage tangible property to include management of digital assets. The act allows fiduciaries to manage digital property like computer files, web domains, and virtual currency, but restricts a fiduciary's access to electronic communications such as email, text messages, and social media accounts unless the original user consented to fiduciary access in a will, trust, power of attorney, or other record.*[44]

13: ESTATE PLANNING

The ULC does not pass laws. Each state must approve, amend, or craft their own laws regarding digital assets. The ULC provides recommendations and language that states can use in creating their own laws. Check with your lawyer or your local state authorities to find out how the laws are established in your state.

Digital content downloaded as eBooks from Amazon or music from iTunes is not owned by the person doing the download. Instead, the person has a license to access or use the content. That license typically expires when the person dies. This means that when your father passes away you will be able to keep all the books in his library if you so choose, but the eBooks on his Kindle or iPad will disappear as soon as the account is closed. Making a list of the content will allow you to know what he had read and perhaps obtain a copy for yourself. But ownership is not only non-transferable, it is not even true ownership; it is more of a lease.

Online Digital Estate Planning Services

Today, a few online services are available to hold and keep your digital legacy in one place. These services allow you to upload your digital assets (word documents, photographs, videos, etc.). You can create a list of all your digital assets, the username and password for each, and specific instructions for each item. In a predetermined way, often a length of time with no activity, these services will share the information with people you choose. Sometimes they will send an email with a code that will allow the person of your choosing to get into your account. Some require verification of death, usually in the form of a death certificate. SecureSafe, a Swiss company, claims that the information in their digital storage area is as safe as a Swiss bank. They do not have access to your information, your password, or your account.

LEGACY PLANNING

Online services keep your digital legacy in one place

In other words, if there has been no activity on your account for six months (you specify how long), online digital estate services will send you an email that basically says, "Are you still alive?" If there is no response, they will send an email to the heirs you have instructed them to send an email to. Based on your instructions, certain heirs will have access to some information while others will have access to other information. Perhaps you want everyone to have access to your photographs, but only your executor to have access to your legal documents and just your designated family historian to have access to the family archives you established.

Email services have different policies on how to close an account and who has permission

EMAIL

Legal standards do not exist for how emails will be handled after a person passes away. Each service provider has different rules. You and your executor will need to be schooled on which service you have and how to close your account after your death. Most service providers believe that their responsibility to keep your information safe, secure, and private extends to your afterlife. This is reasonable since email is correspondence and can be very private and intimate. We may prefer that our account be deleted sight unseen. On the other hand, we may want to share some information and the onus is on us to make these determinations. The policies of the biggest service providers as of this writing are below. As with all things digital, be aware that everything is subject to change. Do your research and establish your desires and directions.

- ✓ Google has a service called Inactive Account Manager that allows your account to be shared with or deleted by someone of your choosing after a period of inactivity. When setting up Inactive Account Manager, you decide the length of time of inactivity (six months, a year) and whether you want the account deleted or shared with a specified person. You also indicate which services (Gmail, Drive, AdSense, Blogger, etc.) you want shared.

- ✓ Alternatively, Google recognizes that many people pass away without leaving instructions for how to handle their online accounts. With this in mind, they allow loved ones to contact them regarding a deceased user's account. They will close the account of a deceased person and in certain circumstances will provide content from a deceased user's account after a careful review. They will not provide passwords or login details. You must upload a death certificate, driver's license, or other documents to verify information.

- ✓ Microsoft has a Next of Kin process that will release the contents of an Outlook account or close the account including emails and attachments, address books, and Messenger contact lists. Passwords on the account will not be provided, the passwords cannot be changed, and ownership cannot be transferred. Contents of the account will be shipped on a DVD. This policy extends to emails with the extensions @outlook.com, @hotmail.com, @live.com,

13: ESTATE PLANNING

@windowslive.com, and @msn.com. It does not include SkyDrive, MSN Dial-up, or Xbox Live. Microsoft will want proof that the user has passed away and that the person making the request has legal executor status or proof of kin.

- ✓ Yahoo will not allow your heir access to passwords, email, or other account information. They will allow the account to be closed, fees to be suspended, and the information to be permanently deleted. A letter of request to close the account must include the user's Yahoo ID, proof that the person making the request is the legal representative of the person or estate, and a copy of the death certificate of the Yahoo account holder.

- ✓ Apple iCloud, including Mac.com and Me.com, stipulates in the iCloud Terms of Service that there is "No Right of Survivorship." They clearly state that the account is non-transferable and that rights to the account, Apple ID, and content terminate upon your death. All content within the account will be deleted once Apple receives a death certificate. If you have an iPhone with iCloud storage, the biggest part of that storage may be your photographs. If this is the only place you have pictures, they will be deleted after your death—unless you take other measures.

If you use another email service provider, be sure to check their policy and instruct your heirs accordingly.

FACEBOOK

Facebook provides several options for handling your account after your death. The account can be memorialized, a legacy contact can be appointed, or the entire account can be deleted.

A memorialized account has "Remembering" next to the profile name. Friends can still share memories on the timeline. This is a nice way for people to express their sorrow or memories after a loved one has passed. Every year people post to my cousin's website on his birthday and the anniversary of

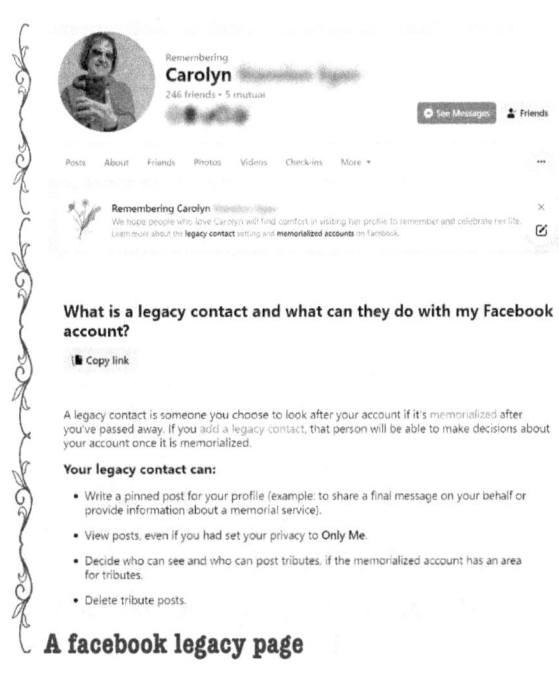

A facebook legacy page

his death. It is a nice way to bond at those times with the community of family and friends who also miss him. Being able to post on the timeline requires that the settings indicate this is permissible. Content already on the site at the time of death is not removed. This makes a stroll down memory lane as easy as scrolling through pictures, postings, and other content shared by loved ones. Memorialized profiles do not appear in public spaces such as "People You May Know," or "Birthday Reminders." Memorialized accounts cannot be logged into and cannot be changed, but they can be removed from Facebook with a valid request.

Alternatively, Facebook recently instituted a system for designating a "legacy contact." Upon your death, the designated person must prove to Facebook that you have passed away. Once your death has been established, the legacy contact can request the removal of your account or set it up as a memorial site. They can also write a pinned post on your profile page sharing a final message on your behalf and provide information about funerals, memorial services, or celebrations. The legacy contact can respond to new friend requests and update the profile picture and cover photo. They can also download a copy of what you have shared on Facebook. However, they cannot log into your account, remove or change past posts or photos, read your messages, remove friends, or make new friend requests. A legacy contact could choose to keep the site memorialized for a certain period of time and then close it after a few months or several years.

Another option is having your account permanently deleted after your death. Look in the account settings for "Your Facebook Information" and click "Delete Your Account and Information." If no action is taken, Facebook will delete your account if they learn of your passing.

*"We are stardust
We are golden
And we've got to
get ourselves back
to the garden."*

JONI MITCHELL
Woodstock

TWITTER

Twitter will deactivate a deceased person's account at the request of a loved one. Upon submitting a request, the loved one will be sent an email from Twitter with instructions for submitting copies of the executor's identification and a copy of your death certificate. While Twitter will deactivate the account, they will not allow anyone access to the account, thereby protecting the confidentiality of the user. The rules are similar if a person has become medically incapacitated. In this case, Twitter requires the requester's ID, the user's ID, and documentation authorizing your Power of Attorney to act on your behalf. Twitter has an additional policy that will allow loved ones to request removal of images and videos taken of the deceased person from the time of injury through the time of death. This will only be done in cases where the images and video are not considered newsworthy. It is a halfhearted, respectful response to the abject voyeurism rampant in the digital age.

DEAD MAN'S SWITCH

An innovation of the digital age is the dead man's switch. Traditionally, a dead man's switch is an automatic "off" or "kill" switch that kicks in when the operator of heavy machinery becomes incapacitated through death or loss of consciousness. The use of these devices increased with the introduction of trains, subways, and streetcars. We may be more familiar with their use in lawn mowers, chainsaws, snowblowers, treadmills, tractors, and amusement park rides.

Digital versions of the dead man's switch function in different ways. We are all familiar with getting locked out of our bank accounts or other sensitive secure sites by failing to enter the right password within a designated number of tries. This is a version of a dead man's switch. Other software might delete or encrypt data in the event a breach has occurred. Many of us have a "Find My Phone" feature that will allow us to destroy the content on our phone if the phone is lost or stolen.

Some dead man's services allow you to send information to loved ones after your death. These could be private letters expressing love, forgiveness, or speaking your truth, or they could be letters that share instructions, passwords, and links needed to dismantle your estate. Google's Inactive Account Manager described above is a form of a dead man's switch.

Some of these services are free, others require monthly or annual fees. Do your research and decide what is best for you.

CHAPTER 14

DISASTER PREPAREDNESS, DISASTER RECOVERY, EMERGENCY MANAGEMENT[45]

Just yesterday mornin', they let me know you were gone
Suzanne, the plans they made put an end to you
I walked out this morning and I wrote down this song
I just can't remember who to send it to

I've seen fire and I've seen rain
I've seen sunny days that I thought would never end
I've seen lonely times when I could not find a friend
But I always thought that I'd see you again

—James Taylor, *Fire and Rain*

Hopefully, you will never experience an emergency or disaster, but it is always best to prepare. To repeat what has been said before in this book, prevention is better than restoration. It is easier and cheaper to prevent damage than it is to restore items to their original glory after damage occurs. One of the main reasons to get your family archive in order is that in the event of a natural disaster or a personal emergency all will not be lost. With all the preparations that you will need to think of when threatened by disaster, and with all the work and responsibilities you will face afterward, it will be a great relief knowing that your family archive is one less thing you need to worry about. If you have followed the advice in this book, all your analog photographs, family documents, analog videos, and audio tapes have been digitized, and they are all backed up using the 3-2-1 Rule. As discussed in Chapter 11, digitizing can be tedious and time consuming but is well worth the effort. If you face a disaster or personal emergency that results in all your photographs being destroyed, having a digital copy of them ensures you can easily print them out again using an online service.

Tornado Waynoka, Oklahoma, May 1898

The National Archives and Records Administration (NARA) identifies an emergency as "a situation or an occurrence of a serious nature, developing suddenly and unexpectedly, and demanding immediate action, generally of short duration… a week or less."[46] A disaster is "an unexpected occurrence inflicting widespread destruction and distress and having long-term adverse effects…"[47] Collection managers who have been through a disaster report that "knowing your collection is the single most important factor to successful recovery."[48] Having your collection processed before a major disaster or even a minor emergency will help identify what is missing or damaged or what needs attention.

We live in an age when watching our fellow Americans suffer catastrophic loss is an almost daily occurrence. From the wildfires in California, the tornados in the Midwest, and hurricanes along the Eastern Seaboard and the Gulf Coast, to floods everywhere and unprecedented snowfalls, the evening news is a parade of images of people suffering the loss of everything to these disastrous events. When faced with such tragedies, people's first concern is that their loved ones, including pets, are safe and accounted for. Their second concern is not for their houses, their cars, or their clothing. Once victims have determined that everyone made it out alive, their next thought is of their memories. If they realize they have lost everything, it is absolutely heart-wrenching to watch their shock and sadness.

> **ARCHIVES TIP**
>
> One of the main reasons to get your family archive in order is that in the event of a natural disaster or a personal emergency all will not be lost.

14: DISASTER PREPAREDNESS, DISASTER RECOVERY, EMERGENCY MANAGEMENT

We live with the knowledge that we could be the next victims of Mother Nature. The work to secure our family archives can be extensive and arduous, yet faced with the uncertainty of our age, we and our descendants will be very grateful that all was not lost in any natural disasters your family faced during the age of global warming. Whether you believe the root cause of the changes in our atmosphere is a result of Earth's natural cycles, or you think it is based on an overload of methane, nitrous oxide, and carbon dioxide being pumped into the air through human activity, it is not going to make a whole lot of difference when you are standing in the burnt-out shell of the building you once called home with not one picture of your grandparents left anywhere.

Everything lost in a house fire

A disaster does not need to be global or far-reaching for everything to be lost. A fire in your home, a burst pipe flooding your basement, a natural gas explosion in your neighborhood, a tree falling in your yard, a roof collapsing from too much snow, the boiler dying in the middle of winter, or a leaky roof are all personal tragedies that can be just as devastating to our memorabilia as a county-wide disaster.

Beyond the digitization project, you probably have family heirlooms and collectibles that you will want to make sure survive a disaster. I am not sure everything can be saved, but I am going to do my best to teach you how to save as much as you can for as long as you can. After reading this chapter and taking the recommendations within, you will have gone a long way toward ensuring that your family archive, your valuables, your story, and your legacy are as protected and as safe as possible.

Much of the advice I give below may be impractical in the event of a real disaster. Some weather events such as hurricanes provide us with days of preparation, while others such as earthquakes, tornados, and wildfires are sudden and unpredictable. In the event of an emergency, we may be lucky to get out with our lives, in which case all

ARCHIVES TIP

An emergency is "a situation or an occurrence of a serious nature, developing suddenly and unexpectedly, and demanding immediate action, generally of short duration... a week or less."

our material objects, including our archives, become secondary. However, when prioritizing our tasks in the event of an impending disaster, knowing what to do before we are panic-stricken will help calm our nerves and focus our attention on what we can do in the moment.

Hurricanes cause extensive damage annually to millions of homes.

I want to also acknowledge that after the devastation, when you are able to return to your home, you will most likely be overwhelmed with the amount of work that needs to be done. Much of the advice below requires clean, distilled or deionized water to repair the damage. Clean water of any kind may not be available for days or even weeks, and the water that can be had must be reserved for drinking. The life and wellbeing of yourself and your family naturally take priority. While you sit reading this well in advance of a disaster, you have no idea what fate might befall you. You can only plan, prepare, and do the best you can. Though you may have it restored in a day, the truth is that you may be without water for a long time. My job is to teach you what the best practices are so that you can apply them to your circumstance using common sense and working within your means.

I have been fortunate to not have sustained a great loss during the natural disasters in my location, which have mostly been hurricanes. I have lost a few trees and large limbs that needed attention. I sustained damage to my house during a record-breaking snowfall season in 2015 that required substantial repair work. So, while I have been affected by the extreme weather that is the hallmark of our age, I have not had my entire house submerged in water, a wildfire nipping at the backyard, or an earthquake or tornado ready to destroy my entire home. Know that if you have suffered such a fate, my thoughts and prayers are with you. I hope the advice in this chapter will be of some service to you.

PREVENTION

Making a Disaster Plan

The greatest value in developing a disaster plan is the forethought that goes into it. Writing everything down in advance is useful in the event of a real emergency. Developing the plan helps you prepare because you will have already gone through the process. Many actions may be completed well in advance of an emergency so that, if and when real disaster strikes, there is less to think about, prepare, and do. In other words, if you have already rehoused your photographs and digitized them, this is one less thing you will have to worry about in the event of an emergency. If important legal and historical documents such as birth certificates, marriage certificates, deeds, and genealogical documents have been digitized and stored in a safety deposit box off-site, these are also items you will not need to be concerned about in a real emergency.

ARCHIVES TIP

A disaster is an unexpected occurrence inflicting widespread destruction and distress and having long-term adverse effect.

Thinking ahead about what to take when being evacuated will make the transition smoother. Planning what will fit in your vehicle and how it will fit is essential. Deciding where in your house valuables would be safest is another consideration. Moving items to the top floor or an attic during a flood, using a cement outbuilding like a garage during a wildfire, and storing furniture in a closet or shed during a hurricane are all simple measures you can take to increase the likelihood that your keepsakes will survive. Another thing to ask yourself is what you should take with you. Working out these details ahead of time will help in the event of a real catastrophe.

A disaster plan should not be too long. It should be well organized, easy to use, easy to understand, and sensible. It should contain all the telephone numbers and contacts needed before and after an emergency. Consider putting it on your phone in a note, but also have a paper copy in the event electricity is unavailable for days. Another idea is to have important numbers on a small card that can be kept in your wallet. Once the disaster plan is completed, all family members should be trained and age-appropriate tasks should be delegated. A simulated drill will help clarify what to do and iron out any bugs that would not work in a real emergency. Here is a list of items and actions that should be included in everyone's disaster plan:

- ✓ **Emergency Telephone List**
    - ✓ Fire/Rescue/Police
    - ✓ All family members
    - ✓ Insurance agents and insurance policy numbers. If you have valuable antiques and artwork, special collections, or rare books, you may need a special rider on your insurance policy to protect against thieves, natural disasters, or home mishaps. Make sure your homeowners policy covers any valuables in your collection. Do this now before disaster strikes.
    - ✓ Utility Companies—Electric, Gas, Water, Sewer. All family members should know how to shut off the utilities in the event of a disaster or personal emergency.

One burst pipe can cause a great deal of damage

- **Document Your Valuables**
  - Photograph and record measurements of valued materials and family heirlooms.
  - Keep purchase receipts of antiques, fine art purchases, and other valuables.
  - Keep historical records of conservation work, special framing materials, archival materials, and other additions to a particular piece.
  - Store copies of documentation in your home and at another location, maybe a safety deposit box. Your insurance broker may also keep a copy of records of important valuables and documents. Digitizing important records and storing them in the cloud will provide easy retrieval after an emergency when internet and electricity is available.

- **Incorporate Preservation Planning**
  - Assess and reduce risks. Repair faulty wiring, install storm shutters, fix a leaky roof, trim or remove trees.
  - Know your area. What types of disasters are you most at risk for? Do you live in a flood zone? What disasters have occurred in the past that your area may be vulnerable to in the future? Think of what you can do to prepare for similar emergencies.
  - Analyze and prioritize risks. Consider the frequency and probability of reoccurrence of certain disasters in your area and take measures accordingly.
  - Treat risks. Take steps that can reduce or minimize your exposure to damage in the event a disaster or personal emergency occurs. If you live in a hurricane zone, fit shutters to windows; if you are at risk of dust storms, seal cracks and purchase heavy curtains; for flood zones, have sandbags ready and make sure nothing is on the floor.

- **Identify Items Most at Risk in Different Emergencies**

  If you processed your collection as outlined earlier in this book, your Finding Aid should contain all the information you need. It will have a list of all the materials in your collection and where they are located.
  - All photo albums
  - All boxes with important documents
  - All boxes with genealogical information

- ✓ A list of antiques and/or family heirlooms and where they are located
- ✓ A list of valuable artwork
- ✓ A list of valuable jewelry
- ✓ A list of important books to grab in an emergency
- ✓ Where journals are stored
- ✓ What special collectibles you have and where they are located
- ✓ A list of heirloom items that may not have monetary value but are important to the family history
- ✓ Business documents
- ✓ Family financial documents

If you have not processed your collection yet, do the survey as recommended. This will at least identify everything you have, even if it is not organized, rehoused, and cataloged. A survey may take only a few hours and will provide the most important information needed in an emergency or after a disaster.

✓ **Supplies Before the Disaster**

Have support materials ready before an emergency strikes:

- ✓ Large plastic storage bins
- ✓ Blankets and sheets to cover furniture or wrap delicate ceramic, glass, or metal
- ✓ Rope to secure furniture
- ✓ Masking tape for windows
- ✓ Duct tape
- ✓ Plastic sheeting to cover materials and to possibly cover doorways and windows

✓ **Supplies After the Disaster**

Think ahead of time what you may need after the disaster to clean up your property. These items may be in short supply after the emergency, so planning ahead may make the difference between being able to cleanup on day one and having to wait until day three or day ten.

- ✓ A few gallons of distilled water will be needed for cleaning photographs, antiques, textiles, and other items. Preparing this ahead of time will be helpful, but in all cases, any water is better than no water.

- A box of disposable nitrile gloves to use when handling archival materials
- Heavy-duty rubber gloves needed for general cleanup
- Trash bags (large and small)
- Tape—paper, masking, duct, and gorilla
- Plastic sheeting to cover materials and possibly cover doorways and windows; if mold growth begins, certain rooms may need to be cordoned off.
- Rolls of clean paper to line surfaces during recovery
- Paper towels
- Cloth towels (soft, clean)
- Soft microfiber cleaning cloths or other lint-free cloths
- Flashlights, lanterns, headlamps, and batteries (Remember you might not have electricity for days and certain rooms or areas may be dark all the time.)
- Isopropyl alcohol
- First aid kit
- Buckets and mops
- Tyvek plastic suits that will be necessary in the event of flood or exposure to other toxic materials; you can find these at many hardware stores.
- A good set of goggles to protect your eyes
- Face mask (N95 or N100)
- Respirator with an organic cartridge if a face mask is not providing enough protection

Keep recovery supplies on hand before disaster strikes

> "It makes you feel more complete. When you know where you come from. It just makes you feel good.... Now I know that I belong and I don't feel like I'm just floating on this planet not knowing and just going day to day. Now I know I'm here because I come from this line of people who have paved the way for me."
>
> **MICHAEL STRAHAN**
> **Finding Your Roots, S5.E5**

or if you have any kind of respiratory issues; (Remember, mold can grow quickly and profusely after a water-soaked disaster, especially if the weather afterward continues to be damp or tropical.)

- ✓ A good pair of rubber boots; hiking boots are a good secondary alternative.

PERSONAL DISASTERS

Look to prevent disasters before they occur. Where are the potential hazards in the home? Assess whether mechanical and electrical systems are potential fire threats. Check fire prevention systems such as smoke alarms. Assess the risk of mold and insect infestations; this is especially important in southern states with high humidity. Prioritize risks. What is the likelihood of your area being flooded in the next ten years?

Identify Risks

Look for and think about leaky pipes, electrical system age and condition, roof age and condition, and outside environmental threats such as trees or wires. Consider regional risks, flood zones, hurricane paths, wildfire risk, earthquakes, and tornados. Determine how each of these threats would affect your home and your collection.

Analyze Risks

Categorize risks by their frequency and likely impact.

Prioritize Risks

Prioritize risks according to the probability of occurrence. For example, you may live in an area that experiences hurricanes, but what is the probability that one will occur? Even if one does occur, what is the likelihood of severe damage to your home? If you live along the coast, your chances are higher than those of someone who lives inland. Consider the level of impact to your collection if the likely scenario manifests itself. What types of damage are you at risk for?

Treat Risks

Take steps now to reduce or minimize the risks that you identified in the Analyze Risks category.

Buildings are often the first and sometimes only line of defense for materials during a disaster. After doing a risk assessment, identify tasks you can complete that will rectify any weaknesses in the structure of your home and yard. This might include trimming trees or cutting them down, fixing leaky pipes or damaged roofs, making sure the electrical system is in good working order, making sure the sump pump works, and replacing old heating systems or hot water tanks.

Security and Theft

Depending on the value of your collection, you may want to consider installing a security system. Are your treasures valuable just to you, or would others consider them valuable too? Art theft is considered the second highest international crime after drug trafficking.[49] Only 10% of stolen items are ever found and returned to their owners. Antiques are also at risk of theft and resale on the black market. Security for your collections is similar to security for your entire house. The main point is to find the vulnerabilities or weaknesses and eliminate them. Would you benefit from security fences and gates, exterior lighting, or having watchdogs? Look at your home through the eyes of a burglar. Is there regular activity? Are there vulnerable doors or windows? Be cautious about discussing your collection with people you are unfamiliar with, especially regarding its value. This means do not brag at parties, as tempting as that might be.

Only 10% of stolen items are ever found

Securing the exterior is of utmost importance. High-security deadbolts with restricted keyways are the best all-around protection.[50] Locksmiths, security companies, and local police can all provide specific advice. Skylights can be vulnerable, and glass sliders are particularly vulnerable. Consider non-breakable polycarbonate glass, security films, or security bars. You can purchase security bars for as little as eleven dollars; they will make a vulnerable window safe. Outdoor lighting also discourages burglars. Statistically speaking, well-lit homes are less likely to be broken into than ones in complete darkness.[51] Floodlights with motion detectors and interior lights with random timers discourage entry. Also be aware of shrubbery close to the building. Does it provide a safe hiding spot for burglars? Alternatively, shrubbery can be used as a deterrent. Prickly or thorny shrubs like holly, roses, or evergreens beneath windows deter access. Thieves are human too. Which house would you rather break into, the one with the prickly bush that will scratch you to shreds, or the one with soft furry shrubs?

14: DISASTER PREPAREDNESS, DISASTER RECOVERY, EMERGENCY MANAGEMENT   263

Ninety percent of burglaries occur in houses without burglar alarms.[52] Purchase a system that is simple and easy to use so you will actually use it. It is not necessary to get the latest, most cutting-edge security system; it is more important that you get one that fits within your budget and that you will use. Security systems include wired or wireless windows, doors, motion detectors, magnetic door contacts, break-glass detectors, duress alarms, a control panel, and communication with either a security company or the police department. Some control panels include fire and water detection. You can set them up to have separate zones. Inside alarm blasts will let an intruder know they have been detected, and hopefully this will scare them off. Closed-circuit televisions or video monitoring is another method that has become increasingly affordable and easy to install.

Do not hide keys in easily detectable places where thieves will look. Never hand over your house keys to strangers. Keep a separate key for your car when having it serviced at garages. Make sure when you are away that the lawn is mowed and the leaves are raked. Police indicate that it is better to have a trusted friend or neighbor pick up your daily mail or newspaper than have the services stopped. Not all postal workers and delivery people are ethical.

If you have a rare or valuable collection, such as artwork, furniture, rugs, or jewelry, it is essential to document and inventory each item for insurance purposes. This also goes for historic documents that you have collected like the history geek I know you are. The task should be easy to do if you have already processed your collection; half the work will already be done. After processing your collection, the only thing you might need to do is identify the items that may have value to a thief or that an insurance company would compensate in the event of loss. Be sure to take pictures of each item and back them up using the 3-2-1 Rule. Also be sure to photograph and note any flaws or distinctive features, especially in antiques or artwork. It could help with identification and will be invaluable to police in their attempt to recover stolen items. Video inventories are also helpful, but police prefer photographs. In addition to having digital photographs, consider printing out copies and storing them in a safety deposit box.

We must from time to time have strangers enter our homes, often to do work. Most contractors and domestic workers are regular people with regular families, have valuables of their own, are honest, and have integrity. But unsavory characters do exist, and sometimes the temptation might be too great. General good advice says make sure whoever enters your home to work is bonded and insured. Though it is helpful if they are referred through a trusted friend, coworker, or relative, it is not always possible

Workers who enter your home should be bonded and insured.

that a guy you know knows a guy who knows a guy. Even if that is the case, it does not mean they will not harm us in some way or that one of their employees would not bring us harm. Be aware that if you leave a key for a trusted friend or contractor, they may bring unsavory characters into your home without you knowing.

A friend of mine had a trusted plumber whom she let go into her house through the bulkhead during the day while she was at work. On one occasion, she was there when the plumber came to fix something, and they started chit-chatting. He revealed that a few years earlier he brought a few teenagers he was mentoring from the training school into her house. As a woman living alone, she did not appreciate his taking such liberties with her safety, something that may never have occurred to him. In fact, he let slip that one of the boys had gotten into trouble for another incident and now as an adult would be facing serious jail time.

When construction is being done on your house, make sure ladders and other equipment are put away at the end of the day. Do not leave ladders leaning against the house, allowing easy entry through a window.

You should always ensure that domestic workers have completed a background check. Today these are easy and inexpensive to do using online services. Whenever a domestic worker leaves your employ, be sure to change the locks and security codes. It is better to err on the side of caution. Trust your instincts. If someone coming into your home gives you a bad feeling, take the necessary steps to secure yourself and your collection even if it seems like paranoia. Gavin de Becker, bestselling author and security specialist, says one of the best security systems is the "gift of fear."[53] If someone gives you an uneasy feeling, he advises to trust that instinct and act on it. Good, honest people think other people are good and honest and therefore often trust more than they should.

Another thing to consider is installing a safe. The best safes are floor mounted in concrete, but there are many options in terms of size, style, and location. Safes can be hidden or in the open. Most safes will protect items from theft and environmental damage such as fire and water. Even cheap safes will protect precious items from fire for a certain number of hours. Photographs, important papers, archival documents, and media such as thumb drives and CDs can all be kept securely in a safe.

If you are the victim of theft, take these precautions:

- ✓ Notify the police immediately.
- ✓ Do not disturb the crime area until the police have arrived.
- ✓ Provide emergency personnel with photographs and detailed information on what was stolen.
- ✓ Contact your insurance company.

Fire

Fire within your home is probably the greatest threat to your collection. With that in mind, it would be worth it to have items stored securely in a fireproof safe and to make sure fire alarms are in good working order. The first line of defense is prevention. Fire prevention is not magical or complicated. Good common sense, regular maintenance of essential equipment, and vigilance is all that is needed to prevent most house fires

Fire in your home may be the greatest threat to your collection

from starting. Go through your home and identify any fire hazards. Be sure to have fire extinguishers handy and know how to use them. Smoking inside your home should always be prohibited. Smoking increases the risk of fire, but the residue from smoke can also damage your collection by causing yellowing and deterioration. Be aware that more fires in homes start during times when construction is taking place.[54] Take extra precautions to protect your collection at these times. Temporarily relocate valuable and vulnerable items during construction.

Smoke detectors can be hardwired and integrated into your security system. Automatic fire sprinkler systems are becoming more common in homes. Depending on the cost of installation and the value of your collection, this may be a reasonable option. Seventy-five percent of fires begin in the winter.[55] Make sure to check your heating systems every winter. If you have oil heat, your boiler should be serviced by a qualified professional.

Fire extinguishers, while not decorative, should not be hidden away. They are your first line of defense in the event of a fire and could save your collection or even you and your family's lives. Know how to use them, make sure they are easily accessible, and be sure that everyone in the house knows where they are. It is not necessary to have a fire extinguisher in every room of a home, but there should be at least one on every floor that is easily accessible. Fire extinguishers come in three classes:

- ✓ Class A extinguishes ordinary combustibles such as paper and wood.
- ✓ Class B is for flammable liquids and solvents including gas and oil.
- ✓ Class C is for live electrical fires.

Fire extinguishers come in different classes. Make sure to buy the right one.

There is a fourth class of combustibles for chemicals and metals, but the extinguishers for this class can only be used by professional firefighters. Fire extinguishers lose pressure overtime, making them useless in an emergency. Be sure to check the pressure gauge periodically or purchase a system that will digitally signify when the pressure is too low. It has become common practice to check our smoke alarm systems when we change the clocks in fall and spring. This would be a good time to check the pressure on fire extinguishers too.

Class A extinguishers typically contain water. Beware that introducing water to your collection, even to save it from fire, could cause damage. Dry chemical extinguishers also exist, but the chemicals could also cause damage. Collections protected with plastic enclosures will obviously fare better with water than with fire. Consider the size of the fire extinguisher too. Getting one that is too large may prohibit everyone in your family from being able to lift it in an emergency. On the other hand, the soda can size extinguishers are cheaply made, may not have enough liquid inside to put out a fire, and may not work in an emergency. They are not recommended by fire personnel. Find and use extinguishers that are not too big and not too small; find ones that are just right—10 lb., 5 lb., or 2 lb.

Water and Floods

Much of your collection can survive water and some floods, depending on what else is in the water. Cleaning items as soon as possible with distilled or deionized water is essential. Localized floods or floods within homes are very common, so taking steps to prevent them is vital. As discussed earlier in this book, storing historical documents in the basement is not recommended because floods can occur from below (if a sump pump does not work or the washing machine overflows) or from above (if a water pipe bursts). In the event of a flood, having your collection stored in a better place is crucial. Even the smallest amount of water can be damaging. An unnoticed slow leak can do extensive damage in a short period of time. A gallon of water can ruin historical documents quickly and irreparably. Papers that are already browned and in a state of deterioration need just a few drops of water to render them unreadable and destroyed.

Flooded homes

In sensitive areas, you can install a water detection system that will sound an alarm when water touches them. Hardware stores have these available for $10–$20. Cellars should have sump pumps and be checked periodically to ensure they are in good working order. Everyone in the family should know the location of the main water shut-off valve and what to do in the event of a flood.

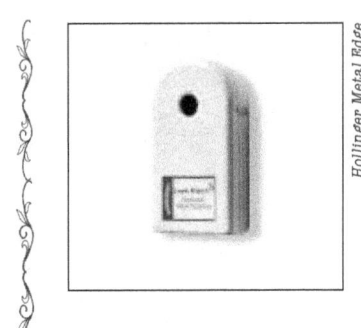

Water Detection Alarm

If you live in a flood zone, having a written flood plan will help you think through the steps you need to take ahead of time in the event a major flood occurs. A written plan gives your family members knowledge of what to do if the ultimate occurs. Your local Red Cross chapter can provide you with official warnings and procedures in your area, and they will let you know how much warning time you will have before flood waters reach you. Identify a friend, relative, or motel to go to in an emergency. Plan the route you will need to take to get out of the area and consider how much congestion may occur and if there will most likely be flooding along the way.

The American Red Cross book, *Repairing Your Flooded Home* offers extensive advice on how to flood-proof your house. (It can be downloaded from my website at https://lenasalina.com/resources/#disaster/.) It is essential to know if you live in a flood zone to ensure you have the proper insurance and to know whether you should take extra precautions for this type of disaster. We all can experience flooded basements when torrential rains come, but being in a flood zone that can be overtaken by a river, stream, pond, or the ocean poses distinct problems and requires special insurance. A separate policy under the National Flood Insurance Program will cover damage to buildings and their contents, storage up to forty-five days after the flood, and expenses for removing debris. It does not cover everything or all kinds of floods, however, so exercise due diligence to make sure you understand what is covered and what is not.

The Federal Emergency Management Agency (FEMA) provides maps of flood risk areas at https://msc.fema.gov/portal/search. Enter your address at this link and see the potential risk for your home.

If you are in a flood area, your local building department will indicate the flood level protection advised for your area. This is the number of feet they predict the water level to rise in your area. With the threat of superstorms ever increasing, you might want to go up a few feet when making this assessment. Some government agencies will purchase homes in flood areas if you decide you would rather move than take the risk. The American Red Cross states that if you have been flooded once, you will most likely be flooded again.

Flood-proofing measures include the following:

- ✓ Elevation – Elevate the house to projected flood stages. This is common along the coast in many areas.
- ✓ Relocation – If you have not already sustained a flood, the structural integrity of your home is intact, and you love your home, you could consider moving it to a new location. My house was built in 1917 but moved to its current site in 1958 when the land was taken over by eminent domain to establish a college.
- ✓ Barrier protection – Floodwalls, berms, and levees made of concrete or thick mud can keep floodwaters from reaching your house. Check with local authorities to see if these are appropriate for your home.
- ✓ Dry floodproofing – This requires coating walls with plastic, rubberized sheeting, or special waterproofing compounds. Openings such as doors, windows, sewer lines, or vents are either closed permanently (if possible) or sealed with removable shields or sandbags in the event of an emergency. This is not recommended in areas where flooding would be more than two to three feet high or where there are basements or crawl spaces.
- ✓ Wet floodproofing – building materials below the flood line are replaced with water-resistant materials. Flood waters are allowed into the home. Only place objects that can be moved easily in the flood zone area. Move permanent objects like furnaces, water heaters, appliances, heavy furniture, and bookcases to a higher floor level. Poet William Butler Yeats lived in Thoor Ballylee in Ireland along the banks of the Streamstown River where it is believed the first floor flooded annually in springtime. The main living area was on the second floor, and the furniture on the first floor was easily moved or able to withstand the annual flooding.

If a flood is imminent, walk through your home with a video camera. Identify the most valuable objects that you will take with you. In a pending emergency, your top priority will be for the safety of yourself, your family, and your pets. Your next thought might be to plan for food and clothing during the time you will be away from your home. But do not forget to consider the most precious objects in your house—your family photographs, artifacts, documents, textiles, and artwork. Having an emergency plan for removing these objects from your house will increase the likelihood you will remember them during a real emergency. If your archive is in order, this could be a matter of simply moving the contents of a closet into the trunk of your car. Alternatively, placing archival materials in sealed plastic bins on the highest level of the home may save them from flood water damage, the aftermath of contaminated mud, and potential mold and mildew. You can also cover cardboard boxes with polyethylene plastic to reduce water damage. For more information on preparing for disasters, see recommendations from the American Institute for Conservation (AIC) at http://www.conservationwiki.com/wiki/Emergency_Preparedness_%26_Response.

For original photographs and documents, textiles, metals, and other objects that would be ruined by water, you can use large plastic bins for storage. While non-archival plastic storage boxes are not recommended for permanent storage, they can be useful in an emergency. Items and boxes may not stay in place during certain natural disasters. Remember Phyllis Puglia whose home was flooded and windswept during Hurricane Sandy on Staten Island? The photographs of her parents were found in debris a mile away from her home. She was lucky she found them at all. Placing items in plastic bins and taping them shut with duct tape to ensure they will not pop open may mean the difference between destruction and survival. Remember to put identifying information in the bins so your items can be returned to you if found.

Hurricanes and Tornados

From a disaster perspective, the main difference between a hurricane and a tornado is that with hurricanes residents generally have a few days to a week to prepare. Tornado victims often have little or no warning. The main forms of damage caused by either disaster are from water and wind. See the above instructions under the section "Water and Floods" to learn more about water damage. To protect

Cover antique furniture before a disaster strikes, if possible.

items from high winds, refer to the advice below for specific items. Many glass companies will board up your house in an emergency. Look for local companies and see if they will provide this service to homeowners.

Secure antique and valuable furniture by covering it with sheets, blankets, and/or plastic sheets. Using duct tape, secure the covering and furniture to the floor or against walls so it does not move. Do not place adhesive tape directly on furniture. Cover furniture first with plastic, towels, or blankets. Placing items in a closet or other area where they are less likely to move around may provide an added level of protection.

You can secure precious artwork the same way. Remove artwork from walls, cover it in blankets, and place it in crates or a closet where it will be less likely to get blown around in the wind. Glass and ceramics should also be wrapped in blankets or towels, placed in plastic or wooden bins, and stored in a secure location.

RECOVERY

Introduction and General Advice

The ultimate has happened. Your home has been damaged in a personal emergency or a natural disaster. In addition to the general advice in this section, see specific advice for different types of objects below and refer to the resources page of my website https://lenasalina.com/resources/#disaster for more links, books, and articles.

Many outside contractors will assist in an emergency. Refer to the *National Resource Guide for Disaster Preparedness* for contact information on specific outside contractors who can provide dehumidification services and assist with the restoration of particular types of materials including film, photographs, paper, textiles, painting, artwork, and computer data (hard drives). The publication also lists conservators and conservation centers that may be able to assist. The Conservation Center for Art & Historic Artifacts provides a PDF link at https://ccaha.org/resources/national-resource-guide-disaster-preparedness. This document is meant for historic institutions, but many contractors will assist homeowners as well.

When assessing all the damage after a disaster, your instinct will be to replace the objects you use on a daily basis. Naturally, food, clothing, and medications will be important to take care of immediately. But in your drive to get back to a normal way of life, do not overlook the archival materials in your collection. Remember, they are irreplaceable. New furniture, clothing, dishes, and towels are easily replaced with insurance money, but the daguerreotype of your great-grandmother can never be replaced.

The following are general guidelines to use after a disaster:

- ✓ Set aside an area where archival materials can be spread out to dry.
- ✓ Protect archival materials by covering them, lifting them off the floor, or moving them to a safer place.
- ✓ Reduce temperature and humidity and increase air circulation to diminish mold growth.

14: DISASTER PREPAREDNESS, DISASTER RECOVERY, EMERGENCY MANAGEMENT

- ✓ Plastic crates, polyethylene sheeting, plywood, and rubber gloves can help with removal and storage.
- ✓ Set up work areas for items that need to be packed or air dried.
- ✓ Use rubber gloves when handling contaminated objects.
- ✓ Take notes and make records of the work you do. This may be invaluable later to both insurance companies and you.

Look in your local yellow pages or other area online services for contractors that specialize in fire and water restoration. These companies will help with carpets, furniture, clothing, and other daily items. Archival materials will still need the specialization of a trained conservator. For antiques or old rugs, do not use fire and water restoration services unless they specialize in these items. Contact a conservator instead.

Mold Recovery

If you have active mold, removing it immediately will be your top priority. Mold grows quickly and is hazardous to your health. Be advised that certain states require specialized licensing for mold recovery services. Refer to the website www.iicrc.org for a list of qualified mold specialists in your area. Remember, mold can be toxic and even life-threatening. Using a facemask or a respirator is essential in

Dirt and Mold after a flood.

mold infected areas. If you have a substantial mold problem after a flood, and you are displaying physical symptoms, local area hospitals can do a mycotoxin test. By sampling urine, they can determine what kind of mold you have been exposed to and whether further precautionary measures need to be taken. They may also prescribe medication. Another good resource is the American Academy of Environmental Medicine at https://www.aaemonline.org.

Active mold is typically dark blue or black. If you see active mold, do not touch it with ungloved hands and, as stated above, wear a mask. Moldy items should be quarantined from people and from other non-moldy materials as soon as possible. Set aside an area of your house, or place items in a container to keep the mold from spreading. As we learned in Chapter 3, mold cannot grow in RH less than 65%. Reducing RH will stop active mold from growing or developing. This could be challenging in a tropical setting or in a flooded or damp area. Air conditioners are the best resource for lowering RH. Obviously, a dehumidifier will also assist in this endeavor. Use fans if nothing else is available, but be careful to not let mold spores spread through the air and infect other items or contaminate other areas of the house. If you already purchased a hygrometer, use it to measure the amount of humidity in the area of affected materials.

Sunshine also kills most molds. While prolonged exposure to sunlight will fade photographs, textiles, and other materials, in the short-term your materials will be fine. If you can, spread documents, photographs, and textiles out so they can air dry—the sooner the better; mold thrives in a wet environment. Books can be a challenge when infected with mold. If possible, lay books spine down and fan the pages out so they will dry and not stick together.

Freezing is a method that can be used particularly on books, photographs, and paper documents that cannot be treated immediately after a disaster. The *National Resource Guide for Disaster Preparedness* includes a list of contractors who provide this service. Your own freezer can suffice as a temporary storage once electricity has been restored. Freezing documents is not as straightforward as you would think. It must be done with care and knowledge of the risks and consequences of unfreezing too quickly. Once you contact a qualified conservator or service provider, your freezer can provide a temporary solution until the experts come in.

FLOODS/WATER DAMAGE

If there is a flood in your area or home, do not go into water that is more than four feet deep. Flood waters are not water, they are toxic wastes from all the materials that have accumulated before reaching your home—including toxic chemicals and human and animal waste. Have the water removed or wait for it to subside before going in. Make sure electricity is turned off before entering an area that is still wet. Never go into standing water when there is a potential for electrical shock. You may need to contact the electric company. If there is a widespread power outage, do not assume that during the time you will be in the water the power will not be restored. If possible, block more water from entering the area and cover drains and other places where water can enter.

Try to pull important items from shelves and bring them to higher areas. After the water has started to subside, use wet vacs, pumps, and fans to help dry the area and reduce the chance of mold growth. You may need the following supplies to dry out archival materials:

- ✓ Plastic containers
- ✓ Clean sheeting
- ✓ Blotter paper or towels
- ✓ Sponges
- ✓ Plastic bags
- ✓ Rubber gloves and rubber boots
- ✓ Clean water

As is mentioned in the section on Prevention, The American Red Cross provides excellent information in the publication "Repairing Your Flooded Home," which can be found on my website at https://lenasalina.com/resources/#disaster. This PDF provides step-by-step procedures outlining what to do in the event of a flood.

Floodwaters affect a home in three ways:

- ✓ **Water** damages interior contents. Wallboards will disintegrate if they remain wet for too long. Wood warps, swells, or rots, and electrical parts short and can cause fire.
- ✓ **Mud** gets everything dirty and contains hazardous contaminants.
- ✓ **Dampness** promotes mildew, mold, and fungus. Take measures to protect yourself from these contaminants by wearing plastic disposable gloves, protective clothing, goggles, and a face mask or respirator.

Drying Out Procedures

Find a cool, dry space and run fans or open windows. Place absorbent materials such as blotter paper or paper towels under wet objects. As paper towels or blotter paper becomes too wet, replace them with new ones. If books, documents, photographs, or textiles cannot be air dried within forty-eight hours, place them in plastic bags in the freezer or keep them as cool as possible with air circulation. Do not hang objects. Water saturation makes paper materials and textiles heavier and weaker, so hanging them could cause further damage.

Running fans helps to dry things after a flood

Lower the humidity by opening the windows, if possible. Open all closet and cabinet doors, use fans, run dehumidifiers, and air conditioners, and use desiccants (materials that absorb moisture). Not all desiccants are safe for archival materials. Choose ones that are easily found at hardware or grocery stores. Kitty litter made of clay is a great, safe desiccant. You can also use calcium chloride pellets used for melting ice in winter, but be aware that calcium chloride can burn skin so be careful when handling it. Place the pellets in a pillowcase, nylon stocking, or cloth bag. Chemical dehumidifier packs used for drying boats and damp closets are another safe desiccant for archival materials.

Segregate the things you want to save in a specific area. A separate room is preferable, such as a second floor as far away from the flood area as possible. Dry everything out as soon as you can. The best way to dry paper is to lay it flat and let it air dry naturally. Placing clean plastic screens on top can help with curling and prevent items from blowing away. Do not try to force papers apart. Just keep drying them and eventually they will usually come apart on their own. If they do not, contact a conservator for assistance. Photocopy or take pictures of important papers as soon as possible before contaminants in the water cause them to deteriorate and become unreadable. For precious archival documents like old birth certificates, marriage certificates, and other valuable papers, the content on the document is more important than the paper itself, even though you might love the old papers and the authenticity of the original. For computer disks, tapes, or thumb drives, put them in plastic bags and place them in the refrigerator until you can bring them to a professional drying center to have the data transferred to a good disk.

In a large-scale catastrophe where no electricity is available for days or weeks, freezing objects may not be possible. If they can be moved to another location such as a relative's home, that would be ideal. Otherwise, do the best you can. Placing them in plastic bags is a good first step. See instructions below for advice on specific materials.

Drying photographs after a disaster

PHOTOGRAPHS

The absolute best protection for photographs is scanning them well in advance of a disaster. Refer to Chapter 11 for further instructions on digitizing your photographs. If you digitize your photographs and store them in the cloud, you can easily print them out and reassemble a photographic collection. No one needs to suffer the fate of Phyllis Puglia and the loss of her parents' images.

Another strategy is storing photographs and their accompanying negatives in separate places. If one is damaged, the other might survive intact. If you must evacuate the area, making room in the car for photo albums might be worth the precious space. Do not leave them behind unless you absolutely have to. You could also place plastic over an area that contains photographs or store them in plastic bins taped shut with duct tape. Again, though plastic bins are not recommended for long-term storage, in an emergency they could be the difference between waterlogged photographs and dry ones. Remember to put identifying information in the bin in the event it ends up far from your home. Remove photographs from plastic as soon as the emergency is over. Trapped moisture could lead to mold growth, a potential disaster of another kind.

Use distilled or deionized water when cleaning photographs, if possible

If flooded, air dry or freeze photographs as soon as possible. Rinse mud off photographs by gently exposing them to a water stream or by totally immersing them in clean water with gentle agitation. Photographs can stay wet in a container of clean water if they have already been saturated.[56] Dry or freeze your photographs within forty-eight hours and interleave them with wax paper before freezing. Partially wet photographs can be air dried or frozen. Photographs that are stuck together or moldy might be beyond saving. Do not tear apart photos that are stuck together. Sometimes you can rewet them and they will pull apart but be gentle. If they start to tear, stop. Dry them face up in a single layer on a clean surface and avoid direct sunlight. Do not worry about curling when the photos dry; you can flatten them later. Placing a clean plastic mesh screen on top will expose photographs to air while keeping them flat and keeping debris off them.

PAPER

Paper documents are another category of archival materials that will greatly benefit from scanning. Scanned documents can be reprinted and restored in archival boxes. All is not lost. I know it is not the same, but a reprinted, scanned birth certificate from 1803 is better than completely losing the document.

Another strategy is making photocopies and storing them in a secure location far from the originals. Oversized paper documents will require more forethought and planning to protect them in the event of an emergency. Professionals can scan large blueprints or artwork, and good quality digital photographs can be reprinted. Like photographs, short-term storage in plastic bins may provide a level of protection against flooding. In the event of fire, the

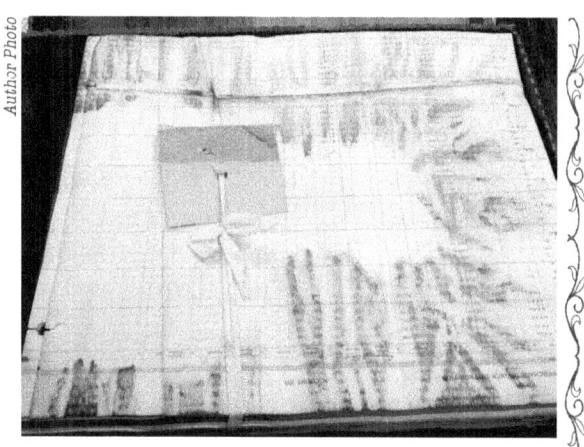
Water damaged paper

only protection will be to remove the document from the disaster area before wildfires occur. When compiling your disaster preparedness list, be sure to identify where important papers are and know which boxes or folders are the most important to grab.

Water is the great enemy of paper. Even the smallest of leaks can do extensive damage, especially to older documents that may be in a weakened condition and may be highly acidic. Inks can discolor or wash out quickly if wet. Some flooded documents may be rinsed with clean water and placed in a frost-free freezer until you have time to work on them or can contact a conservator. If you are unsure whether adding more water to the document will cause more damage, freeze it as-is and then contact a conservator as soon as possible.

TEXTILES

If your textile is insured, take photographs before taking steps to salvage and repair it. Document everything you do. Tending to textiles as soon as possible after a disaster reduces the likelihood of permanent damage. Textiles become weaker when wet and will need support and careful handling in that condition. Use common sense. Because we separate our laundry every week, we know that colors need to be separate from lights or whites due to dye transference. Rewet the textiles and gently rinse mud and debris from them with clean water. You can also use a fine hose spray or mist. Be careful that the water pressure does not damage delicate fibers.

Dab or blot the textile dry with a clean absorbent cloth. Air dry by laying fabrics flat in an area with good ventilation. Keeping lights on will inhibit mold growth. Circulate the air with air conditioning, fans, or by opening windows. Dehumidifiers will also reduce humidity and the potential for mold growth. Cover textiles with clean, thin cotton to provide protection during drying and to absorb dirt and impurities embedded in the material. Do not wring or hang fabric on a line, and do not stack textiles during the drying process. Reshape them while they are still wet. If they cannot be dried within forty-eight hours, place them in plastic bags and freeze them. If materials are already dry, they can be dry-brushed or gently vacuumed using a low suction vacuum and a mesh protective screen as described in Chapter 8. Due to their extremely delicate or fragile fabrics, do not try to unfold textiles if they are stuck together. Let them dry, then contact a conservator.

Fire, soot, and smoke damage can result in long-term or permanent damage of textiles. It is recommended you contact a conservator before handling soot-damaged articles. Handling sooty textiles can drive soiling deeper into the fibers and cause irreversible damage. Handle smoke-damaged textiles with gentle care using nitrile or cotton gloves. Gently place them in a plastic or paper bag or surround them with tissue paper until you can contact a conservator.

METALS

The biggest threat to metals is corrosion from water. Silver and gold are considered noble metals and will fare much better than base metals. Gold does not corrode, and silver can tarnish but is fairly stable. All other metals corrode. The best strategy is to rinse them with distilled or deionized water as soon as possible. If necessary, tap water will suffice. Dry metal objects as quickly as possible with clean cotton cloths. Soft microfiber cleaning cloths or

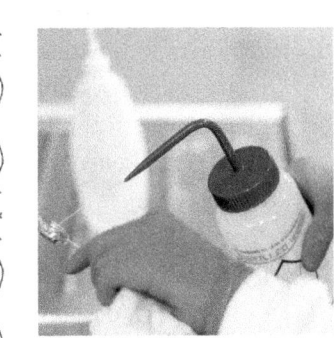

Cleaning silver spoon with distilled water

other lint-free cloths are preferable. You can use paper towels but be careful not to scratch metal surfaces. It is better to tap with paper towels than to rub. The next best thing to do is air dry metals using fans or by placing them in the sun as quickly as possible.

If objects are soot-covered after being in a fire, refer to cleaning instructions on my website at https://lenasalina.com/secrets-from-the-stacks-guides/. Depending on the temperature of a fire, metal objects can become permanently damaged and inscriptions and etchings on them can be lost. With high enough temperatures, they will melt into their original ore state. Contact a conservator to see whether damaged metal objects in your care can be restored.

BOOKS

Wet books on a shelf will be heavy and may cause the shelf to break. Remove books as soon as possible if they have been flooded. If you have made an inventory of your books as part of your archives project, you can easily identify which books are valuable because of age, rarity, or signature by the author. Identify the irreplaceable books and concentrate your attention on them first. If possible, put them in a place with low humidity and low temperatures. Mold growth is likely if books are stored for more than forty-eight hours in temperatures over 70°F and

RH of 60% or more. Stand books upright, opening covers to give them support. Do not force books open. If books are covered in mud or contamination, you can wash them in clean water before drying them. A particularly old or precious book such as a family Bible from the 18th century, an old artbook from the 16th century, or another rare and valuable object, should be placed in a plastic bag or wrapped loosely with freezer paper or wax paper. Then place them in the freezer until you can contact a conservator.

Air drying is the best line of defense, or if possible, using a fan in the room will increase evaporation. Most books will air dry well. There may be some staining or distortion, but otherwise they will be fine. Books are dry when they feel warm to the touch. After drying them, lay them flat with a heavy weight to reduce warping. Glossy paper will stick together and will remain stuck unless the pages are separated when the book is still wet. This is a delicate process. The paper is weakened by the water and can easily tear. If you can unstick the pages, place a piece of interleaving absorbent paper between them until they no longer cling to each other. Otherwise, wrap the book in paper and place it in the freezer until you can contact a conservator. Before a disaster, or when removing them for transport to a conservator, pack books spine down in waterproof containers.

Furniture damaged in natural disaster

FURNITURE

Most likely you will not be able to take any furniture with you in the event of an evacuation due to a natural disaster. The best you can do is take protective measures. Storing antique pieces in closets or securing them with ropes may prevent them from becoming dislodged in the event of a disaster. Covering pieces with blankets and plastic may keep furniture clean and dry. Secure plastic in place with ropes or string. Lift furniture off the floor in the event minor flooding will take place.

To clean soiled and wet furniture, dab it with clean cloths. Do not rub since dirt on the object can scratch hard surfaces or tear cloth. You can rinse and clean many pieces with clean water while they are still wet. Take note of running dyes and do not proceed if adding water will cause further damage. Contact a conservator at your earliest convenience for further advice and remedial attention.

AUDIO AND VIDEO TAPES

As recommended in Chapters 9 and 11, the best preservation technique for audio and video tapes is digitization. Audio and video tapes are highly sensitive and may not survive submersion in water. They will quickly melt in a fire or high heat situation. For that reason, all audio and video files should be digitized as soon as possible. It is okay to keep a copy on CD, but all digitized documents should be backed up using the 3-2-1 Rule. If you have taken these steps, you will have nothing to worry about in the event of a disaster. If you have not taken these steps and you have time to plan an evacuation, grab the most important video and audio tapes in your collection and bring them with you.

If disaster strikes and you are unable to grab the video of your child's graduation or fifth-grade recital, all may not be lost. Contact a conservator to see if the video or audio tape can be restored. If the video was a group event, someone else in the group (another parent) may have a copy. Due to the high sensitivity and fragility of audio and video tapes, I hope you will take steps to get them digitized as soon as possible.

Original audio and video tapes should be stored rewound, off the floor, with spines up, and in an enclosure. Plastic cases and containers are preferred. In "Magnetic Tapes Can Survive Flood Exposure," Peter Brothers notes that tapes that have been submerged for extended periods of time have been recovered by experts. He says, no matter how bad tapes might look, "most wet tapes can now be saved and restored if they are treated properly."[57] How much it will cost to do this is another matter. Digitizing before the storm will be much more cost effective than trying to restore a wet tape after the storm.

Do not attempt to play media that is still wet. It can damage both the tape and the playback equipment. Audio and video media will need to be cleaned in distilled water first and thoroughly dried.

It is important to identify what types of materials have affected the tapes. If they have been submerged in contaminated water, try to identify what types of contaminants may have been present. Tapes submerged in salt water will need to be cleaned in distilled water as soon as possible because the salt is highly corrosive to metal parts such as rollers.

For instructions on how to salvage and stabilize audio and visual media, please go to my website at https://lenasalina.com/secrets-from-the-stacks-guides/.

FRAMED ARTWORK

Keep artwork in a horizontal position with the paint side up. If framed photographs or paintings are stuck to the glass, leave them in the frame and dry them glass side down. It may be possible to rewet the object to unstick it but be careful!

If it does not work easily, leave it alone, let it dry, and contact a conservator. A conservator should be able to get it unstuck.

GLASS, CERAMICS, POTTERY, EARTHENWARE, CRYSTAL

Scratching, cracking, and breakage are the most serious threats to ceramic and glass objects during an emergency. Protecting the surface from scratches and the body from breakage is the main concern. Do not allow objects to come in direct contact with each other. If possible, package precious glass and ceramics before the impending storm. Ideally these items should be packaged in acid-free, lignin-free tissue and stored in acid-free boxes. Placing the cardboard boxes in sturdier boxes such as wood, plastic, or metal would provide an extra level of protection during a disaster. Also, if you do not have easy access to acid-free, lignin-free materials before an impending storm, use what you have on hand such as wrapping paper, commercial tissue paper, dish towels, or bath towels. Newspaper is acidic and can cause discoloration over the long term, but for the short-term in an emergency, it will suffice. Beware that newsprint can transfer to soft ceramic or pottery and permanently stain. If you live in an earthquake prone area, beware that glass and ceramics can "walk" off a shelf due to minor (non-disaster-related) below-the-surface vibrations. Glass and ceramics on display should be secured to the shelf. Museums use tiny dots of wax for this purpose. Consult your local museum or contact a conservator for advice on the best materials for the glass and ceramic you want to display.

Broken ceramic bowl

After the disaster, rinse glass and ceramic objects in clean distilled or deionized water, if possible; otherwise, tap water will suffice. Dry the items with clean cotton or paper towels. Be careful not to scratch the surface of glass by rubbing it with a dirty or gritty towel. You can also sun dry or air dry the items. Porous ceramics are permeable and will draw in dirty water and stains. Clean and dry them as quickly as possible. The AIC recommends contacting a local conservator if an earthenware article is waterlogged. They can offer advice about proper drying and rinsing techniques.

I hope a natural disaster or personal emergency never befalls your domestic sanctuary. But if it does, I hope the information in this chapter will assist in your being prepared ahead of time and your recovery afterward.

CONCLUSION

I have this dream, we're all at the table
Sharing verses, stories and song
Vaudeville Nanna and The Banjolele
She hands it to me and I play along

The best days of my life
Are somewhere up the road
With my family and friends
I can close my eyes
And I can see them, see them.

—**Peter Frampton,** *Vaudeville Nanna and the Banjolele*

I volunteer at a local historic home that was built in 1810. Louisa Meader owned the house from 1890–1901. Louisa was regularly active in the local community. She was president of the Women's Christian Temperance Union of Moshassuck, a Quaker Eldress, and a suffragist. She campaigned for prohibition, fair labor laws, and prison reform and was active in eleven different clubs or societies. Louisa's activity as a suffragist opened the door for the house to celebrate the 100-year anniversary of suffrage. Local and national history can only be presented to the public if that history connects to the house in some way. I was thrilled a suffragist lived in the house so we could celebrate this historic event. As a women's historian, I had looked forward to celebrating the anniversary of suffrage for many years.

In 2019, a small group of us gathered to plan activities for the following year. We planned to go to local archives and research the state's suffrage groups and activities. To bring the history closer to home, we had an initiative to ask people in the immediate community if there were any stories in their families detailing the first time women voted in America or if they had any pictures or documents related to the event. We hoped that after gathering stories and acquiring local artifacts (posters, pins, cards, newspaper articles) the information would be kept in the house's archives to be used again in other museum activities or for researchers to discover in the future.

In January 2020, a group of us gathered to plan attending other local events taking place in our area. The first two National Women's Rights Conventions were held in Worcester, MA, in 1850 and 1851. This was shortly after the historic first meeting took place in Seneca Falls in 1848, during which Elizabeth Cady Stanton boldly pushed for the passage of universal suffrage for women. We live near Worcester, MA, and planned to attend their celebrations as well as many other local events. Some of us were planning a trip to our nation's Capital where other celebrations, museum exhibits, lectures, and events would be taking place.

And then the world went silent. The novel coronavirus put an abrupt end to all the activities everyone had planned. Meetings were canceled, lectures were postponed, and exhibits stood silent while patrons feared leaving their homes. Instead of digging into archives in search of evidence of the passage of the 19th Amendment, people began to search for what happened during the pandemic of 1918. Pictures began to appear on social media of women walking arm in arm down city streets with masks covering their faces. Knowing the history of the catastrophic events of 1918, many leaders acted quickly to contain the effects of the virus as best as possible. When people protested wearing masks, we learned that similar protests took place 100 years earlier. Many of us knew about the devastating influenza virus of 1918, but others had never heard of it. Suddenly that history was more important than ever.

Learning from our past helped us deal with our current circumstances. As encouragement for my relatives in the early scary days of the 2020 pandemic, I listed the people in our family who had lived through and survived the 1918 pandemic. "If they survived, so can we," I said. And while we dug into our pasts to discover and learn from that history, we also realized that we were living through a historic moment. Baby 2135 will want to know what you did when COVID-19 stopped the world.

I cannot think of a more compelling demonstration of why putting your family archive in order is important and significant. Begin today. Go through your home. Gather the documents, birth certificates, marriage certificates, divorce papers, and house purchase and sales agreements. Weed through photographs to find the most significant ones that tell the story of who you are, who your father was, and who was part of your family. Look for the quilts your great-grandmother made, the afghans your grandmother made, the wedding dresses you and your mother wore. Find your father's purple heart and the military uniform your great-great-grandfather wore in WWI. Digitize old movies. Clean up your email. Take screenshots of your Facebook page. Write down your passwords and leave instructions for your executor. Survey all you have. Purchase archival materials. Find the best place in your home to store your archive. Strive to create a room with stable climate control. Decide whether something should be donated to a local or national archive. Tell your story through writing, audio recording, or video recording. Rehouse magnetic photo albums in archival-safe photo books. Make a disaster plan. Decide what aspects of creating your family archive you want to do yourself and what you would be better hiring a professional to do.

And by all means, have fun!

Be creative. Enjoy the process. Leave a legacy.

If you had just a minute to breathe,
And they granted you one final wish
Would you ask for something
Like another chance?

—**Steve Winwood,** *Low Spark of High-Heeled Boys*

NOTES

1. Eric S. Blake, et.al., *Tropical Cyclone Report Hurricane Sandy (AL 182012) 22 – 29 October 2012, PDF file*, National Hurricane Center, February 12, 2013, https://www.nhc.noaa.gov/data/tcr/AL182012_Sandy.pdf.

2. Sidebar Quote: Segomotso Keakopa, as quoted in Carolyn Hamilton's "Oral Archives: Introduction," *S.A. Archives Journal* 40 (1998):78, https://www.researchgate.net/profile/Segomotso_Keakopa.

3. *Dictionary of Archives Terminology* s.v. "Series," accessed January 6, 2020, https://dictionary.archivists.org/entry/series.html.

4. *Dictionary of Archives Terminology* s.v. "Finding Aid," accessed January 6, 2020, https://www2.archivists.org/glossary/terms/f/finding-aid.

5. Granville S. W. Olney Records, RI Historical Society, MSS 1134, Providence.

6. Beaumont Newhall, *The History of Photography, from 1839 to the Present Day* (New York: Museum of Modern Art, 1982), 94.

7. Paul N. Banks and Roberta Pilette, *Preservation: Issues and Planning* (Chicago: American Library Association, 2000), 121–122.

8. Smithsonian Institution Archives, "Preserve Your Treasures: How To Remove Photos from a Sticky Album," YouTube, October 21, 2010, video, 4:07, https://www.youtube.com/watch?v=fcDlbNi-9D0.

9. Image Permanence Institute, *A Consumer Guide for the Recovery of Water-Damaged Traditional and Digital Prints* (Rochester, NY: 2007).

10. Tammy Lamourex, "70 Inspirational Quotes for Photographers," PetaPixel, entry posted May 29, 2014, accessed February 9, 2020, https://petapixel.com/2014/05/29/70-inspirational-quotes-photographers/.

11. University of Illinois at Urbana-Champaign, "Preservation Self-Assessment Program: Daguerreotypes, Ambrotypes, and Tintypes," Institute of Museum and Library Services, accessed January 29, 2016, https://psap.library.illinois.edu/format-id-guide/directimage.

12. Beaumont Newhall, The History of Photography, from 1839 to the Present Day (New York: Museum of Modern Art, 1982), 129.

13. Newhall, The History of Photography, 30.

14. Newhall, The History of Photography, 117.

15. James M Reilly, *Storage Guide for Color Photographic Materials* (New York: University of the State of New York, New York State Program for the Conservation and Preservation of Library Material, 1998), 7.

16. George Eastman speaking of the Brownie camera, 1900, from Anthony Bannon's *"1000 Photo Icons"* (Rochester, NY: George Eastman House, 2003), 347, https://photoquotes.com/author/george-eastman.

17. Hannibal Goodwin, a minister from New Jersey, applied for the patent in early 1889 but did not receive the actual patent until 1898. In the meantime, George Eastman adopted the technology in his factory using a method that Goodwin developed. Eastman combined the film with a lightweight camera, introducing photography to an amateur audience. In 1914, Eastman lost a lawsuit from Goodwin's company and had to pay restitution of $5 million.

18. Maria Fernanda Valverde, *Photographic Negatives: Nature and Evolution of Processes* (New York: Image Permanence Institute, 2005), 24.

19. "Acetate Film Base Deterioration – The Vinegar Syndrome," Image Permanence Institute (Rochester, NY), accessed January 12, 2016. https://www.imagepermanenceinstitute.org/resources/newsletter-archive/v12/vinegar-syndrome.

20. Resource on cold storage of film is the National Park Service online interactive training program, "Cold Storage: A Long-Term Preservation Strategy for Film-Based Photographic Materials" and is available at http://www.nps.gov/museum/coldstorage/NPSColdStorage.swf. Keep in mind this information was put together for archivists and museum preservationists, not lay people or home archivists. I provide this information to demonstrate the extensive care needed in employing cold storage, which is why I recommend either disposing of film or donating it to a qualified archive.

21. Northeast Document Conservation Center, "Session 4: Caring for Paper Collections," accessed February 2, 2016, https://www.nedcc.org/preservation101/session-4/4-papermaking.

22. *Dictionary.com*, s.v. "Groundwood Pulp," accessed February 2, 2016, http://dictionary.reference.com/browse/groundwood-pulp.

23. See https://lenasalina.files.wordpress.com/2016/05/preservationhistory-brittle-paper.pdf.

24. International Organization for Standardization Online Browsing Platform, "3.3 Permanent Paper," accessed September 26, 2021, https://www.iso.org/obp/ui/#iso:std:iso:9706:ed-1:v1:en.

25. The National Archives of Australia, "What is Thermal Paper: Early Thermal Papers," accessed February 2, 2016, https://www.naa.gov.au/information-management/store-and-preserve-information/preserving-information/managing-records-thermal-papers.

26. Northeast Document Conservation Center, "7.8 Removal of Damaging Fasteners from Historic Documents," accessed February 8, 2016, https://www.nedcc.org/free-resources/preservation-leaflets/7.-conservation-procedures/7.8-removal-of-damaging-fasteners-from-historic-documents.

27. Don Williams and Louisa Jaggar, *Saving Stuff: How to Care for and Preserve Your Collectibles, Heirlooms, and Other Prized Possessions* (New York: Simon & Schuster, 2005), 250.

28. VELCRO® is a registered trademark of Velcro IP Holdings LLC.

29. "About Us," ISO, accessed August 19, 2018, https://www.iso.org/about-us.html.

30. Per Christensson, "Optical Media," TechTerms, last modified February 28, 2008, https://techterms.com/definition/opticalmedia.

31. Elizabeth Leggett, *Digitization and Digital Archiving: A Practical Guide for Librarians* (Lantham, MD: Rowman & Littlefield, 2014), 68.

32. Leggett, *Digitization and Digital Archiving*, 71.

33. Leggett, *Digitization and Digital Archiving*, 72.

34. "Why Is Magnetic Tape Still Used?" Quora, accessed August 25, 2018, https://www.quora.com/Why-is-magnetic-tape-still-used.

35. Andy Patrizio, "Humidity, Not Heat, Is a Hard Drive's Biggest Threat," Network World, March 30, 2016, https://www.networkworld.com/article/3049428/humidity-not-heat-is-a-hard-drives-biggest-threat.html.

36. Paul William et. al., "Predicting Archival Life of Removable Hard Disk Drives," ResearchGate (January 2008): 188–192, https://www.researchgate.net/publication/290550670_Predicting_archival_life_of_removable_hard_disk_drive.

37. David George, "Family Reunited with Seabed Camera Dropped Overboard," BBC News, September 20, 2012, https://www.bbc.com/news/av/uk-19667430.

NOTES

38. Elizabeth Leggett, *Digitization and Digital Archiving: A Practical Guide for Librarians* (Lantham, MD: Rowman & Littlefield, 2014), 109.
39. Leggett, *Digitization and Digital Archiving*, 183.
40. Leggett, *Digitization and Digital Archiving*, 124.
41. Donald T. Hawkins, *Personal Archiving: Preserving Our Digital Heritage* (Medford, NJ: Information Today, Inc., 2013), 6.
42. Andrew Chaikivsky, "Everything You Need to Know About Password Managers," *Consumer Reports*, February 7, 2017, https://www.consumerreports.org/digital-security/everything-you-need-to-know-about-password-managers-a5624939418/.
43. Daniel Bates, "Facebook Will Become the World's Biggest Virtual Graveyard with More Profiles of Dead People than Living Users by the End of the Century, Say Experts," last modified March 6, 2016, http://www.dailymail.co.uk/news/article-3479288/Facebook-world-s-biggest-virtual-graveyard-profiles-dead-people-living-users-end-century-say-experts.html.
44. Uniform Law Commission, *"Fiduciary Access to Digital Assets Act, Revised,"* revised in 2015, accessed September 19, 2021, https://www.uniformlaws.org/committees/community-home?CommunityKey=f7237fc4-74c2-4728-81c6-b39a91lecdf22.
45. The recommendations in this chapter are intended for guidance only. The author does not assume responsibility or liability.
46. National Archives, Resources – *Vital Records and Records Disaster Mitigation and Recovery*, accessed October 22, 2018, https://www.archives.gov/records-mgmt/vital-records.
47. National Archives, *Resources*.
48. Northeast Document Conservation Center, "Fundamentals of AV Preservation – Chapter 5," Section 1: Disaster and Prevention Mitigation, accessed August 5, 2018, https://www.nedcc.org/fundamentals-of-av-preservation-textbook/chapter-5introduction/chapter-5-section-1.
49. Arthur Schultz, ed., *Caring for Your Collections* (New York: Henry N. Abrams, Inc., 1992), 157.
50. Schultz, *Caring for Your Collections*, 159.
51. Schultz, *Caring for Your Collections*, 159.
52. Schultz, *Caring for Your Collections*, 159.
53. Gavin de Becker, *The Gift of Fear: Survival Signals that Protect Us from Violence* (New York: Little, Brown and Company, 1997).
54. Arthur W. Schultz, ed., *Caring for Your Collections* (New York: Henry N. Abrams, Inc., 1992), 162.
55. Per E. Guldbeck, *The Care of Antiques and Historical Collections (American Association for State and Local History)*, originally published 1985, revised by MacLeish and A. Bruce (Walnut Creek, CA: Altamira Press, 1995), 52.
56. "Emergency Preparedness & Response," AIC Conservation Wiki: Preventive Care, accessed October 22, 2018, http://www.conservation-wiki.com/wiki/Emergency_Preparedness_%26_Response.
57. Peter Brothers, "Magnetic Tapes Can Survive Flood Exposure," August 5, 2018, http://www.specsbros.com/disaster-recovery-magnetic-tapes-can-survive-flood-exposure.html.

FAMILY HISTORIAN LEGACY PROMISE

AS THE FAMILY HISTORIAN, I PROMISE TO TAKE THE RESPONSIBILITIES OF FAMILY HISTORIAN SERIOUSLY.

I PROMISE TO HOUSE, STORE, PRESERVE, CONSERVE, AND DESCRIBE THE ITEMS IN MY CARE USING BEST PRACTICES TO THE BEST OF MY ABILITIES AND RESOURCES.

I PROMISE TO DO NO HARM WHILE CARING FOR THE COLLECTIONS IN MY CARE.

I PROMISE TO CREATE A FAMILY ARCHIVE WITH FUTURE GENERATIONS IN MIND.

WHEN I AM NO LONGER ABLE OR WILLING TO CARE FOR THE COLLECTION, I WILL FIND A QUALIFIED FAMILY MEMBER TO TAKE MY PLACE.

_____   _____
            SIGNATURE   DATE

SUGGESTED RESOURCES

Books

The Care of Antiques and Historical Collections, *Per E. Guldbeck and A. Bruce MacLeish* – Although this book was originally written in 1972, and revised in 1995, the information about material preservation is sound and still relevant. It includes chapters on conservation of wooden objects, skin and leather, ceramics, glass, bone, ivory and animal teeth, and stone artifacts. The back of the book has several great appendixes including one that instructs how to make padded coat hangers for historical garments.

Caring for Your Collections, *Arthur W. Schultz, ed.* – This book is produced by the National Institute for the Conservation of Cultural Property. It is a beautiful book with many pictures and is a treasure in and of itself. It includes chapters on paintings, works of art on paper, furniture, decorative arts, stone objects, musical instruments, and ethnographic materials. Since it is geared toward collectors, it includes chapters on security for cultural objects in the home, authenticating your collections, donating your collections, appraising and insuring your collections, and obtaining professional conservation services.

Caring for Your Family Treasures, *Jane S. Long and Richard W. Long* – This book has information on saving scrapbooks and albums, genealogy and family treasures, LPs, paintings, furniture, clocks and watches, ceramics and glass, family holiday treasures, musical instruments, natural artifacts, military mementos, dolls, teddy bears, and toy soldiers.

Digitization and Digital Archiving: A Practical Guide for Librarians, *Elizabeth R. Leggett* – This book is written by a librarian for librarians, but if you want to understand the inner workings of the digital world and receive great advice on digital preservation, this is the book to buy. I would have included more information from this book but was unable to because I was writing about many other things and for a general audience. For those with a higher level of computer expertise and who want a greater understanding of digital preservation, you will find it here. While some of the chapters are not relevant to non-librarians, you will walk away with a better understanding of the complexity and issues regarding long-term storage and digital preservation.

The History of Photography: from 1839 to the present, *Beaumont Newhall* – For the photographers in the room, this is a great book that provides a wonderful in-depth history of photography from its roots to around 1982 when the book was last published. This book is considered a scholarly classic on photography. It does not contain archival advice but provides historical context for the photographs in your collection. Newhall was a curator, art historian, and photographer who was the first director of the Museum of Modern Art's Photography Department. He also worked at the Museum of Photography at the George Eastman House in Rochester, NY.

How to Save Your Stuff from a Disaster, Scott M. Haskins – Haskins is the owner and director of the Fine Art Conservation Laboratory in Santa Barbara, CA. This book covers the usual materials: photographs, paper, and books, but also has chapters on ceramics and glass, art on paper including watercolors and pastels, paintings, framing, rugs, tapestries, old clothes, sculpture, and furniture. There is an appendix in the back on emergency preparedness.

Personal Archiving: Preserving Our Digital Heritage, Donald T. Hawkins, ed. – This book is a compilation written by several experts in the field of digital preservation. While the world of digital moves swiftly, this book written in 2013 is still relevant and discusses many issues important to personal digital archiving.

Saving Stuff: How to Care for and Preserve Your Collectibles, Heirlooms, and Other Prized Possessions, Don Williams and Louisa Jaggar – This book contains information on preserving toys, stuffed animals, puppets, dolls, your child's art projects, holiday ornaments, electrical devices such as lamps, chandeliers, and fans, cast iron, baskets, tools, botanical specimens, furniture including wicker and rattan, sports and political memorabilia, entertainment memorabilia including vinyl records, comic books, newspapers, magazines, coins and stamps, fine art including oil paintings, and musical instruments.

The Winterhur Guide to Caring for Your Collections, Gregory J. Landrey, et.al. – The Winterhur Museum, Garden, and Library in Delaware is the leading museum of American decorative arts with a collection of almost 90,000 objects. This book is written by different experts in the field, and contains information on preserving ceramics and glass, works of art on paper, paintings, furniture, and gilded frames as well as photographs, metals, textiles and books.

Websites

American Institute for Conservation of Historic and Artistic Works (AIC)

AIC is dedicated to the preservation of cultural materials and plays a crucial role in establishing and upholding professional standards, promoting research and publications, providing educational opportunities, and fostering the exchange of knowledge among conservators, allied professionals, and the public. To find information related to personal archives, go to: http://www.conservation-us.org/about-conservation/caring-for-your-treasures#.Vyd31_krLb0

You can do a national search to find a conservator at this link: https://www.culturalheritage.org/about-conservation/find-a-conservator#.WlOgHvCnFhE

For information about what to do in an emergency or disaster see: https://www.culturalheritage.org/resources/emergencies/disaster-response-recovery

Association of Personal Historians

This is a great national website where you can find help with genealogy, writing memoir, creating ethical wills, oral history, and much more.

https://www.personalhistorians.org/

The Conservation Center for Art & Historic Artifacts (CCAHA)

The Conservation Center for Art & Historic Artifacts is one of the largest nonprofit conservation centers in the country. Employing a wide array of services, sophisticated treatment facilities, innovative approaches, and highly trained and experienced staff, they provide expertise and leadership in the preservation of the world's cultural heritage. CCAHA specializes in the treatment of works of art and artifacts on paper, such as drawings, prints, maps, posters, historic wallpaper, photographs, rare books, scrapbooks, and manuscripts, as well as related materials such as parchment and papyrus. CCAHA also offers on-site consultation services, educational programs and seminars, internships, and emergency conservation services.

http://www.ccaha.org/publications

Family History Metadata Working Group

The Family History Metadata Working Group's goal is to make sure the descriptions you add to digital photographs are retained regardless of the program they are created in or if they are uploaded online or transferred to another platform. Keep watching this group to see when they accomplish their goal.

https://fhmwg.wordpress.com/

Image Permanence Institute

IPI® is a nonprofit, university-based laboratory devoted to preservation research on anything that captures an image including photographs, film, and video. They are the world's largest independent laboratory with this specific scope and are the resource archivists and conservators turn to for expertise. IPI provides information, consulting services, practical tools, and preservation technology to libraries, archives, and museums worldwide. The imaging and consumer preservation industries also use IPI's consulting, testing, and educational services. While IPI limits their conservation services to institutions, their resources section has the best information on photographic and film preservation.

https://www.imagepermanenceinstitute.org/resources/publications

LenaSalina Legacy Preservation

This is the author's website. The Resources page has many of the PDF articles listed in the bibliography. Also see the Secrets from the Stacks page for demonstration videos and specific step-by-step instructions on how to do many of the things discussed in this book. Please be advised that the Guides page can only be accessed by using the link below and is not searchable through a search engine.

www.lenasalina.com/resources

https://lenasalina.com/secrets-from-the-stacks-guides/

Library of Congress

The Library of Congress has an initiative to assist the public in archiving digital content and material items. These links provide a starting point for the information on their website.

https://digitalpreservation.gov/personalarchiving/

https://blogs.loc.gov/thesignal/2016/05/how-to-begin-a-personal-archiving-project/

The National Archives and Records Administration (NARA)

Your national archives at work, NARA provides great information on the basics of personal preservation. There is a section specific to family archives, but there are also sections on digitizing family papers and photographs and much more.

https://www.archives.gov/preservation/family-archives/

http://www.archives.gov/preservation/

Northeast Document Conservation Center (NEDCC)

NEDCC is the local authority archivists and librarians turn to for assistance. Founded in 1973, they were the first independent conservation laboratory in the United States to specialize exclusively in the conservation and preservation of paper and film-based collections. Today NEDCC provides professional conservation treatment for books, maps, photographs, documents, parchment, papyrus, manuscripts, architectural plans, and works of art on paper. In addition to conservation assistance, they have a free online course called *Preservation 101* that is a great resource for information about all types of materials.

https://www.nedcc.org/preservation-training/training-about

The Photo Detective

Maureen Taylor is the Photo Detective. She can help you to identify family members lost to time. Maureen has a great deal of educational materials on her website and has a regular podcast where she interviews many people with great tips and tricks on saving family photographs and identifying who is in the pictures.

https://maureentaylor.com/

The Photo Managers

The Photo Managers is a community of professionals helping individuals and families manage photo collections and tell their stories. They will help with organizing, scanning, converting old media, or finding creative ways to share. If you are overwhelmed with the thought of organizing your paper photographs or digital photographs, a professional can assist or do it for you. Their website has a national database to help you find a qualified photo organizer in your area.

https://thephotomanagers.com/

Genealogy Shows

Finding Your Roots

Hosted by Dr. Henry Louis Gates Jr., the show explores the ancestry of dozens of influential people from diverse backgrounds, taking millions of viewers deep into the past to reveal the connections that bind us all. It can be seen on most PBS stations.

Genealogy Roadshow

Part detective story, part emotional journey, Genealogy Roadshow combined history and science to uncover the fascinating stories of diverse Americans. Each individual's past links to a larger community history, revealing the rich cultural tapestry of America. Genealogy Roadshow aired for three seasons from 2013-2016. It can be watched on many local PBS stations.

Who Do You Think You Are?

This docuseries researches the family histories of celebrities around the world. There is an American version, a British version, and an Australian version. Episodes can be watched on many streaming devices or can be purchased.

Supplies

For archival supplies, see these websites:

Gaylord https://www.gaylord.com/

GMI Companies https://waddellfurniture.com/products/floor-cases.html

Hollinger Metal Edge https://www.hollingermetaledge.com/

Hollinger has a family photo album kit. See: https://www.hollingermetaledge.com/family-album-kit/

University Products https://www.universityproducts.com/

LIST OF TERMS

Acid-Free Paper – wood pulp cellulose paper that is purified to remove lignin and acids so paper will have the longest shelf life.

Acrylic – first produced in the United States in 1950, acrylic fibers resemble wool and are known for their softness and warmth. Acrylic improves upon wool by being quick-drying and resistant to moths, sunlight, oil, and chemicals. It can also be machine-washed. It comes under the trade names Orlon, Acrilan, and Cresian.

Activated Carbon – a type of carbon used chiefly for absorbing gases or solutes; it can be used to absorb sulfur compounds.

Allotropic – the chemical property of an element that can occur in two or more forms that differ in molecular structure.

Ambrotypes – a type of photography developed by Frederick Scott Archer, they were popular in America between 1851 and 1880. Ambrotypes used a wet plate collodion process on glass plates which revolutionized photography.

Backward Compatible in computer programs – means that newer versions can read older versions.

Binary Systems – relate to, are composed of, or involve two things, the two "things" inside a computer are categorized as 0s and 1s.

Biographical Background – in an archival Finding Aid it provides researchers with basic information about the creator of a collection.

Bit Rot – this happens when tiny bits of magnetic encoding on a hard drive are erased by temperature fluctuations.

Bitonal – scanner term that refers to scanning two-tone black-and-white scans such as printed or handwritten text.

Blu-Ray – is the largest capacity optical storage medium, having multiple layers that allow up to 128 GB of storage. It requires a specialized reader that uses a blue laser instead of a red laser to read it. The blue laser allows more information to be stored and read. Blu-ray discs come in BD-ROM, for use with computers, BD-R, which are recordable, and BD-RE, which are rewritable.

Born Digital Documents – are items that were created in the digital world. This includes correspondence, reports, presentations, photographs, audio and video files, email, text, websites, and social media.

Buffered – materials that contain an agent that reduces the harmful effects of the acid in paper; the most common buffering agent is calcium carbonate.

Calcium Carbonate – an alkaline-based product designed to absorb the natural acidity of paper and slow down the deterioration process.

Calotypes – a type of photography invented by William Henry Fox Talbot and patented in 1841. Photographic images were captured on chemically treated paper.

Carpet Beetles – a small insect about the size of a ladybug with white and brown stripes that are attracted to proteins in animal-based materials such as wool, silk, and leather.

Carte des Visites – a type of photography patented by André Adolphe-Eugène Disdéri in France in 1854. Cartes-de-visite used a wet plate process employing a special camera with four lenses and a plate holder. The photographs were cut up into individual prints, then pasted on a mount measuring 4" x 2½". They were very popular in the 19th century and were accessible to a wide range of customers. They replaced calling cards and were collected to form the first photo albums.

CD-Compact Disc – a form of optical media that are read by a laser.

CD-DA-Compact Disc Digital Audio – discs used for commercially produced music that can be played in any CD player including a computer, an automobile media player, or a dedicated CD player.

CD-R-Compact Disc Recordable – blank CDs with no information encoded until the user "burns" the information onto them. Information can be recorded but not written over.

CD-ROM-Compact Disc Read-Only-Memory – CDs that can only be read by computers. The information on a CD-ROM cannot be altered by computers, which makes them a great backup storage mechanism for archival purposes.

CD-RW-Compact Disc Rewritable – CDs that can be overwritten.

Chromogenic Development – in color photographs the process by which the color dyes in the final picture are formed during processing. All color photographs are made using this technology except for Polaroid, invented in 1963, which is non-chromogenic.

Cibachrome or **Ilfochrome** – non-chromogenic photographs that are made of silver dye bleach rather than organic colors. These are rare but are thought to be able to last several hundred years. Cibachrome or Ilfochrome are typically used in large format cameras.

Clothes Moths – an insect that is attracted to the protein in animal-based materials such as wool, silk, fur, and leather. They prefer dark areas and they are more likely to be found in areas that are undisturbed such as closets and attics.

Cloud Storage – The basic concept of cloud storage is that the information is stored on a highly powerful remote computer not in your control, and the information is accessed through the internet. With cloud computing, you, as the user, agree to allow a company to store your data. Usually, though not always, there is a fee for this service

CoDec – short for "coder-decoder." In media files, encoded data must be decoded to be played back. CoDec is different from compression/decompression, but most CoDecs do compress the original data and reduce the original file size. CoDecs can be lossless, meaning the quality of the original medium is not reduced, or lossy, meaning some data is lost and can result in reduced quality.

Color – a scanner term. Palettes have a range of 256 gray tones to thousands of color tones. Select this when scanning color photographs, maps, illustrations, graphics, diagrams, and other color images.

Compression – a term used to describe the reduction in file size created when saving a digital document, image, audio, or video file. When a file is compressed, two actions occur. First, it is compressed upon saving. Second, it is decompressed when opened or during playback.

Cotton – a plant-based fiber at risk of deterioration by acids.

CSV-Comma Separated Values – a standard way to store structured data separated by comma values in plain text. CSV is a common export option especially for spreadsheet import.

Daguerreotypes – a type of photography invented by Louis-Jacques-Mandé Daguerre and Nicéphore Niépce, it used a silver-plated copper base which was cleaned and polished until the surface looked black when held up in a darkened room. Daguerreotypes were most popular between 1839 and 1860.

Dark Fading – when the organic dyes in color photographs fade even when photos are kept in a dark, cool environment.

DCIM-Digital Camera Images – the default directory or folder on digital cameras including cell phones.

Dead Man's Switch – an automatic "off" or "kill" switch that kicks in when the operator of heavy machinery becomes incapacitated through death or loss of consciousness. Digital versions of the dead man's switch function to prevent hackers from gaining entry to password protected sites such as bank accounts, it deletes or encrypts data in the event a breach has occurred, or allows users to send information to loved ones after their death.

Descriptive Metadata – the description users add to photographs explaining the who, what, where, why, and when depicted in the photograph.

Digital Archiving – the preservation of born digital information.

Digital Assets – any digital entity owned by an individual or company including digital photos, videos, songs, or documents.

Digital Legacy – digital assets passed down after a person dies including digital photographs, video files, audio files, and documents. It also includes digital subscriptions that may need to be altered or terminated after a person dies such as social media accounts, retail accounts, email services, and organizational memberships.

Digital Preservation – the preservation of print materials through digitization.

Direct Access – a term used to describe the motion of a magnetic computer data reader head, which includes the up-and-down movement of an arm, and the back-and-forth movement of the tape itself.

Disaster – an unexpected occurrence inflicting widespread destruction and distress and having long-term adverse effects.

Distilled Water – chemically pure water.

DPI-Dots Per Inch – used to describe the capabilities of a printer, it refers to the dots per inch used when printing a digital document.

DVD-Digital Versatile Discs – large-capacity compact discs that can hold multiple layers of data, they contain two layers of information on one disc, or they can both be double sided, quadrupling the information capacity of a regular CD.

Dye Stability – a term used to describe the stability level of different dyes used in the creation of CD-Rs, DVD-Rs, and BD-Rs.

Emergency – a situation or an occurrence of a serious nature, developing suddenly and unexpectedly, and demanding immediate action, generally of short duration, a week or less.

Encryption – a process that converts data to an unrecognizable form, it is commonly used to protect sensitive information from unauthorized parties.

Enduring Value – the concept that some items have usefulness or significance related to a family archive or a personal history.

Ethafoam – inert polyethylene foam padding used in archives and sold by archival stores, it can be custom made to support artifacts during storage or transportation and can be cut to specific sizes. It is soft enough to embed objects such as jewelry, military metals, or decorative pins to keep them stationary and prevent scratching, denting, and breakage.

Extension – the three or four letters after a file name, preceded by a dot, that are automatically added and identify the type of file. Examples are .docx, .pdf, .jpeg, and .mov.

Ferrotypes – see tintypes.

File Formats – a standard way information is encoded for storage in a computer file.

Finding Aid – a tool that facilitates discovery of information within a collection of records. It provides a description of records that gives the repository or user physical and intellectual control over the materials and assists users to gain access to and understand the materials.

Flash Memory – computer data storage drives that writes data to transistors using silicon.

Glassine – a highly polished, semitransparent interleaving paper, it can be used to interleaf photographs, documents, or other items. Glassine comes in buffered and unbuffered varieties.

Grayscale – a scanner term that describes a type of palette that provides up to 256 gray tones.

Historical Note – in an archival Finding Aid it provides researchers with basic information about the collection.

HTML-HyperText Markup Language – as a coding language, rather than a file format, documents stored using HTML coding may have a lengthier life expectancy for long-term digital storage preservation.

Hydroscopic – absorbing moisture from the air.

Hygrometer – a device that measures relative humidity (RH). Many hygrometers also display the temperature.

Inert – materials will not cause further damage.

Inherent Vice – a condition that occurs when an object can be destroyed by the materials that were used in the manufacturing process or during the construction of the object.

Intellectual Preservation – a term used to describe keeping the integrity and authenticity of the information as it was originally recorded.

ISO-International Standard Organization – an independent, non-governmental international organization with a membership of 161 national standards bodies, it brings together experts to share knowledge and develop voluntary, consensus-based, and market-relevant international standards. ISO provides specifications for products, services, and systems to ensure quality, safety, and efficiency to facilitate international trade.

Kodachrome – the first color film introduced by Kodak in 1935.

Laser Rot – a term that describes damage that has occurred in optical media discs through corrosion, discoloration, or pitting, rendering the information unreadable. Laser rot often occurs when the lacquer or polycarbonate protective layers have been compromised in some way and atmospheric conditions penetrate to the metallic layer.

Lignin-Free Paper – paper free of lignin, an acid-forming component of paper causing brittleness and discoloration, resulting in the longest shelf life.

Linen – a plant-based fiber made from flax used in making cloth. It is highly absorbent and will change shape and strength in high humidity environments.

Lossless – digital compression that is mathematically reversible and results in no loss of quality. It allows the decompressed data to be exactly the same, bit for bit. The disadvantage is larger file size.

Lossy – digital compression that results in permanent loss of data usually associated with image, audio, and video files. The decompressed data will not be identical to the original. Typically, the lost data is imperceptible to the human eye or ear. If it is perceptible, it may appear as jagged edges, pixelated areas, a watery sound in audio files, or blurred video images. The tradeoff between using lossy or lossless is file size over image quality.

Magnetic Media – one of the oldest methods of data storage originally invented in 1898, magnetic tape was used to record sound by 1928 and to record speeches and radio programs before the advent of computers. It is still a viable digital storage mechanism for computer data.

Magnetic Photo Albums – sold in the 1960s and 1970s, these albums are not actually magnetic. They use heavy glue to hold photographs to pages that are covered with PVC plastic.

Mathematically Lossless – a term to describe when no digital data is lost during compression and decompression.

Metadata – data about data. There are two types of metadata. The first describes the technical and structural data that is automatically created by a file format. Technical metadata may include the file format (docx, jpg), the size of the document in pixels, and who it was created by. The second type of metadata is the information users add to describe a computer file as a document, an image, an audio file, or a video file.

MOV Files – videos created on phones or digital cameras.

Native Formats – digital file formats that are created in certain software programs, are native to that software, and can only be read by that specific software program. PSD, created by Photoshop, is an example.

Nonionic Detergent – a synthetic detergent that is electrically neutral.

Non-Proprietary or Free – a published specification usually maintained by a standards organization which can be used and implemented by anyone.

Nylon – the first "true" synthetic fiber to be manufactured in 1931, it is the second most used synthetic fiber in the United States after polyester. Nylon's first use was to replace women's silk stockings in 1939. It can be found under the trade names Antron, Durasoft, and Supplex.

Open – a file format that is freely available online.

Open Document Format (ODF) – a non-proprietary, open-source format that is available for text documents, spreadsheets, charts, and presentations. It was developed by the Organization for the Advancement of Structured Information Standards (OASIS) consortium as an XML-based file format that uses ZIP compression.

Original Order – the order documents or photographs were put in by their creator.

Palette – similar to an artist's palette, it describes the range of gray tones or colors in an image when scanning objects.

Parchment – any animal skin prepared for use in writing, typically sheepskin.

PDF-A – a specialized format standard designed to be used for **A**rchiving and long-term digital preservation of electronic documents. The PDF-A standards are developed and maintained by a working group that has representatives in government, industry, and academia and is supported by Adobe Systems, Inc. Because PDF-As are an ISO standard, they are guaranteed the ability to be opened and rendered by future generations.

PDF-Portable Document Format – an "as printed" format that is portable between applications and systems, it was officially released as an open standard in 2008 under ISO 3200-1:2008 and is now controlled by the ISO committee. PDF is also referred to as Portable Digital File.

Permanent Paper – paper which will undergo little or no change in properties that affect use during long-term storage in protected environments.

Photographic Activity Test (PAT©) – documents that have passed this test will say "Passed PAT" somewhere in the description. PAT is a test developed by the Image Permanence Institute (IPI) that guarantees the enclosure will not react chemically with the photographs. The institute tests specific products and adds its seal of approval only if the products meet certain standards. The institute does not guarantee that a product is the best or will last the longest, it guarantees that the product will not do further damage to an item.

Polaroid film – introduced to the market in 1963, it is self-developing film that is non-chromogenic.

Polyester – a synthetic fabric first commercially produced in 1953, during the 1960s and 1970s, it was introduced as wash and wear and wrinkle-free. It can resemble cotton, silk, or wool and is often blended with natural fibers. Trade names for polyester include Dacron, Fortrel, Thermoloft, and Microloft.

Polyurethane – fabric commercially produced beginning in the early 1950s, polyurethane products include spandex, fake suede, fake leather, water-repellent materials and "wet-look" fabrics used for belts, shoes, purses, and jackets in the 1960s and 1970s. It is extremely sensitive to light, heat, and atmospheric chemicals, discoloration, cracking, delamination, or bubbling, and is highly susceptible to mold and mildew.

Polyvinyl or Polyvinyl Chloride (PVC) Plastic – a cheaper grade of plastic found in most loose-leaf binders and non-archival photo albums. Enclosures made from PVC release harmful elements that can affect the stability and appearance of photographs or papers. When PVC plastic begins to deteriorate, especially in hot conditions, it gets soft and sticks to pages. Over time, plastic sheets and binders will turn to goop, damaging the very items they were meant to protect.

PPI-Pixels per Inch – is the proper term to use when working within the computer and describes how many pixels per inch of color or shading are contained within one inch of an image. The more PPI, the finer the image. Higher PPI also results in a larger file size.

Preservation Week – an initiative started in 2005 to have libraries connect with the community and teach individuals about preservation. Preservation Week is usually in April or sometime in the spring. Many libraries sponsor digitization events where they teach digitization basics and sometimes provide equipment, including specialized equipment they may have on site. Contact your local library for more information.

Proprietary – a file format that is developed and owned by a software company, organization, or individual that keeps secret its properties and structure.

Provenance – refers to the individual, family, or organization that created or received the items in a collection.

Rayon – a synthetic fiber first produced in the 1880s, rayon is regenerated cellulose fiber. Since it is made from wood pulp, it is considered semi-synthetic. It was often called artificial silk, but it can imitate the look and feel of silk, wool, cotton, and linen. Rayon is easily dyed and the fibers are soft, smooth, comfortable, and highly absorbent, they do not insulate body heat, making rayon ideal for hot and humid climates. Most rayon needs to be dry-cleaned. Trade names are Viscose, Bemberg, Modal, Tencel, Accordis, and Lyocell.

Red Rot – a type of deterioration found in leather book covers from the late-19th to early-20th centuries, it is a result of the decaying of sulfuric acid used in the tanning process and appears as a red or reddish-brown powder or dust. It is highly contagious to other books that it comes in direct contact with, books containing red rot should be encapsulated as soon as possible.

Resolution – a scanner term that refers to a measurement that reflects the sharpness of an image.

Respect du Fonds – the principle in archival theory that states collections should be organized according to their creator.

Scope and Content – a section of the Finding Aid that provides summary information on what kind of documents are found in the collection.

Series List – A group of similar records that are arranged according to a filing system and that are related as the result of being created, received, or used in the same activity; a file group; a record series.

Silica Gel – a chemical compound sold in gel packs that can be used to help keep an interior environment at a low moisture level. Silica gel is "conditioned" to a particular RH.

Silk – an animal-based fiber made from silkworms composed primarily of proteins.

SIM Card-Subscriber Identification Module Card – a removable chip that identifies a mobile device on a cellular network having a unique identifier on an integrated circuit. It is required for cell phones to be used on a cellular network.

Spandex – a synthetic fiber that is a common form of polyurethane that became popular in the 1960s as a replacement for natural rubber. Because of its stretchability, it was used primarily in swimwear and undergarments, but it has also been used in jackets, skiwear, and exercise clothing. It is manufactured under the names Lycra, Cleerspan, Dorlastan, and Glospan.

Stereoscopic Photography – a type of photography that was produced by using twin-lens cameras resulting in a 3-D image that was similar to human binocular vision. Use of these photographs became popular after Sir David

Brewster invented a device for easily viewing them in 1849. Stereoscopic images provided the first vehicle for action photography and was the foundation of the development of motion pictures.

Sticky Shed Syndrome – occurs when excess moisture causes the binders in a magnetic tape to deteriorate leaving a deposit of sticky residue. It is most often found in polyester-urethane binders from the 1970s onward and can be damaging to playback equipment.

Stray Magnetic Fields – produced by AC-powered motors or transformers, dynamic sound equipment such as microphones, headphones, loudspeakers, and moving coil instruments are examples of objects that emit stray magnetic field and should be kept at least six inches away from magnetic tapes which can be demagnetized or erased.

Structural Metadata – information that is automatically generated when a digital object is created.

Synthetic – any manufactured fiber made from chemical synthesis, first produced in the 20th century. Synthetics were made to replace and replicate natural fibers by maintaining the desirable qualities of natural fibers while eliminating the undesirable ones.

Technical Metadata - data that is automatically created and stored with a digital file. To obtain technical metadata of a file, right-click on the file name and select Properties.

Technology Preservation – the concept that preserving digital information requires original software programs, operating systems, and media drives, sometimes referred to as a "computer museum," to allow digital information to be read.

Tintypes – a type of photography that uses the same wet plate collodion process as the ambrotype using a thin sheet of iron as the support layer, patented by Hamilton I. Smith in 1856.

Unpublished – a file format code that is kept by the developer.

Vellum – parchment paper made from calfskin for use in writing.

Vinegar Syndrome – decomposing acetate film. Film in an active state of vinegar syndrome can be hazardous to your health.

Visually lossless – in digital compression it is the same as lossy compression. Loss of data occurs but not enough to be visible to the naked eye.

VOB-Video OBject – files found on DVDs that have been made on video recorders or directly on a video recording device.

Wool – an animal-based fiber made from sheep composed primarily of proteins.

Wrapper – the container all digital video files wrap the video and audio streams in. Wrappers are identified by the video file's extension such as AVI, JP2, MOV, mp2, mp4, MXF, WMV.

ZIP File – a file archive that contains one or more compressed files using zip compression. Files are stored separately from each other allowing them to be compressed using different methods and extracted without compressing or decompressing the entire archive.

BIBLIOGRAPHY

1. About Inactive Account Manager. Google Support. Accessed August 5, 2018. https://support.google.com/accounts/answer/3036546?hl=en.
2. *About Us*, ISO, accessed August 19, 2018, https://www.iso.org/about-us.html.
3. *Acetate Film Base Deterioration – The Vinegar Syndrome*, Image Permanence Institute (Rochester, NY), accessed January 12, 2016. https://www.image-permanenceinstitute.org/resources/newsletter-archive/v12/vinegar-syndrome.
4. Adelstein, Peter Z. *IPI Media Storage Quick Reference*, 2nd ed., Rochester, NY: Image Permanence Institute, 2009.
5. AIC Conservation Wiki: Preventive Care is "Emergency Preparedness & Response." Accessed October 22,2018. http://www.conservation-wiki.com/wiki/Emergency_Preparedness_%26_Response.
6. Alper, Diana, "How to Flatten Folded or Rolled Paper Documents," *Conserve O Gram*, Number 13/2, (July 1993), 1-4.
7. *American Institute for Conservation Learning Community, Disaster Response & Recovery Guides: Guides and Information.* Accessed October 22, 2018. www.conservation-us.org/disaster.
8. American Red Cross. *Repairing Your Flooded Home.* Jessup, MD: FEMA, 1992.
9. Banks, Paul N. and Roberta Pilette, *Preservation: Issues and Planning* Chicago: American Library Association, 2000, 121–122.
10. Bannon, Anthony "1000 Photo Icons" Rochester, NY: George Eastman House, 2003 https://photoquotes.com/author/george-eastman.
11. Bates, Daniel "Facebook Will Become the World's Biggest Virtual Graveyard with More Profiles of Dead People than Living Users by the End of the Century, Say Experts," last modified March 6, 2016, http://www.dailymail.co.uk/news/article-3479288/Facebook-world-s-biggest-virtual-graveyard-profiles-dead-people-living-users-end-century-say-experts.html.
12. *Best Solutions to the Top Five Disaster Recovery Mistakes.* Iron Mountain, General Articles. Accessed July 21,2018. http://www.ironmountain.com/resources/general-articles/b/best-solutions-to-the-top-five-disaster-recovery-mistakes
13. Bigourdan, Jean-Louis and James M. Reilly. *Effectiveness of Storage Conditions in Controlling the Vinegar Syndrome: Preservation Strategies for Acetate Base Motion-Picture Film Collections.* Rochester, NY: Image Permanence Institute, Rochester Institute of Technology, 2002.

14. Bigourdan, Jean-Louis and James M. Reilly. *Environment and Enclosures in Film Preservation: Final Report to the Office of Preservation National Endowment for the Humanities.* Rochester, NY: Image Permanence Institute, Rochester Institute of Technology, September 15, 1997.
15. Bigourdan, Jean-Louis, et.al. *From Silver Image to Silver Anniversary: A look back at 25 years of award-winning preservation research at RIT's Image Permanence Institute.* Rochester, NY: Image Permanence Institute, 2010.
16. Blake, Eric S., et. al., *Tropical Cyclone Report Hurricane Sandy (AL 182012) 22 – 29 October 2012, PDF file,* National Hurricane Center, February 12, 2013, https://www.nhc.noaa.gov/data/tcr/AL182012_Sandy.pdf
17. Blyth, Val. *Carpet & Rug Care.* Victoria and Albert Museum. Accessed January 18, 2017. http://www.vam.ac.uk/content/articles/c/carpetandrugcare/.
18. Bradley, Tony. "Facebook 'Legacy Contact' Lets You Decide What Happens To Your Social Network When You Die." *Forbes,* February13, 2015. Accessed August 5, 2018 https://www.forbes.com/sites/tonybradley/2015/02/13/facebook-legacy-contact-lets-you-decide-what-happens-to-your-social-network-when-you-die/#68e892cf39ad.
19. Bradley, Tony, "What Happens To Your Data When You Die?" *Forbes.com.* Accessed August 5, 2018. https://www.forbes.com/sites/tonybradley/2015/02/20/what-happens-to-your-data-when-you-die/#4d0fc34737ca.
20. Brittle Paper. *Preservation History.* Accessed February 2, 2016. https://preservationhistory.wikispaces.com/Brittle+Paper
21. Brothers, Peter "Magnetic Tapes Can Survive Flood Exposure," August 5, 2018, http://www.specsbros.com/disaster-recovery-magnetic-tapes-can-survive-flood-exposure.html
22. Broussard, Mitchel. "How to Password Protect Notes in iOS 9.3 and OS X 10.11.4." *MacRumors,* Accessed July 22, 2018. https://www.macrumors.com/how-to/password-protect-notes-ios-os-x/.
23. Byers, Fred R. *Care and Handling of CDs and DVDs: A Guide for Librarians and Archivists.* Council on Library and Information Resources. National Institute of Standards and Technology, October 2003.
24. CERF+ The Artists Safety Net, Studio Protector. "The Artist's Guide to Emergencies." Accessed October 10, 2018. https://cerfplus.org/get-ready/studio-protector/help-yourself-portal/)
25. Chaikivsky, Andrew, "Everything You Need to Know About Password Managers," *Consumer Reports,* February 7, 2017, https://www.consumerreports.org/digital-security/everything-you-need-to-know-about-password-managers-a5624939418/.
26. Choe, D.H.. "Carpet Beetles.," *Pest Notes,* Publication 7436. Davis, CA: University of California, Davis. November 2012.

27. Christensson, Per, *"Optical Media,"* TechTerms, last modified February 28, 2008, https://techterms.com/definition/opticalmedia.
28. Claremont Rug Company. "Antique Oriental Rug Care." Accessed January 18, 2017. https://www.claremontrug.com/antique-rugs-information/rug-care/.
29. Clark Historical Library, "Preserving Memories- Caring for Your Heritage." Accessed January 12, 2016. https://www.cmich.edu/library/clarke/Public Programs/Advice_and_Resources/Pages/Preserving-Memories--Caring-for-Your-Heritage.aspx.
30. Conn, Donia. "Preserving a Christening Gown and Petticoat." Chicago, IL: American Library Association, 2016. Accessed May 13, 2017. http://www.ala.org/alcts/preservationweek/advice/christininggown
31. Conn, Doina. "Preserving Diaries." Chicago, IL: American Library Association, 2016. Accessed February 2, 2016. http://www.ala.org/alcts/preservationweek/advice/diaries.
32. Conn, Donia. "Preserve Onion Skin Paper." Chicago, IL: American Library Association, 2016. Accessed February 2, 2016. http://www.ala.org/alcts/preservationweek/advice/onionskin.
33. Council of State Archivists (COSA). Accessed October 22, 2018. https://www.statearchivists.org/programs/emergency-preparedness/
34. Cox, Richard J., *Personal Archives and a New Archival Calling: Readings, Reflections, and Ruminations,* Duluth, MN: Litwin Books, LLC, 2008.
35. Daw, David. "Designing your digital legacy," *PC World*, April 29, 2013. Accessed July 21, 2018. https://www.pcworld.com/article/2036372/designing-your-digital-legacy.html
36. Dead Man's Switch. *Stochastic Technologies*. Accessed July 21, 2018. https://www.deadmansswitch.net/.
37. Death in the Family need access to Microsoft Account Locked Computer., Microsoft.com. Accessed August 5, 2018. https://support.microsoft.com/en-us/help/189126/microsoft-policy-about-lost-or-forgotten-passwords.
38. Decide when Google should consider your Google Account Inactive. Accessed August 5, 2018. https://myaccount.google.com/inactive.
39. *Dictionary of Archives Terminology* s.v. "Finding Aid," accessed January 6, 2020, https://www2.archivists.org/glossary/terms/f/finding-aid.
40. *Dictionary of Archives Terminology* s.v. "Series," accessed January 6, 2020, https://dictionary.archivists.org/entry/series.html.
41. *Dictionary.com*, s.v. "Groundwood Pulp," accessed February 2, 2016, http://dictionary.reference.com/browse/groundwood-pulp.
42. Eastman Kodak Company. "Super 8 mm Film History." Rochester, NY: Eastman Kodak Company, 2016. Accessed March 21, 2016. http://www.kodak.com/ek/US/en/corp/websiteterms/default.html)

43. *Emergency Preparedness & Response*, AIC Conservation Wiki: Preventive Care, accessed October 22, 2018, http://www.conservation-wiki.com/wiki/Emergency_Preparedness_%26_Response.
44. Everplans. "Death and Email: How to Manage a Deceased Person's Accounts," *TransAmerica*, May 28, 2018. Accessed August 5, 2018. https://knowledgeplace.wealthmeethealth.com/individual/be-smart/article/death-and-email-how-to-manage-a-deceased-persons-accounts/.
45. Facebook to become world's biggest virtual graveyard by 2098, *Massachusetts Sun (IANS)*, Monday, March 7, 2016. Issue 1003/2016, p.1.
46. Fernanda Valverde, Maria, *Photographic Negatives: Nature and Evolution of Processes* New York: Image Permanence Institute, 2005, 24.
47. Fernanda Valverde, Maria. *Photographic Negatives: Nature and Evolution of Processes, 2nd Edition*. Advanced Residency Program in Photograph Conservation sponsored by the Andrew W. Mellon Foundation, George Eastman House, Rochester, NY: Image Permanence Institute, 2005.
48. Fischer, Monique, "Photographs: 5.1 A Short Guide to Film Base Photographic Materials: Identification, Care, and Duplications." Northeast Document Conservation Center, Andover, MA: 2007.
49. Frey, Franziska S., and James M. Reilly. *Photographic Collections: Foundations for Technical Standards*. Rochester, NY: Image Permanence Institute, 2006.
50. Gavin de Becker, *The Gift of Fear: Survival Signals that Protect Us from Violence* New York: Little, Brown and Company, 1997.
51. Gaylord Archival. "Conditioning Silica Gel." Accessed June 5, 2017 http://www.gaylord.com/resources/conditioningsilicagel.
52. General Accounts Settings. Facebook.com. Accessed August 5, 2018. https://www.facebook.com/settings?tab=account&section=account_management&view
53. George, David "Family Reunited with Seabed Camera Dropped Overboard," BBC News, September 20, 2012, https://www.bbc.com/news/av/uk-19667430.
54. Granville S. W. Olney Records, RI Historical Society, MSS 1134, Providence, RI
55. Guide to Photographic Photo Paper. *Photography Life*, 2016. Accessed December 5, 2016. https://photographylife.com/guide-photographic-photo-paper.
56. Guldbeck, Per E., *The Care of Antiques and Historical Collections American Association for State and Local History*, originally published 1985, revised by MacLeish and A. Bruce Walnut Creek, CA: Altamira Press, 1995.
57. Hamel, Annajean. *What's Behind Your Frame?* Andover, MA: Northeast Document Conservation Center, 2014.

58. Harris, Mark, "Converting and Digitizing Audio Cassettes to MP3," September 13, 2021, http://lifewire.com/how-to-convert-audio-cassettes-to-mp.3-2438827.
59. Haskins, Scott M. *How to Save Your Stuff from a Disaster*. Santa Barbara, CA: Preservation Help Publications, 1996.
60. Hawkins, Donald T. *Personal Archiving: Preserving Our Digital Heritage* Medford, NJ: Information Today, Inc., 2013, 6.
61. Hawkins, Donald T., ed. *Personal Archiving: Preserving Our Digital Heritage.*, Medford, NJ: Information Today, Inc., 2013.
62. Hope, Michele, "Can Secure Cloud Storage Solve the Long-Term Archiving Dilemma?" *Iron Mountain.com, 2016*. Accessed July 21, 2018.
63. How to contact Twitter about a deceased family member's account. Twitter Help Center. Accessed July 21, 2018. https://help.twitter.com/en/rules-and-policies/contact-twitter-about-a-deceased-family-members-account.
64. Image Permanence Institute, *A Consumer Guide for the Recovery of Water-Damaged Traditional and Digital Prints*, Rochester, NY: 2007.
65. Image Permanence Institute, *A Consumer Guide to Modern Photo Papers*, Rochester, NY: 2009.
66. Image Permanence Institute, *A Consumer Guide to Traditional and Digital Print Stability*, Rochester, NY: 2004.
67. Image Permanence Institute, *A Consumer Guide to Understanding Permanence Testing*, Rochester, NY: 2009.
68. Image Permanence Institute. *Acetate Film Base Deterioration – The Vinegar Syndrome*. Rochester, NY. Accessed January 12, 2016.
69. Image Permanence Institute, *Preserving Film-Based Photographic Collections*, Rochester, NY: 2016. https://www.imagepermanenceinstitute.org/resources/newsletter-archive/v12/vinegar-syndrome.
70. Industry Fact: By 2018, more than 60 percent of enterprises will have at least half of their infrastructure and applications in the cloud. *Iron Mountain Cloud Archive, Solution Brief*. Downloaded July 21, 18.
71. International Organization for Standardization Online Browsing Platform, "3.3 Permanent Paper," accessed September 26, 2021, https://www.iso.org/obp/ui/#iso:std:iso:9706:ed-1:v1:en.
72. Jennings, Richi, "Oops: Google "loses" your cloud data (sky falling; film at 11)," *Computerworld, IT Blogwatch*. Accessed July 21, 2018. https://www.computerworld.com/article/2973600/cloud-computing/google-cloud-loses-data-belgium-itbwcw.html
73. Jewish Women's Archive, "Basic Preservation Tips for Family Papers and Personal Archives." Accessed February 2, 2016. http://jwa.org/stories/howto/preservation.

74. Jimenez, Mona and Liss Platt. *Videotape Identification and Assessment Guide.* Austin, TX: Texas Commission on the Arts, 2004.
75. Johns, Darby, "Archival Quality – What Type of Enclosures should I buy?," May 2005. Accessed February 5, 2016. http://www.albox.com.au/pages/Archivalquality%252dwhattypeofenclosuresshouldIbuy%3F.html.
76. Lamourex, Tammy, "70 Inspirational Quotes for Photographers," PetaPixel, entry posted May 29, 2014, accessed February 9, 2020, https://petapixel.com/2014/05/29/70-inspirational-quotes-photographers/.
77. *Landrey, Gregory J., et.al., The Winterhur Guide to Caring for Your Collections,* Winterthur, DE: Henry Francis du Pont Winterther Museum, 2000.
78. Leggett, Elizabeth R., *Digitization and Digital Archiving: A Practical Guide for Librarians.* Lantham, MD: Rowman & Littlefield, 2014.
79. Library of Congress, Preservation. Accessed October 22,2018. www.loc.gov/preservation.
80. Library of Congress: Prints & Photographs Online Catalog. "Daguerreotypes." Accessed January 29, 2016. http://www.loc.gov/pictures/collections/dag/medium.html
81. Long, Jane S. and Richard W. Long, *Caring for Your Family Treasures,* New York, NY: Henry N. Abrams, Inc, 2000.
82. Lovelace, Jesse. "Deadman," *Deadman 2012.* http://www.deadman.io/. Accessed July 21, 2018.
83. Make a Plan for your Google Account if you pass away or stop using Google. Accessed August 5, 2018. https://myaccount.google.com/inactive.
84. Mayo, Benjamin. "Digital property after death issues continue as Apple requires court order for widow to get late husband's Apple ID password." 9to5Mac, 1/19/16. Accessed August 5,2018. https://9to5mac.com/2016/01/19/digital-property-after-death-issues-continue-as-apple-requires-court-order-for-widow-to-get-late-husbands-apple-id-password/.
85. Mediati, Nick, Melissa Riofrio, and Michael Simon. "How to delete, disable or limit your Facebook account." *PC World.* Accessed July 21,2018. https://www.pcworld.com/article/2050324/how-to-delete-or-disable-your-facebook-account.html.
86. Mellor, Chris, "StorageTek leaps into electronic vaulting," *Computerworld.* Accessed July 21,2018. https://www.computerworld.com/article/2557847/disaster-recovery/storagetek-leaps-into-electronic-vaulting.html.
87. Microsoft policy about lost or forgotten passwords. Microsoft. Accessed August 5,2018. https://support.microsoft.com/en-us/help/189126/microsoft-policy-about-lost-or-forgotten-passwords.

88. Muchachos, Tumblr post, August 22, 2012 (15:06), accessed November 29, 2019, https://muchachos.tumblr.com/post/29959960960
89. My family member died recently/is in a coma, what do I need to do to access their Microsoft account? Microsoft. Accessed August 5,2018. https://answers.microsoft.com/en-us/outlook_com/forum/oaccount-omyinfo/my-family-member-died-recently-is-in-coma-what-do/308cedce-5444-4185-%E2%80%A6%201/3 .
90. National Archives of Australia. "Managing Records on Thermal Papers." Australian Capital Territory, Australia. Accessed February 2, 2016. http://naa.gov.au/recordsmanagement/agency/preserve/physicalpreservation/thermalpapers.aspx.
91. National Archives: Additional Resources. Accessed March 20, 2016. https://www.archives.gov/preservation/records-emergency/additional-resources
92. National Archives, *Recovery Procedures*, Accessed October 22, 2018. https://www.archives.gov/preservation/records-emergency/recovery.
93. National Archives, *Resources – Vital Records and Records Disaster Mitigation and Recovery*, accessed October 22, 2018, https://www.archives.gov/records-mgmt/vital-records.
94. National Conference of Commissioners on Uniform State Laws, "Revised Uniform Fiduciary Access to Digital Assets Act (2015)," Chicago, IL: National Conference of Commissioners on Uniform State Laws, 2015.
95. National Parks Service, "Caring for Blueprints and Cyanotypes," *Conserve O Gram*, Number 19/9. Washington, DC: July 1995.
96. National Parks Service, "Caring for Photographs: General Guidelines," *Conserve O Gram*, Number 14/4, Washington, DC: June 1997.
97. National Park Service *Cold Storage: A Long-Term Preservation Strategy for Film-Based Photographic Materials* http://www.nps.gov/museum/coldstorage/NPSColdStorage.swf.
98. National Parks Service, "Salvage at a Glance, Part V: Textiles," *Conserve O Gram*, Number 21/8. Washington, DC: June 2003.
99. National Parks Service, "Synthetic Fibers in Costume Collections," *Conserve O Gram*, Number 16/4, Washington, DC: September 2002.
100. NBC News, "Sandy Survivor: 'You're Homeless in the Place You Love,'" November 8, 2012, accessed November 29, 2019, http://www.nbcnews.com/video/rock-center/49753888.
101. Newhall, Beaumont. *The History of Photography, from 1839 to the Present Day*. New York: Museum of Modern Art, 1982.

102. Northeast Documents Conservation Center, "Caring for Family and Private Collections." Accessed February 2, 2016. https://www.nedcc.org/freeresources/preservingprivateandfamilycollections/caringforprivateandfamilycollections
103. Northeast Document Conservation Center, "Fundamentals of AV Preservation - Chapter 5," Section 1: Disaster and Prevention Mitigation, accessed August 5, 2018, https://www.nedcc.org/fundamentals-of-av-preservation-textbook/chapter-5introduction/chapter-5-section-1.
104. Northeast Document Conservation Center, "Session 4: Caring for Paper Collections," accessed February 2, 2016, https://www.nedcc.org/preservation101/session-4/4-papermaking.
105. Northeast Document Conservation Center, "7.8 Removal of Damaging Fasteners from Historic Documents," accessed February 8, 2016, https://www.nedcc.org/free-resources/preservation-leaflets/7.-conservation-procedures/7.8-removal-of-damaging-fasteners-from-historic-documents.
106. Nova PDF, *Softland*."Convert a web page to PDF," Jan 27, 2015. Accessed June 24, 2017. http://www.novapdf.com/kb/convertawebpagetopdf100.html.
107. O'Toole, James M. and Richard J. Cox. *Understanding Archives and Manuscripts*. Chicago: Society of American Archivists, 2006.
108. Patrizio, Andy, "Humidity, Not Heat, Is a Hard Drive's Biggest Threat," Network World, March 30, 2016, https://www.networkworld.com/article/3049428/humidity-not-heat-is-a-hard-drives-biggest-threat.html.
109. Pinola, Melanie. "How to Backup Your Gmail: Gmail backup instructions for saving your emails and folders." Updated 5/31/2017. Dotdash, *Livewire*, 2017. Accessed June 5, 2017. https://www.lifewire.com/howtobackupyourgmail 2378049
110. Potter, Michael F.. "ENT-609 Clothes Moths." UK Cooperative Extension Service, Lexington, KY: University of Kentucky, College of Agriculture. Accessed January 23, 2017. https://entomology.ca.uky.edu/ef609.
111. Reilly, James M. *Storage Guide for Color Photographic Materials*. New York: University of the State of New York, New York State Program for the Conservation and Preservation of Library Material, 1998.
112. Reilly, James M. and Kaspars M. Cupriks. *Sulfiding Protection for Silver Images: Final Report to the Office of Preservation, National Endowment for the Humanities, Grant #PS-20152-87*. Rochester, NY: Image Permanence Institute, 1991.
113. Ritzenthaler, Mary Lynn. "Preservation of Archival Records: Holdings Maintenance at the National Archives, Technical Information Paper Number 6." Washington, D.C.: National Archives and Records Administration, 1990).

Accessed December 12, 2016. https://www.archives.gov/preservation/holdings-maintenance/general-guidance.html#repairs

114. Robinson, Katie. "National Conference of State Legislature: Uniform Law Commission: An Update for Legislative Lawyers." NCSL. Accessed July 22, 2018. http://www.ncsl.org/legislators-staff/legislative-staff/research-editorial-legal-and-committee-staff/uniform-law-commission-an-update-for-legislative-lawy... ¼.

115. Roe, Kathleen D. *Arranging and Describing Archives and Manuscripts.* Chicago: Society of American Archivists, 2005.

116. Roosa, Mark. "Care, Handling and Storage of Photographs," Reviewed by Andrew Robb in *IFLA-PAC International Preservation Issues*, No.5, Paris, France: International Federation of Library Associations and Institutions (IFLA) Core Activity on Preservation and Conservation (PAC). 2004.

117. Santoro, Karen. *IPI Storage Guide for Acetate Film.* Image Permanence Institute, Rochester, NY: 1996.

118. Schultz, Arthur, ed., *Caring for Your Collections* New York: Henry N. Abrams, Inc., 1992.

119. Segomotso Keakopa, as quoted in Carolyn Hamilton's "Oral Archives: Introduction," *S.A. Archives Journal* 40 (1998):78, https://www.researchgate.net/profile/Segomotso_Keakopa

120. Silverman, Sue William. *Fearless Confessions: A Writer's Guide to Memoir.* Athens, GA: The University of Georgia Press, 2009.

121. Smithsonian Institution Archives, "Preserve Your Treasures: How To Remove Photos from a Sticky Album," YouTube, October 21, 2010, video, 4:07, https://www.youtube.com/watch?v=fcDlbNi-9D0.

122. Special Request for Medically Incapacitated or Deceased Person's Account. Facebook Help Center. Accessed July 21, 2018. https://www.facebook.com/help/contact/?id=228813257197480.

123. Standard Terms and Condition of Business (T&C). *SecureSafe.* Accessed July 21, 2018. https://www.securesafe.com/en/terms/

124. Submit a request regarding a deceased user's account. Google Troubleshooter. Accessed August 5, 2018. https://support.google.com/accounts/troubleshooter/6357590?hl=en.

125. The American Museum of Photography, "A Brief History of the Carte De Visite." Accessed January 29, 2016. www.photographymuseum.com/histw.htm.

126. The British Film Institute. *Identifying and Handling Nitrate Film.* London, England: December 2008.

127. The National Archives, "Archive Principles and Practice: An Introduction to Archives for Non-archivists," 2016. Accessed October 22, 2018. https://www.nationalarchives.gov.uk/documents/archives/archive-principles-and-practice-an-introduction-to-archives-for-non-archivists.pdf .

128. The National Archives. *Archive Principles and Practice: and introduction to archives for non-archivists*. Kew, Richmond, Surrey, England: the National Archives, 2016

129. The National Archives of Australia, "What is Thermal Paper: Early Thermal Papers," accessed February 2, 2016, https://www.naa.gov.au/information-management/store-and-preserve-information/preserving-information/managing-records-thermal-papers.

130. Tips For the Care for Water-Damaged Family Heirlooms and Other Valuables. AIC Publications & Resources, Disaster Response & Recovery. Accessed October 22,2018. http://www.conservationus.org/publicationsresources/disasterresponserecovery/guidesandinformation/waterdamagetips#Vu7akuIrLb0.

131. Tom. "How to Print Text Messages from iPhone 6/6s/7WE and 5/5s/5c/4/4s." *iMoblie, Inc.,* 2017. Accessed June 24, 2017. https://www.imobie.com/support/howtoprinttextmessagesfromiphone.htm.

132. U.S. National Archives and Records Administration. "Motion Picture Film Guidance: Identifying Motion Picture Film Formats."Washington, DC. Accessed March 21, 2016. http://www.archives.gov/preservation/formats/motion-picture-film-important_Characteristics.html.

133. U.S. National Archives and Records Administration. "Motion Picture Film Guidance: Important Characteristics of Motion Picture Film Formats." Washington, DC. Accessed March 21, 2016.

134. U. S. National Archives and Records Administration, "Video Guidance: Identifying Video Formats." Washington, DC. Accessed March 21, 2016. https://www.archives.gov/preservation/formats/video-identify-formats.html.

135. U.S. Patents & Trademarks, Discover Education, *September 13, 1898: Patent issued for celluloid photographic film*. Accessed August 21, 2016). https://www.cosmeo.com/viewEvents.cfm?guidAssetId=7B4B1A06-8752-4F37-B265-FE322A6D2EDF&&nodeid=.

136. Uniform Law Commission, *"Fiduciary Access to Digital Assets Act, Revised,"* revised in 2015, accessed September 19, 2021, https://www.uniformlaws.org/committees/community-home?CommunityKey=f7237fc4-74c2-4728-81c6-b39a91lecdf22.

137. University of Illinois at Urbana-Champaign, "Preservation Self-Assessment Program: Daguerreotypes, Ambrotypes, and Tintypes," Institute of Museum and Library Services, accessed January 29, 2016, https://psap.library.illinois.edu/format-id-guide/directimage.
138. Vogt O'Connor, Diane. *NPS Museum Handbook, Part I.* "Appendix M: Management for Cellulose Nitrate and Cellulose Ester Film." Washington, DC: National Parks Service, 1999.
139. What is a legacy contact and what can they do? Facebook Help Center. Accessed August 5, 2018. https://www.facebook.com/help/1568013990080948 (accessed 8/5/18).
140. What will happen to my Facebook account if I pass away?" Facebook Help Center. Accessed July 21, 2018. //https://www.facebook.com/help/103897939701143.
141. *Why Is Magnetic Tape Still Used?* Quora, accessed August 25, 2018, https://www.quora.com/Why-is-magnetic-tape-still-used.
142. Wilhelm, Henry. *The Permanence and Care of Color Photographs.* Grinnell, IA: The Center for the Image.org in association with Wilhelm Imaging Research, Inc., 2013.
143. Willeford, Tim. "IBM Completes Acquisition of Arsenal Digital Solutions." *Marketwired News Room.* Accessed July 21,2018. http://www.marketwired.com/press-release/ibm-completes-acquisition-of-arsenal-digital-solutions-816563.htm.
144. William, Paul et. al., "Predicting Archival Life of Removable Hard Disk Drives," ResearchGate January 2008: 188–192, https://www.researchgate.net/publication/290550670_Predicting_archival_life_of_removable_hard_disk_drive
145. Williams, Don and Louisa Jaggar, *Saving Stuff: How to Care for and Preserve Your Collectibles, Heirlooms, and Other Prized Possessions* New York: Simon & Schuster, 2005, 250.

PHOTOGRAPH CREDITS

p.20 - Library of Congress: Prints and Photographs Division, *Charlotte Gilman, Head-and-Shoulders Portrait, Facing Left,* c1900, cph 3c06490, accessed January 20, 2022, https://www.loc.gov/pictures/item/93500552/.

p.61 - Image Permanence Institute, *A Consumer Guide for the Recovery of Water-Damaged Traditional and Digital Prints* (Rochester, NY: 2007), cover photo, http://www.imagepermanenceinstitute.org/consumerguide_waterdamage.pdf.

p.64 - Wikimedia Commons contributors, "File: You press the button, we do the rest (Kodak).jpg," *Wikimedia Commons,* original 1889, taken from the George Eastman Collection at the George Eastman Museum in Rochester, NY, accessed June 9, 2022, https://commons. wikimedia.org/w/index.php?title=File:Making_Paper_4.PNG&oldid=199152612.

p.67 - David Octavius Hill and Robert Adamson, *Newhaven Fisherboy,* ca.1845, calotype, Library of Congress: Prints and Photographs Division, cph 3g08401, accessed July 6, 2020, https://www.loc.gov/item/00652572/.

p.68 - Sam A. Cooley, *Sam. A. Cooley, photographer Tenth Army Corps*, between 1861 and 1865, Stereograph, 2 15/16 x 6, Library of Congress: Prints and Photographs Division, https://www.loc.gov/item/2012649704/.

p.69 - Library of Congress: Prints and Photographs Division, Two Unidentified Soldiers in Union Uniforms, One in Denim Jeans, with Bugle and Bayoneted Musket, between 1861 and 1865, Tintype, plate 108 x 82 mm (quarter plate format), frame 161 x 136 mm, accessed July 6, 2020, https://www.loc.gov/item/2019646742/.

p.70 - William Abel, Full-Length Portrait of an Unidentified African American Woman, Standing Beside a Chair, between 1860 and 1870, carte de visite mount: albumen, 10 x 6 cm, Library of Congress: Prints and Photographs Division, accessed July 6, 2020, https://www.loc.gov/item/2010647809/.

p.72 - Sears, Roebuck & Company, publisher, *Just a Few Talking Machine Records,* between 1900 and 1910, stereograph, mount 9 x 18 cm, Library of Congress: Prints and Photographs Division, accessed July 6, 2020, https://www.loc.gov/resource/stereo.1s08724/.

p.75 - Detroit Publishing Co., publisher, *Eastman Kodak Co., State St[reet] Factory and Main Office, Rochester, N.Y.,* between 1900 and 1910, stereograph, card mount 9 x 18 cm, Library of Congress: Prints and Photographs Division, accessed July 7, 2020, https://www.loc.gov/item/2016814734/.

p.77 - James M. Reilly, *Storage Guide for Color Photographic Materials: Caring for Color Slides, Prints, Negatives, and Movie Films* (New York: University of the State of New York, New York State Program for the Conservation and Preservation of Library Material, 1998), 7.

p.79 - Creative Image Photography by David Cruz, cip.dcruz@gmail.com.

p.83 - Lance Aram Rothstein, "Tag Archives: Nitrate Film: Letting Go of My Last Three Rolls of Eastman Super-XX Film," September 21, 2014, Labeauratoire Beautiful Experimentation, https://labeauratoire.wordpress.com/tag/nitrate-film/.

p.87 - SunOfErat, *Filmmuseum Berlin - Frame By Frame - Archive Simulation*, Wikimedia Commons, November 7, 2021, 13:11:01, https://commons.wikimedia.org/wiki/File:Filmmuseum_Berlin_-_Frame_By_Frame_-_Vinegar_Syndrome.jpg.

p.91 - Wikimedia Commons contributors, "File:Making Paper 4.PNG," *Wikimedia Commons*, last revised June 16, 2016, https://commons.wikimedia.org/w/index.php?title=File:Making_Paper_4.PNG&oldid=199152612.

p.104 - Library of Congress: Rare Book and Special Collections Division, Men's League for Woman Suffrage, Miller Scrapbook, 1910 and 1911, published in American Women: A Library of Congress Guide for the Study of Women's History and Culture in the United States, ed. Sheridan Harvey (Washington: Library of Congress, 2002), 113, https://www.loc.gov/item/2002719620/.

p.106 - Massachusetts Historical Society, "Adams Family Papers," accessed June 15, 2022, https://www.masshist.org/adams/adams-family-papers

p.107 - John Adams and Charles Francis Adams, *The Works of John Adams Vol. 1: Life of John Adams (Annotated)* (Altenmünster, Germany: Jazzybee Verlag, 2015), cover photo.

p.107 - David McCullough, *John Adams* (New York, NY: Simon & Schuster, 2001), cover.

p.108 - Finn Årup Nielsen, "File:Ugeskrift for Retsvæsen, Børsen, 2016-05-14.JPG," *Wikimedia Commons*, May 14, 2016, 15:06:28, https://commons.wikimedia.org/wiki/File:Ugeskrift_for_Retsv%C3%A6sen,_B%C3%B8rsen,_2016-05-14.JPG.

p.113 - Holly Prochaska, "Prepping for a Shift," *The Preservation Lab* (blog), March 11, 2016, https://blog.thepreservationlab.org/tag/red-rot.

PHOTOGRAPH CREDITS

p.115 - Falcon® Photography, "File:D-DAY 76 (49978059006).jpg," *Wikimedia Commons*, June 5, 2019, 16:26, https://commons.wikimedia.org/wiki/File:D-DAY_76_(49978059006).jpg.

p.129 - Melanie Pereira, "File:US Navy 030328-N-2775P-001 Preservation workshop at Naval Historical Center, Wash., D.C.jpg," *Wikimedia Commons*, March 28, 2003, https://commons.wikimedia.org/wiki/File:US_Navy_030328-N-2775P-001_Preservation_workshop_at_Naval_Historical_Center,_Wash.,_D.C.jpg

p.145 - Wikimedia Commons contributors, "File:Side Chairs (England), 18th century (CH 18475769-3).jpg," *Wikimedia Commons*, original 18th century, taken from the Cooper Hewitt Collection at the Smithsonian Design Museum in NYC, last updated May 31, 2019, https://commons.wikimedia.org/wiki/File:Side_Chairs_(England),_18th_century_(CH_18475769-3).jpg.

p.186 - *Sisters*, directed by Jason Moore (Little Stranger/Everyman Productions, 2015), 1:18:00, movie DVD cover, https://www.imdb.com/title/tt1850457/.

p.194 - Cigdem, *Modern Scanner Isolated on White Background. 3D Illustration*, Shutterstock, ID 1402233032, accessed January 27, 2022, https://www.shutterstock.com/image-illustration/modern-scanner-isolated-on-white-background-1402233032.

p.274 - Northeast Documents Conservation Center, *3.7 Emergency Salvage of Wet Photographs: Air Drying Photographs*, https://www.nedcc.org/free-resources/preservation-leaflets/3.-emergency-management/3.7-emergency-salvage-of-wet-photographs.

p.277 - Fourre, *Closeup Picture of Female Researcher Rinsing a Weighing Spoon with Distilled Water from a Squeeze Bottle. Only Hands are Visible. Blue Gloves and White Lab Coat. Scientifically Accurate Image!* Shutterstock, ID 1354725980, accessed May 11, 2022, https://www.shutterstock.com/image-photo/closeup-picture-female-researcher-rinsing-weighing-1354725980

ACKNOWLEDGEMENTS

Jenn T. Grace and everyone at PYP Press have been awesome and have consistently gone above and beyond to hold my hand throughout this process. I have been constantly impressed (and relieved) with the level of professionalism everyone has demonstrated and am grateful to have found a trustworthy publisher. Thanks to Bailly Morse, Project Manager extraordinaire and Nancy Graham-Tillman, the best editor ever. Nelly Murariu, great book cover designer and life-saving graphic artist, went into the Underworld with me and never faltered. Every time she sent another revision back and said, "I'll be right here for you," I felt supported and protected.

My archives mentors deserve honorable mention for teaching me the tricks of the trade and for taking me under their wings in different ways. I want to express appreciation to Karen Eberhart and Jennifer Betts who gave me a chance and never lost faith in me, even in my darkest hour. My archives professor Donna Webber, and history professors Laurie Crumpacker and Laura Prieto opened up amazing doors for me. Clare Sheridan and Jane Ward from the American Textile History Museum, and Elaine Robinson, partner in my first archives business supported me and helped forge my archival skills. Thanks also to Clare for reading through the final manuscript.

I started giving library lectures in 2016 and that experience gave me first-hand awareness of the needs of people in the family history and genealogical communities. I want to thank all the librarians who booked me to speak at their libraries and all the patrons who came to my lectures and showed me or told me what they had in their collections, their worries and concerns and for teaching me what they needed.

I want to thank Jacki Rose for suggesting that I put my library lectures in book form and my many friends who pushed me along in the process: Susan Wiedner and I were a sort of writers group of two for the first few years of writing this book. Helen Litterst has been my biggest fan and has opened the door to many opportunities with different genealogical groups and read through the final manuscript. Dave Cruz has been a consistent cheerleader and contributed many great ideas to the layout. I want to thank my sister Donna, and friends Al and Jane for their patience and steadfastness throughout this process. It's been much appreciated.

My father and I shared a love of history and a love of photography which influenced the choices I made in life ultimately resulting in my becoming an archivist and historian. My mother had a deep sense of family and shared the stories of her mother, grandmother, and grandfather which inspired me to do genealogy and write about family history. I remember their sacrifices and honor them by naming my business after them and keeping their legacy alive.

INDEX

A

Accordis, 119
Accounts of social interactions, identifying, 7–8
Acetate film, 86–88
Acid-free materials, 12
    boxes, 50, 52, 55, 72, 89, 137, 138, 280
    folders, 50, 52, 53, 55, 56, 72, 81, 82, 89, 100
    paperboard, 111
    tissue paper, 10, 50, 55, 59, 66, 69, 70, 97, 110, 111, 136, 137, 138, 139
    tubes, 101
Acrilan, 120
Acrylic materials, 50, 120, 140, 143–144, 146
Adams, Charles Francis, 107
Adobe Photoshop, 57, 79, 155, 200, 201
Adobe Scan, 199
Agfacolor, 86
AIFF (Audio Interchange File Format), 160
Air circulation, 123
Air conditioners, 122, 123, 273, 276
Air drying, 277–278
Air pollution and textiles, 126
Alumrosin sizing agent, 93
Ambrotype photographs, 65, 68–69, 73–74
American Academy of Environmental Medicine, 271
American Institute for Conservation (AIC), 269, 280
American National Standards Institute (ANSI) standard, 93
American Textile History Museum (ATHM), 24
Ammonia, 126
Antique furniture, 269
Anti-static storage bags, 174–175
Antron Durasoft, 119
Apache Open Office, 157, 213
Apple, 161, 162
Archer, Frederick Scott, 68
Archival basics
    checklist, 17–18
    concepts, 3–5
    enclosures, 12–13
    environment, 8–11
    family archive, 5–8
    handy supplies, 14–15

    location, 11–12
    prevention
        from dirt and dust, 10–11
        from environment, 8
        from environmental pollutants, 11
        from humidity, 9
        from light, 9–10
        from temperature, 9
    workspace creation, 15–17
Archival mat, 144
Arms, Caroline, 156
Artificial silk, 119
Art theft, 262
Asthma, 123
Atmospheric chemicals, 120
Audio tapes, 89, 204–207, 278–279
Audio data formats, 160–161
Audio file formats, 223
Automatic backup programs, 185
AV (audio/video) tapes, 89
AVI (Audio Video Interleaved file), 162
Azo dyes, 167

B

Backup
    creating, 183–185
    digital, 185
    of website, 230
Backward compatible format, 158, 212
Bemberg, 119
Binary systems, 150–151, 167
Biographical background, 33–34
Bitonal scanning, 198
Bit rot, 171
Black-and-white negatives, 88
Blanquart-Evrard, Louis Desire, 71
Bleach, 131
Blogs, 216, 234
Blotting paper, 59, 131, 273
Blotting wet wool, 133
Blueprints, 100–101
Blu-ray discs, 164, 165–166
BMP (Bitmap), 159
Body oils stains, 124
Bonded polyurethane, 120
Books, 105–113
    appraisal, 106–108

book making, 106
caring for and handling books, 108–110
disaster preparedness and recovery of, 277–278
protection, 111
repairing damage, 112–113
shelving, 111
storage boxes, 110
Born digital documents, 211–214
   born digital documents
      HTML, 213
      Letters, Spreadsheets, FileMaker Pro, Access, PowerPoint, 211–212
      open document format (ODF), 213
      PDF-A, 212–213
      saving documents, 214
   born digital photographs, 215–216
   digital audio, 223–224
   digital video, 224–225
   emails, 226–228
      desktop, 227
      online services, 227–228
   Flickr, 234
   Instagram, 234
   MySpace, 234
   obsolescent media, 210–211
      libraries, 211
      paid services, 211
      purchasing external hard drive reader, 211
   organizing photographs, 217–222
   other social media sites, 234
   overview, 209–210
   social media, 231–235
   text messages, 234–235
   transferring photos to computer, 216–217
   Twitter, 234
   websites, 228–231
      backup, 230
      copy and paste, 229
      saving or printing the pages, 229
      saving the code, 230
      screenshots, 230–231
Born digital photographs, 215–216
Brewster, David, Sir, 72
Broken spine of books, 112
Browning, 112
Bubbling, 120
Buffered materials, 12
   boxes, 118
   paper products, 56
   paper sleeves, 87
Buffering agents, 101, 118
BWF (Broadcast Wave Format), 160

C

Calcium carbonate, 12, 118
Calcium chloride pellets, 273–274
Calotypes, 66–67, 73–74
Camphor, 83
Canned air, 197–198
Cardboard boxes, 135, 145, 280
Carpet beetles, 124, 125–126, 132, 136
Carpets, 132–133, 141–143
Cartes-de-visite, 70–71, 73–74
Caster cups, 142
CDs (Compact disks)
   handling, 165
   preservation of, 152–153
   readers, 167
CD-DA (Compact Disc Digital Audio) discs, 163
CD-R (Compact Disc Recordable) discs, 163
CD-ROM (Compact Disc Read-Only-Memory) discs, 163
CD-RW (Compact Disc Rewritable) discs, 164
Cedar chests, 136
Cellulose acetate, 204
Cellulose fiber, 119
Cellulose nitrate, 46, 83, 84
Century boxes, 52
Ceramics, disaster preparedness and recovery of, 279–280
Checklist, processing basics, 17–18
Chemical pollutants, 126
Chemical toxins, 169
Chiffon, 133
Chopin, Kate, 20
Chromogenic development, 76
Chromogenic dyes, 76, 88
Cibachrome photographs, 80
Clamshell boxes, 12, 14, 52, 82, 111
Cleaning
   and maintenance, 166
   solutions, 126
Cleerspan, 121
Closed proprietary formats, 155
Clothing moths, 124–125, 132
Cloud storage, 185, 189–190
CoDec, 154, 162, 224–225
Collodion positive, 68–69
Color bleeding, 130, 131
Colorfastness, 131
Color loss, 130
Comma separated documents (CSV), 227, 234

INDEX

Commercial cloud storage services, 189–190
Conservation Center for Art & Historic Artifacts, 270
Consumer guide, 61
A Consumer Guide for the Recovery of Water-Damaged Traditional and Digital Prints, 61
CopyTrans Contacts (Windows only), 234
Cotton, 124
    gloves, 120, 127–128
    muslin, 142
    twill, 137
Cracking, 120
Cresian, 120
Crystal, disaster preparedness and recovery of, 279–280
CSV (comma separated values) format, 227, 234
Curled photographs, 58–59
Curled reports, 97–98
Curtains, 122
Cyanine, 167

D

Dacron, 120
Daguerre, Louis-Jacques-Mande, 64–65
Daguerreotype photographs, 64–66, 73–74
Daly, Mary, 107
Dampness, 76, 78, 82, 122, 127, 273
Dark fading, 57, 76
Dashlane, 243
Data storage, 162–163
    archival storage of optical media, 164–167
    cloud storage, 176–179
    flash memory, 172–176
    hard drives, 170–172
    magnetic tapes, 167–170
    optical storage, 163–164
DCIM (Digital Camera IMages), 217
Defrosting film, 48
Dehumidifiers, 113, 122, 123, 271–272, 273–274, 276
Delamination, 120
Desiccants, 273
Desktop email programs, 227
Detergents, 131, 133
Diaries, 96
Digital archive, online, 244–245
Digital archivists, 187–189, 211
Digital assets, 245–246

Digital audio, 223–224
Digital backup, 185
Digital camera, 196
Digital content, ownership of, 247
Digital inkjet photo papers, 81
Digital legacy, planning
    digital afterlife, 241–243
        identify, 241
        passwords, 242
    emails, 247–249
        dead man's switch, 250–251
        Facebook, 249–250
        Twitter, 250
    non-digital afterlife, 240–241
    overview, 239–240
    password managers
        access, 243
        online digital estate planning services, 247
        rights and ownership, 243–247
Digital preservation
    born digital vs. digitized, 151–153
        intellectual preservation, 153
        preservation of medium, 152–153
        technology preservation, 153
    data storage, 162–163
        archival storage of optical media, 164–167
        cloud storage, 176–179
        flash memory, 172–176
        hard drives, 170–172
        magnetic tapes, 167–170
        optical storage, 163–164
    terms, 153–155
        audio data formats, 160–161
        file formats, 155–157
        images/photographs, 159–160
        text formats, 157–159
        video data formats, 162
Digital Preservation (Hawkins), 189
Digital scanners, 89
Digital video, 224–225
Digitization, 87–88, 95, 99
    audio and video tapes, 204–207
    choosing a scanner, 194–197
        portable scanners, 195–197
        scanner apps, 194
    color photographs, 79
    converting audio tape to digital, 207–208
    converting videotape to digital, 208
    dust and canned air, 197–198
    photographing objects, 203
    of photographs, 57
    preparing documents for scanning, 197

of a print, 49–50
scanning
  documents, 198–199
  objects, 202–203
  photographs, 199–200
  slides and negatives, 200–202
videotaping objects, 203–204
Digitizing material items
  commercial services, problem with, 189–190
  creating backups, 183–185
  long-term digital storage and access, 186–189
  overview, 181–183
  printing digital documents, 190–191
Direct access, 168
Dirt, damage caused by, 10–11, 60, 126, 129, 168
Disaster, defined, 254
Disasters, preparedness and recovery
  audio and video tapes, 278–279
  books, 277–278
  floods/water damage, 273–274
  framed artwork, 279
  furniture, 269, 278
  glass, ceramics, pottery, earthenware, crystal, 279–280
  metals, 277
  overview, 253–256
  paper documents, 275–276
  personal disasters
    analyzing risks, 261
    fire, 265–266
    hurricanes and tornados, 269–270
    identifying risks, 261
    prioritizing risks, 261
    security and theft, 262–264
    treating risks, 261–262
    water and floods, 266–269
  photographs, 274–275
  prevention, making plan, 256–261
  recovery
    introduction and general advice, 270–271
    mold recovery, 271–272
  textiles, 276
Discoloring
  of photographs, 47, 56
  of textiles, 120, 135
Disderi, Andre Adolphe-Eugene, 71
Distilled water, 131, 133, 139, 259, 277, 279
Distortion of form, 130
DOC or DOCX format, 158
Dorlastan, 121
Drawings, 100–101
Dropbox, 177, 189–190, 216
Dry-cleaning, 125, 130–131, 132–134
Dust, 168, 197–198
DVDs (Digital Versatile Discs), 164, 165–166
Dyes, 121, 127, 136
  bleeding, 130, 142
  stability, 167

E

Earthenware, recovery and protection of, 279–280
Eastman, George, 64, 75, 80, 83–84
Eastman Kodak, 64, 75, 80, 83–84, 86
eBay, 9
eBooks, 247
Emails, 226–228, 247–249
  dead man's switch, 250–251
  desktop, 227
  Facebook, 249–250
  online services, 227–228
  Twitter, 250
Embrittlement, 112
Embroidery/cross-stitch works/lace doilies, 143–144
Emergency, defined, 255
Encryption, 156
Enduring value, 5, 7, 32, 209
Environment, damage caused by, 8–11, 174–175
Environmental pollutants, 11, 78, 111
Evernote, 230–231
Evidence of events, identifying, 6–7
Excel spreadsheet, 23, 31, 108, 211–214, 242
Extension, file, 154
Exterminator, 132
External media storage, 184–185
Ezine, 234

F

Facebook, 216, 231–233, 246, 249–250
Face mask, 260
Fading
  of photographs, 57–58
  of textiles, 121
Family archive
  accounts of social interactions, 7–8
  evidence of events, 6–7
  functional documents, 6
  items with financial value, 6

INDEX

legal documents, 6
records of the inner life, 7
sentimental items, 7
Family History Metadata Work Group (FHMWG), 219
Fasteners, 101–103
Federal Agency Digitization Guidelines, 225
Federal Emergency Management Agency, 267
Felting, 131, 133
Ferrotypes, 69–70
fhmwg.wordpress.com, 219
Fiberglass screen, 129–130, 131, 133
File compression types, 153–154
File formats, 154, 155–157, 160, 213–214
FileMaker Pro, 211–212
Film
    acetate film, 86–88
    deformity, 87
    nitrate film, 83–86
    polyester film, 88
    storage of slides and negative film, 89–90
Finding aid
    creating, 29–33
    historical note, 33–34
    inventory, 36
    provenance, 35–36
Finding Your Roots (genealogy show), 4
Firebrats, 124
Fire extinguishers, 265–266
FLAC (Free Format Lossless Audio CoDec) file format, 155, 160
Flags, 139–140, 145
Flaking
    of books, 112
    of photographs, 57–58
Flash drives, 153, 173
Flash format, 162
Flash memory, 172–173
    archival storage of, 174–176
    types of, 173–174
Flatbed scanners, 194, 197
Flea medication, 132
Fleischhauer, Carl, 156
Flickr, 216, 234
Fliptop boxes, 6
Floods/water damage, drying out procedures, 273–274
Floor carpets, 141–143
Floor sweeper model, 143
Floppy disks, 167
Fluorescent bulbs, 145

Fluorescent light, 121
Food stains, 124, 135–136
Fortrel, 120
Framed artwork, disaster preparedness and recovery of, 279
Framing, 50, 143–144
Free file format, 154, 155
Freezing, 132, 272
Functional documents, identifying, 6
Fur, 124
Furniture, disaster preparedness and recovery of, 278

G

Gazette de France, 64
Genealogy Roadshow (genealogy show), 4
Georgette, 133
GIF (Graphics Interchange Format), 159
Gilman, Charlotte Perkins, 20
Glass
    bookcases, 111
    disaster preparedness and recovery of, 279–280
    frames, 143
Glassine, 14, 101, 140
Glospan, 121
Glossy paper, 278
Gloves, 16, 120, 127–128, 138–139, 201, 260
Glue, 144
Gmail, 227
Goggles, 260
Gold CD-Rs, 164
Gone with the Wind (film), 84
Google, 216, 248, 251
    Books, 107
    Doc, 227
    Drive, 189–190
    Photos (formerly Picasa), 79, 200, 215, 219
Graphite pencils, 53
Grayscale images, 159, 198
Greeting cards, 98–99
Gutenberg, Johannes, 91–92

H

Hair shampoo, 142
Halogen-produced lights, 121
Handmade paper, 92
Hands, cleaning, 16, 127–128, 131
Hanger, 137–138
Hard drives, 153, 170–172, 184

Harper's Magazine, 64
Hats, 138
Hawkins, Donald T., 189
Hawthorn, Nathaniel, 108
Health hazards, 123
Heat, 47, 120, 121, 124, 127, 131
HEPA
    vacuum bags, 126
    vacuums, 11
Herringbone, 133
Historical Note, 34–35
Hollinger Metal Edge, 52
Holmes, Oliver Wendall, Sr., 72
@Hotmail.com, 248
HTML (HyperText Markup Language), 155, 158–159, 213
    coding, 213, 229
    file extensions, 232
    page, 230
Humidifiers, 122
Humidity, 124, 127, 273
    and CDs, 165
    fluctuations, 126
    gauge, 14
    and hard drives, 171–172
    and magnetic tapes, 169
    and photographs, 47
    relative humidity (RH), 9, 122, 123, 165, 271
    and textiles, 122
Hurricanes, 256
Hydroscopic materials, 204
Hygrometer, 9, 14, 122

I

IBM, 161
iCloud, 189–190, 234, 249
Identifying items, 5
    accounts of social interactions, 7–8
    evidence of events, 6–7
    with financial value, 6
    functional documents, 6
    legal documents, 6
    records of the inner life, 7
    sentimental items, 7
iExplorer, 234
Ilfochrome photographs, 80
Image Permanence Institute (IPI), 13, 61, 81–82, 85
Images, 159–160; *see also* Photographs
Inactive Account Manager, 248, 251
Incandescent lights, 10, 121

Inert materials, 12, 13, 57–58, 94, 100, 103, 104, 111, 136
Inherent vice
    and paper, 92–93
    and textiles, 126–127
Inspections, conducting, 133
Instagram, 234
Intellectual control over documents, 29
Intellectual order of items, 22–23
Intellectual preservation, 153
International Association of Sound and Audiovisual Archives (IASA), 206
Internet Archive, 229
iPhone, 234
iPhoto, 57, 79, 215
ISO Standard, 155
iTunes, 223–224, 247
Ivory liquid dishwashing detergent, 131, 133, 139, 142

J

JavaScripts, 158, 213, 230
Journals, 96
JPEG or JPG (Joint Photographic Experts Group) format, 160, 194, 199, 201, 202, 212, 215, 217, 230

K

KeePass, 243
"Kodachrome" film, 76
Kodacolor, 86
Kodak, 64, 75, 80, 83–84, 86
Kondo, Marie, 37

L

Labeling
    CDs, 165–166
    digital documents, 188–189
    films, 85
    folders, 53
    large prints, 50–51
Lanolin-rich wool, 142
Laser rot, 166
LastPass, 243
Leather, 124, 125
    covers, 112
    fake, 120
LED light, 10
Legal documents, 6, 98
Letters, 96–98, 211–212

INDEX

Library book, 107
Library of Congress, 38, 85–86, 155–161, 181, 183, 186, 191, 197, 198–199, 201, 210, 212, 213, 234
The Life-Changing Magic of Tidying Up (Kondo), 37
Light, 120
    and CDs, 165
    exposure, 127
    fluorescent, 121
    halogen-produced, 121
    incandescent, 10, 121
    LED, 10
    and magnetic tapes, 169
    prevention from, 9–10
    and textiles, 121–122
    ultraviolet (UV), 10, 89, 121
Lignin-free materials, 12
Lignin-free tissue, 280
Linen, 118, 124
LinkedIn, 216
Lint-free cloths, 197, 260, 277
Liquid air, 60
Liquid detergent, 142
@Live.com, 248
Loose-leaf photo album, 78–79
The Lord of the Rings trilogy, 201
Lossy or lossless compression, 154–155, 159, 160, 162
Lubricants, 204–205
Lycra, 121
Lyocell, 119

M

Mac.com, 249
Machine paper making, 92
Machine washing, 131, 133
Magnetic fields and hard drives, 172
Magnetic media, 162, 167–168, 170, 173, 175
    Magnetic photo albums, 21, 54, 282
Magnetic tapes
    archival storage of, 169–170
    audio and video, 204–207
    data storage, 167–168
Maps, 100–101
Massachusetts Historical Society, 106
Mathematically lossless compression, 154
Matting, 131, 133
maureentaylor.com, 74
McCullough, David, 107
Me.com, 249
Melville, Herman, 108

Mesh netting, 131
Metadata, 90, 136, 139, 184
    descriptive, 218, 219
    structural, 218
    technical, 155, 156
    types of, 218
Metallic salts, 127
Metals, disaster preparedness and recovery of, 277
Microfiber cleaning cloths, 260, 277
Microloft, 120
MicroSD, 174
Microsoft, 31, 155, 161, 162, 212, 248
Microsoft Access, 211–212
Microspatulas, 14
MIDI (Musical Instrument Digital Interface), 161
MiniSD, 174
Mirroring, 46
Moby Dick, 108
Modal, 119
Moisture and photographs, 59
Mold
    and magnetic tapes, 205
    and photographs, 56–57
    recovery from, 271–272
    and textiles, 123
Moths, 124–125, 132, 133–134, 136
Motion JPEG 2000, 162
Motion picture film, 84, 89
Mounting
    fabric, 141
    photographs, 53
MOV files, 162, 208
MPEG (Moving Pictures Experts Group), 161, 162
MP3s, 161, 173, 208, 223
@Msn.com, 248
MSN Dial-up, 248
Muslin cloth, 137, 138, 142, 145
Mycotoxin test, 271
MySpace, 234

N

Naphthalene, 125
National Archives (NARA.org), 85–86, 88, 95, 123, 254
National Endowment for the Humanities Newspaper Program, 94–95
National Resource Guide for Disaster Preparedness, 270, 272
Native formats, 160

Natural fibers, 135
Newspapers, 93–95, 280
Next of Kin process, 248
Nitrate film, 75, 83–86
Nitrile gloves, 16, 87, 120, 127–128, 201, 260
Non-proprietary or free file format, 154
Note app, 242
Notepad, 234
Nylon, 119

O

Obsolescence, 186, 187, 225, 235
Obsolescent media, 210–211
    libraries, 211
    paid services, 211
    purchasing external hard drive reader, 211
ODF (Open Document Format), 157, 213
Odor, 113
ODP format, 157, 213
ODS format, 157, 213
ODT format, 157, 213
Oil stains, 120, 135–136
OneDrive, 189–190
Online digital archive, 244–245
Online storage sites, 216
Open document format (ODF), 157, 213
Open source file format, 154, 155
Optical discs, 165
Optical media, 166
Organization of materials
    appraisal, 36–39
        identifying, 36–37
        reviewing, 37–39
    finding aid
        creating a, 29–36
        historical note, 33–34
        inventory, 36
        provenance, 35–36
        scope and content, 34–35
    intellectual *vs.* physical order, 22–29
    original order, 21–22
    photographs, 217–222
    Respect du Fonds, 19–21
    survey, 40–41, 44
Orlon, 120
Outlook, 227
@Outlook.com, 248
Over-wetting, 131, 133

P

Padded hanger, 137–138
Padding rugs, 141–142
Paper
    clips, 102
    documents, disaster preparedness and recovery of, 275–276
    enclosures, 76
    materials, 135
    permanent, 93
    resin-coated, 81
    towels, 273
Paper-based storage materials, 135
Paperboard enclosures, 89–90
Paper making
    binding documents, 103–104
    books, 105–113
        appraisal, 106–108
        book making, 106
        caring for and handling books, 108–110
        protection, 111
        repairing damage, 112–113
        shelving, 111
    diaries, 96
    fasteners, 101–103
    greeting cards, 98–99
    history, 91–93
    journals, 96
    keeping things straight, 101
    legal documents, 98
    letters, important papers, reports, 96–98
    maps, blueprints, drawings, and oversize items, 100–101
    newspapers, 93–95
    report, 100
    tape or glue, 104–105
    thermal paper, 95–96
    transcription, 99
Paradichlorobenzene, 125
Parchment, 106
1Password, 243
Password managers
    access, 243
    online digital estate planning services, 247
    rights and ownership, 243–247
Passwords and digital afterlife, 242
Past Book, 233
Patents and file formats, 156
PDF-A (Portable Document Format/Archives), 158, 212–213

INDEX

PDF (Portable Document Format), 157, 234
Pencil marks, 112
Permanent paper, 93
Persian rugs, 142, 143
Perspiration in fabrics, 136
Pests and textiles, 124–126
PhoneView (Mac only), 234
Photo editing software programs, 79, 202, 219
Photo-enhancing program, 57
Photographic activity test (PAT©), 13, 56, 58, 78, 82, 90
Photographing objects, 203
Photographs, 159–160; *see also* Digital preservation
   cheat sheet, 73
   digitization of, 57, 79
   disaster preparedness and recovery of, 274–275
   discoloring of, 47, 56
   enclosures, 81–82
   fading of, 57–58
   flaking of, 57–58
   and humidity, 47
   and moisture, 59
   and molds, 56–57
   mounting, 53
   organizing, 217–222
   scanning of, 199–200
   stuck, 60–61
Photographs, preservation concerns and processing instructions for
   ambrotype, 68–69, 73–74
   calotypes, 66–67, 73–74
   cartes-de-visite, 70–71, 73–74
   daguerreotype, 64–66, 73–74
   damage to photographs, 56–61
      curled photographs, 58–59
      digitizing, 57
      dirt on photographs, 60
      fading, 57–58
      flaking, 57–58
      rips and tears, 60
      stuck photographs, 60–61
      water damage, 61
   determining the year of a photograph, 73–74
   processing photographs, 49–56
      large prints, 49–51
      photo albums, 54–56
      snapshots, small photos, 51–53
   stereoscopic slides, 71–72
   technical aspects, 46–49
   tintypes, 69–70

Photographs, 20th-century
   color prints and film, 76–79
   non-chromogenic, 80
   processing modern photographs, 81–82
   20th-century paper, 80–81
Photo Managers, 217–218
Photoshop, 60, 160
Phthalocyanine, 167
Physical order of items, 22–23
Picasa (photo storage software program), 219
Pile rugs, 129
Pinterest, 216
PPI (pixels per inch), 198
Plant-based fibers, 118
Plastic containers, 135
Plastic enclosures, 13, 51–52, 76
Plastic sheeting, 260
PNG (Portable Network Graphics) file format, 155, 159–160
Polaroid film, 76, 80
Pollutants
   chemical, 126
   environmental, 11, 78, 111
   and magnetic tapes, 169
Polyester, 104, 119–120, 124
   batting, 137–138, 139
   films, 88
   sheets, 82, 111
Polyethylene
   cardboard, 90
   laminate, 81
Polypropylene, 90, 111, 135
   enclosures, 82
   records boxes, 78
   sheets, 51, 52, 58–59, 94, 104, 136
Polystyrene enclosures, 82
Polyurethane, 120–121, 134, 204
Polyvinyl, 13
Portable scanners, 195–197
Pottery, disaster preparedness and recovery of, 279–280
PowerPoint, 211–212
Preservation planning, 258
Preservation-quality cardboard, 90
Preservation Week, 195–196
Printing digital documents, 190–191
Proprietary file format, 154, 155
Protein-based natural fibers (wool and silk), 135
The Providence Journal, 94
PSD (PhotoShopDocument-closed proprietary formats), 155
Purses, 139

Q

QT (QuickTime), 161, 162
QuickBooks financial software, 212
Quilt, 136–137

R

Ransomware, 190
RA (Real Audio), 161
Rare books, 107
Rayon, 119, 124
RC (resin-coated) papers, 76
Records of the inner life, identifying, 7
Red rot, 113
Relative humidity (RH), 9, 122, 123, 165, 271
Repairing Your Flooded Home (American Red Cross book), 61, 267
Residential freezer, 126
Resin-coated paper, 81
Respirator, 260–261
Rhode Island Historical Society, 20
Rodents, 124
Rolled items, 137
RTF (Rich Text Format), 157
Rubber
    bands, 103
    boots, 260–261
    gloves, 260
Rugs, 129, 132–133, 136–137, 141–143
Rust stains, 139

S

SafeCoat® boxes, 52
Safety film, 84–85
Saving documents as PDFs, 214
Scanner apps, 194
Scanning
    documents, 197, 198–199
    objects, 202–203
    photographs, 199–200
    slides and negatives, 200–202
The Scarlet Letter, 108
Scope and content, 34–35
Screenshots, 230–231
SD (Secure digital) cards, 173, 174, 217, 234
SecureSafe, 247
Security systems, 262–263
Selfie stick, 203–204
Sentimental items, identifying, 7
Series list, creating, 23–29
Service providers, 234

Shellac, 134
Shoes, 139
Shrinkage, 87, 130–131
Shutterfly, 57, 79, 191, 216
Silk clothing, 119, 124, 125, 127, 129, 134, 135, 138
Silverfish, 124
SIMS file, 234
Single-lens reflex (SLR) camera, 81
SkyDrive, 248
Smith, Hamilton I., 69
Smithsonian Institution, 56
Smog and magnetic tapes, 169
Smoke detectors, 265
Smoking, 16, 17, 265
Snapchat, 216
Snip-it, 230–231
Social media, 231–235
Software editing program (Adobe), 215
Solid-state drives/disks (SSDs), 173
Sooty textiles, 276
Spandex, 120, 121
Spiders, 124
Spreadsheets, 23, 31, 108, 211–214, 242
Stacking textiles, 135
Staining on textiles, 118, 123, 124, 135–136
    and dyes, 127
    and humidity fluctuations, 126
    oil, 120
    rust, 139
Staples, 102
Stereoscopic photography, 72
Sticky-shed syndrome (SSS), 204
Stop-action photography, 72
Storage and maintenance
    of hard drives, 172
    magnetic tapes, 169–170
    textiles, 134–136
Storage on optical media, 167
Straight pins, 102–103
Stray magnetic fields, 205
String ties, 103
Structural metadata, 218
Stuck photographs, 60–61
Subject guides, 28–29, 32–33
Suede, fake, 120
Sulfur dioxides, 126
Sunlight, 109, 113, 272
Supplex, 119
SVG (Scalable Vector Graphics) format, 160
Syncing, 224

T

Talbot, William Henry Fox, 66
Tape or glue, 104–105
Tapestry, 136–137
Technical metadata, 155
Technology preservation, 153
Temperature
    and CDs, 165
    gauge, 14
    and hard drives, 171
    and magnetic tapes, 169
    and textiles, 122
Tencel, 119
Terms of Use, 245
Text formats, 157–159
Textiles
    caring for
        air pollution, 126
        inherent vice, 126–127
        light, 121–122
        mold and mildew, 123
        pests, 124–126
        temperature and relative humidity, 122
    cleaning and maintenance
        dry cleaning, 130–131
        eliminating infestations, 132–134
        vacuuming, 129–130
        wet cleaning, 130–131
    disaster preparedness and recovery, 276
    display
        embroidery/cross-stitch works/lace doilies, 143–144
        flags, 145
        floor carpets and rugs, 141–143
        upholstery, 145–146
        wall hangings, 140–141
    fiber types, 118
        cotton and linen, 118
        natural, 118
        wool and silk, 118
    handling, 127–128
    overview, 115–117
    storage
        general considerations for, 134–136
        specific items, 136–140
    synthetic
        acrylic, 120
        nylon, 119
        polyester, 119–120
        polyurethane, 120–121
        rayon, 119
Text messages, 234–235

TEXT-reading program, 227
Thermal paper, 95–96
Thermoloft, 120
3M Company, 95
3-2-1 rule, 183–185, 188, 210, 263, 278
TIFF (Tagged Image File Format), 159, 199, 201, 202, 217
Tintypes, 69–70
Tissue paper, 14, 101, 118, 128, 135, 137, 138
Torn pages, 112
Transcription, 99
Transferring photos to computer, 216–217
Turpentine, 126
Twill strip, 138
Twitter, 216, 234, 250
TXT format, 234
Tyvek plastic suits, 260

U

Unbuffered materials, 143
Unbuffered tissue paper, 135, 138
Uniform Laws Commission (ULC), 246
Unpublished file format, 154, 155
Upholstery, 145–146
USB
    port, 207, 217
    stick drive, 188–189
UV-blocking glass, 50
UV-filtering acrylic frames, 143
UV (Ultraviolet) light, 10, 89, 121

V

Vacuuming, 123, 126, 129–130, 132, 139, 146
VELCRO® brand fasteners, 140–141
Vellum, 106
Velvets rugs, 129
Ventilation, 123
Vermin, 125
VHS player, 208
VHS tape, 89, 208
Video data formats, 162
Video OBject, 208
Video tapes, 89
    digitization, 204–207
    disaster preparedness and recovery of, 278–279
Videotaping objects, 203–204
View-Masters, 71–72
Vinegar syndrome, 86, 204
Vinyl garment bags, 138

Viscose, 119
Visually lossless compression, 154
VOB (Video OBject) files, 208
Voice memos, 223–224

W

Wall hangings, 140–141
Wand scanners, 195
Washing hands, 16, 127–128, 131
Water
    damage, 61, 273–274
    detection alarm, 267
    and floods, 266–269
Waterborne polyurethane varnish, 134
Water-repellent materials, 120
WAV (Waveform Audio File), 161, 208, 223
Wayback Machine, 229
Webmail, 227–228
WebM file format, 155
Websites, 216, 228–231
    backup, 230
    copy and paste, 229
    saving or printing the pages, 229
    saving the code, 230
    screenshots, 230–231
Wedding dresses for storage, 137–138
"Weighted" silk, 127
Wet cleaning, 130–131
"Wet-look" fabrics, 120
WhatsApp, 234
White archival gloves, 201
White vinegar for stain removal, 142
Who Do You Think You Are (genealogy show), 4
@Windowslive.com, 248

WMA (Windows Media Audio), 155, 161
WMV (Windows Media File), 162
Wondershare TunesGo, 234
Wooden shelves for fabrics storage, 134–135
Wool clothing, 124, 125, 129, 131, 133–134, 138
Woolite brand detergent, 131, 133, 139
WordPress, 229
The Works of John Adams (Adams), 107
Workspace creation, 15–17
Wrappers, 224
www.aaemonline.org, 271
www.archive.org, 229
www.iicrc.org, 271

X

Xbox Live, 248
XML-based file format, 213

Y

Yahoo, 248–249
Yarns, 133
Yellowing
    and fire, 265
    of paper, 96
    of textiles, 135
Yellow pages, 271
The Yellow Wallpaper (Gilman), 20
YouTube videos, 56, 79, 196, 198

Z

ZIP format, 212

www.ingramcontent.com/pod-product-compliance
Lightning Source LLC
Chambersburg PA
CBHW060407010526
44107CB00005B/611